Sallust's *Bellum Catilinae*

AMERICAN PHILOLOGICAL ASSOCIATION

TEXTBOOK SERIES

Gilbert W. Lawall, Series Editor

NUMBER 9
SALLUST'S *BELLUM CATILINAE*
Edited with Introduction and Commentary
by J. T. Ramsey

Sallust's *Bellum Catilinae*

Edited, with Introduction and Commentary,

by
J. T. Ramsey

Scholars Press
Atlanta, Georgia

SALLUST'S *BELLUM CATILINAE*

Edited with Introduction and Commentary
by J. T. Ramsey

©1984
American Philological Association

Library of Congress Cataloging in Publication Data

Sallust, 86–34 B.C.
Sallust's Bellum Catilinae.

(Textbook series / American Philological Association ; no. 9) (ISSN 0278–6400)
Bibliography: p.
Includes Index.
1. Catiline, ca. 108–62 B.C. 2. Rome—History—Conspiracy of Catiline, 65–62 B.C. I. Ramsey, J. T. (John T.) II. Title. III. Title: Bellum Catilinae. IV. Series: Textbook series (American Philological Association) ; no. 9.
PA6653.A4R35 1982   937'.05   81–21281
ISBN 0–89130–560–2   AACR2

Printed in the United States of America

For Sarah

CONTENTS

PREFACE ix

INTRODUCTION 1

   I.   LIFE OF SALLUST 1

           Date of Birth
           Family and Boyhood
           Political Career
           Service under Caesar
           Retirement from Public Life

   II.   THE WRITINGS OF SALLUST 5

           The Genuine Works
           Time of Writing

   III.   SALLUST'S CONTRIBUTION TO ROMAN HISTORIOGRAPHY 7

           State of Roman Historiography before Sallust
           Choice of Topic
           Sources of the BELLUM CATILINAE

   IV.   SALLUST'S STYLE 10

           Influence of Thucydides
           Debt to Cato
           Sallustian Traits: Brevity
                       Vocabulary
                       Grammar and Syntax
                       Inconcinnitas

   V.   THE TEXTUAL TRADITION 14
   VI.   SUMMARY OF THE CATILINARIAN CONSPIRACY 15
   VII.   STRUCTURE OF THE *BELLUM CATILINAE* 22

VARIATIONS FROM THE TEXTS OF ERNOUT
   AND KURFESS 24

SIGLA 26

TEXT 27

COMMENTARY 55

APPENDICES

   I.   Catiline's Birth Date and Early Career 235
   II. Evidence for the "First Catilinarian Conspiracy" 237

SELECTED BIBLIOGRAPHY 241

   I.   Texts and Commentaries 241

   II. Books and Articles 241

INDEX NOMINUM 247

INDEX RERUM 253

INDEX VERBORUM 259

PREFACE

The plans to write this textbook were made in 1974 when I was completing my graduate studies at Harvard University. At that time, the most recent annotated editions in English of Sallust's *Catiline* still generally available were those by Charles Merivale (revised ed., London 1882) and Walter Summers (Pitt Press, Cambridge 1900). My proposal to produce a new edition was presented to the editor of the APA Textbook Series in the spring of 1975 and accepted by the Editorial Board one year later. The bulk of the writing was done during the following two years in between teaching duties, mainly during the summers of 1977 and 1978. During the latter period, my work was assisted by a Faculty Summer Fellowship from the University of Illinois at Chicago.

The text printed here is based on that of A. Ernout (3rd ed., Paris 1958) with the modifications noted at the end of the Introduction (p. 24). My reason for basing the text on Ernout's edition rather than on the Teubner text by A. Kurfess (3rd ed., Leipzig 1957) is explained in footnote 12 of the Introduction. In composing the notes, I have tried to strike a balance between comments designed to aid the reader in translating the text and discussions of historical topics and points of style. In this respect, my commentary differs from the recent school edition of the *Catiline* by Patrick McGushin (Bristol 1980), which places more emphasis on historical matters and Sallust's treatment of the conspiracy than on points of grammar. Where I have offered help with translation, I have preferred, whenever possible, to present a grammatical analysis so that the reader can unravel the syntax for himself rather than offer a ready-made translation. Occasionally, square brackets have been employed within the commentary to segregate more detailed comments on a particular topic from the basic information needed by the less advanced student.

A work of this nature inevitably draws upon the fruits of scholarship represented by previous annotated editions, and I have indicated in the bibliography the works that were found to be of greatest service. The recent full-scale commentaries on the *Catiline* in German by Karl Vretska (Heidelberg 1976) and in English by Patrick McGushin (Leiden 1977) appeared at a most opportune time when my own work was still in progress, and they proved invaluable guides on a number of thorny problems. I have not tried to signal my debt to predecessors within the notes themselves since this did not seem appropriate in an edition primarily intended for undergraduates. Those familiar with the works listed in the bibliography, however, will be aware of the instances where scholarship, past and present, has been pressed into service, and I want to take this opportunity to acknowledge the aid received from these secondary sources.

The delay in publication since the commentary was completed in September 1978 has afforded a welcome opportunity to seek advice and criticism from various friends and colleagues. At this university, my colleague, Michael Alexander, shared with me his expertise in Roman law, and my colleague, Alexander MacGregor, assisted me on several paleographical points. I am grateful to Professor Ernst Badian for suggestions on a number of specific topics, and I received many useful recommendations for revisions or corrections from Professor George Paul and Professor George Goold, who read through the entire commentary. Their detailed comments saved me from many errors and blunders. Likewise, Professor Roger Hornsby, the former editor of the APA Textbook Series, and the current editor, Professor Gilbert Lawall, rendered yeoman's service. Under Professor Hornsby's guiding hand, my manuscript assumed its final form, and the subsequent task of editing this manuscript and seeing it through the press was cheerfully and very ably performed by Professor Lawall and his colleagues on the APA Editorial Board for Textbooks, Professors Richard Hamilton and Judith Sebesta. All gave generously of their time and offered many helpful suggestions for improvements. The blemishes that remain are, of course, the author's responsibility.

It remains to thank my principal typist, Miss Lilliam Alvarez, who transcribed the final typescript in the summer of 1980, and the other members of our office staff, Mrs. Jeanette Uyeda and Mrs. Vivian Woolfolk, who retyped pages needing further revision. Lastly, it is only fair to say this work would never have been possible without the constant support and encouragement of my wife, Sarah. Much of the writing was done while we were still living in a one-bedroom apartment and adjusting to the arrival of a new-born son. The conditions were far from ideal and would have been impossible without an understanding wife.

July, 1983

John T. Ramsey
University of Illinois
Chicago

INTRODUCTION

I. LIFE OF SALLUST

Date of Birth

Jerome's *Chronicle* records the birth of C. Sallustius Crispus[1] under the year corresponding to 86 B.C. and his death in 36 B.C. (R. Helm, *Die Chronik des Hieronymus* [Berlin 1956]):

> (1) *ann. Abr.* 1931 [= *Ol.* 173.2/3 = 86 B.C.] (87 B.C., cod. B) p. 151 *Sallustius Crispus scriptor historicus in Sabinis Amiterni nascitur.*
> (2) *ann. Abr.* 1981 [= *Ol.* 185.4/186.1 = 36 B.C.] p. 159 *Sallustius diem obiit quadriennio ante Actiacum bellum.*

The former date receives some confirmation from two lesser chronicles, the *Consularia Constantinopolitana* (Mommsen, *Chron. Min.* 1.214) and the *Chronicon Paschale* (Dindorf 347), which likewise give 86 B.C. as the year of S.'s birth and add that he was born on October 1st. Since, however, the second notice in Jerome reports that S.'s death occurred four years before the Battle of Actium (2 September 31 B.C.), clearly the date given for his death is too early by one year or possibly two if we reckon inclusively. Unfortunately, the *Consul. Constant.* (p. 217) and the *Chron. Pasch.* (p. 359) cannot be used to decide between the two possible adjustments to the date in Jerome because they are even farther from the mark and place S.'s death earlier still in 38 and 39 B.C. respectively, although they agree in stating that S. died on May 13th. Certainty is impossible, but it seems safest to modify the year given by Jerome for S.'s death to 35 B.C. so as to bring it into line with *quadriennio ante Actiacum bellum*, and to accept 86 and 35 B.C. as the approximate dates of S.'s birth and death. Presumably the information about S. in Jerome goes back to the no longer extant portion of Suetonius' *De Viris Illustribus* on the lives of the Roman historians, and this work in turn may have drawn upon the lost biography of S. by the first-century A.D. scholar Asconius.

---

[1] His full name is found in the *tituli* of several of the chief MSS (e.g., **P** and **B**) and in the *Bellum Africanum* (8.3). For the sake of convenience, the abbreviation "S." will be used henceforth.

Family and Boyhood

Nothing is known about the boyhood or family of S. apart from the notice in Jerome that he was born at Amiternum. This town, which was situated in a remote upland region of the Sabine countryside, about 50 miles northeast of Rome, had been incorporated into the Roman state by the grant of full citizen rights before the Social War (91–87 B.C.). Therefore, by the date of S.'s birth, many of the local families of prominence, probably including S.'s own, must have been thoroughly Romanized. However, the social prestige and influence of these municipal aristocrats (*domi nobiles* as they are called, e.g., *Cat.* 17.4) counted for little in the capital where honors and political office were commonly the prerogatives of a select circle of well-established families. Those young men who were the first in their family to enter Roman politics, such as S. and Cicero (vid. 23.6n. *homo novos*), had to overcome the barriers that their municipal origin placed in the way of easy access to political office and rapid advancement. Local ties were seldom forgotten; pride in personal achievement based upon merit rather than birth was almost inevitable; and the outlook of the select few who ennobled their families by holding the consulship could never be quite the same as that of the hereditary aristocracy to whom power and prestige belonged as a right of birth. Much of the bitterness and scorn for these aristocrats that is to be found in the pages of S. is to be explained by his municipal origin.

Political Career

S. tells us (*Cat.* 3.3) that he was attracted to a career in politics at an early age. His first attested office is his tribunate in 52 B.C. (Ascon. p. 37C. 18–19). Prior to this, it is reasonable to assume that he held the quaestorship since this office was the first in the *cursus honorum* and entitled the holder to automatic admission to the senate. Unfortunately the only source to mention S.'s quaestorship is the invective ascribed to Cicero which is plainly a late forgery emanating from the rhetorical schools under the empire.[2] Although one cannot rule out the possibility that S. may have gained his seat in the senate by holding merely the tribunate,[3] in the absence of positive evidence to the contrary, it is probably best to assume a normal pattern for his career. If he was indeed born in 86, he would have been eligible to be quaestor in 55 under the second consulship of Pompey and Crassus, and this date suits the

---

[2] M. Tulli Ciceronis *In C. Sallustium Crispum Invectiva*, ed. A. Kurfess, *Appendix Sallustiana* II, ed. 4 (Leipzig 1962); attributed to Didius by Diomedes (I.387.4K).

[3] R. Syme, *Sallust* (Berkeley, 1964) 28.

chronology of his tribunate three years later.[4]

During his tribunate, S. came into prominence in the political crisis that was precipitated by the murder of the demagogue P. Clodius. The year opened without any consuls since the elections had been impeded during the previous year by violence and obstruction. Three candidates were seeking the office: T. Annius Milo, who had the support of the conservative Optimate faction, and Q. Metellus Scipio and P. Plautius Hypsaeus, who had the backing of Pompey and Clodius, who was himself a candidate for the praetorship. Milo and Clodius were leaders of rival gangs of ruffians that had been recruited earlier in the decade when violence and intimidation became typical features of the Roman political scene. Clodius set the precedent when he was tribune in 58 and settled an old grudge against Cicero by driving him into exile. For nearly a year, Clodius was able to dominate his opponents by means of open violence until those who wished to curb his power and secure the recall of Cicero called upon Milo to organize a rival band of thugs. Finally an end was put to their rivalry when Clodius was murdered on the *via Appia* by Milo's gang on 18 January 52. Riots ensued when Clodius' body was brought to Rome, and the senate-house was burned down in the turmoil. A state of emergency was declared, and Pompey was eventually made sole consul for the first part of the year. Steps were taken to bring Milo to trial for the murder, and despite Cicero's efforts to defend him in court, he was condemned and went into exile.

During this stormy period, S. is found allied with two of his colleagues in the tribunate, T. Munatius Plancus Bursa and Q. Pompeius Rufus, who incited the people to hostility against Milo and against Cicero because he was defending him. S.'s motives for taking such an active part in this affair are difficult to ascertain with certainty. There is no evidence for close ties between S. and Clodius as there is for the other two tribunes. Possibly his role is to be explained by assuming that he was a supporter of Pompey's candidates who were running against Milo.[5] If so, the standard view that S. was a life-long partisan of Caesar may need qualification.[6] There was a rumor, in fact, that S. later settled his quarrel with Milo and Cicero (Ascon. p. 37C. 23–24). Significantly Plancus and Pompeius Rufus were brought to trial in the following year and condemned for their part in the turmoil that had attended their tribunate,[7] while S. apparently escaped unscathed.

---

[4] T.R.S. Broughton, *The Magistrates of the Roman Republic* (New York, 1952) II.217.

[5] Syme (above, n. 3) p. 31f.

[6] The only evidence that tends to connect S. with Caesar in this year is the bill that was passed by all ten of the tribunes granting Caesar an exemption from the requirement of canvassing in person when he became eligible to stand for a second consulship. This bill, it should be noted, apparently had Pompey's blessing (Caes. *BCiv.* 1.32.3; Cic. *Att.* 7.1.4).

[7] Plancus was successfully prosecuted by Cic. (*Fam.* 7.2.2; Plut. *Pomp.* 55) and sought

The reprieve was only temporary, however. Two years later, in 50 B.C., S. was expelled from the senate by the censor Appius Claudius (Dio 40.63.4). A reference to this severe setback in his career is clearly implied by the words *mihi multa advorsa fuere* (*Cat.* 3.3). Ordinarily senators were stripped of their rank on the grounds of moral or political misconduct, but a word of caution is in order before judgment is passed on this disgrace suffered by S. Later sources indeed give the impression that S.'s private life reeked of scandal. They delight in contrasting the censorious tone of S.'s strictures on the moral corruption of others with the shocking character of his own conduct. One story in particular reports that S. was caught *in flagrante delicto* by Milo and flogged for his affair with Milo's wife, the notorious Fausta, daughter of Sulla. The invective ascribed to Cicero retails a host of unnatural crimes of the flesh (5.13) and dabbling in the mysticism of a Pythagorean sect (5.14). All of these charges, however, are the stock material of rhetorical abuse, and the trustworthiness of these *testimonia* is rightly questioned by the cautious scholar.[8] Significantly Dio does not attribute S.'s expulsion from the senate to moral turpitude but implies that the motive of the censor was a political purge. S. will have paid the price for throwing in his lot with the wrong faction. Others were more fortunate. Caesar's agent, the tribune Scribonius Curio, barely escaped the same fate through the intervention of Appius' colleague, Calpurnius Piso, who was Caesar's father-in-law.

Service under Caesar

Apparently S. sought refuge in the camp of Caesar. He is next found in command of one of Caesar's legions in Illyricum late in 49. He was outmaneuvered by Pompey's generals and failed to relieve C. Antonius, Caesar's legate, who had been trapped on the island of Curicta (Orosius 6.15.8). Following this setback, S. disappears from sight until 47 when, as praetor-elect, he was sent to quell a mutiny in Caesar's legions that were stationed in Campania. Once again the task proved to be beyond S.'s ability, and he barely escaped from the riotous soldiers with his life (App. *BCiv.* 2.92; Dio 42.52.1f.). Caesar himself was forced to intervene, and it took all the diplomacy and tact at his command to bring these restive troops back into line so that they were willing to forgo their long-overdue discharge and cash bounties until after the completion of the African campaign.

It was during Caesar's campaign against the Republican forces in Africa in 46 that S.'s fortunes began to turn. In this year he regained his

---

refuge in the camp of Caesar (*Fam.* 8.1.4); Pompeius Rufus met with a similar fate at the hands of Caelius Rufus (Val. Max. 4.2.7) and withdrew to Campania.

[8] Syme (above, n. 3) p. 278ff.

seat in the senate by holding the praetorship and rendered valuable service to Caesar by securing supplies for his troops from the island of Cercina (*Bell. Afr.* 8.3, 34.1–3). Following the Battle of Thapsus, S. was handsomely rewarded by being made governor of the new province of Africa Nova, which Caesar created out of part of the former Numidian kingdom of Juba (*Bell. Afr.* 97.1). Apparently Caesar had formed a high estimate of S.'s administrative ability to entrust him with this important assignment which included the command of three legions. The trust, however, may have been misplaced. According to Dio (43.9.2), S. plundered the province and lined his own pockets. He was accused of extortion when he returned to Rome in 45, and he may have escaped the disgrace of losing his rank as senator a second time by sharing some of his ill-gotten gains with Caesar, who is said to have been willing to shield other malefactors in exchange for a share of the spoils (Dio 43.47.4).

Retirement from Public Life

Whether S. made up his mind at this point to renounce further political aspirations or was driven into retirement by the assassination of Caesar, his benefactor, in March of 44, his private resources appear to have been more than adequate to support a life of leisure. If the famous and elegant *horti Sallustiani*, situated on the outskirts of Rome between the Pincian and Quirinal, which later became the property of the imperial family, were indeed laid out by the historian rather than his adoptive heir of the same name, they provide evidence of considerable wealth. At the same time, the outspokenness of S. in his writings and the fact that he survived the proscriptions of the triumvirs unscathed imply that he continued to enjoy favor with Caesar's successors.

II. THE WRITINGS OF SALLUST

The Genuine Works

Of S.'s historical works, two monographs survive intact, the *Bellum Catilinae*[9] and the *Bellum Jugurthinum*, and we possess four speeches

---

9 The work is sometimes called *De Catilinae Coniuratione* or simply *Catilina* in modern editions. Neither title rests upon the authority of the manuscripts. The former is taken from the text itself (4.3) and does not appear to have been current in antiquity. The MSS preserve the monograph under a variety of headings: *Bellum Catilinarium, Liber Catilinarius, In Catilinario* (sc. *bello*), and *Bellum Catilinae*. Even within one of our best MSS, P, the title fluctuates between *Bellum Catulinarium* [*sic*] in the *praescriptio* and *Bellum Catilinae* in the *subscriptio*. The grammarians as well show considerable latitude in the way they describe this work. Apparently, however, the word *bellum* belongs in the title, and by Quintilian's day the work seems to have been known as the *Bellum Catilinae* since he refers to the two monographs as *in bello Iugurthino et Catilinae* (3.8.9). Likewise Florus, who drew heavily upon S. for his chapter on the Catilinarian conspiracy,

and two letters in addition to about 500 fragments from his *Historiae*, which was published in five books. The two *Epistulae ad Caesarem*, which are sometimes attributed to S. by modern scholars and preserved in only one MS that contains the speeches and letters excerpted from his genuine works, appear to be the product of the imperial schools of rhetoric. Some scholars still cling to the belief that these two short essays are genuine and may be useful for revealing the development of S.'s ideas and style. For the purposes of this commentary, however, these two letters to Caesar are assumed to be spurious and are not included in the statistics that are occasionally given in the notes for Sallustian usage.

Time of Writing

Very little evidence is available for determining the precise date of composition for each of the three genuine works. It is generally assumed that the *Catiline* is S.'s maiden effort. One notes a more apologetic and uncertain tone in the preface to this work than in the preface to the *Jugurtha*. Apparently S.'s confidence in the value of his occupation grew as time went on. One may also detect in the preface to the *Jugurtha* signs that S. was repelled further from politics by the events that followed the inception of the so-called Second Triumvirate in November of 43 B.C. He speaks of politicians whose personal safety was no longer assured by the prestige of political office (*Jug.* 3.1). Later in the same chapter, he appears to allude to the proscriptions and bloodletting of the Triumvirs, who revived a reign of terror on the Sullan model to crush their enemies and raise cash for the war with Brutus and Cassius.

Within the *Catiline* itself, a probable *terminus post quem* is furnished by the reference to Cato and Caesar in the past tense (53.6 *fuere viri duo*). Clearly S. is writing after the Ides of March of 44, but how long after remains in doubt. Various theories have been advanced to prove that the work was published before or after the death of Cicero in December of 43. None, unfortunately, can establish the fact with certainty one way or the other, but on the grounds of sheer probability it is perhaps best to assume that S. brought out his monograph on the Catilinarian conspiracy after the death of the leading personalities, Cicero included. If so, the *Bellum Catilinae* may have been published towards the end of 42. If we allow another year or two for the composition of the *Bellum Jugurthinum*, S.'s more ambitious work, the *Historiae*, may have had its inception in 39. It appears from the

---

calls this section of his history (2.12) the *Bellum Catilinae*. Possibly S. deliberately called his first essay the *Bellum Catilinae* in reaction to Cicero's contention (*Cat.* 3.23) that he had averted the war which threatened the state by means of a bloodless victory in the garb of peacetime. Cic. (*Fam.* 5.12.2) later prefers to describe the affair as a *civilis coniuratio* rather than a full-scale *bellum*.

surviving fragments and *testimonia* that the *Historiae* covered a dozen years of history from 78 to 67. Possibly S.'s intention was to bring his account of the post-Sullan period down to the point at which the *Bellum Catilinae* takes up the narrative. Since book five of the *Historiae* shows signs of lacking completion, it may be that S. was still working on this final project when death overtook him in 35.

III. SALLUST'S CONTRIBUTION TO ROMAN HISTORIOGRAPHY

State of Roman Historiography before Sallust

In his preface to the *Catiline*, S. argues that the writing of history is no less valuable to the state than the services performed by those who involve themselves in political affairs. Both occupations are praiseworthy, and the writer's task may even prove to be a greater challenge because an author must not only do justice to the deeds that he sets out to record, but he also runs a very grave risk of being faulted by his readers. Some will accuse him of malice if he censures misconduct in his historical works, and others will suspect him of exaggeration if they read about deeds beyond their own capability (*Cat.* 3.1–2). Yet S. is convinced that a memorial of past achievements is valuable as a model for future generations (*Jug.* 4.5–6), and he laments the fact that his nation has lacked men of genius, such as Athens had in the field of history, to lend glory to the noteworthy accomplishments of the Roman people (*Cat.* 8).

This judgment is in accord with the opinion of Cicero. S.'s Roman predecessors in the field of history were a sorry lot (*De Or.* 2.51ff.; *Leg.* 1.5ff.; *Brut.* 228). They were merely *narratores rerum* (*De Or.* 2.54) and were sadly lacking in prose style. Brevity and truthfulness were their only virtues. Eloquence at Rome had been directed to public speaking rather than the writing of history. Those who wrote history were content to record events year after year without any attempt at analysis. A few recent historians had tried to infuse their works with interest. L. Cornelius Sisenna, who died in 67 B.C. and wrote an account of the Social War and the Civil War of the Sullan period, had achieved *puerile quiddam* (*Leg.* 1.7), but in the field of history no Roman had yet achieved the stature of the Greek historians of the 5th and 4th centuries B.C.

Ironically, there survives a letter of Cicero (*Fam.* 5.12) to the contemporary Roman historian L. Lucceius in which he recommends both the form and to some extent the subject matter that S. later chose for his first historical work. Cicero wrote to Lucceius in 56 B.C. to persuade him to postpone further work on his extended history, covering the Social War and Sullan period, in favor of publishing a separate monograph on the suppression of the Catilinarian conspiracy and the events in Cicero's life down to his triumphant return from exile in 57.

Cicero was eager to have his deeds celebrated within his own lifetime, and the letter cites the works of several Greek historians as precedents for preferring the format of a monograph to a continuous history for recording a period charged with dramatic possibilities and unified by a single protagonist.

Choice of Topic

More than a decade after Cicero sent his request to Lucceius, S. began composing an account of the crisis that occurred during Cicero's consulship, and he adopted the vehicle that Cicero had recommended to Lucceius for such a work. His first venture in the field of history was to be a monograph,[10] and it was to represent a significant departure from the bulk of his Roman predecessors, who had composed annals, personal memoirs, or outline histories.

The affair of Catiline was ideally suited to S.'s purposes. It presented an opportunity to examine the moral degeneracy of the late Republic, it involved most of the leading personalities of S.'s own lifetime, and the sources were abundant. As S. himself remarks, this affair was particularly noteworthy because of the singular nature of the crime and the danger it posed to the state (*Cat.* 4.4). Catiline may be taken as a prime representative of the decadent noble who sought political advancement by espousing the cause of the downtrodden, while all the time his chief concern was to maintain and further his own *dignitas* (vid. *Cat.* 35.3, 4nn.). Of noble birth himself (5.1n.), Catiline gathered into his following many of the same class (17.5n.) who recalled the revolutionary days of Sulla (5.6, 37.6nn.) and were willing to burn the city of Rome and incite the Gauls to make war on the Roman people so that they could seize power for themselves in the confusion. Ironically the savior in this crisis was an outsider, the new man from Arpinum, Cicero, who brought the conspiracy to light and frustrated the aims of the revolutionaries.

Sources of the BELLUM CATILINAE

The sources for this period were almost superabundant if nevertheless one-sided, since few would care to defend the memory of Catiline or present his failure in a favorable light. Cicero never tired of recounting the services that he had rendered to his country during his consulship, and he published within his own lifetime a prose memoir in

---

[10] L. Coelius Antipater, who wrote a history of the 2nd Punic War in seven books (*post* 121 B.C.), appears to be the first Roman historian to break away from the annalistic treatment of history in favor of the historical monograph which deals with a single topic. He surpassed his predecessors by writing in a more flowing style but is faulted for lacking polish and variety (Cic. *De Or.* 2.54; *Leg.* 1.6).

Greek and a poem in three books on his consulship, *de Consulatu Suo*. A second prose account in Latin was projected but perhaps never published. A second poem, also in three books, *de Temporibus Suis*, appears to have been completed sometime after 54.

In addition, there was a large number of orations and published documents pertinent to this chapter in Roman history. Cicero's consular orations were revised and in circulation within a few years after he left office. The influence of the four *Catilinarians* may be detected here and there in S. (vid. *Cat.* 15.2, 20.9, 51.9nn.). Much could be learned from the *Oratio in Toga Candida*, which had been delivered before the consular elections in 64, (e.g., *Cat.* 19.2n.) and from the *pro Murena* of November 63 (vid. *Cat.* 31.9n.). The *pro Sulla* in particular, which was delivered in 62, appears to have greatly influenced S.'s conception of Catiline's role in the earlier coup d'état, allegedly planned for 65 B.C. (vid. *Cat.* 18.5n.). As a result of Cicero's foresight and caution, the minutes of the senate's deliberations on the fate of the conspirators arrested in early December had been taken down and published (vid. *Cat.* 47.1-4 introd. n.). Even the speech of Cato Uticensis, who played such a significant role in the senatorial debate on December 5th, had been preserved (Plut. *Cato Min.* 23).

Although he is extremely reticent about the nature of his sources, in at least two instances S. appears to reproduce contemporary documents that he had discovered in his research (vid. *Cat.* 34.3, 44.4nn.). A number of contemporary rumors and hearsay evidence are offered concerning facts or events on which the author refuses to pass judgment (*Cat.* 14.7, 17.7, 19.4, 22.1, 48.7). A remark that S. claims to have heard from Crassus himself is preserved (vid. *Cat.* 48.9n.), and it is safe to assume that he was acquainted with many contemporary witnesses who could provide valuable insight.

Accordingly, S. partially fulfilled the request that Cicero addressed to Lucceius more than a decade before S. began writing. The momentous events of the year 63 would be duly celebrated by an author of genius. Lucceius was apparently receptive to Cicero's suggestion. He even received the material that Cicero promised to supply, but the project appears to have been postponed indefinitely. Cicero was cheated of the glory that he hoped to derive from Lucceius' account. Another historian was to reap the benefit of this missed opportunity. Furthermore, if the *Catiline* was published earlier than 42, as some scholars believe, then S. may have even satisfied Cicero's desire to have the year of his consulship made the subject of an historical work within his own lifetime. S., however, must have gravely disappointed the hopes of Cicero on two counts. First, he chose to make not Cicero but the villain Catiline the central figure in his essay. Next, he went out of his way to disregard the precepts on style that Cicero hoped would elevate

Roman historiography and make it a respectable branch of literature. S. struck out on his own to forge a new style that was consciously un-Ciceronian and reminiscent of the antique prose that was so characteristic of earlier historical writing.

IV. SALLUST'S STYLE

Influence of Thucydides

S.'s verdict on the inadequacy of his Roman predecessors in the field of history caused him to turn elsewhere for a suitable model. His choice, not perhaps surprisingly, settled on the fifth century Athenian historian Thucydides. As we happen to know from Cicero, Thucydides' *History of the Peloponnesian War* seems to have enjoyed a sudden access of popularity at Rome in the mid 1st century B.C. shortly before S. began writing. Apparently the interest in Thucydides was revived by the crisis precipitated when Caesar crossed the Rubicon and civil war broke out. Readers turned to the historian of the decline and fall of the Athenian empire for grim consolation or enlightenment under the pressure of similar circumstances which Thucydides (1.22.4) argues are controlled by human nature and therefore are likely to recur so long as human nature remains unchanged.

Soon, however, this renewed interest in Thucydides carried the author into the center of a literary debate. Some Roman orators, in reaction to the ornate and flowing style of Cicero, attempted to adopt a plain and unadorned style of speaking by taking the Attic orators as their models. These "Atticists," as they are called, challenged the supremacy of Cicero as Rome's leading orator, and Cicero responded by writing several treatises on oratory in 46 B.C. in which he defends the merits of his style. In both the *Brutus* (287ff.) and the *Orator* (30ff.), Cicero examines the possibility of using Thucydides as a model for oratory. His verdict is that many of his contemporaries who were attracted to Thucydides failed to appreciate that his abrupt and obscure style was inappropriate to forensic oratory, although this manner of writing might be effective for presenting an account of *res gestae*.

S. appears to have concurred with this judgment, and his ancient critics did not fail to appreciate his debt and resemblance to Thucydides. The two men had much in common. Both had been generals and had been forced to retire from the political arena. Both took as their theme contemporary events: Thucydides the collapse of the Athenian empire; S. the decadence of the Roman Republic. The treatment is selective and realistic. Above all, both seek to bring out the character of the main participants. The personality and morals of these leading figures, rather than social or economic factors, are used to explain the chain of events.

Hence both historians place great emphasis on speeches which they compose to portray the personality of the speaker and capture the mood of the times. The direct and indirect borrowings from Thucydides in S. are many, and attention is drawn to most of them in the notes.

Debt to Cato

Once S. decided upon Thucydides as a model, it remained to fashion a suitable style in Latin to capture the spirit of Thucydides' prose, which was characterized by rapidity, abruptness, a fondness for poetical words, inconcinnity, and grammatical peculiarities. The polished prose that Cicero recommended as the ideal medium for history would hardly satisfy an author who wished to emulate the sometimes obscure, tortuous, and archaic prose of Thucydides. Clearly S. had to turn to a comparable writer in his own language, if one could be found, and Cicero in fact points the way. In the same literary polemic that involved the name of Thucydides, Cicero suggests that those who wish to adopt a plain and simple style would do well to read the orations and *Origines* of the Elder Cato, which were sadly neglected (*Brut.* 65ff.). In Cato they would find brevity and a vigorous style of speaking. His vocabulary would, of course, be archaic and antiquated, but this could be altered in the light of contemporary usage. Certainly the arrangement of his words could also stand improvement, and his prose would need to be recast in the proper rhythms. With these slight modifications, Cicero affirms that Cato can be ranked with the Greek orator Lysias, who was so much admired by the new Attic orators.[11]

In Cato, S. discovered the perfect model for capturing the flavor of Thucydidean prose. Not only in language but also in outlook, Cato was ideally suited to the needs of S. Like S., the Elder Cato was the first in his family to enter Roman politics. His humble origins and conservative temperament caused him to clash frequently with the aristocracy, and he was noted for being a sharp critic of the corruption and decadence of his own age. This anti-aristocratic bias was carried over into his *Origines*, which was the first history of Rome to be composed in Latin. In this work, Cato deliberately suppressed the names of generals and commanders who fought in Rome's wars lest he appear to celebrate the deeds of the aristocracy. Instead, he chose to emphasize the accomplishments of the Roman nation as a whole and included a generous treatment of the Italian states other than Rome. These characteristics of the Elder Cato, together with the fame earned by his great-grandson in S.'s own lifetime, are doubtless what first attracted the

---

[11] This extravagant claim concerning the merits of Cato's style need not be taken at face value. Cicero indulges in special pleading to turn the flank of his critics and later qualifies his praise of Cato (*Brut.* 293ff.).

historian's attention to the writings of this early Roman annalist.

S.'s resemblance to Cato is one of the most commonly noticed characteristics of his style. His most severe ancient critics accused him of plundering the works of the Elder Cato, and not without justice, since, although the remains of Cato's writings are slight, his influence on S. may be detected on almost every page. Most of these borrowings are indicated in the commentary on the relevant passages.

Sallustian Traits: Brevity

Out of these ingredients, S. fashioned a style that was characterized by brevity, novelties in vocabulary and syntax, and *inconcinnitas*. Brevity is one of the qualities that S. admired most in Cato, and it was essential for any writer who wished to emulate Thucydides to achieve the same abrupt and rapid form of prose in Latin. *Brevitas* and *velocitas* are the words that S.'s ancient critics used most often to describe his style. To achieve this rapidity and sense of breathlessness, S. employed a number of common devices including (1) ellipsis (often the verb *sum* must be supplied, e.g., 5.3–4; sometimes a whole clause is left to the reader's imagination, e.g., 7.2n.); (2) asyndeton, which is especially noticeable in the way sentences are strung together without any particle showing the logical connection (e.g., 5.3–5) and in long lists of words (e.g., 21.2) or clauses (e.g., 31.3); (3) frequent use of the historical infinitive (e.g., 6.4n.); (4) the use of the polar opposites to suggest the full range of possibilities without tiresome enumeration (e.g., 11.3, 11.6, 15.4, 20.7, 30.4, 52.32); and (5) a decided preference for parataxis in lieu of the more complex and flowing periods of Ciceronian Latin (e.g., 2.1 parenthetical *nam*; the demonstrative adverb and coordinate conjunction in place of a subordinate relative clause, e.g., 3.3; and the demonstrative pronoun in the nominative to resume the subject contained in the previous sentence, vid. 8.1n.).

Vocabulary

S.'s choice of vocabulary was often censured by the purists, who objected to the rare and archaic, for which they had an abhorrence. S., however, revelled in the archaic. In several instances he appears to have deliberately revived the archaic meaning of words in current usage (e.g., 11.3 *venenum*; 26.2 *dolus*) or rehabilitated the literal meaning of words that had assumed a pejorative connotation (e.g., 11.5 *ductare*; 18.8n. *patrare*). He shows a fondness for adverbs in -*tim* (vid. 4.2n.), adjectives in -*osus* (e.g., 18.4), and abstract nouns in -*tudo* (vid. 17.2n.), while substitutes are found for a number of words common in Cicero (vid. 3.5n. *cupido*; 53.3n. *facundia*). A variety of obsolete or obsolescent forms and spellings are revived (vid. 7.5n. *labor*; 18.1n. *quibus*; 30.3n. *senati*;

37.1n. *plebes*), and the MSS preserve traces of the archaic orthography which is commonly adopted by most modern editors of S.'s text (e.g., *-umus* for *-imus* in superlatives; *-undus* for *-endus* in gerunds and gerundives; *vivos* and *vivom* for *vivus* and *vivum*, vid. 11.2n. *ignavos*).[12] S. was also noted as an innovator of new words (e.g., 42.2 *portatio*; 61.7 *incruentus*) and was blamed for his bold figures of speech.

Grammar and Syntax

A similar freedom and boldness may be observed in the grammar and syntax of S. One notes a much freer use of the infinitive (vid. 5.9n. *repetere*). Contrary to the standard usage, *quippe qui* is invariably construed with the indicative (vid. 48.2n.), and *quo* is used as equivalent to *ut* to introduce purpose clauses that contain no word in the comparative degree (vid. 11.5n.). Adverbs are used in place of predicate adjectives (vid. 20.2n.), prepositional phrases are made to modify substantives (vid. 6.1n.), and examples of synesis are abundant (e.g., 16.1n. *ex illis* referring to the collective noun *iuventus*; 23.6n. the collective noun *nobilitas* construed with one verb in the sing. and another in the pl.). The historical infinitive is employed extensively and in a variety of novel ways (e.g., twice in the passive voice in the *Cat.*, 10.6, 27.2; in combination with a finite verb having the same subject, 24.2; extended to copulative and modal verbs, 20.7 *esse*, 38.1 *fieri*, 25.5 *posse*). Occasionally a perfect passive participle is used by itself to form an ablative absolute (e.g., *Hist.* 5.13M *comperto*; *Hist.* 5.14M *audito*), and the modal ablative of the gerund is sometimes substituted for a present participle (vid. 61.2n.). The genitive of the gerundive is used to express tendency or purpose (vid. 6.7n.), and one notices a freer use of the partitive genitive (e.g., 45.3 *ad id loci* where the neut. pron. is the object of a prep.).

Inconcinnitas

In combining all of these ingredients, S. went out of his way to

---

12 This archaizing tendency on the part of modern editors of S. is carried to an extreme by Kurfess in his Teubner edition (1957) in which, for instance, *quom* is restored for the conjunction *cum*, *quoius* for *cuius*, *quoi* for *cui*, and most compounds are resolved into their unassimilated forms, e.g., 30.4 *inpediti*, 31.6 *conmotus*, 56.1 *conplet*. The MSS of S. doubtless reflect a tendency on the part of scribes to modernize orthography in the light of subsequent conventions and are therefore unreliable for determining the spelling that S. himself favored. The editor can only reach a probable solution to this complex problem based upon the evidence of contemporary usage that is furnished by inscriptions and the grammarians (see the judicious remarks of Maurenbrecher, *Historiarum Reliquiae*, Appendix II, pp. 212ff.). For the purposes of this commentary, the more moderate course followed by Ernout in his Budé edition (1958) is adopted.

present the unusual and unexpected. The result was variety and dissymmetry. To achieve this *inconcinnitas*, S. deliberately varied the order of words in standard expressions (e.g., 14.2 *alienum aes*; cf. 18.2, 23.6nn.) and phrases (e.g., 10.1 *maria terraeque*; cf. 36.4, 53.2nn.). The same verb is sometimes construed with a variety of constructions (vid. 5.9n. *disserere*). Balanced phrases are deliberately avoided by pairing a prepositional phrase with an *ubi* clause (9.3n.), by combining two different prepositional phrases (51.6n.), or by pairing an adverb with a modal ablative (e.g., 51.4 *recte atque ordine*) or with *per* + the accusative (e.g., 42.2). The striving for inconcinnity may be observed on almost every page, and by means of this device S. sought to enhance the interest of his account and avoid the risk of monotony.

Quintilian's verdict provides a fitting conclusion to this essay on S.'s style and achievement in the field of history. In his judgment (2.5.19), S. was a greater historian than Livy, whose style he compares with the flowing and diffuse prose of the Greek historian Herodotus (10.1.101), but he cautions his readers to avoid S. as a model for forensic oratory. Brevity and abruptness are ideally suited to the narration of *res gestae*, but the reader must be intelligent and attentive (10.1.32; cf. 4.2.45).

V. THE TEXTUAL TRADITION

Two of the manuscripts that preserve the *Bellum Catilinae* and the *Bellum Jugurthinum* are of the 9th century (**P** and **A**); the rest are mainly of the 11th. They may be divided into two classes, the *mutili* and the *integri*. The former are so named because they share the common feature of a lacuna in the text of the *Jugurtha* (103.2 *quinque delegit . . . 112.3 et ratam*) which is sometimes filled in by a later hand from an outside source, and they are clearly descended ultimately from a common archetype. The MSS in this class are our oldest and most reliable witnesses for the text of S., although they do not always agree among themselves despite their common ancestry. In addition to individual errors in transcription, there are signs of contamination from a source other than the archetype; numerous corrections are made by later hands; and in quite a few instances the genuine text appears to have been glossed by the scribe. Sometimes a more familiar word or form is substituted for an archaism; word order is tampered with to achieve a more normal sequence; and occasionally words that S. deliberately omitted are supplied. For a list of the principal witnesses to the text and their *sigla*, see p. 26.

Besides these sources, a single MS, **V** (Vaticanus 3864), which alone preserves the speeches and letters from the *Historiae*, also contains the text of the letters and speeches excerpted from the *Catiline* and *Jugurtha*. About contemporary with **P**, this MS shows a tendency to modernize the spelling of words and alter word order. We also possess for the *Catiline* two short papyrus fragments, one of the 5th (*Pap. Oxyrh.* VI no. 884) and one of the 4th century (*Pubblicazioni della Società Italiana*, vol. I, 1912, no. 110). Although both antedate our earliest MSS by a considerable interval, they are too short to be of much value, and the latter is extremely fragmentary. The text of the former, which preserves a portion of chapter 6 (6.1 *liberum atque solutum . . . 6.7 eo modo minime*), contains a remarkable number of corruptions which at least give us some idea of the state of S.'s text under the late Empire. It is chiefly useful for establishing the probable solution to two textual problems (vid. 6.2nn.).

Lastly, we have, in addition to the evidence of our medieval MSS, a large number of citations from the works of S. and reminiscences in ancient authors. His writings were culled for the unusual and the apropos by later historians, philosophers, grammarians, and rhetoricians who had access to texts of S. that predate the recension of the 4th or 5th century which doubtless produced the parent of all our extant MSS. Frequently these quotations are designed to illustrate a particular form or locution, and the immediate context in which the relevant words occur is of little concern and therefore likely to be altered or abridged by the author who may even be quoting from memory. These ancient *testimonia*, however, provide a useful check on the manuscript tradition and in a number of instances permit the editor to recover the genuine text of S. which would otherwise be lost (e.g., 5.9, 6.2nn.).

VI. SUMMARY OF THE CATILINARIAN CONSPIRACY

S. attributes to Catiline a long-standing desire to seize absolute power and make himself master of Rome as Sulla had done in the Civil War of 83–82 B.C. (5.6). His account of the conspiracy commences with the description of a meeting held in June of 64, shortly before the consular elections, at which Catiline outlined to his supporters his plans for revolution (17, 20–22). Inserted in this context is a flash-back to an earlier occasion when Catiline allegedly plotted to murder the consuls of 65 and seize control of the government. The details of this previous scheme, the so-called first conspiracy of Catiline, are discussed in Appendix II, where it is argued that the earlier conspiracy has no basis in historical fact. Accordingly, we shall take the meeting in June of 64 as our starting point for relating the stages in Catiline's schemes. As it will be seen, however, even this date precedes by more than a year the formation of a true conspiracy, despite S.'s claim to the contrary.

At the time of the consular elections in 64, Catiline had already suffered one setback in the advancement of his political career. Praetor in 68 and governor of Africa in 67 (vid. App. I), Catiline had been prevented from being a candidate for the consulship in 66 as he had intended. When he returned from Africa in 66 and announced his intention to stand for the consulship (vid. 18.2–3nn.), the consul L. Volcacius Tullus, who was to preside at this election, disallowed Catiline's candidacy on the advice of a *consilium* (Ascon. p. 89C). Apparently the consul's advisors based their decision on the fact that Catiline faced charges for extortion (*res repetundae*) arising from his conduct as governor of Africa, and they felt he should not be allowed to gain immunity from prosecution by securing election to the consulship. The prosecution itself was set in motion in 65 (Ascon. p. 85C), and the case came to trial during the summer of that year (Cic. *Att.* 1.1.1, 1.2.1). Although Catiline received support from many influential consulars (Cic. *Sull.* 81) and eventually gained an acquittal, the prosecution appears to have further delayed his ambition to reach the consulship by preventing him from being a candidate until the following year, 64.

Contrary to S.'s account, there is no reason to suspect that Catiline was plotting a bloody revolution when he was standing for office in 64. We learn from the fragments of Cicero's *Oratio in Toga Candida*, delivered shortly before the elections in 64, and the comments of Asconius on this speech, that Catiline enjoyed the support of powerful backers during this campaign. Catiline and another candidate, C. Antonius, had formed a coalition to defeat Cicero and secure the consulship for themselves. It is reasonable to suppose, with Asconius (p. 83C), that Crassus, and possibly Caesar, stood behind the candidacy of Catiline and Antonius and hoped to use these two friendly consuls to smooth the way for passage of several pieces of reform legislation in 63 (vid. 23.5n.). Catiline and Antonius would then proceed as proconsuls in 62 to hold the important provinces of Cisalpine Gaul and Macedonia where they would command armies and provide a counterbalance to the immense military power of Pompey, who was expected to return soon from the East (vid. 17.7n.).

As it turned out, Cicero, despite the disadvantage of being a *novus homo* (vid. 23.6n.), succeeded in alarming the voters against Catiline and Antonius. Although the latter was successful in securing one of the two consulships, Cicero rallied sufficient support among the nobility, *equites*, and followers of Pompey to come in at the head of the poll and defeat Catiline (vid. 24.1n.). The tribunes of 63 proceeded, nonetheless, to sponsor a series of reform proposals (including an agrarian law, relief for debtors, and a cancellation of the disabilities imposed by Sulla on the descendants of the proscribed), but thanks to Cicero's staunch opposition these measures failed to pass (Dio 37.25.4). Meanwhile, shortly after the elections in 64, Catiline was brought to trial by L. Lucceius for his role in the Sullan proscriptions and successfully weathered this second judicial threat to his career thanks, perhaps, to the support of Julius

Caesar, who presided over the court that acquitted him (vid. 24.2n.). Once again, many consulars came to Catiline's defense at his trial, and this fact reveals that he was not yet perceived as a dangerous revolutionary by these important figures in government (Cic. *Sull.* 81).

A far different picture emerges from S.'s account which makes Catiline the ringleader of a sinister plot at the time of his candidacy in 64. S. fails to allow for a gradual shift in Catiline's strategy and aims as his hopes of reaching the consulship faded, because S. prefers to present Catiline as a thoroughgoing villain, the product of a corrupt age, who was bent on the destruction of the state from the very beginning of his career. The weakness of this view becomes apparent when we examine the details of S.'s narrative covering the period between the elections in 64 and 63. Surprisingly little activity is assigned to the conspirators in the latter half of 64 and the first half of 63, and S. is hard pressed to sustain the notion that a full-scale revolution was already in the making. Chapters 24–26 covering this phase of the conspiracy report the recruitment of followers, the acquisition of money and arms, and the dispatch of lieutenants to various points in Italy (mere filler, anticipating events belonging more properly to the latter half of the year 63, 27.1–2). It is not until after the defeat of Catiline at the elections in 63 that our other sources begin to confirm that preparations for revolution had been set in motion.

It appears from these sources, and from a close reading of S. himself, that Catiline still entertained some hope of achieving supreme power by legitimate means until his final rejection by the voters in 63. This assumption explains why several months elapsed after the elections in 63 before rumors of a conspiracy began to be taken seriously by the senate. If Catiline and his followers had been pursuing revolutionary designs against the government since mid 64, it is remarkable that these plans were not farther along when the conspiracy came out into the open in the latter half of 63 and that the senate delayed so long in adopting countermeasures against the revolutionaries. This is not to argue, however, that Catiline continued to pursue his goal of being elected consul with the same strategy and resources as before his defeat by Cicero in 64. Rather, during his final campaign in 63, Catiline appears to have been deserted by his powerful backers who supported him in 64. He was forced, therefore, to appeal to a less respectable constituency, voters who longed for relief from financial woes (vid. 14.2n.) and a change in the status quo (vid. 20.1n.). This group comprised the urban poor, the veterans of Sulla who had squandered their bounties, the political enemies of Sulla who had survived the Civil War and proscriptions, and various ruined aristocrats who were hopelessly in debt. So bitter and heated was the campaigning in 63 that new legislation against corrupt electioneering (*ambitus*) was introduced and passed under the sponsorship of the consuls Cicero and Antonius in an attempt to curb the violence and bribery being practiced by Catiline and some of his competitors (Cic. *Mur.* 47, 67–68; *Schol. Bob.* p. 79St.).

S.'s account of this phase of Catiline's career, the period immediately preceding the elections in 63 and the plotting of revolution which followed—that phase which can more properly be called a conspiracy—leaves something to be desired. Several weaknesses are apparent. On the one hand, a number of significant events are passed over in silence. On the other, only one precise date is supplied in the narrative (30.1), and the narrative itself is so arranged that without the aid of more prominent signposts it is easy to become confused concerning the correct order of events. Fortunately, however, our other sources are fairly full and allow us to reconstruct with some precision the events leading up to the outbreak of armed revolution and the crushing of Catiline's army in January 62.

Shortly before the elections in 63, Catiline held a meeting of his supporters (called a *contio domestica* by Cic. *Mur.* 50) at which he made certain threatening remarks. Cicero learned of this meeting—possibly through informers recruited among Catiline's followers as S. reports (26.3), although S. does not relate this incident. Alarmed by Catiline's behavior, the senate postponed the elections and met on the day the elections were to have been held to consider Catiline's conduct. The meeting was inconclusive and no stringent measures were adopted against Catiline (Cic. *Mur.* 51). It was on this occasion, according to Cicero, that Catiline threatened general destruction against those who were stirring up conflagrations against his fortunes—a remark that S. transfers to the meeting in November just before Catiline's departure from Rome (vid. 31.9n.). It is also, perhaps, not fanciful to suppose that the *contio domestica* in 63 was taken by S. as his model for the meeting that he assigns to June of the previous year. In any case, the elections were held in due course, presumably in July after a brief delay, and Catiline was defeated by L. Licinius Murena and D. Iunius Silanus. To alarm the people to the threat posed by Catiline and his followers, Cicero wore a breastplate underneath his toga on the day he conducted the consular elections and surrounded himself with a loyal bodyguard (vid. 26.5n.).

Goaded by defeat at the polls and the hostile attacks of his political enemy Cicero, Catiline now resolved to have recourse to armed revolt (vid. 35.2–3nn.). Since the details of the revolution and suppression of the conspiracy are numerous and discussed in their proper place within the commentary, developments after the elections in 63 are presented below in outline form. References are given to the text for events reported by S. This annotation will enable the reader to see at a glance the order of S.'s presentation and will provide a convenient guide to topics treated in the commentary. Material derived from sources other than S. is enclosed in square brackets, and the reader is occasionally referred to particular notes for a more detailed discussion of controversial points such as specific dates and the relative order of certain events.

mid-July–Oct.	Manlius collects forces in Etruria at Faesulae; other followers of Catiline arrange disturbances in other parts of Italy (27.1).
20 Oct.	[Crassus and other leading nobles hand over to Cic. anonymous letters warning of an impending massacre in Rome (vid. 29.1n.).]
21 Oct.	Senate arms the coss. with *senatus consultum ultimum* to defend the state from harm (for date, vid. 29.2n.); watches posted in Rome (vid. 30.7n.).
27 Oct.	Manlius raises the standard of revolt at Faesulae (30.1).
28 Oct.	[Intended massacre of leading citizens in Rome (Cic. *Cat*. 1.7).]
late Oct.–early Nov.	[The quaestor P. Sestius sent with military forces by Cic. to secure Capua against the conspirators (Cic. *Sest*. 9).]
1 Nov.	[Attempt by conspirators to seize the town of Praeneste, ca. 23 miles SE of Rome, foiled (Cic. *Cat*. 1.8).]
ca. 1 or 2 Nov.	Senate learns of uprising at Faesulae from a letter sent to a senator L. Saenius; military commanders dispatched to threatened areas; rewards offered for betrayal of the conspiracy (30).
early Nov.	Catiline indicted by L. Aemilius Paulus under the *lex Plautia de vi* (31.4).
night of 6–7 Nov.	Meeting of the conspirators at the house of M. Porcius Laeca (for date, vid. 27.3n.).
morning of 7 Nov.	Failed assassination attempt against Cic. (28.1–3).
8 Nov.	Meeting of the senate [in temple of Jupiter Stator (vid. 31.5n.)]; delivery of Cicero's *First Catilinarian* urging Catiline to leave Rome (31.5–9; for date, vid. 31.6n.).
night of 8–9 Nov.	Departure of Catiline from Rome (32.1). Within a few days, he joins Manlius at Faesulae (36.1).
9 Nov.	[Delivery of Cicero's *Second Catilinarian*

justifying his policies to the people, (for date, vid. Cic. *Cat.* 2.12).]

ca. mid-Nov.

Catiline and Manlius declared *hostes* by the senate; date fixed for extending amnesty to deserters of the conspiracy; coss. authorized to levy an army, and Antonius instructed to crush the rebel forces (36.2–3).

Catiline's associate, the praetor P. Lentulus, attempts to recruit the support of the Allobroges, a Gallic nation, through their ambassadors in Rome (40). The Allobroges betray the negotiations to Cic. and promise cooperation (41).

late Nov.–early Dec.

Disturbances in the two Gauls, Picenum, the territory of the Bruttii, and Apulia put down (42.1–3).

late Nov.

Catiline evacuates his camp near Faesulae to avoid the approach of Antonius' army (56.4).

night of 2–3 Dec.

Arrest of the conspirator Volturcius and the Allobroges on the Mulvian Bridge (45).

3 Dec.

Meeting of the senate in the temple of Concord; documentary evidence and testimony presented against the conspirators; five of the leading conspirators placed under house arrest (46.3–47). [Cic. honored with a vote of thanks and declaration of a *supplicatio* (vid. 47.3n.); Cic. caused a written record of the senate's meetings on the 3rd, 4th, and 5th to be made and published (vid. 47.1–4 introd. n.).]

[Delivery of Cicero's *Third Catilinarian* reporting to the people the arrest of the conspirators and the senate's findings (for date, vid. Cic. *Cat.* 3.5).]

Conspirators lose sympathy among the common people when they learn of the plans to set fire to the city (48.1–2).

4 Dec.

Meeting of the senate; further testimony against the conspirators; attempt by L. Tarquinius to implicate M. Crassus (48.3–9); rewards voted to the informers (50.1).

Abortive attempt to rescue the conspirators under house arrest (50.1–2).

5 Dec.

Senate debates the punishment of the conspirators; Caesar advocates confiscation of property and life imprisonment in the towns of Italy; [Cic. delivers *Fourth Catilinarian* to rally senators who wavered after the speech of Caesar (vid. 52.1n.)]; Cato advocates the death penalty, and the senate supports this motion (50.3–53.1).

Five of the leading conspirators executed in the *Tullianum* towards evening (55). [Cic. makes a brief address to the crowd gathered outside the prisonhouse in the Forum and is given a triumphal escort to his home by torch light (vid. 56.1n.).]

ca. 10 Dec.   The tribune L. Bestia was to attack the policies of Cic. at a public meeting, and this *contio* was to provide a signal for the conspirators to set fire to Rome and begin the massacre on the following night (43.1–2). [Possibly these plans had been postponed to 16/17 Dec. (vid. 43.1n. *contione*).]

ca. 15 Dec.   News of the arrest and execution of the conspirators in Rome reaches Catiline's camp in the hills north of Faesulae; massive desertions occur in his army following this disclosure (57.1).

ca. 25 Dec.   Catiline's attempt to break out of Etruria into Gaul with his remaining forces blocked by Q. Metellus Celer (57.1–3).

29 Dec.   [Cic. prevented by the tribunes Bestia and Metellus Nepos from addressing the Roman people when laying down his office on the grounds that he executed Roman citizens without a trial (vid. 17.3n. *Bestia*).]

early Jan. 62 B.C.   Catiline arrives in the vicinity of Pistoria. Catiline's forces [numbering approximately 3,000 men (Dio 37.40.1)] join battle with Antonius' army under the command of his legate M. Petreius near Pistoria; Catiline and his army are annihilated (57.5–61).

3 Jan.   [The tribune Q. Metellus Nepos attempts to pass a bill recalling Pompey to put down the insurrection of Catiline; the bill is vetoed and rioting ensues; the senate passes the *senatus consultum ultimum*, and Nepos withdraws from Rome to join Pompey in the East (Dio 37.43; Cic. *Fam.* 5.2.8).]

ca. mid-Jan.	[Catiline's head is brought to Rome to establish proof of his death (Dio 37.40.2).]
spring of 62	[The praetors Q. Cicero and M. Bibulus are credited with putting down disturbances in central and southern Italy caused by Catiline's followers (vid. 42.1n.).]

VII. STRUCTURE OF THE *BELLUM CATILINAE*

The following analysis is designed to show the arrangement of S.'s narrative. Attention is drawn to digressions (marked with two vertical strokes and presented at the far right), speeches and documents (set in italics), and S.'s technique of interweaving his account of the conspiracy in Rome with reports of events occurring elsewhere in Italy (marked with single vertical strokes and indented to the near right).

MAIN EVENTS
I EVENTS OCCURRING ELSEWHERE
II DIGRESSIONS

1–4	II Preface: justification for writing history, choice of topic
5.1–8	Portrait of Catiline
5.9–13	II Early history of Rome: growth and moral decline
14–16	Corruption of Catiline and his associates
17	Meeting of conspirators, June 64
18–19	II First Catilinarian Conspiracy
20–22	Resumption of meeting
20.2–20.17	*Speech of Catiline*
23	Alarm caused by rumors of Catiline's intentions
24	Election of Cicero; history of conspiracy to end of 64
25	II Portrait of Sempronia
26	Defeat of Catiline at consular elections in 63
27.1	I Manlius and others dispatched to various parts of Italy
27.2–28.3	Activities of conspirators in Rome; attempt on life of Cicero
28.4–31.3	I Activities of Manlius in Etruria and counter-measures of government

31.4–32.2   Departure of Catiline from Rome

32.3–34.1 | Negotiations with Manlius
33 | *Dispatch of Manlius* to Marcius Rex

34.2–36.3   Reaction of government against Catiline
35   *Letter of Catiline* to Catulus

36.4–39.5 || Reflection on the corrupt state of
                    Roman society

39.6–41   Negotiations of Lentulus with Allobroges

42 | Disturbances in various regions of Italy and
                    Gaul

43   Plans of conspirators to set fires in Rome and carry out
                    massacre
44–45   Betrayal of conspirators by Allobroges and arrest
44.5   *Letter of Lentulus* to Catiline
46–48   Examination of conspirators and informers by senate
49   Attempt to implicate Caesar in conspiracy
50–53.1   Debate in senate on fate of conspirators in custody
51   *Speech of Caesar*
52.2–36   *Speech of Cato*

53.2–54 || Reflection on character of Caesar and
                    Cato

55   Execution of conspirators

56–57 | Movements of Catiline's army
58-61 | Final Battle
58 | *Speech of Catiline*

VARIATIONS FROM THE TEXTS OF ERNOUT
AND KURFESS

The text of this edition is based on that of Ernout (3rd ed., 1958) with the following alterations, not including minor differences in orthography.

	This edition	Ernout
title:	*Bellum Catilinae*	*De Coniuratione Catilinae*
3.5	*eadem qua*	*eadem quae*
6.1	*cumque his*	*cumque is*
7.4	*usum militiae*	*usu militiam*
10.2	*otium divitiaeque*	*otium divitiae*
30.4	*hi*	*i*
31.3	*<omni rumore>*	
	<adripere omnia>	
31.5	*sicut*	*sicubi*
33.1	*patriae, sed*	*patria sed<e>*
36.5	*atque uti*	*ac veluti*
42.3	*in citeriore Gallia*	*in ulteriore Gallia*
43.1	*suum quodque*	*suum quoique*
51.27	*ignaros eius*	*ignaros [eius]*
51.40	*coepere, tum*	*coepere. Tum*
51.42	*illis*	*in illis*
52.13	*existumans ea quae*	*existumans quae*
52.29	*prospere*	*prospera*
53.5	*sicuti effeta parentum*	*sicuti <esset> effeta pariendo*
	<vi>	
53.6	*possum*	*possem*
57.4	*expeditos*	*expeditus*
59.5	*inermis*	*inermos*

The following list of variants, apart from differences in orthography (vid. Introd. n.12), is presented for the convenience of readers who may wish to consult the Teubner text of Sallust, edited by A. Kurfess (3rd ed., 1957).

This edition		Kurfess
2.8	*transiere*	*transigere*
3.2	*exaequanda*	*exequenda*
	dehinc	*dein*
3.5	*eadem qua*	*eadem quae*
6.1	*cumque his*	*et cum his*
15.5	*colos ei exsanguis*	*colos exanguis*
18.1	*in quibus*	*in quis*
19.2	*Cn. Pompei*	*Pompei*
20.2	*forent*	*foret*
22.2	†*dictitare*†	*dicationem*
23.3	*interdum*	*etiam*
25.2	*Graecis et Latinis*	*Graecis Latinis*
28.4	*fecerat*	*fecerant*
31.9	*restinguam*	*extinguam*
33.2	*miseriti*	*miserti*
35.3	*solvere possem*	*solvere non possem*
43.1	†*Faesulanum*†	*Aefulanum*
50.4	*dixerat qui*	*dixit quod*
51.5	*atque advorsa*	*et advorsa*
51.35	*Atque ego haec*	*atque haec ego*
52.36	*maxuma pericula*	*summa pericula*
53.5	*magnitudine sua*	*magnitudine sui*
	sicuti effeta parentum *<vi>*	*sicuti effeta <esset> partu*
55.6	*exitium vitae*	*exitum [vitae]*
57.4	*expeditos*	*expeditus*
59.2	*et ab dextra rupe<m>* *aspera<m>*	*et ab dextra rupe aspera*
59.3	*Ab eis centuriones,* *omnis lectos et* *evocatos*	*ab his omnis evocatos et* *centuriones*
	quemque armatum	*quemque [armatum]*
61.2	*quisque vivos*	*quisque [vivos]*
61.3	*paulo divorsius, sed* *omnes*	*paulo divorsius, <alis alibi* *stantes>, sed omnes*

SIGLA

V = cod. Vaticanus 3864 (9th cent.)

codices mutili

P = cod. Parisinus 16024 (9th cent.)
A = cod. Parisinus 16025 (late 9th cent.)
C = cod. Parisinus 6085 (10th/11th cent.)
B = cod. Basileensis A.N. IV 11 (11th cent.)
Q = cod. Parisinus 5748 (10th/11th cent.)
N = cod. Palatinus 889 (11th cent.)
K = cod. Palatinus 887 (10th/11th cent.)
H = cod. Berolinensis 205 (11th cent.)
M = cod. Monacensis 4559 (11th/12th cent.)
T = cod. Turicensis bibl. reip. C143a (11th/12th cent.)
D = cod. Parisinus 10195 (11th cent.)
F = cod. Hauniensis 25 (11th cent.)
R = cod. Vaticanus 3325 (12th cent.)

codices integri

l = cod. Leidensis Voss. lat. 73 (11th cent.)
s = cod. Lipsiensis bibl. sen. rep. I fol. 4 (11th cent.)
n = cod. Parisinus 6086 (11th cent.)
m = cod. Monacensis 14477 (11th cent.)
e = cod. Einsidelensis (11th cent.)
π = cod. Palatinus 883 (12th cent.)

P^1A^1 signify the first hand, P^2A^2 a correcting hand.

BELLUM CATILINAE

I. [1]Omnis homines qui sese student praestare ceteris animalibus summa ope niti decet ne vitam silentio transeant veluti pecora, quae natura prona atque ventri oboedientia finxit. [2]Sed nostra omnis vis in animo et corpore sita est; animi imperio, corporis servitio magis utimur; alterum nobis cum dis, alterum cum beluis commune est. [3]Quo mihi rectius videtur ingeni quam virium opibus gloriam quaerere et, quoniam vita ipsa qua fruimur brevis est, memoriam nostri quam maxume longam efficere. [4]Nam divitiarum et formae gloria fluxa atque fragilis est, virtus clara aeternaque habetur.

[5]Sed diu magnum inter mortalis certamen fuit vine corporis an virtute animi res militaris magis procederet. [6]Nam et prius quam incipias consulto et, ubi consulueris, mature facto opus est. [7]Ita utrumque per se indigens alterum alterius auxilio eget.

II. [1]Igitur initio reges—nam in terris nomen imperi id primum fuit—divorsi, pars ingenium, alii corpus exercebant; etiam tum vita hominum sine cupiditate agitabatur, sua cuique satis placebant. [2]Postea vero quam in Asia Cyrus, in Graecia Lacedaemonii et Athenienses coepere urbis atque nationes subigere, lubidinem dominandi causam belli habere, maximam gloriam in maximo imperio putare, tum demum periculo atque negotiis compertum est in bello plurumum ingenium posse. [3]Quod si regum atque imperatorum animi virtus in pace ita ut in bello valeret, aequabilius atque constantius sese res humanae haberent, neque aliud alio ferri neque mutari ac misceri omnia cerneres. [4]Nam imperium facile eis artibus retinetur quibus initio partum est. [5]Verum ubi pro labore desidia, pro continentia et aequitate lubido atque superbia invasere, fortuna simul cum moribus immutatur. [6]Ita imperium semper ad optumum quemque a minus bono transfertur.

[7]Quae homines arant, navigant, aedificant, virtuti omnia parent. [8]Sed multi mortales, dediti ventri atque somno, indocti incultique vitam sicuti peregrinantes transiere. Quibus profecto contra naturam corpus voluptati, anima oneri fuit. Eorum ego vitam mortemque iuxta aestumo, quoniam de utraque siletur. [9]Verum enim vero is demum mihi vivere atque frui anima videtur, qui aliquo negotio intentus praeclari facinoris aut artis bonae famam quaerit. Sed in magna copia rerum aliud alii natura iter ostendit.

III. [1]Pulchrum est bene facere rei publicae, etiam bene dicere haud absurdum est; vel pace vel bello clarum fieri licet; et qui fecere, et qui facta aliorum scripsere, multi laudantur. [2]Ac mihi quidem, tametsi haudquaquam par gloria sequitur scriptorem et auctorem rerum, tamen in primis arduum videtur res gestas scribere: primum, quod facta dictis exaequanda sunt; dehinc, quia plerique, quae delicta reprehenderis, malivolentia et invidia dicta putant; ubi de magna virtute atque gloria bonorum memores, quae sibi quisque facilia factu putat, aequo animo accipit, supra ea veluti ficta pro falsis ducit.

[3]Sed ego adulescentulus initio, sicuti plerique, studio ad rem publicam latus sum, ibique mihi multa advorsa fuere. Nam pro pudore, pro abstinentia, pro virtute, audacia, largitio, avaritia vigebant. [4]Quae tametsi animus aspernabatur, insolens malarum artium, tamen inter tanta vitia imbecilla aetas ambitione corrupta tenebatur; [5]ac me, cum ab relicuorum malis moribus dissentirem, nihilo minus honoris cupido eadem qua ceteros fama atque invidia vexabat.

IV. [1]Igitur, ubi animus ex multis miseriis atque periculis requievit et mihi relicuam aetatem a re publica procul habendam decrevi, non fuit consilium socordia atque desidia bonum otium conterere, neque vero agrum colundo aut venando, servilibus officiis, intentum aetatem agere; [2]sed a quo incepto studioque me ambitio mala detinuerat eodem regressus, statui res gestas populi Romani carptim, ut quaeque memoria digna videbantur, perscribere; eo magis quod mihi a spe, metu, partibus rei publicae animus liber erat. [3]Igitur de Catilinae coniuratione quam verissume potero paucis absolvam; [4]nam id facinus in primis ego memorabile existumo sceleris atque periculi novitate. [5]De cuius hominis moribus pauca prius explananda sunt quam initium narrandi faciam.

V. [1]L. Catilina, nobili genere natus, fuit magna vi et animi et corporis, sed ingenio malo pravoque. [2]Huic ab adulescentia bella intestina, caedes, rapinae, discordia civilis grata fuere, ibique iuventutem suam exercuit. [3]Corpus patiens inediae, algoris, vigiliae, supra quam cuiquam credibile est. [4]Animus audax, subdolus, varius, cuius rei lubet simulator ac dissimulator; alieni adpetens, sui profusus; ardens in cupiditatibus; satis eloquentiae, sapientiae parum. [5]Vastus animus inmoderata, incredibilia, nimis alta semper cupiebat. [6]Hunc post dominationem L. Sullae lubido maxuma invaserat rei publicae capiundae, neque id quibus modis adsequeretur, dum sibi regnum pararet, quicquam pensi habebat. [7]Agitabatur magis magisque in dies animus ferox inopia rei familiaris et conscientia scelerum, quae utraque eis artibus auxerat quas supra memoravi. [8]Incitabant praeterea corrupti civitatis mores, quos pessuma ac divorsa inter se mala, luxuria atque avaritia, vexabant.

[9]Res ipsa hortari videtur, quoniam de moribus civitatis tempus admonuit, supra repetere ac paucis instituta maiorum domi militiaeque, quomodo rem publicam habuerint quantamque reliquerint, ut, paulatim *ut* immutata, ex pulcherruma <atque optuma> pessuma ac flagitiosissuma facta sit, disserere.

VI. [1]Urbem Romam, sicuti ego accepi, condidere atque habuere initio Troiani qui, Aenea duce profugi, sedibus incertis vagabantur, cumque his Aborigines, genus hominum agreste, sine legibus, sine imperio, liberum atque solutum. [2]Hi postquam in una moenia convenere, dispari genere, dissimili lingua, alius alio more viventes, incredibile memoratu est quam facile coaluerint: <ita brevi multitudo diversa atque vaga concordia civitas facta erat.>

[3]Sed postquam res eorum civibus, moribus, agris aucta satis prospera satisque pollens videbatur, sicuti pleraque mortalium habentur, invidia ex opulentia orta est. [4]Igitur reges populique finitumi bello temptare, pauci ex amicis auxilio esse; nam ceteri, metu perculsi, a periculis aberant. [5]At Romani, domi militiaeque intenti festinare, parare, alius alium hortari, hostibus obviam ire, libertatem, patriam parentesque armis tegere. Post, ubi pericula virtute propulerant, sociis atque amicis auxilia portabant, magisque dandis quam accipiundis beneficiis amicitias parabant. [6]Imperium legitumum, nomen imperi regium habebant. Delecti, quibus corpus annis infirmum, ingenium sapientia validum erat, rei publicae consultabant; ei vel aetate vel curae similitudine patres appellabantur. [7]Post, ubi regium imperium, quod initio conservandae libertatis atque augendae rei publicae fuerat, in superbiam dominationemque se convortit, inmutato more annua imperia binosque imperatores sibi fecere; eo modo minume posse putabant per licentiam insolescere animum humanum.

VII. [1]Sed ea tempestate coepere se quisque extollere magisque ingenium in promptu habere. [2]Nam regibus boni quam mali suspectiores sunt, semperque eis aliena virtus formidulosa est. [3]Sed civitas incredibile memoratu est adepta libertate quantum brevi creverit; tanta cupido gloriae incesserat. [4]Iam primum iuventus, simul ac belli patiens erat, in castris per laborem usum militiae discebat, magisque in decoris armis et militaribus equis quam in scortis atque conviviis lubidinem habebant. [5]Igitur talibus viris non labor insolitus, non locus ullus asper aut arduus erat, non armatus hostis formidulosus; virtus omnia domuerat. [6]Sed gloriae maxumum certamen inter ipsos erat; se quisque hostem ferire, murum ascendere, conspici dum tale facinus faceret, properabat; eas divitias, eam bonam famam magnamque nobilitatem putabant. Laudis avidi, pecuniae liberales erant; gloriam ingentem, divitias honestas volebant. [7]Memorare possum quibus in locis maxumas hostium copias

except that this topic would draw us away

populus Romanus parva manu fuderit, quas urbis natura munitas pugnando ceperit, ni ea res longius nos ab incepto traheret.

VIII. [1]Sed profecto fortuna in omni re dominatur; ea res cunctas ex lubidine magis quam ex vero celebrat obscuratque. [2]Atheniensium res gestae, sicuti ego aestumo, satis amplae magnificaeque fuere, verum aliquanto minores tamen quam fama feruntur. [3]Sed quia provenere ibi scriptorum magna ingenia, per terrarum orbem Atheniensium facta pro maxumis celebrantur. [4]Ita eorum qui fecere virtus tanta habetur, quantum eam verbis potuere extollere praeclara ingenia. [5]At populo Romano numquam ea copia fuit, quia prudentissumus quisque maxume negotiosus erat; ingenium nemo sine corpore exercebat; optumus quisque facere quam dicere, sua ab aliis bene facta laudari quam ipse aliorum narrare malebat.

IX. [1]Igitur domi militiaeque boni mores colebantur; concordia maxuma, minuma avaritia erat. Ius bonumque apud eos non legibus magis quam natura valebat. [2]Iurgia, discordias, simultates cum hostibus exercebant, cives cum civibus de virtute certabant. In suppliciis deorum magnifici, domi parci, in amicos fideles erant. [3]Duabus his artibus, audacia in bello, ubi pax evenerat aequitate, seque remque publicam curabant. [4]Quarum rerum ego maxuma documenta haec habeo, quod in bello saepius vindicatum est in eos qui contra imperium in hostem pugnaverant quique tardius revocati proelio excesserant, quam qui signa relinquere aut pulsi loco cedere ausi erant; [5]in pace vero quod beneficiis magis quam metu imperium agitabant, et accepta iniuria ignoscere quam persequi malebant.

X. [1]Sed ubi labore atque iustitia res publica crevit, reges magni bello domiti, nationes ferae et populi ingentes vi subacti, Carthago, aemula imperi Romani, ab stirpe interiit, cuncta maria terraeque patebant, saevire fortuna ac miscere omnia coepit. [2]Qui labores, pericula, dubias atque asperas res facile toleraverant, eis otium divitiaeque, optanda alias, oneri miseriaeque fuere. [3]Igitur primo pecuniae, deinde imperi cupido crevit; ea quasi materies omnium malorum fuere. [4]Namque avaritia fidem, probitatem ceterasque artis bonas subvortit; pro his superbiam, crudelitatem, deos neglegere, omnia venalia habere edocuit. [5]Ambitio multos mortalis falsos fieri subegit, aliud clausum in pectore, aliud in lingua promptum habere, amicitias inimicitiasque non ex re, sed ex commodo aestumare; magisque voltum quam ingenium bonum habere. [6]Haec primo paulatim crescere, interdum vindicari; post, ubi contagio quasi pestilentia invasit, civitas inmutata, imperium ex iustissumo atque optumo crudele intolerandumque factum.

XI. [1]Sed primo magis ambitio quam avaritia animos hominum exercebat, quod tamen vitium propius virtutem erat. [2]Nam gloriam, honorem, imperium bonus et ignavos aeque sibi exoptant; sed ille vera via nititur, huic, quia bonae artes desunt, dolis atque fallaciis contendit. [3]Avaritia pecuniae studium habet, quam nemo sapiens concupivit; ea, quasi venenis malis imbuta, corpus animumque virilem effeminat; semper infinita, insatiabilis est, neque copia neque inopia minuitur. [4]Sed, postquam L. Sulla, armis recepta re publica, bonis initiis malos eventus habuit, rapere omnes, trahere, domum alius, alius agros cupere, neque modum neque modestiam victores habere, foeda crudeliaque in civis facinora facere. [5]Huc accedebat quod L. Sulla exercitum quem in Asia ductaverat, quo sibi fidum faceret, contra morem maiorum luxuriose nimisque liberaliter habuerat. Loca amoena, voluptaria facile in otio ferocis militum animos molliverant. [6]Ibi primum insuevit exercitus populi Romani amare, potare, signa, tabulas pictas, vasa caelata mirari, ea privatim et publice rapere, delubra spoliare, sacra profanaque omnia polluere. [7]Igitur ei milites, postquam victoriam adepti sunt, nihil relicui victis fecere. [8]Quippe secundae res sapientium animos fatigant; ne illi corruptis moribus victoriae temperarent.

XII. [1]Postquam divitiae honori esse coepere et eas gloria, imperium, potentia sequebatur, hebescere virtus, paupertas probro haberi, innocentia pro malivolentia duci coepit. [2]Igitur ex divitiis iuventutem luxuria atque avaritia cum superbia invasere; rapere, consumere, sua parvi pendere, aliena cupere, pudorem, pudicitiam, divina atque humana promiscua, nihil pensi neque moderati habere. [3]Operae pretium est, cum domos atque villas cognoveris in urbium modum exaedificatas, visere templa deorum quae nostri maiores, religiosissumi mortales, fecere. [4]Verum illi delubra deorum pietate, domos suas gloria decorabant; neque victis quicquam praeter iniuriae licentiam eripiebant. [5]At hi contra, ignavissumi homines, per summum scelus omnia ea sociis adimere, quae fortissumi viri victores reliquerant: proinde quasi iniuriam facere, id demum esset imperio uti.

XIII. [1]Nam quid ea memorem quae nisi eis qui videre nemini credibilia sunt, a privatis compluribus subvorsos montis, maria constrata esse? [2]Quibus mihi videntur ludibrio fuisse divitiae; quippe quas honeste habere licebat abuti per turpitudinem properabant. [3]Sed lubido stupri, ganeae ceterique cultus non minor incesserat: viri muliebria pati, mulieres pudicitiam in propatulo habere; vescendi causa terra marique omnia exquirere, dormire prius quam somni cupido esset, non famem aut sitim, neque frigus neque lassitudinem opperiri, sed ea omnia luxu antecapere. [4]Haec iuventutem, ubi familiares opes defecerant, ad facinora incendebant. [5]Animus inbutus malis artibus haud facile lubidinibus carebat; eo profusius omnibus modis quaestui atque sumptui deditus erat.

XIV. [1]In tanta tamque corrupta civitate Catilina, id quod factu facillumum erat, omnium flagitiorum atque facinorum circum se tamquam stipatorum catervas habebat. [2]Nam quicumque inpudicus, adulter, ganeo, manu, ventre, pene, bona patria laceraverat, quique alienum aes grande conflaverat quo flagitium aut facinus redimeret, [3]praeterea omnes undique parricidae, sacrilegi, convicti iudiciis aut pro factis iudicium timentes, ad hoc quos manus atque lingua periurio aut sanguine civili alebat, postremo omnes quos flagitium, egestas, conscius animus exagitabat, ei Catilinae proxumi familiaresque erant. [4]Quod si quis etiam a culpa vacuus in amicitiam eius inciderat, cottidiano usu atque illecebris facile par similisque ceteris efficiebatur. [5]Sed maxume adulescentium familiaritates adpetebat; eorum animi molles etiam et fluxi dolis haud difficulter capiebantur. [6]Nam ut cuiusque studium ex aetate flagrabat, aliis scorta praebere, aliis canes atque equos mercari, postremo neque sumptui neque modestiae suae parcere dum illos obnoxios fidosque sibi faceret. [7]Scio fuisse nonnullos qui ita existumarent iuventutem, quae domum Catilinae frequentabat, parum honeste pudicitiam habuisse; sed ex aliis rebus magis quam quod cuiquam id compertum foret haec fama valebat.

XV. [1]Iam primum adulescens Catilina multa nefanda stupra fecerat, cum virgine nobili, cum sacerdote Vestae, alia huiuscemodi contra ius fasque. [2]Postremo captus amore Aureliae Orestillae, cuius praeter formam nihil umquam bonus laudavit, quod ea nubere illi dubitabat, timens privignum adulta aetate, pro certo creditur necato filio vacuam domum scelestis nuptiis fecisse. [3]Quae quidem res mihi in primis videtur causa fuisse facinus maturandi. [4]Namque animus impurus, dis hominibusque infestus, neque vigiliis neque quietibus sedari poterat; ita conscientia mentem excitam vastabat. [5]Igitur colos ei exsanguis, foedi oculi, citus modo, modo tardus incessus; prorsus in facie voltuque vecordia inerat.

XVI. [1]Sed iuventutem quam, ut supra diximus, inlexerat, multis modis mala facinora edocebat. [2]Ex illis testis signatoresque falsos commodare; fidem, fortunas, pericula vilia habere, post, ubi eorum famam atque pudorem adtriverat, maiora alia imperabat. [3]Si causa peccandi in praesens minus suppetebat, nihilo minus insontis sicuti sontis circumvenire, iugulare; scilicet ne per otium torpescerent manus aut animus, gratuito potius malus atque crudelis erat. [4]His amicis sociisque confisus Catilina, simul quod aes alienum per omnis terras ingens erat, et quod plerique Sullani milites, largius suo usi, rapinarum et victoriae veteris memores, civile bellum exoptabant, opprimundae rei publicae consilium cepit. [5]In Italia nullus exercitus; Cn. Pompeius in extremis terris bellum gerebat; ipsi consulatum petenti magna spes; senatus nihil sane intentus; tutae tranquillaeque res omnes; sed ea prorsus opportuna Catilinae.

XVII. [1]Igitur circiter Kalendas Iunias, L. Caesare et C. Figulo consulibus, primo singulos appellare, hortari alios, alios temptare; opes suas, inparatam rem publicam, magna praemia coniurationis docere. [2]Ubi satis explorata sunt quae voluit, in unum omnis convocat quibus maxuma necessitudo et plurumum audaciae inerat. [3]Eo convenere senatorii ordinis P. Lentulus Sura, P. Autronius, L. Cassius Longinus, C. Cethegus, P. et Ser. Sullae Ser. filii, L. Vargunteius, Q. Annius, M. Porcius Laeca, L. Bestia, Q. Curius; [4]praeterea ex equestri ordine M. Fulvius Nobilior, L. Statilius, P. Gabinius Capito, C. Cornelius; ad hoc multi ex coloniis et municipiis, domi nobiles. [5]Erant praeterea complures paulo occultius consili huiusce participes nobiles, quos magis dominationis spes hortabatur quam inopia aut alia necessitudo. [6]Ceterum iuventus pleraque, sed maxume nobilium, Catilinae inceptis favebat; quibus in otio vel magnifice vel molliter vivere copia erat, incerta pro certis, bellum quam pacem malebant. [7]Fuere item ea tempestate qui crederent M. Licinium Crassum non ignarum eius consili fuisse; quia Cn. Pompeius invisus ipsi magnum exercitum ductabat, cuiusvis opes voluisse contra illius potentiam crescere, simul confisum, si coniuratio valuisset, facile apud illos principem se fore.

XVIII. [1]Sed antea item coniuravere pauci contra rem publicam, in quibus Catilina; [2]de qua quam verissume potero dicam. L. Tullo et M.' Lepido consulibus, P. Autronius et P. Sulla, designati consules, legibus ambitus interrogati, poenas dederant. [3]Post paulo Catilina pecuniarum repetundarum reus, prohibitus erat consulatum petere, quod intra legitimos dies profiteri nequiverat. [4]Erat eodem tempore Cn. Piso, adulescens nobilis, summae audaciae, egens, factiosus, quem ad perturbandam rem publicam inopia atque mali mores stimulabant. [5]Cum hoc Catilina et Autronius, circiter Nonas Decembris consilio communicato, parabant in Capitolio Kalendis Ianuariis L. Cottam et L. Torquatum consules interficere, ipsi fascibus correptis Pisonem cum exercitu ad optinendas duas Hispanias mittere. [6]Ea re cognita, rursus in Nonas Februarias consilium caedis transtulerant. [7]Iam tum non consulibus modo, sed plerisque senatoribus perniciem machinabantur. [8]Quod ni Catilina maturasset pro curia signum sociis dare, eo die post conditam urbem Romam pessumum facinus patratum foret. Quia nondum frequentes armati convenerant, ea res consilium diremit.

XIX. [1]Postea Piso in citeriorem Hispaniam quaestor pro praetore missus est, adnitente Crasso, quod eum infestum inimicum Cn. Pompeio cognoverat. [2]Neque tamen senatus provinciam invitus dederat, quippe foedum hominem a re publica procul esse volebat; simul, quia boni complures praesidium in eo putabant, et iam tum potentia Cn. Pompei formidulosa erat. [3]Sed is Piso in provincia ab equitibus Hispanis quos in exercitu ductabat, iter faciens occisus est. [4]Sunt qui ita dicant imperia eius iniusta, superba, crudelia barbaros nequivisse pati; [5]alii autem equites illos, Cn. Pompei veteres fidosque clientis, voluntate eius Pisonem adgressos; numquam Hispanos praeterea tale facinus fecisse, sed imperia saeva multa antea perpessos. Nos eam rem in medio relinquemus. [6]De superiore coniuratione satis dictum.

XX. [1]Catilina, ubi eos, quos paulo ante memoravi, convenisse videt, tametsi cum singulis multa saepe egerat, tamen in rem fore credens univorsos appellare et cohortari, in abditam partem aedium secedit atque ibi, omnibus arbitris procul amotis, orationem huiuscemodi habuit:

[2]"Ni virtus fidesque vostra satis spectata mihi forent, nequiquam opportuna res cecidisset; spes magna, dominatio in manibus frustra fuissent, neque ego per ignaviam aut vana ingenia incerta pro certis captarem. [3]Sed quia multis et magnis tempestatibus vos cognovi fortis fidosque mihi, eo animus ausus est maxumum atque pulcherrumum facinus incipere, simul quia vobis eadem quae mihi bona malaque esse intellexi: [4]nam idem velle atque idem nolle, ea demum firma amicitia est.

[5]"Sed ego quae mente agitavi omnes iam antea divorsi audistis. [6]Ceterum mihi in dies magis animus accenditur, cum considero quae condicio vitae futura sit, nisi nosmet ipsi vindicamus in libertatem. [7]Nam postquam res publica in paucorum potentium ius atque dicionem concessit, semper illis reges, tetrarchae vectigales esse, populi, nationes stipendia pendere; ceteri omnes, strenui, boni, nobiles atque ignobiles, volgus fuimus sine gratia, sine auctoritate, eis obnoxii quibus, si res publica valeret, formidini essemus. [8]Itaque omnis gratia, potentia, honos, divitiae apud illos sunt aut ubi illi volunt; nobis reliquere repulsas, pericula, iudicia, egestatem. [9]Quae quousque tandem patiemini, o fortissumi viri? Nonne emori per virtutem praestat quam vitam miseram atque inhonestam, ubi alienae superbiae ludibrio fueris, per dedecus amittere? [10]Verum enim vero, pro deum atque hominum fidem, victoria in manu nobis est. Viget aetas, animus valet; contra illis annis atque divitiis omnia consenuerunt. Tantum modo incepto opus est; cetera res expediet. [11]Etenim quis mortalium, cui virile ingenium est, tolerare potest illis divitias superare quas profundant in exstruendo mari et montibus coaequandis, nobis rem familiarem etiam ad necessaria deesse? illos binas aut amplius domos continuare, nobis larem familiarem nusquam ullum esse? [12]Cum tabulas, signa, toreumata emunt, nova diruunt, alia aedificant, postremo omnibus modis pecuniam trahunt, vexant, tamen summa lubidine divitias suas vincere nequeunt. [13]At nobis est domi inopia, foris aes alienum, mala res, spes multo asperior;

denique, quid relicui habemus, praeter miseram animam?

[14]"Quin igitur expergiscimini? En illa, illa quam saepe optastis, libertas, praeterea divitiae, decus, gloria in oculis sita sunt; fortuna omnia ea victoribus praemia posuit. [15]Res, tempus, pericula, egestas, belli spolia magnifica magis quam oratio mea vos hortantur. [16]Vel imperatore vel milite me utimini; neque animus neque corpus a vobis aberit. [17]Haec ipsa, ut spero, vobiscum una consul agam, nisi forte me animus fallit et vos servire magis quam imperare parati estis."

XXI. [1]Postquam accepere ea homines, quibus mala abunde omnia erant, sed neque res neque spes bona ulla, tametsi illis quieta movere magna merces videbatur, tamen postulavere plerique ut proponeret quae condicio belli foret, quae praemia armis peterent, quid ubique opis aut spei haberent. [2]Tum Catilina polliceri tabulas novas, proscriptionem locupletium, magistratus, sacerdotia, rapinas, alia omnia quae bellum atque lubido victorum fert. [3]Praeterea esse in Hispania citeriore Pisonem, in Mauretania cum exercitu P. Sittium Nucerinum, consili sui participes; petere consulatum C. Antonium, quem sibi collegam fore speraret, hominem et familiarem et omnibus necessitudinibus circumventum; cum eo se consulem initium agendi facturum. [4]Ad hoc maledictis increpabat omnis bonos; suorum unumquemque nominans laudare; admonebat alium egestatis, alium cupiditatis suae, compluris periculi aut ignominiae, multos victoriae Sullanae, quibus ea praedae fuerat. [5]Postquam omnium animos alacris videt, cohortatus ut petitionem suam curae haberent, conventum dimisit.

XXII. [1]Fuere ea tempestate qui dicerent Catilinam, oratione habita, cum ad ius iurandum popularis sceleris sui adigeret, humani corporis sanguinem vino permixtum in pateris circumtulisse; [2]inde cum post exsecrationem omnes degustavissent, sicuti in sollemnibus sacris fieri consuevit, aperuisse consilium suum, atque eo †dictitaret† fecisse quo inter se fidi magis forent, alius alii tanti facinoris conscii. [3]Nonnulli ficta et haec et multa praeterea existumabant ab eis qui Ciceronis invidiam, quae postea orta est, leniri credebant atrocitate sceleris eorum qui poenas dederant. Nobis ea res pro magnitudine parum comperta est.

XXIII. [1]Sed in ea coniuratione fuit Q. Curius, natus haud obscuro loco, flagitiis atque facinoribus coopertus, quem censores senatu probri gratia moverant. [2]Huic homini non minor vanitas inerat quam audacia; neque reticere quae audierat, neque suamet ipse scelera occultare, prorsus neque dicere neque facere quicquam pensi habebat. [3]Erat ei cum Fulvia, muliere nobili, stupri vetus consuetudo; cui cum minus gratus esset quia inopia minus largiri poterat, repente glorians, maria montisque polliceri coepit, et minari interdum ferro, ni sibi obnoxia foret; postremo ferocius agitare quam solitus erat. [4]At Fulvia, insolentiae

Curi causa cognita, tale periculum rei publicae haud occultum habuit, sed sublato auctore de Catilinae coniuratione quae quoque modo audierat compluribus narravit. [5]Ea res in primis studia hominum accendit ad consulatum mandandum M. Tullio Ciceroni. [6]Namque antea pleraque nobilitas invidia aestuabat, et quasi pollui consulatum credebant, si eum quamvis egregius homo novos adeptus foret. Sed ubi periculum advenit, invidia atque superbia post fuere.

XXIV. [1]Igitur comitiis habitis, consules declarantur M. Tullius et C. Antonius; quod factum primo popularis coniurationis concusserat. [2]Neque tamen Catilinae furor minuebatur, sed in dies plura agitare, arma per Italiam locis opportunis parare, pecuniam sua aut amicorum fide sumptam mutuam Faesulas ad Manlium quendam portare, qui postea princeps fuit belli faciundi. [3]Ea tempestate plurumos cuiusque generis homines adscivisse sibi dicitur, mulieres etiam aliquot, quae primo ingentis sumptus stupro corporis toleraverant, post, ubi aetas tantummodo quaestui neque luxuriae modum fecerat, aes alienum grande conflaverant. [4]Per eas se Catilina credebat posse servitia urbana sollicitare, urbem incendere, viros earum vel adiungere sibi vel interficere.

XXV. [1]Sed in eis erat Sempronia, quae multa saepe virilis audaciae facinora commiserat. [2]Haec mulier genere atque forma, praeterea viro liberis satis fortunata fuit; litteris Graecis et Latinis docta, psallere, saltare elegantius quam necesse est probae, multa alia, quae instrumenta luxuriae sunt. [3]Sed ei cariora semper omnia quam decus atque pudicitia fuit; pecuniae an famae minus parceret haud facile discerneres; lubido sic accensa ut saepius peteret viros quam peteretur. [4]Sed ea saepe antehac fidem prodiderat, creditum abiuraverat, caedis conscia fuerat, luxuria atque inopia praeceps abierat. [5]Verum ingenium eius haud absurdum: posse versus facere, iocum movere, sermone uti vel modesto, vel molli, vel procaci; prorsus multae facetiae multusque lepos inerat.

XXVI. [1]His rebus conparatis, Catilina nihilo minus in proxumum annum consulatum petebat, sperans, si designatus foret, facile se ex voluntate Antonio usurum. Neque interea quietus erat, sed omnibus modis insidias parabat Ciceroni. [2]Neque illi tamen ad cavendum dolus aut astutiae deerant. [3]Namque a principio consulatus sui multa pollicendo per Fulviam effecerat ut Q. Curius, de quo paulo ante memoravi, consilia Catilinae sibi proderet. [4]Ad hoc collegam suum Antonium pactione provinciae perpulerat ne contra rem publicam sentiret; circum se praesidia amicorum atque clientium occulte habebat. [5]Postquam dies comitiorum venit, et Catilinae neque petitio neque insidiae quas consulibus in Campo fecerat prospere cessere, constituit bellum facere et extrema omnia experiri, quoniam quae occulte temptaverat aspera foedaque evenerant.

XXVII. [1]Igitur C. Manlium Faesulas atque in eam partem Etruriae, Septimium quendam Camertem in agrum Picenum, C. Iulium in Apuliam dimisit; praeterea alium alio, quem ubique opportunum sibi fore credebat.

[2]Interea Romae multa simul moliri, consulibus insidias tendere, parare incendia, opportuna loca armatis hominibus obsidere, ipse cum telo esse, item alios iubere, hortari uti semper intenti paratique essent, dies noctisque festinare, vigilare, neque insomniis neque labore fatigari. [3]Postremo, ubi multa agitanti nihil procedit, rursus intempesta nocte coniurationis principes convocat per M. Porcium Laecam, [4]ibique multa de ignavia eorum questus, docet se Manlium praemisisse ad eam multitudinem quam ad capiunda arma paraverat, item alios in alia loca opportuna, qui initium belli facerent, seque ad exercitum proficisci cupere, si prius Ciceronem oppressisset; eum suis consiliis multum officere.

XXVIII. [1]Igitur perterritis ac dubitantibus ceteris C. Cornelius, eques Romanus, operam suam pollicitus, et cum eo L. Vargunteius senator constituere ea nocte paulo post cum armatis hominibus sicuti salutatum introire ad Ciceronem, ac de improviso domi suae imparatum confodere. [2]Curius ubi intellegit quantum periculum consuli impendeat, propere per Fulviam Ciceroni dolum qui parabatur enuntiat. [3]Ita illi ianua prohibiti tantum facinus frustra susceperant.

[4]Interea Manlius in Etruria plebem sollicitare egestate simul ac dolore iniuriae novarum rerum cupidam, quod Sullae dominatione agros bonaque omnia amiserat, praeterea latrones cuiusque generis, quorum in ea regione magna copia erat, nonnullos ex Sullanis coloniis, quibus lubido atque luxuria ex magnis rapinis nihil relicui fecerat.

XXIX. [1]Ea cum Ciceroni nuntiarentur, ancipiti malo permotus, quod neque urbem ab insidiis privato consilio longius tueri poterat, neque exercitus Manli quantus aut quo consilio foret satis compertum habebat, rem ad senatum refert, iam antea volgi rumoribus exagitatam. [2]Itaque, quod plerumque in atroci negotio solet, senatus decrevit darent operam consules ne quid res publica detrimenti caperet. [3]Ea potestas per senatum more Romano magistratui maxuma permittitur, exercitum parare, bellum gerere, coercere omnibus modis socios atque civis, domi militiaeque imperium atque iudicium summum habere; aliter sine populi iussu nullius earum rerum consuli ius est.

XXX. [1]Post paucos dies L. Saenius senator in senatu litteras recitavit, quas Faesulis adlatas sibi dicebat, in quibus scriptum erat C. Manlium arma cepisse cum magna multitudine ante diem VI Kalendas

Novembris. [2]Simul, id quod in tali re solet, alii portenta atque prodigia nuntiabant, alii conventus fieri, arma portari, Capuae atque in Apulia servile bellum moveri.

[3]Igitur senati decreto Q. Marcius Rex Faesulas, Q. Metellus Creticus in Apuliam circumque ea loca missi—[4]hi utrique ad urbem imperatores erant, impediti ne triumpharent calumnia paucorum quibus omnia honesta atque inhonesta vendere mos erat—, [5]sed praetores Q. Pompeius Rufus Capuam, Q. Metellus Celer in agrum Picenum, eisque permissum uti pro tempore atque periculo exercitum conpararent. [6]Ad hoc, si quis indicavisset de coniuratione quae contra rem publicam facta erat, praemium servo libertatem et sestertia centum, libero inpunitatem eius rei et sestertia ducenta [milia]; [7]itemque decrevere uti gladiatoriae familiae Capuam et in cetera municipia distribuerentur pro cuiusque opibus, Romae per totam urbem vigiliae haberentur eisque minores magistratus praeessent.

XXXI. [1]Quibus rebus permota civitas atque inmutata urbis facies erat. Ex summa laetitia atque lascivia, quae diuturna quies pepererat, repente omnis tristitia invasit: [2]festinare, trepidare, neque loco nec homini cuiquam satis credere, neque bellum gerere neque pacem habere, suo quisque metu pericula metiri. [3]Ad hoc mulieres, quibus rei publicae magnitudine belli timor insolitus incesserat, adflictare sese, manus supplicis ad caelum tendere, miserari parvos liberos, rogitare omnia, <omni rumore> pavere, <adripere omnia,> superbia atque deliciis omissis, sibi patriaeque diffidere.

[4]At Catilinae crudelis animus eadem illa movebat, tametsi praesidia parabantur et ipse lege Plautia interrogatus erat ab L. Paulo. [5]Postremo, dissimulandi causa aut sui expurgandi, sicut iurgio lacessitus foret, in senatum venit. [6]Tum M. Tullius consul, sive praesentiam eius timens, sive ira commotus, orationem habuit luculentam atque utilem rei publicae, quam postea scriptam edidit. [7]Sed ubi ille adsedit, Catilina, ut erat paratus ad dissimulanda omnia, demisso voltu, voce supplici postulare a patribus coepit ne quid de se temere crederent; ea familia ortum, ita se ab adulescentia vitam instituisse ut omnia bona in spe haberet; ne existumarent sibi patricio homini, cuius ipsius atque maiorum pluruma beneficia in plebem Romanam essent, perdita re publica opus esse, cum eam servaret M. Tullius, inquilinus civis urbis Romae. [8]Ad hoc maledicta alia cum adderet, obstrepere omnes, hostem atque parricidam vocare. [9]Tum ille furibundus: "Quoniam quidem circumventus," inquit, "ab inimicis praeceps agor, incendium meum ruina restinguam."

XXXII. [1]Deinde se ex curia domum proripuit. Ibi multa ipse secum volvens, quod neque insidiae consuli procedebant et ab incendio intellegebat urbem vigiliis munitam, optumum factu credens exercitum augere ac, prius quam legiones scriberentur, multa antecapere quae bello usui forent, nocte intempesta cum paucis in Manliana castra profectus est. [2]Sed Cethego atque Lentulo ceterisque quorum cognoverat promptam audaciam mandat quibus rebus possent opes factionis ? confirment, insidias consuli maturent, caedem, incendia aliaque belli facinora parent: sese prope diem cum magno exercitu ad urbem accessurum.

[3]Dum haec Romae geruntur, C. Manlius ex suo numero legatos ad Marcium Regem mittit cum mandatis huiuscemodi:

XXXIII. [1]"Deos hominesque testamur, imperator, nos arma neque contra patriam cepisse, neque quo periculum aliis faceremus, sed uti corpora nostra ab iniuria tuta forent, qui miseri, egentes, violentia atque crudelitate feneratorum plerique patriae, sed omnes fama atque fortunis expertes sumus; neque cuiquam nostrum licuit more maiorum lege uti, neque amisso patrimonio liberum corpus habere: tanta saevitia feneratorum atque praetoris fuit. [2]Saepe maiores vostrum, miseriti plebis Romanae, decretis suis inopiae eius opitulati sunt; ac novissume memoria nostra propter magnitudinem aeris alieni volentibus omnibus bonis argentum aere solutum est. [3]Saepe ipsa plebs, aut dominandi studio permota aut superbia magistratuum, armata a patribus secessit. [4]At nos non imperium neque divitias petimus, quarum rerum causa bella atque certamina omnia inter mortalis sunt, sed libertatem, quam nemo bonus nisi cum anima simul amittit. [5]Te atque senatum obtestamur, consulatis miseris civibus, legis praesidium, quod iniquitas praetoris eripuit, restituatis, neve nobis eam necessitudinem inponatis ut quaeramus quonam modo maxume ulti sanguinem nostrum pereamus."

XXXIV. [1]Ad haec Q. Marcius respondit, si quid ab senatu petere vellent, ab armis discedant, Romam supplices proficiscantur; ea mansuetudine atque misericordia senatum populi Romani semper fuisse, ut nemo umquam ab eo frustra auxilium petiverit.

[2]At Catilina ex itinere plerisque consularibus, praeterea optumo cuique litteras mittit, se falsis criminibus circumventum, quoniam factioni inimicorum resistere nequiverit, fortunae cedere, Massiliam in exilium proficisci, non quo sibi tanti sceleris conscius esset, sed uti res publica quieta foret neve ex sua contentione seditio oreretur. [3]Ab his longe divorsas litteras Q. Catulus in senatu recitavit, quas sibi nomine Catilinae redditas dicebat. Earum exemplum infra scriptum est.

XXXV. [1]"L. Catilina Q. Catulo. Egregia tua fides re cognita, grata mihi magnis in meis periculis, fiduciam commendationi meae tribuit. [2]Quam ob rem defensionem in novo consilio non statui parare, satisfactionem ex nulla conscientia de culpa proponere decrevi, quam me dius fidius veram licet cognoscas. ³Iniuriis contumeliisque concitatus, quod fructu laboris industriaeque meae privatus statum dignitatis non obtinebam, publicam miserorum causam pro mea consuetudine suscepi; non quin aes alienum meis nominibus ex possessionibus solvere possem— et alienis nominibus liberalitas Orestillae suis filiaeque copiis persolveret—sed quod non dignos homines honore honestatos videbam, meque falsa suspicione alienatum esse sentiebam. ⁴Hoc nomine satis honestas pro meo casu spes relicuae dignitatis conservandae sum secutus. ⁵Plura cum scribere vellem, nuntiatum est vim mihi parari. ⁶Nunc Orestillam commendo tuaeque fidei trado; eam ab iniuria defendas, per liberos tuos rogatus. Haveto."

XXXVI. ¹Sed ipse paucos dies commoratus apud C. Flaminium in agro Arretino, dum vicinitatem antea sollicitatam armis exornat, cum fascibus atque aliis imperi insignibus in castra ad Manlium contendit. ²Haec ubi Romae comperta sunt, senatus Catilinam et Manlium hostis iudicat, ceterae multitudini diem statuit, ante quam liceret sine fraude ab armis discedere, praeter rerum capitalium condemnatis. ³Praeterea decernit uti consules dilectum habeant, Antonius cum exercitu Catilinam persequi maturet, Cicero urbi praesidio sit.

⁴Ea tempestate mihi imperium populi Romani multo maxume miserabile visum est. Cui cum ad occasum ab ortu solis omnia domita armis parerent, domi otium atque divitiae, quae prima mortales putant, affluerent, fuere tamen cives qui seque remque publicam obstinatis animis perditum irent. ⁵Namque duobus senati decretis ex tanta multitudine neque praemio inductus coniurationem patefecerat, neque ex castris Catilinae quisquam omnium discesserat: tanta vis morbi atque uti tabes plerosque civium animos invaserat.

XXXVII. ¹Neque solum illis aliena mens erat qui conscii coniurationis fuerant, sed omnino cuncta plebes novarum rerum studio Catilinae incepta probabat. ²Id adeo more suo videbatur facere. ³Nam semper in civitate quibus opes nullae sunt bonis invident, malos extollunt; vetera odere, nova exoptant; odio suarum rerum mutari omnia student; turba atque seditionibus sine cura aluntur, quoniam egestas facile habetur sine damno. ⁴Sed urbana plebes, ea vero praeceps erat de multis causis. ⁵Primum omnium, qui ubique probro atque petulantia maxume praestabant, item alii per dedecora patrimoniis amissis, postremo omnes quos flagitium aut facinus domo expulerat, ei Romam sicut in sentinam confluxerant. ⁶Deinde multi memores Sullanae victoriae, quod ex gregariis militibus alios senatores videbant, alios ita divites ut regio victu atque cultu aetatem agerent, sibi quisque, si in armis foret, ex victoria talia sperabat. ⁷Praeterea iuventus, quae in agris manuum mercede inopiam toleraverat, privatis atque publicis largitionibus excita, urbanum otium ingrato labori praetulerat. Eos atque alios omnis malum publicum alebat. [8]Quo minus mirandum est homines egentis, malis moribus, maxuma spe, rei publicae iuxta ac sibi consuluisse. [9]Praeterea quorum victoria Sullae parentes proscripti, bona erepta, ius libertatis inminutum erat, haud sane alio animo belli eventum exspectabant. [10]Ad hoc quicumque aliarum atque senatus partium erant, conturbari rem publicam quam minus valere ipsi malebant. [11]Id <ad>eo malum multos post annos in civitatem revorterat.

XXXVIII. [1]Nam, postquam Cn. Pompeio et M. Crasso consulibus tribunicia potestas restituta est, homines adulescentes summam potestatem nacti, quibus aetas animusque ferox erat, coepere senatum criminando plebem exagitare, dein largiundo atque pollicitando magis incendere, ita ipsi clari potentesque fieri. [2]Contra eos summa ope nitebatur pleraque nobilitas senatus specie pro sua magnitudine. [3]Namque, uti paucis verum absolvam, post illa tempora quicumque rem publicam agitavere honestis nominibus, alii sicuti populi iura defenderent, pars quo senatus auctoritas maxuma foret, bonum publicum simulantes pro sua quisque potentia certabant. [4]Neque illis modestia neque modus contentionis erat; utrique victoriam crudeliter exercebant.

XXXIX. [1]Sed postquam Cn. Pompeius ad bellum maritumum atque Mithridaticum missus est, plebis opes imminutae, paucorum potentia crevit. [2]Ei magistratus, provincias aliaque omnia tenere; ipsi innoxii, florentes, sine metu aetatem agere ceterosque iudiciis terrere, quo plebem in magistratu placidius tractarent. [3]Sed ubi primum dubiis rebus novandi spes oblata est, vetus certamen animos eorum adrexit. [4]Quod si primo proelio Catilina superior aut aequa manu discessisset, profecto magna clades atque calamitas rem publicam oppressisset, neque illis qui victoriam adepti forent diutius ea uti licuisset, quin defessis et exsanguibus qui plus posset imperium atque libertatem extorqueret. [5]Fuere tamen extra coniurationem complures, qui ad Catilinam initio profecti sunt. In eis erat Fulvius, senatoris filius, quem retractum ex itinere parens necari iussit.

[6]Isdem temporibus Romae Lentulus, sicuti Catilina praeceperat, quoscumque moribus aut fortuna novis rebus idoneos credebat, aut per se aut per alios sollicitabat; neque solum civis, sed cuiusque modi genus hominum, quod modo bello usui foret.

XL. [1]Igitur P. Umbreno cuidam negotium dat uti legatos Allobrogum requirat eosque, si possit, inpellat ad societatem belli, existumans publice privatimque aere alieno oppressos, praeterea quod natura gens Gallica bellicosa esset, facile eos ad tale consilium adduci posse. [2]Umbrenus, quod in Gallia negotiatus erat, plerisque principibus civitatium notus erat atque eos noverat. Itaque sine mora, ubi primum legatos in foro conspexit, percontatus pauca de statu civitatis et quasi dolens eius casum, requirere coepit quem exitum tantis malis sperarent. [3]Postquam illos videt queri de avaritia magistratuum, accusare senatum quod in eo auxili nihil esset, miseriis suis remedium mortem exspectare, "At ego," inquit, "vobis, si modo viri esse voltis, rationem ostendam qua tanta ista mala effugiatis." [4]Haec ubi dixit, Allobroges in maxumam spem adducti Umbrenum orare uti sui misereretur: nihil tam asperum neque tam difficile esse quod non cupidissume facturi essent, dum ea res civitatem aere alieno liberaret. [5]Ille eos in domum D. Bruti perducit, quod foro propinqua erat neque aliena consili propter Semproniam; nam tum Brutus ab Roma aberat. [6]Praeterea Gabinium arcessit, quo maior auctoritas sermoni inesset; eo praesente coniurationem aperit, nominat socios, praeterea multos cuiusque generis innoxios, quo legatis animus amplior esset; deinde eos pollicitos operam suam domum dimittit.

XLI. [1]Sed Allobroges diu in incerto habuere quidnam consili caperent. [2]In altera parte erat aes alienum, studium belli, magna merces in spe victoriae; at in altera maiores opes, tuta consilia, pro incerta spe certa praemia. [3]Haec illis volventibus, tandem vicit fortuna rei publicae. [4]Itaque Q. Fabio Sangae, cuius patrocinio civitas plurumum utebatur, rem omnem uti cognoverant aperiunt. [5]Cicero per Sangam consilio cognito legatis praecipit ut studium coniurationis vehementer simulent, ceteros adeant, bene polliceantur, dentque operam uti eos quam maxume manufestos habeant.

XLII. [1]Isdem fere temporibus in Gallia citeriorc atque ulteriore, item in agro Piceno, Bruttio, Apulia motus erat. [2]Namque illi, quos ante Catilina dimiserat, inconsulte ac veluti per dementiam cuncta simul agebant: nocturnis consiliis, armorum atque telorum portationibus, festinando, agitando omnia, plus timoris quam periculi effecerant. [3]Ex eo numero compluris Q. Metellus Celer praetor, ex senatus consulto causa cognita, in vincula coniecerat, item in citeriore Gallia C. Murena, qui ei provinciae legatus praeerat.

XLIII. [1]At Romae Lentulus cum ceteris qui principes coniurationis erant, paratis ut videbatur magnis copiis, constituerant uti, cum Catilina in agrum †Faesulanum† cum exercitu venisset, L. Bestia tribunus plebis contione habita quereretur de actionibus Ciceronis bellique gravissumi invidiam optumo consuli inponeret; eo signo proxuma nocte cetera multitudo coniurationis suum quodque negotium exsequeretur. [2]Sed ea divisa hoc modo dicebantur: Statilius et Gabinius uti cum magna manu duodecim simul opportuna loca urbis incenderent, quo tumultu facilior aditus ad consulem ceterosque quibus insidiae parabantur fieret;

Cethegus Ciceronis ianuam obsideret eumque vi aggrederetur; alius autem alium, sed filii familiarum, quorum ex nobilitate maxuma pars erat, parentes interficerent; simul, caede et incendio perculsis omnibus, ad Catilinam erumperent. [3]Inter haec parata atque decreta Cethegus semper querebatur de ignavia sociorum: illos dubitando et dies prolatando magnas opportunitates corrumpere; facto, non consulto in tali periculo opus esse, seque, si pauci adiuvarent, languentibus aliis, impetum in curiam facturum. [4]Natura ferox, vehemens, manu promptus erat, maximum bonum in celeritate putabat.

XLIV. [1]Sed Allobroges ex praecepto Ciceronis per Gabinium ceteros conveniunt. Ab Lentulo, Cethego, Statilio, item Cassio postulant ius iurandum quod signatum ad civis perferant: aliter haud facile eos ad tantum negotium impelli posse. [2]Ceteri nihil suspicantes dant; Cassius semet eo brevi venturum pollicetur ac paulo ante legatos ex urbe proficiscitur. [3]Lentulus cum eis T. Volturcium quendam Crotoniensem mittit ut Allobroges, prius quam domum pergerent, cum Catilina data atque accepta fide societatem confirmarent. [4]Ipse Volturcio litteras ad Catilinam dat, quarum exemplum infra scriptum est:

[5]"Qui sim ex eo quem ad te misi cognosces. Fac cogites in quanta calamitate sis, et memineris te virum esse. Consideres quid tuae rationes postulent; auxilium petas ab omnibus, etiam ab infimis."

[6]Ad hoc mandata verbis dat: cum ab senatu hostis iudicatus sit, quo consilio servitia repudiet? In urbe parata esse quae iusserit; ne cunctetur ipse propius accedere.

XLV. [1]His rebus ita actis, constituta nocte qua proficiscerentur, Cicero, per legatos cuncta edoctus, L. Valerio Flacco et C. Pomptino praetoribus imperat ut in ponte Mulvio per insidias Allobrogum comitatus deprehendant. Rem omnem aperit cuius gratia mittebantur; cetera uti facto opus sit ita agant permittit. [2]Illi, homines militares, sine tumultu praesidiis conlocatis, sicuti praeceptum erat, occulte pontem obsidunt. [3]Postquam ad id loci legati cum Volturcio venerunt et simul utrimque clamor exortus est, Galli, cito cognito consilio, sine mora praetoribus se tradunt. [4]Volturcius primo cohortatus ceteros gladio se a multitudine defendit; deinde, ubi a legatis desertus est, multa prius de salute sua Pomptinum obtestatus, quod ei notus erat, postremo timidus ac vitae diffidens veluti hostibus sese praetoribus dedit.

XLVI. [1]Quibus rebus confectis omnia propere per nuntios consuli declarantur. [2]At illum ingens cura atque laetitia simul occupavere. Nam laetabatur intellegens coniuratione patefacta civitatem periculis ereptam esse; porro autem anxius erat, dubitans in maxumo scelere tantis civibus deprehensis quid facto opus esset; poenam illorum sibi oneri, inpunitatem perdundae reipublicae fore credebat. [3]Igitur confirmato animo vocari ad sese iubet Lentulum, Cethegum, Statilium, Gabinium, itemque Caeparium Terracinensem, qui in Apuliam ad concitanda servitia proficisci parabat. [4]Ceteri sine mora veniunt; Caeparius, paulo ante domo egressus, cognito indicio ex urbe profugerat. [5]Consul Lentulum, quod praetor erat, ipse manu tenens in senatum perducit; relicuos cum custodibus in aedem Concordiae venire iubet. [6]Eo senatum advocat, magnaque frequentia eius ordinis Volturcium cum legatis introducit; Flaccum praetorem scrinium cum litteris quas a legatis acceperat eodem adferre iubet.

XLVII. [1]Volturcius interrogatus de itinere, de litteris, postremo quid aut qua de causa consili habuisset, primo fingere alia, dissimulare de coniuratione; post, ubi fide publica dicere iussus est, omnia uti gesta erant aperit, docetque se, paucis ante diebus a Gabinio et Caepario socium adscitum, nihil amplius scire quam legatos, tantummodo audire solitum ex Gabinio P. Autronium, Ser. Sullam, L. Vargunteium, multos praeterea in ea coniuratione esse. [2]Eadem Galli fatentur ac Lentulum dissimulantem coarguunt praeter litteras sermonibus quos ille habere solitus erat: ex libris Sibyllinis regnum Romae tribus Corneliis portendi; Cinnam atque Sullam antea, se tertium esse cui fatum foret urbis potiri; praeterea ab incenso Capitolio illum esse vicesimum annum, quem saepe ex prodigiis haruspices respondissent bello civili cruentum fore. [3]Igitur perlectis litteris, cum prius omnes signa sua cognovissent, senatus decernit uti abdicato magistratu Lentulus itemque ceteri in liberis custodiis habeantur. [4]Itaque Lentulus P. Lentulo Spintheri, qui tum aedilis erat, Cethegus Q. Cornificio, Statilius C. Caesari, Gabinius M. Crasso, Caeparius—nam is paulo ante ex fuga retractus erat—Cn. Terentio senatori traduntur.

XLVIII. [1]Interea plebs, coniuratione patefacta, quae primo cupida rerum novarum nimis bello favebat, mutata mente, Catilinae consilia exsecrari, Ciceronem ad caelum tollere: veluti ex servitute erepta gaudium atque laetitiam agitabat. [2]Namque alia belli facinora praedae magis quam detrimento fore, incendium vero crudele, inmoderatum ac sibi maxume calamitosum putabat, quippe cui omnes copiae in usu cotidiano et cultu corporis erant.

[3]Post eum diem, quidam L. Tarquinius ad senatum adductus erat, quem ad Catilinam proficiscentem ex itinere retractum aiebant. [4]Is cum se diceret indicaturum de coniuratione si fides publica data esset, iussus a consule quae sciret edicere, eadem fere quae Volturcius de paratis incendiis, de caede bonorum, de itinere hostium senatum docet; praeterea se missum a M. Crasso, qui Catilinae nuntiaret ne eum Lentulus et Cethegus aliique ex coniuratione deprehensi terrerent, eoque

magis properaret ad urbem accedere, quo et ceterorum animos reficeret et illi facilius e periculo eriperentur. [5]Sed ubi Tarquinius Crassum nominavit, hominem nobilem, maxumis divitiis, summa potentia, alii rem incredibilem rati, pars tametsi verum existumabant, tamen quia in tali tempore tanta vis hominis magis leniunda quam exagitanda videbatur, plerique Crasso ex negotiis privatis obnoxii, conclamant indicem falsum esse, deque ea re postulant uti referatur. [6]Itaque consulente Cicerone frequens senatus decernit Tarquini indicium falsum videri, eumque in vinculis retinendum, neque amplius potestatem faciundam, nisi de eo indicaret cuius consilio tantam rem esset mentitus. [7]Erant eo tempore qui aestumarent illud a P. Autronio machinatum quo facilius, appellato Crasso, per societatem periculi relicuos illius potentia tegeret. [8]Alii Tarquinium a Cicerone inmissum aiebant ne Crassus, more suo suscepto malorum patrocinio, rem publicam conturbaret. [9]Ipsum Crassum ego postea praedicantem audivi tantam illam contumeliam sibi a Cicerone inpositam.

XLIX. [1]Sed isdem temporibus Q. Catulus et C. Piso neque precibus neque gratia neque pretio Ciceronem inpellere potuere uti per Allobroges aut alium indicem C. Caesar falso nominaretur. [2]Nam uterque cum illo gravis inimicitias exercebant: Piso oppugnatus in iudicio pecuniarum repetundarum propter cuiusdam Transpadani supplicium iniustum, Catulus ex petitione pontificatus odio incensus quod extrema aetate, maxumis honoribus usus, ab adulescentulo Caesare victus discesserat. [3]Res autem opportuna videbatur quod is privatim egregia liberalitate, publice maxumis muneribus, grandem pecuniam debebat. [4]Sed ubi consulem ad tantum facinus inpellere nequeunt, ipsi singillatim circumeundo atque ementiundo quae se ex Volturcio aut Allobrogibus audisse dicerent, magnam illi invidiam conflaverant, usque eo ut nonnulli equites Romani, qui praesidi causa cum telis erant circum aedem Concordiae, seu periculi magnitudine seu animi mobilitate inpulsi, quo studium suum in rem publicam clarius esset, egredienti ex senatu Caesari gladio minitarentur.

L. [1]Dum haec in senatu aguntur et dum legatis Allobrogum et T. Volturcio, conprobato eorum indicio, praemia decernuntur, liberti et pauci ex clientibus Lentuli divorsis itineribus opifices atque servitia in vicis ad eum eripiundum sollicitabant; partim exquirebant duces multitudinum, qui pretio rem publicam vexare soliti erant. [2]Cethegus autem per nuntios familiam atque libertos suos, lectos et exercitatos, orabat in audaciam, ut grege facto cum telis ad sese inrumperent. [3]Consul ubi ea parari cognovit, dispositis praesidiis ut res atque tempus monebat, convocato senatu refert quid de eis fieri placeat qui in custodiam traditi erant. Sed eos paulo ante frequens senatus iudicaverat contra rem publicam fecisse. [4]Tum D. Iunius Silanus, primus sententiam rogatus quod eo tempore consul designatus erat, de eis qui in custodiis tenebantur et praeterea de L. Cassio, P. Furio, P. Umbreno, Q. Annio, si deprehensi forent, supplicium sumundum decreverat; isque postea, permotus oratione C. Caesaris, pedibus in sententiam Ti. Neronis iturum se dixerat qui de ea re, praesidiis additis, referundum censuerat. [5]Sed Caesar, ubi ad eum ventum est, rogatus sententiam a consule, huiuscemodi verba locutus est:

LI. [1]"Omnis homines, patres conscripti, qui de rebus dubiis consultant, ab odio, amicitia, ira atque misericordia vacuos esse decet. [2]Haud facile animus verum providet ubi illa officiunt, neque quisquam omnium lubidini simul et usui paruit. [3]Ubi intenderis ingenium, valet; si lubido possidet, ea dominatur, animus nihil valet. [4]Magna mihi copia est memorandi, patres conscripti, quae reges atque populi, ira aut misericordia inpulsi, male consuluerint; sed ea malo dicere quae maiores nostri contra lubidinem animi sui recte atque ordine fecere. [5]Bello Macedonico, quod cum rege Perse gessimus, Rhodiorum civitas magna atque magnifica, quae populi Romani opibus creverat, infida atque advorsa nobis fuit. Sed postquam bello confecto de Rhodiis consultum est, maiores nostri, ne quis divitiarum magis quam iniuriae causa bellum inceptum diceret, inpunitos eos dimisere. [6]Item bellis Punicis omnibus, cum saepe Carthaginienses et in pace et per indutias multa nefaria facinora fecissent, numquam ipsi per occasionem talia fecere: magis quid se dignum foret quam quid in illos iure fieri posset quaerebant. [7]Hoc item vobis providendum est, patres conscripti, ne plus apud vos valeat P. Lentuli et ceterorum scelus quam vostra dignitas, neu magis irae vostrae quam famae consulatis. [8]Nam si digna poena pro factis eorum reperitur, novom consilium adprobo; sin magnitudo sceleris omnium ingenia exsuperat, his utendum censeo quae legibus conparata sunt.

[9]"Plerique eorum qui ante me sententias dixerunt composite atque magnifice casum rei publicae miserati sunt. Quae belli saevitia esset, quae victis acciderent, enumeravere: rapi virgines, pueros, divelli liberos a parentum complexu, matres familiarum pati quae victoribus conlibuissent; fana atque domos spoliari; caedem, incendia fieri; postremo armis, cadaveribus, cruore atque luctu omnia compleri. [10]Sed, per deos inmortalis, quo illa oratio pertinuit? An uti vos infestos coniurationi faceret? Scilicet quem res tanta et tam atrox non permovit, eum oratio accendet! [11]Non ita est; neque cuiquam mortalium iniuriae suae parvae videntur; multi eas gravius aequo habuere. [12]Sed alia aliis licentia est, patres conscripti. Qui demissi in obscuro vitam habent, si quid iracundia deliquere, pauci sciunt; fama atque fortuna pares sunt. Qui magno imperio praediti in excelso aetatem agunt, eorum facta cuncti mortales novere. [13]Ita in maxuma fortuna minuma licentia est: neque studere, neque odisse, sed minume irasci decet. [14]Quae apud alios

iracundia dicitur, ea in imperio superbia atque crudelitas appellatur. [15]Equidem ego sic existumo, patres conscripti, omnis cruciatus minores quam facinora illorum esse. Sed plerique mortales postrema meminere, et, in hominibus impiis sceleris eorum obliti, de poena disserunt, si ea paulo severior fuit.

[16]"D. Silanum, virum fortem atque strenuum, certo scio quae dixerit studio rei publicae dixisse, neque illum in tanta re gratiam aut inimicitias exercere: eos mores, eamque modestiam viri cognovi. [17]Verum sententia eius mihi non crudelis—quid enim in talis homines crudele fieri potest?—sed aliena a re publica nostra videtur. [18]Nam profecto aut metus aut iniuria te subegit, Silane, consulem designatum, genus poenae novom decernere. [19]De timore supervacuaneum est disserere, cum praesertim diligentia clarissumi viri consulis tanta praesidia sint in armis. [20]De poena possum equidem dicere, id quod res habet, in luctu atque miseriis mortem aerumnarum requiem, non cruciatum esse; eam cuncta mortalium mala dissolvere; ultra neque curae neque gaudio locum esse. [21]Sed, per deos immortalis, quam ob rem in sententiam non addidisti uti prius verberibus in eos animadvorteretur? [22]An quia lex Porcia vetat? At aliae leges item condemnatis civibus non animam eripi, sed exilium permitti iubent. [23]An quia gravius est verberari quam necari? Quid autem acerbum aut nimis grave est in homines tanti facinoris convictos? [24]Sin quia levius est, qui convenit in minore negotio legem timere, cum eam in maiore neglegeris?

[25]"At enim quis reprehendet quod in parricidas rei publicae decretum erit? Tempus, dies, fortuna, cuius lubido gentibus moderatur. Illis merito accidet quicquid evenerit; [26]ceterum vos, patres conscripti, quid in alios statuatis considerate. [27]Omnia mala exempla ex rebus bonis orta sunt. Sed ubi imperium ad ignaros eius aut minus bonos pervenit, novom illud exemplum ab dignis et idoneis ad indignos et non idoneos transfertur. [28]Lacedaemonii devictis Atheniensibus triginta viros imposuere qui rem publicam eorum tractarent. [29]Ei primo coepere pessumum quemque et omnibus invisum indemnatum necare: ea populus laetari et merito dicere fieri. [30]Post, ubi paulatim licentia crevit, iuxta bonos et malos lubidinose interficere, ceteros metu terrere. [31]Ita civitas, servitute oppressa, stultae laetitiae gravis poenas dedit. [32]Nostra memoria, victor Sulla cum Damasippum et alios eius modi, qui malo rei publicae creverant, iugulari iussit, quis non factum eius laudabat? Homines scelestos et factiosos, qui seditionibus rem publicam exagitaverant, merito necatos aiebant. [33]Sed ea res magnae initium cladis fuit. Nam uti quisque domum aut villam, postremo vas aut vestimentum alicuius concupiverat, dabat operam ut is in proscriptorum numero esset. [34]Ita illi quibus Damasippi mors laetitiae fuerat paulo post ipsi

trahebantur, neque prius finis iugulandi fuit quam Sulla omnis suos divitiis explevit. [35]Atque ego haec non in M. Tullio neque his temporibus vereor; sed in magna civitate multa et varia ingenia sunt. [36]Potest alio tempore, alio consule, cui item exercitus in manu sit, falsum aliquid pro vero credi. Ubi hoc exemplo per senatus decretum consul gladium eduxerit, quis illi finem statuet aut quis moderabitur?

[37]"Maiores nostri, patres conscripti, neque consili neque audaciae umquam eguere; neque illis superbia obstabat quo minus aliena instituta, si modo proba erant, imitarentur. [38]Arma atque tela militaria ab Samnitibus, insignia magistratuum ab Tuscis pleraque sumpserunt; postremo, quod ubique apud socios aut hostis idoneum videbatur, cum summo studio domi exsequebantur: imitari quam invidere bonis malebant. [39]Sed eodem illo tempore, Graeciae morem imitati, verberibus animadvortebant in civis, de condemnatis summum supplicium sumebant. [40]Postquam res publica adolevit et multitudine civium factiones valuere, circumveniri innocentes, alia huiuscemodi fieri coepere, tum lex Porcia aliaeque leges paratae sunt, quibus legibus exilium damnatis permissum est. [41]Hanc ego causam, patres conscripti, quo minus novom consilium capiamus in primis magnam puto. [42]Profecto virtus atque sapientia maior illis fuit, qui ex parvis opibus tantum imperium fecere, quam in nobis, qui ea bene parta vix retinemus.

[43]"Placet igitur eos dimitti et augeri exercitum Catilinae? Minume. Sed ita censeo: publicandas eorum pecunias, ipsos in vinculis habendos per municipia quae maxume opibus valent, neu quis de eis postea ad senatum referat neve cum populo agat; qui aliter fecerit, senatum existumare eum contra rem publicam et salutem omnium facturum."

LII. [1]Postquam Caesar dicundi finem fecit, ceteri verbo alius alii varie adsentiebantur. At M. Porcius Cato rogatus sententiam huiuscemodi orationem habuit:

[2]"Longe mihi alia mens est, patres conscripti, cum res atque pericula nostra considero et cum sententias nonnullorum ipse mecum reputo. [3]Illi mihi disseruisse videntur de poena eorum qui patriae, parentibus, aris atque focis suis bellum paravere; res autem monet cavere ab illis magis quam quid in illos statuamus consultare. [4]Nam cetera maleficia tum persequare ubi facta sunt; hoc nisi provideris ne accidat, ubi evenit, frustra iudicia implores: capta urbe nihil fit relicui victis. [5]Sed, per deos immortalis, vos ego appello, qui semper domos, villas, signa, tabulas vostras pluris quam rem publicam fecistis: si ista, cuiuscumque modi sunt, quae amplexamini, retinere, si voluptatibus vostris otium praebere voltis, expergiscimini aliquando et capessite rem publicam. [6]Non agitur de vectigalibus neque de sociorum iniuriis; libertas et anima nostra in

dubio est.

[7]"Saepe numero, patres conscripti, multa verba in hoc ordine feci; saepe de luxuria atque avaritia nostrorum civium questus sum, multosque mortalis ea causa advorsos habeo. [8]Qui mihi atque animo meo nullius umquam delicti gratiam fecissem, haud facile alterius lubidini malefacta condonabam. [9]Sed ea tametsi vos parvi pendebatis, tamen res publica firma erat: opulentia neglegentiam tolerabat. [10]Nunc vero non id agitur bonisne an malis moribus vivamus, neque quantum aut quam magnificum imperium populi Romani sit, sed haec, cuiuscumque modi videntur, nostra an nobiscum una hostium futura sint. [11]Hic mihi quisquam mansuetudinem et misericordiam nominat? Iampridem equidem nos vera vocabula rerum amisimus: quia bona aliena largiri liberalitas, malarum rerum audacia fortitudo vocatur, eo res publica in extremo sita est. [12]Sint sane, quoniam ita se mores habent, liberales ex sociorum fortunis; sint misericordes in furibus aerari; ne illi sanguinem nostrum largiantur et, dum paucis sceleratis parcunt, bonos omnis perditum eant.

[13]"Bene et composite C. Caesar paulo ante in hoc ordine de vita et morte disseruit, credo, falsa existumans ea quae de inferis memorantur, divorso itinere malos a bonis loca taetra, inculta, foeda atque formidulosa habere. [14]Itaque censuit pecunias eorum publicandas, ipsos per municipia in custodiis habendos, videlicet timens ne, si Romae sint, aut a popularibus coniurationis aut a multitudine conducta per vim eripiantur: [15]quasi vero mali atque scelesti tantummodo in urbe et non per totam Italiam sint, aut non ibi plus possit audacia ubi ad defendundum opes minores sunt. [16]Quare vanum equidem hoc consilium est, si periculum ex illis metuit; si in tanto omnium metu solus non timet, eo magis refert me mihi atque vobis timere. [17]Quare cum de P. Lentulo ceterisque statuetis, pro certo habetote vos simul de exercitu Catilinae et de omnibus coniuratis decernere. [18]Quanto vos attentius ea agetis, tanto illis animus infirmior erit; si paululum modo vos languere viderint, iam omnes feroces aderunt.

[19]"Nolite existumare maiores nostros armis rem publicam ex parva magnam fecisse. [20]Si ita res esset, multo pulcherrumam eam nos haberemus, quippe sociorum atque civium, praeterea armorum atque equorum maior copia nobis quam illis est. [21]Sed alia fuere quae illos magnos fecere, quae nobis nulla sunt: domi industria, foris iustum imperium, animus in consulendo liber, neque delicto neque lubidini obnoxius. [22]Pro his nos habemus luxuriam atque avaritiam, publice egestatem, privatim opulentiam; laudamus divitias, sequimur inertiam; inter bonos et malos discrimen nullum; omnia virtutis praemia ambitio possidet. [23]Neque mirum: ubi vos separatim sibi quisque consilium

capitis, ubi domi voluptatibus, hic pecuniae aut gratiae servitis, eo fit ut impetus fiat in vacuam rem publicam.

[24]"Sed ego haec omitto. Coniuravere nobilissumi cives patriam incendere; Gallorum gentem infestissumam nomini Romano ad bellum arcessunt; dux hostium cum exercitu supra caput est: [25]vos cunctamini etiam nunc et dubitatis quid intra moenia deprehensis hostibus faciatis? [26]Misereamini, censeo: deliquere homines adulescentuli per ambitionem; atque etiam armatos dimittatis; [27]ne ista vobis mansuetudo et misericordia, si illi arma ceperint, in miseriam convortat. [28]Scilicet res ipsa aspera est, sed vos non timetis eam. Immo vero maxume; sed inertia et mollitia animi alius alium exspectantes cunctamini, videlicet dis immortalibus confisi qui hanc rem publicam saepe in maxumis periculis servavere. [29]Non votis neque suppliciis muliebribus auxilia deorum parantur: vigilando, agundo, bene consulundo prospere omnia cedunt. Ubi socordiae te atque ignaviae tradideris, nequiquam deos implores; irati infestique sunt.

[30]"Apud maiores nostros A. Manlius Torquatus bello Gallico filium suum, quod is contra imperium in hostem pugnaverat, necari iussit, [31]atque ille egregius adulescens immoderatae fortitudinis morte poenas dedit; vos de crudelissumis parricidis quid statuatis cunctamini? Videlicet cetera vita eorum huic sceleri obstat. [32]Verum parcite dignitati Lentuli, si ipse pudicitiae, si famae suae, si dis aut hominibus umquam ullis pepercit; [33]ignoscite Cethegi adulescentiae, nisi iterum patriae bellum fecit. [34]Nam quid ego de Gabinio, Statilio, Caepario loquar? quibus si quicquam umquam pensi fuisset, non ea consilia de re publica habuissent.

[35]"Postremo, patres conscripti, si mehercule peccato locus esset, facile paterer vos ipsa re corrigi, quoniam verba contemnitis. Sed undique circumventi sumus; Catilina cum exercitu faucibus urget; alii intra moenia atque in sinu urbis sunt hostes, neque parari neque consuli quicquam potest occulte: quo magis properandum est.

[36]"Quare ego ita censeo: cum nefario consilio sceleratorum civium res publica in maxuma pericula venerit, eique indicio T. Volturci et legatorum Allobrogum convicti confessique sint caedem, incendia, aliaque se foeda atque crudelia facinora in civis patriamque paravisse, de confessis, sicuti de manufestis rerum capitalium, more maiorum supplicium sumundum."

LIII. [1]Postquam Cato adsedit, consulares omnes itemque senatus magna pars sententiam eius laudant, virtutem animi ad caelum ferunt; alii alios increpantes timidos vocant. Cato clarus atque magnus habetur; senati decretum fit sicuti ille censuerat.

[2]Sed mihi multa legenti, multa audienti quae populus Romanus domi militiaeque, mari atque terra, praeclara facinora fecit, forte lubuit adtendere quae res maxume tanta negotia sustinuisset. [3]Sciebam saepe numero parva manu cum magnis legionibus hostium contendisse; cognoveram parvis copiis bella gesta cum opulentis regibus; ad hoc saepe fortunae violentiam toleravisse; facundia Graecos, gloria belli Gallos ante Romanos fuisse. [4]Ac mihi multa agitanti constabat paucorum civium egregiam virtutem cuncta patravisse, eoque factum uti divitias paupertas, multitudinem paucitas superaret. [5]Sed postquam luxu atque desidia civitas corrupta est, rursus res publica magnitudine sua imperatorum atque magistratuum vitia sustentabat ac, sicuti effeta parentum <vi>, multis tempestatibus haud sane quisquam Romae virtute magnus fuit. [6]Sed memoria mea ingenti virtute, divorsis moribus fuere viri duo, M. Cato et C. Caesar. Quos quoniam res obtulerat, silentio praeterire non fuit consilium quin utriusque naturam et mores, quantum ingenio possum, aperirem.

LIV. [1]Igitur eis genus, aetas, eloquentia, prope aequalia fuere; magnitudo animi par, item gloria, sed alia alii. [2]Caesar beneficiis ac munificentia magnus habebatur, integritate vitae Cato. Ille mansuetudine et misericordia clarus factus, huic severitas dignitatem addiderat. [3]Caesar dando, sublevando, ignoscendo, Cato nihil largiundo gloriam adeptus est. In altero miseris perfugium erat, in altero malis pernicies. Illius facilitas, huius constantia laudabatur. [4]Postremo Caesar in animum induxerat laborare, vigilare, negotiis amicorum intentus sua neglegere, nihil denegare quod dono dignum esset; sibi magnum imperium, exercitum, bellum novom exoptabat ubi virtus enitescere posset. [5]At Catoni studium modestiae, decoris, sed maxume severitatis erat. [6]Non divitiis cum divite neque factione cum factioso, sed cum strenuo virtute, cum modesto pudore, cum innocente abstinentia certabat. Esse quam videri bonus malebat; ita, quo minus petebat gloriam, eo magis illum assequebatur.

LV. [1]Postquam, ut dixi, senatus in Catonis sententiam discessit, consul optumum factu ratus noctem quae instabat antecapere ne quid eo spatio novaretur, tresviros quae [ad] supplicium postulabat parare iubet; [2]ipse, praesidiis dispositis, Lentulum in carcerem deducit; idem fit ceteris per praetores. [3]Est in carcere locus, quod Tullianum appellatur, ubi paululum ascenderis ad laevam, circiter duodecim pedes humi depressus. [4]Eum muniunt undique parietes atque insuper camera lapideis fornicibus iuncta; sed incultu, tenebris, odore foeda atque terribilis eius facies est. [5]In eum locum postquam demissus est Lentulus, vindices rerum capitalium, quibus praeceptum erat, laqueo gulam fregere. [6]Ita ille patricius ex gente clarissuma Corneliorum, qui consulare imperium Romae habuerat, dignum moribus factisque suis exitium vitae invenit.

De Cethego, Statilio, Gabinio, Caepario eodem modo supplicium sumptum est.

LVI. [1]Dum ea Romae geruntur, Catilina ex omni copia quam et ipse adduxerat et Manlius habuerat, duas legiones instituit; cohortis pro numero militum complet. [2]Deinde, ut quisque voluntarius aut ex sociis in castra venerat, aequaliter distribuerat, ac brevi spatio legiones numero hominum expleverat, cum initio non amplius duobus milibus habuisset. [3]Sed ex omni copia circiter pars quarta erat militaribus armis instructa; ceteri, ut quemque casus armaverat, sparos aut lanceas, alii praeacutas sudis portabant. [4]Sed postquam Antonius cum exercitu adventabat, Catilina per montis iter facere; modo ad urbem, modo Galliam vorsus castra movere; hostibus occasionem pugnandi non dare: sperabat propediem magnas copias sese habiturum, si Romae socii incepta patravissent. [5]Interea servitia repudiabat, cuius initio ad eum magnae copiae concurrebant, opibus coniurationis fretus, simul alienum suis rationibus existumans videri causam civium cum servis fugitivis communicavisse.

LVII. [1]Sed postquam in castra nuntius pervenit Romae coniurationem patefactam, de Lentulo et Cethego ceterisque quos supra memoravi supplicium sumptum, plerique, quos ad bellum spes rapinarum aut novarum rerum studium inlexerat, dilabuntur; relicuos Catilina per montis asperos magnis itineribus in agrum Pistoriensem abducit, eo consilio uti per tramites occulte perfugeret in Galliam Transalpinam. [2]At Q. Metellus Celer cum tribus legionibus in agro Piceno praesidebat, ex difficultate rerum eadem illa existumans, quae supra diximus, Catilinam agitare. [3]Igitur, ubi iter eius ex perfugis cognovit, castra propere movit ac sub ipsis radicibus montium consedit, qua illi descensus erat in Galliam properanti. [4]Neque tamen Antonius procul aberat, utpote qui magno exercitu locis aequioribus expeditos in fuga sequeretur. [5]Sed Catilina, postquam videt montibus atque copiis hostium sese clausum, in urbe res advorsas, neque fugae neque praesidi ullam spem, optumum factu ratus in tali re fortunam belli temptare, statuit cum Antonio quam primum confligere. [6]Itaque contione advocata huiuscemodi orationem habuit:

LVIII. [1]"Conpertum ego habeo, milites, verba virtutem non addere, neque ex ignavo strenuum, neque fortem ex timido exercitum oratione imperatoris fieri. [2]Quanta cuiusque animo audacia natura aut moribus inest, tanta in bello patere solet. Quem neque gloria neque pericula excitant, nequiquam hortere; timor animi auribus officit. [3]Sed ego vos quo pauca monerem advocavi, simul uti causam mei consili aperirem.

[4]"Scitis equidem, milites, socordia atque ignavia Lentuli quantam ipsi nobisque cladem attulerit, quoque modo, dum ex urbe praesidia

opperior, in Galliam proficisci nequiverim. [5]Nunc vero quo loco res nostrae sint iuxta mecum omnes intellegitis. [6]Exercitus hostium duo, unus ab urbe, alter a Gallia obstant. Diutius in his locis esse, si maxume animus ferat, frumenti atque aliarum rerum egestas prohibet. [7]Quocumque ire placet, ferro iter aperiundum est. [8]Quapropter vos moneo uti forti atque parato animo sitis et, cum proelium inibitis, memineritis vos divitias, decus, gloriam, praeterea libertatem atque patriam in dextris vostris portare. [9]Si vincimus, omnia nobis tuta erunt; commeatus abunde, municipia atque coloniae patebunt. [10]Si metu cesserimus, eadem illa advorsa fient, neque locus neque amicus quisquam teget quem arma non texerint. [11]Praeterea, milites, non eadem nobis et illis necessitudo impendet: nos pro patria, pro libertate, pro vita certamus; illis supervacuaneum est pugnare pro potentia paucorum. [12]Quo audacius adgredimini, memores pristinae virtutis. [13]Licuit vobis cum summa turpitudine in exilio aetatem agere; potuistis nonnulli Romae, amissis bonis, alienas opes expectare. [14]Quia illa foeda atque intoleranda viris videbantur, haec sequi decrevistis. [15]Si haec relinquere voltis, audacia opus est; nemo nisi victor pace bellum mutavit. [16]Nam in fuga salutem sperare, cum arma quibus corpus tegitur ab hostibus avorteris, ea vero dementia est. [17]Semper in proelio eis maxumum est periculum qui maxume timent; audacia pro muro habetur.

[18]"Cum vos considero, milites, et cum facta vostra aestumo, magna me spes victoriae tenet. [19]Animus, aetas, virtus vostra me hortantur, praeterea necessitudo, quae etiam timidos fortis facit. [20]Nam multitudo hostium ne circumvenire queat prohibent angustiae loci. [21]Quod si virtuti vostrae fortuna inviderit, cavete inulti animam amittatis, neu capti potius sicuti pecora trucidemini quam virorum more pugnantes cruentam atque luctuosam victoriam hostibus relinquatis."

LIX. [1]Haec ubi dixit, paululum commoratus, signa canere iubet atque instructos ordines in locum aequom deducit. Dein, remotis omnium equis quo militibus exaequato periculo animus amplior esset, ipse pedes exercitum pro loco atque copiis instruit. [2]Nam uti planities erat inter sinistros montis et ab dextra rupe<m> aspera<m> octo cohortis in fronte constituit, relicuarum signa in subsidio artius conlocat. [3]Ab eis centuriones, omnis lectos et evocatos, praeterea ex gregariis militibus optumum quemque armatum in primam aciem subducit. C. Manlium in dextra, Faesulanum quendam in sinistra parte curare iubet: ipse cum libertis et colonis propter aquilam adsistit, quam bello Cimbrico C. Marius in exercitu habuisse dicebatur.

[4]At ex altera parte C. Antonius, pedibus aeger, quod proelio adesse nequibat, M. Petreio legato exercitum permittit. [5]Ille cohortis veteranas,

quas tumulti causa conscripserat, in fronte, post eas ceterum exercitum in subsidiis locat. Ipse equo circumiens unum quemque nominans appellat, hortatur, rogat ut meminerint se contra latrones inermis pro patria, pro liberis, pro aris atque focis suis certare. [6]Homo militaris, quod amplius annos triginta tribunus aut praefectus aut legatus aut praetor cum magna gloria in exercitu fuerat, plerosque ipsos factaque eorum fortia noverat; ea commemorando militum animos accendebat.

LX. [1]Sed ubi omnibus rebus exploratis Petreius tuba signum dat, cohortis paulatim incedere iubet; idem facit hostium exercitus. [2]Postquam eo ventum est unde a ferentariis proelium committi posset, maxumo clamore cum infestis signis concurrunt; pila omittunt, gladiis res geritur. [3]Veterani, pristinae virtutis memores, comminus acriter instare; illi haud timidi resistunt: maxuma vi certatur. [4]Interea Catilina cum expeditis in prima acie vorsari, laborantibus succurrere, integros pro sauciis arcessere, omnia providere, multum ipse pugnare, saepe hostem ferire; strenui militis et boni imperatoris officia simul exsequebatur. [5]Petreius, ubi videt Catilinam contra ac ratus erat magna vi tendere, cohortem praetoriam in medios hostis inducit, eosque perturbatos atque alios alibi resistentis interficit; deinde utrimque ex lateribus ceteros adgreditur. [6]Manlius et Faesulanus in primis pugnantes cadunt. [7]Catilina postquam fusas copias seque cum paucis relicuom videt, memor generis atque pristinae suae dignitatis, in confertissumos hostis incurrit ibique pugnans confoditur.

LXI. [1]Sed confecto proelio, tum vero cerneres quanta audacia quantaque animi vis fuisset in exercitu Catilinae. [2]Nam fere quem quisque vivos pugnando locum ceperat, eum amissa anima corpore tegebat. [3]Pauci autem, quos medios cohors praetoria disiecerat, paulo divorsius, sed omnes tamen advorsis volneribus conciderant. [4]Catilina vero longe a suis inter hostium cadavera repertus est, paululum etiam spirans ferociamque animi, quam habuerat vivos, in voltu retinens. [5]Postremo ex omni copia neque in proelio neque in fuga quisquam civis ingenuus captus est: [6]ita cuncti suae hostiumque vitae iuxta pepercerant. [7]Neque tamen exercitus populi Romani laetam aut incruentam victoriam adeptus erat; nam strenuissumus quisque aut occiderat in proelio aut graviter volneratus discesserat. [8]Multi autem, qui e castris visundi aut spoliandi gratia processerant, volventes hostilia cadavera, amicum alii, pars hospitem aut cognatum reperiebant; fuere item qui inimicos suos cognoscerent. [9]Ita varie per omnem exercitum laetitia, maeror, luctus atque gaudia agitabantur.

COMMENTARY

Ancient authors and their works are cited in the commentary according to the abbreviations employed in the *Oxford Classical Dictionary*[2] (Oxford 1970). Collections of fragments, standard works of reference, and editions of specific authors referred to in the commentary are as follows.

Ascon.   Clark, A.C., *Q. Asconii Pediani Commentarii*. Oxford, 1907.

Cato   Jordan, H., *M. Catonis praeter librum De re rustica quae exstant*. Leipzig, 1860.

CIL   *Corpus Inscriptionum Latinarum*.

Ennius   Vahlen, J., *Ennianae Poesis Reliquiae*. 2nd ed. 1903. rp. Leipzig, 1928.

Festus   Lindsay, W.M., *Festi de Verborum Significatu*. Leipzig, 1913.

Fronto   Haines, C.R., *The Correspondence of Marcus Cornelius Fronto*. 2 vols. London, 1928–29.

HRR   Peter, H., *Historicorum Romanorum Reliquiae*. vol. 1[2] (1914), vol. 2 (1906), Leipzig.

Ibycus   Page, D.L., *Poetae Melici Graeci*. Oxford, 1962.

ILS   Dessau, H., *Inscriptiones Latinae Selectae*. 3 vols. Berlin, 1892–1916.

K-S   Kühner, R., and C. Stegmann, *Ausführliche Grammatik der lateinischen Sprache: Satzlehre*. 2 vols. 5th ed. Hannover, 1976.

L-S   Lewis, C., and C. Short, *A Latin Dictionary*. Oxford, 1879.

Nonius   Lindsay, W.M., *Nonii Marcelli de Compendiosa Doctrina*. Leipzig, 1903.

ORF[3]   Malcovati, H., *Oratorum Romanorum Fragmenta Liberae Rei Publicae*. 3rd ed. Turin, 1966.

S. *Hist.*   Maurenbrecher, B., *C. Sallusti Crispi Historiarum Reliquiae*. Leipzig, 1891–93.

Sappho   Lobel, E., and D. Page, *Poetarum Lesbiorum Fragmenta*. Oxford, 1955.

Schol. Bob.   *Scholia Bobiensia*: T. Stangl, *Ciceronis Orationum Scholiastae*. Vienna, 1912.

CHAPTER 1

(1)   *Omnis homines*: acc. object of *decet*, the impersonal subject of which is supplied by the inf. *niti*.

sese . . . praestare: this use of the reflexive pron. as subject acc. of the inf., rather than a simple prolative inf. depending on *student*, seems to be a deliberate archaism. In Cic. and Caes., the reflexive pron. is generally expressed after verbs of wishing and striving only when the inf. takes a pred. noun or adj. (K-S i.714).

ceteris animalibus: dat. after *praestare*; the unusual position of these words within the relative clause emphasizes the antithesis with *omnis homines*. Although the word *animal* is sometimes used to denote all living creatures including man, here the contrast, which is further developed from different aspects by *pecora* and *beluis* below, probably restricts the sense to forms of life other than man.

summa ope: S. uses this abl. of manner five times in all. The phrase has an archaic flavor reminiscent of a similar expression in Ennius (*Ann.* 161V *summa nituntur opum vi*).

silentio: abl. of manner, "in silence," i.e., without any notice being taken of them, while at 53.6 the sense is active "without taking notice."

transeant: lit., "pass through," i.e., as we say, "let life pass them by" (cf. 2.8); this expression describes just the opposite of living a full and active life (*vitam agere*; cf. 51.12 *aetatem agunt*).

veluti pecora: *pecora*, meaning "cattle," "beasts in the field" (not wild animals but the docile domestic kind), frequently has the nuance of contempt or abuse, especially when it is applied to human beings, as it is here.

prona . . . oboedientia: pred. adjs. agreeing with *quae*, which is the neut. pl. acc. object of *natura finxit*. The observation that men who pursue sensual pleasures are no better than beasts whose gaze is directed towards the ground is a *topos* as old as Plato (*Rep.* 586A).

(2)   *Sed*: this conj. opposes *nostra* to *pecora* in the previous sentence; *omnis* means "taken as a whole" rather than "all our power" (which would be *omnis nostra vis*).

animi imperio: the notion that the proper function of the *animus*, the rational or spiritual element, is to rule the body may be found in Plato (*Phaedo* 80A). The following observation that men approximate the gods through the soul may also be traced to the same passage in the *Phaedo*.

alterum . . . alterum: ordinarily these words would stand for the two concepts set forth in the previous clause (*animi imperio uti* and *corporis servitio uti*), but here the context limits the reference to *animus* and *corpus* since *beluae* do not employ their bodies as servants of the soul.

beluis: this word, in contrast with *pecora*, usually denotes wild animals, esp. those noted for their size or ferocity. The notion here of brute strength, as opposed to the intellect, makes this word more appropriate than *pecora*, which was used above to suggest the type of person who is a slave to his body and primarily devoted to sensual pleasures.

(3) *Quo*: the rel. adv. used in a causal sense (= *qua re:* "wherefore").

videtur: the subj. is provided by the infs. *quaerere* and *efficere* which are modified by the pred. adj. *rectius*.

opibus: "resources," abl. of means; contrast this meaning with *ope* above (1.1) and *plebis opes* (39.1) = "power," "influence" in the sense of political resources.

nostri: objective gen. with *memoriam* to designate the person towards whom the recollection is directed, while the possessive adj. *nostram* would express the subjective relationship (i.e., our memory of someone or something).

quam maxume longam: the adj. forms a pred. acc. agreeing with *memoriam*, the object of *efficere*; the adv. *quam* is to be taken with the superlative *maxume longam* which stands for *longissimam*. This means of forming the superlative is generally confined to adjs. for which the usual superlative in *-issimus* is rare (e.g., 41.5 *maxume manufestos*) or unattested in classical Latin (e.g., 8.5 *maxume negotiosus*; 36.4 *maxume miserabile*), but occasionally it is used, as it is here (cf. 48.2), to emphasize the contrast with a preceding adj. in the positive degree—in this instance, *brevis*. The view that one approaches immortality through fame is a *topos* (e.g., Sappho, fr. 147 L-P; Ibycus, fr. 282 P. 47–48; Thuc. 2.43.2).

(4) *fluxa atque fragilis*: "fleeting and frail"; the first word describes the tendency of internal properties to cause the object to decay and waste away, while *fragilis* (lit., "easily broken") concerns primarily the effect of external forces. These two adjs. are nearly synonymous and are paired for the sake of the alliteration produced by *f*, which is found as well in *formae*. S. is fond of this device which contributes an archaic flavor to his prose, and frequently the words forming the pair merely reinforce each other with little or no emphasis placed on the difference in their meaning. Both of these adjs. mean the opposite of *aeterna*, and S. deliberately disturbs the apparent balance in the grammatical structure by making *clara*, the first adj.

in the second pair, resume the notion contained in *gloria* rather than making the two pairs of adjs. correspond to each other.

virtus: the abstract quality of "excellence," not just in the limited sense of moral worth. *Virtus animi* is one manifestation of this quality, but *virtus* by itself has a broader significance. It is an essential ingredient in all human activity, and it is the foundation on which Rome rose to greatness. S. singles out two of his contemporaries, Caesar and Cato, who possessed *virtus* (53.6), yet the two men were very different in character (*divorsis moribus*). *Virtus* is essentially a quality that is manifested by *egregia facinora*, and it presupposes the right use of a person's ability (*ingenium*).

habetur: not in the common sense "is considered," "regarded," but with its literal meaning "is possessed," i.e., "is a possession."

(5)   *mortalis*: this word is used freely by S. as a substitute for *homines*. It is especially common in the alliterative combination *multi mortales* (e.g., 2.8, 10.5, 52.7), which seems to be archaic and is found only twice in the speeches of Cic., who prefers *omnes mortales*. [S. never writes *multi homines*, but with the adj. *omnes*, *homines* and *mortales* are used interchangeably. There is no evidence that S. ever uses *mortales* in the more comprehensive sense (= men, women, and children) which Fronto (ap. Gell. 13.29) claims that this word can have as opposed to *homines*.]

vine . . . an: S. prefers this means of introducing alternative indirect questions to *utrum . . . an*. These indirect questions depend upon *certamen fuit* = "there was a dispute."

procederet: "turned out successfully," "succeeded," a common meaning in S. which is related to its lit. sense of "go forward" (e.g., 61.8).

(6)   *incipias*: subjn. because the subject is the indefinite second pers. sing. (= the indefinite "one") in a generalizing clause; likewise *consulueris*, pf. subjn. of completed action after *ubi*, "when one has deliberated."

consulto . . . facto: the pf. pass. part. is used in the neut. sing. to represent a verbal substantive in the abl. depending on *opus est*: "deliberation . . . action." This construction is common in S., and sometimes the part. modifies a noun in the abl. while the leading idea is still contained in the part. (e.g., 31.7 *perdita re publica opus esse*: "need for the destruction of the state"). The observation that success depends upon reflection and planning followed by timely action is a *topos* (e.g., Thuc. 1.70.2, 7; 2.40.2).

✳ (7)   *utrumque*: pronouns referring to things rather than persons are generally neut. in S., even when the pronoun stands for a series of nouns that all have the same m. or f. gender—here *vis corporis* and *virtus animi.*

alterum: standing in apposition with *utrumque* and redundant: "needs the help, the one of the other." It is apparently added under the influence of the following *alterius*, since *alter*, like *alius*, is frequently paired in different cases to denote a reciprocal relationship (= "each other").

auxilio: abl. with *eget*, which S. construes more often (8:3) with the gen. (e.g., 51.37), although the abl. is the case preferred by Cic. and is more common in post-Augustan prose.

CHAPTER 2

(1)   *Igitur*: "and so," merely resuming the argument which was interrupted by the parenthetical remarks contained in 1.6–7. In S., this word always stands first in its own clause except in interrogative sentences (e.g., 20.14, 51.43) where it is postpositive, which is the preferred classical usage. This is a deliberate archaism for which the Elder Cato and earlier historians may have provided S. with a model.

nam: S. is fond of using this conj. to introduce an explanation (e.g., 6.4) or an aside (as here) in parataxis, which he favors over subordination as being more archaic and typical of the early Latin prose authors whom he set out to emulate. The theory that monarchy was the first form of government (*imperium*, lit., "supreme power") was commonly held by the ancients.

divorsi: lit., "turned in different directions," i.e., pursuing opposite courses.

pars . . . alii: standing in partitive apposition with *reges*. Instead of the more usual *alii . . . alii* in a distributive sense, which S. uses sparingly, various combinations with *pars* are employed more frequently for the sake of variety.

cupiditate: a general term for "greed" or "avarice" which is later analyzed (10.3–5) into *avaritia* and *ambitio*; here it is opposed to the honorable pursuit of *gloria*.

agitabatur: one of the most common of the frequentative verbs which S. employs to give his prose an archaic flavor often with little or no difference in meaning between these forms and the more common simple verbs to which they are related. [S. uses *agitare* so often and in such a variety of senses that it becomes rather colorless (here = *vitam agere*, simply "to live"; 5.7 with *animus ferox* = "torment," "disturb"; 9.5 *imperium* = "exercise"; 23.3 *ferocius* = "behave"; 48.1 *gaudium* = "display"; 53.4 *multa* = "ponder"). Therefore, S. must resort to *exagitare* on those occasions when a more vivid word seems to be called for.]

sua cuique: the reflexive (lit., "his own possessions") refers to *cuique* which is the leading idea ("each one was satisfied"), although it is not the grammatical subject.

(2) *Cyrus*: not the first ruler of a great empire, but noted (esp. from the account in Herodotus) for his conquest of the Medes, Lydians, and Babylonians in the mid 6th cent. B.C. Out of these former kingdoms he fashioned the vast Persian Empire which occupied most of the Middle East and Asia Minor including the many Greek colonies on the coast and nearby islands.

coepere: S. prefers the more archaic and poetic ending -ere for the 3rd person pl. in the pf. act. indic. to the standard prose form in -*erunt*, which is found only four times in the *Cat.* (20.10, 45.3, 51.9, 51.38). Both endings were still current in his day according to Cic. (*Orat.* 157), although the shorter ending is far less common even in Plautus and Terence as well as in the best prose writers. This seems to be a conscious borrowing from Cato in whom -*ere* is the more frequent form.

urbis atque nationes: the former mainly refers to the conquests of the Spartans (*Lacedaemonii*) and Athenians (*Athenienses*) who exercised control in the 6th and 5th cents. B.C. over various city-states in mainland Greece and in the Aegean, while *nationes* is commonly applied to loosely organized populations and must refer especially to the conquests of Cyrus. The arrangement of the corresponding terms in these two pairs in the reverse order produces the rhetorical figure known as chiasmus.

habere: the 2nd in a series of three complementary infs. depending on *coepere*; their lust for power constituted a justification for war: i.e., "to possess (in) their lust for power . . ."

putare: instead of an indirect statement with *esse*, S. invariably construes this verb with a double acc. in the sense of "consider," "regard (as)" (e.g., 7.6, 36.4, 51.41), or sometimes, as here, with a prepositional phrase taking the place of the pred. acc. where *putare* = "see," "reckon."

tum demum: the adv. *demum* (in origin a superlative form from *de*) used enclitically with advs. of time, such as *tum*, and demonstrative pronouns, expresses the exclusion of prior occasions or other instances: "only then," "then at last."

periculo atque negotiis: although *periculum* is sometimes equivalent to *experimentum* (= "trial," usu. with *facere*), *periculo* is best taken with *negotiis* (= simply *rebus*) as standing by hendiadys for *periculosis negotiis*: "hazardous enterprises."

(3) *Quod*: the usual adversative conj. with *si* or *nisi*.

imperatorum: a general word for any ruler who holds *imperium* but does not possess the title *rex*.

valeret: the impf., rather than plupf. subjn., is used in this contrary to fact condition both in the protasis and apodosis since it is general and refers to present as well as past time; i.e., the action is repeated or continued and not limited to one fixed occasion in the past.

sese . . . haberent: lit., "to be situated (in such and such a manner)," virtually èquivalent to *essent*.

neque . . . neque: the first *neque* is merely coordinate to the one following rather than supplying a conj. (*et non*) to join *cerneres* to the previous clause: "one would see neither power shifting to and fro nor everything in chaos and confusion." Asyndeton is normal in sentences of this type, which S. is fond of adding to explain a previous statement.

aliud alio ferri: *alius* repeated in diff. cases within the same clause, usu. in the sing., or with a cognate adv. (here *alio*), often has the meaning "various" or "different": here = "things carried in different directions."

(4) *artibus*: a favorite word in S. meaning "qualities" or "practices," especially those related to the sphere of morality as can be seen from the examples given immediately below at 3.3 and 10.4. Cato appears to use this word several times in a similar sense (45.6J; 60.1J). For the view that power is best retained by the same practices that established it in the first place, cf. Polybius (10.36.5) on the Carthaginians.

(5) *continentia*: "self-restraint," "temperance," as opposed to *lubido*, "unrestrained desire," "wantonness."

invasere: "have burst in," a common word in S. used to describe the onset of emotions or sudden and radical changes. Sometimes it is used absolutely as here; more often with an acc. direct object.

fortuna: virtually = *condicio*, i.e., the "standing" of kings and rulers. Their position in the state declined together with their morals, as the next sentence makes clear.

(6) *quemque*: intensifies the superlative *optumum* (lit., "each one in the order of his excellence"); trans. "the best man." The use of the superlative in contrast with the comparative *minus bono* is typical of S.'s deliberate *inconcinnitas*.

(7) *Quae*: inner acc. object of *arant, navigant, aedificant* standing for the activity itself denoted by each of these vbs. (= *quae homines arando navigando aedificando agunt*). These three pursuits are selected merely as typical examples of the various occupations that

might be subsumed under the heading of private life as opposed to politics or military affairs. *Omnia* is best taken as the subject which gathers up and generalizes the specific examples in the relative clause to include other fields: "all occupations, agriculture, shipping, and building. . . ."

parent: "depend on," "be subject to" with the dat. *virtuti*.

(8) *multi mortales*: vid. 1.5n.

dediti ventri atque somno: "given over to gluttony and sloth"; taken as a model by Tacitus (*Ger.* 15.1), who writes *dediti somno ciboque*.

indocti incultique: paired for the sake of alliteration without special reference to the soul as opposed to the body; the former refers to intellectual, the latter to cultural refinement.

transiere: this vb. (= "pass through"), as opposed to *transigere* or *transegere* ("conduct," "bring to a conclusion"), which are found in the bulk of the MSS, suits better the comparison with a traveler in a foreign land (*sicuti peregrinantes*) who merely passes through without feeling a part of his surroundings. [*Transigere* commonly describes the completion or performance of a task, and it does not appear to be used as an equivalent of *agere* ("pass," "spend") until the post-Augustan period. S. uses *transigere* only once elsewhere (*Jug.* 29.5) meaning "to transact (through negotiation)."]

contra naturam: to the man who cultivates his soul rather than his body, the *corpus* is at best merely the servant (1.2) and is frequently viewed as a burden (*onus*) standing in the way of the perfection of the soul (e.g., Plato, *Phaedo* 66B).

anima: elsewhere in S., this word generally means the "vital principle" or "life" itself, but in this passage it must stand for *animus* in contrast with the body (likewise in *Jug.* 2.1, 2.2). The choice of *anima* here, rather than *animus*, need not imply that the soul in these men is being regarded as so degraded that it cannot be called *animus*. Possibly *anima* is substituted for *animus* to avoid the jingle *corpus . . . animus*.

iuxta: a common adv. in S., = *pariter* ("alike"). Usually the two things that are likened to each other are joined by a conj., but once S. uses the archaic *iuxta mecum* (58.5).

(9) *Verum enim vero*: "but in very truth"; *verum* is made more emphatic by the addition of *enim vero*. This rhetorical pleonasm is rare in Cic., quite common in Livy.

is demum: vid. 2.2n. *tum demum*.

frui anima: virtually synonymous with *vivere*, but added to reinforce and clarify the sense in which *vivere* is being used: "to live and really enjoy life." *Anima* is used in its normal sense, = the "vital principle," which man has in common with all living creatures, as opposed to the *animus*, which sets man apart from other *animalia*.

aliquo negotio intentus: *intentus* is frequently used absolutely by S. with the meaning "eager," "alert," but when it is accompanied by a noun, it is usually construed with the abl. as here (= "occupied with," "absorbed by"; cf. *Jug.* 44.3 *expectatione . . . intentos*). Sometimes, however, it is impossible to decide whether the noun is being used in the abl. or dat. (= "intent upon"), e.g., 4.1, 54.4.

praeclari facinoris: a defining adj. is generally required when *facinus* means a "deed" (= *factum*) rather than a crime (cf., however, 4.4n.). This literal sense of *facinus*, which is found quite often in S., is archaic.

artis bonae: "good conduct."

aliud alii: best expanded in trans.: "one path to one, another (path) to another"; *via* is also used several times by S. in this metaphorical sense of the course or means employed to reach a goal—in this case, *gloria* or *fama bonae artis*.

CHAPTER 3

(1)   *bene facere . . . bene dicere*: the stock and conventional comparison which contrasts action with words. The chiastic arrangement of the infs. and pred. adjs. is designed to strengthen the antithesis. The fact that *scripsere* is substituted for *dicere* when the comparison is restated below indicates that *dicere* is being used in a wider sense than simply public speaking with which it might be tempting to understand *rei publicae*. Therefore the dat. should be taken only with *bene facere* (= "to perform a good deed").

haud absurdum: i.e., *praeclarum*, an example of litotes (an assertion made by denying its contrary), which is common in S.; *absurdus* (lit., "out of tune"), which has an archaic ring, is used once elsewhere by S. (25.5), also in litotes, to mean "having merit."

vel pace vel bello: these nouns are usu. accompanied by the prep. *in* when temporal unless modified by an adj.; therefore best taken as instrumental standing for the deeds that are performed in peacetime or in war.

fecere: used absolutely as at 8.5 and 23.2 where it is also paired with *dicere*: "those who have performed deeds."

multi: modifying the subject of *laudantur*, which is supplied by the unexpressed antecedent of *qui fecere* and *qui . . . scripsere*. When *multi* is thus added late in a sentence, it is usually to be taken in the predicate and means "in great numbers."

(2) *Ac mihi quidem*: with *videtur*, whose subj. is *scribere*, a very common idiom in Cic. meaning "I think."

haudquaquam par gloria: another example of litotes; the man of action, esp. a military leader, commonly receives greater recognition than the man who devotes himself to intellectual pursuits.

auctorem rerum: the reading *actorem*, which is found in several MSS, would provide a stronger antithesis with *scriptorem*, since *auctor rerum* is frequently synonymous with *scriptor rerum* and means the author of historical works. *Auctor*, however, is perhaps deliberately selected by S. to convey the notion of responsibility or initiative for a deed as well as the actual performance, which would be the primary sense of *actor*—the mere "agent" or "doer."

arduum: construe with *scribere*, which in this context means "to write appropriately" (cf. *vivere* above 2.9).

dictis exaequanda: "must be matched with words" (abl. of means). This reading, rather than the less well attested *ex(s)equenda*, better suits the context and the *topos* that it is difficult to find words that are adequate or appropriate to the subject matter (e.g., Isoc. *Paneg.* 13).

dehinc, quia: *dehinc* is rare in enumerations in place of the more usu. *deinde*, which has crept into several MSS as a correction; *quia* is deliberately substituted for a second *quod* for the sake of variation.

delicta: standing in apposition with *quae*, the object of *reprehenderis*: "those things that you censure as faults." The potential subjn. is used because the subject is the indefinite 2nd pers. sing., and the clause is virtually conditional (cf. *memores* below).

general condition
A+ G S14 D

malivolentia et invidia: abls. of cause.

dicta: sc. *esse*, = "mentioned"; the acc. subj. of the inf. in this indirect statement is supplied by the unexpressed antecedent of *quae*.

ubi . . . ducit: in asyndeton; an adversative conj. has been suppressed here and below after *accipit*. This observation may be compared with the very similar statement attributed to Pericles by Thucydides (2.35.2) in his funeral oration, but the danger of arousing jealousy in the listener when he hears another man's virtue praised is a common rhetorical theme (e.g., Isoc. *Evag.* 6; Demos. *Epitaph.* 14).

memores: also found with *de* + abl. at 26.3, 52.13, but often construed with a direct object acc., e.g., 5.7, 20.1.

sibi quisque: as usu., the distributive *quisque* stands immediately after the reflexive and is placed in the subordinate clause, although it must be taken as the subj. of *accipit* and *ducit* as well as *putat*.

facilia factu: the alliteration here and below (*ficta pro falsis*) adds forcefulness to the assertion.

supra ea: = *quae supra ea sunt*; the prepositional phrase imitates the Greek usage of forming a substantive by means of the definite article plus a prepositional phrase; it supplies the direct object of *ducit*.

pro falsis: to be taken with *ducit* as the predicate complementing *supra ea*: "<those things that are> beyond that (i.e., the realm of his own capabililty), like made-up stories, he regards as unhistorical."

(3) *Sed*: introduces a digression to explain why S. turned to the writing of history late in life. S.'s description of his youthful attraction to politics closely resembles a similar confession in Plato (*Ep.* 7.324B).

adulescentulus: the diminutive is perhaps intended to suggest the naive simplicity of youth (cf. 3.4 *imbecilla aetas*) in contrast with mature reflection based upon experience, but the word is extremely flexible and applied elsewhere by S. (49.2) to Julius Caesar at a time when he was 37 years old. Possibly S. has in mind the period around his 30th birthday when he became eligible under the *lex Cornelia* to stand for the quaestorship, the first office in the *cursus honorum* leading to the consulship. S.'s earliest attested office is his tribunate in 52 B.C. at the age of about 34 (vid. Introd. p. 2).

sicuti plerique: an exaggeration, since political affairs remained almost exclusively in the hands of a relatively small number of well-established families, and it was not very common or easy for an outsider, whose ancestors had never held office, to play an important role in government. To the members of this governing class, however, and to men like Cic. (vid. 23.6) and S. himself who wished to distinguish themselves, few careers outside of politics were regarded as acceptable.

studio: an abl. of manner with *latus sum*, which although passive, expresses what is essentially an active idea: "I threw myself eagerly into politics."

ibique: = *in eaque*, lit., "there," i.e., in the pursuit of his career; *-que* has the force of an adversative. S. is fond of substituting a demonstrative or relative adv. for a prepositional phrase (a colloquial usage, found also in poetry) and employs parataxis here in preference to subordination (i.e., *in qua*).

advorsa: the first attested major setback in S.'s career is his expulsion from the senate in 50 B.C. Later, after serving with distinction in Caesar's African campaign as praetor in 46, he seems to have been forced to retire from politics owing to a scandal arising from his governorship of Africa Nova (vid. Introd. pp. 4–5).

audacia, largitio, avaritia: a triad in asyndeton consisting of three vices. Each is paired with one of the preceding virtues, which are emphasized by the anaphora of *pro*. The first members in the two series correspond as opposites, while *largitio* and *avaritia* are contrasted with *virtute* and *abstinentia* respectively so that the arrangement is chiastic. Bribery (*largitio*) was employed by men who lacked merit (*virtus*) to gain advancement (cf. 11.2), and conduct in office was characterized by a desire for personal enrichment (*avaritia*) rather than restraint in refusing graft (*abstinentia*). The sound rather than sense probably led S. to bracket the first series with *pudore* and *virtute* and the second with *audacia* and *avaritia*.

(4)   *Quae*: neut. pl., although the pronoun has the preceding three f. substantives as its antecedent.

animus: here and at 4.1 virtually = *ego*, while still maintaining the emphasis on the rational spirit that sets men apart from animals.

malarum artium: gen. supplying the object of reference for the adj. *insolens*: "unaccustomed to evil practices."

corrupta tenebatur: the participle is best taken as nom. agreeing with *aetas*: "was seduced and held prisoner." According to S.'s analysis (cf. 10.3–5), *ambitio* (= "the desire for power") is one of the two evils that corrupted the state. It closely resembles *virtus* because it aims at the same ends (*gloria*, *honor*, and *imperium*), but it leads men to adopt any means at their disposal to satisfy their desire for advancement.

(5)   *me*: emphasized by being placed so early in the sentence and so far from *vexabat* of which it is the direct object.

relicuorum: "the rest" in contrast with S. who set himself apart by refusing to adopt the corrupt practices of his age, while *ceteros* below = "the others" who resembled S. in so far as they were motivated by *honoris cupido*.

nihilo: in origin an abl. of degree of difference with the comparative adv. *minus*; sometimes written as one word and used like *tamen* to introduce the main statement after a concessive or conditional clause.

cupido: never used by Cic. or Caes. who prefer *cupiditas*, which is found only three times in S. (2.1, 5.4, 21.4) as opposed to twenty instances of *cupido*. In general, S. shows a tendency to avoid the frequent use of abstracts in *-tas* (e.g., *saevitia* 8 times as opposed to *crudelitas* 4 times), and may have borrowed *cupido* from Cato (e.g., 47.14J) as being more archaic. Following S., Livy and Tacitus used *cupido* quite freely.

eadem qua: if *eadem* is to be construed with the instrumental abls. *fama* and *invidia*, the reading *qua*, which is found in only three MSS, is preferable to the nom. *quae*, which is offered by all the rest. Since S. invariably places *idem*, meaning "the same," before the word it modifies, *eadem* is not likely to modify *cupido*. With *eadem qua* is understood *honoris cupido vexabat*: "troubled me with the same reputation and envy as the others."

fama atque invidia: *fama* in conjunction with *invidia* would ordinarily refer to the "fame" or "prominence" of a public figure, but in this context, the sense seems to be "ill repute," while *invidia* describes the jealousy aroused by successfully advancing one's political career in the face of opposition.

CHAPTER 4

(1) *ex multis miseriis atque periculis*: the *multa advorsa* of 3.3; *ex* is used in the sense of "following," "after."

a re publica: with *procul*, which probably influences the choice of *habere* rather than *agere*: "at a distance from public life" (cf. 3.3 for this meaning of *res publica*).

habendam: sc. *esse*, forming an indirect statement depending on *decrevi*; *mihi*, the dat. of agent with the pass. periphrastic, is made prominent by being put first in the clause.

bonum otium: acc. obj. of the inf. *conterere*, which with *agere* below, supplies the subj. of the impersonal expression *non fuit consilium*. The adj. *bonum* ("felicitous") is used to contrast *otium* with *ambitio mala* ("destructive") below and to set it apart from *desidia* (= "idleness"), with which *otium* is sometimes synonymous.

agrum colundo aut venando: abls. depending on *intentum* which agrees with *me*, the unexpressed acc. subject of *agere*. S. quite often retains the gerund with an acc. object in preference to the more common gerundive equivalent, esp. when it is accompanied by one or more gerunds used absolutely.

servilibus officiis: "servile tasks," in apposition with *colundo* and *venando*. By contrast, Cato (*Agr.*, praef.) and Cic. (*Off.* 1.151) single out agriculture as one of the most worthy occupations for a free man, and their judgment appears to reflect the conventional attitude of the Romans towards farming. Possibly S. rejects this traditional view because he is still thinking primarily in terms of the proper exercise of one's *ingenium* and regards these two pursuits as involving the *corpus* rather than the *animus*. At the same time, he may be sneering at the vast pleasure parks and country estates that were maintained in his day by leading members of the aristocracy and staffed with slaves. Ironically, S. himself may have been the owner of a very elegant pleasure park or garden (the *horti Sallustiani*) which was located on the outskirts of Rome between the Quirinal and Pincian Hills (vid. Introd. p. 5).

(2) *a quo incepto studioque*: the neut. substs. *incepto* (= "undertaking") and *studio* should logically form the antecedent of *quo*, but they have been attracted into the relative clause since it has been placed first to stress the contrast with the adv. *eodem* which stands for *ad idem inceptum studiumque*.

carptim: adv., lit., "in parts," "separately," i.e., in monographs or separate essays on a limited period rather than a continuous history of R. from the foundation. On the choice of this vehicle for writing history, vid. Introd. pp. 7–8. [S.'s fondness for adverbs in *-tim* may have been influenced by the practice of his predecessor Sisenna who was noted for employing a number of new and unusual adverbs ending in this suffix (Gell. 12.15). In addition to *carptim*, which is first attested here, and the rare *confertim* (*Jug.* 50.5), we also find a host of such common words as *paulatim* (5.9), *privatim* (11.6), *singillatim* (49.4), *partim* (50.1), and *separatim* (52.23).]

ut quaeque: as elsewhere in S., virtually a periphrasis for *quaecumque*.

perscribere: the compound conveys the notions of completeness and accuracy.

eo magis: sc. *statui res gestas p. R. perscribere*; *eo* is abl. of degree of diff.

a spe, metu, partibus rei publicae: a triad in asyndeton; *partibus r. p.* refers to the two factions within the government, which S. defines elsewhere (38.1–4) as the conservatives, who controlled the senate, and the reformers, who sought power by appealing to the popular assemblies. It was traditional for an historian to assert his objectivity near the beginning of his work, and often he explained the circumstances which made it possible for him to write without bias and from a detached point of view (cf. Hecateus, bk.1 fr.1; Thuc. 1.22.2ff.; Livy, *praef.* 5).

erat: past rather than present because the statement is expressed as holding true with respect to the time of the main vb. *statui*.

(3) *de Catilinae coniuratione*: this phrase has supplied the modern title by which the work is commonly known rather than the *Bellum Catilinae* (vid. Introd. n. 9).

paucis: sc. *verbis*, a colloquial expression found chiefly in comedy before S. Brevity is a quality that S. greatly admired in his predecessor the Elder Cato, and it is one of the chief characteristics of his own style (vid. Introd. p. 12).

absolvam: "set forth" (lit., "unbind," "set free"); S. is apparently the first prose author to use this verb in the sense of *narrare*. Elsewhere in S., *absolvere* is construed with the acc. and is found only here with *de* + abl.

(4) *id facinus*: usually pejorative in S. in the absence of a defining adj., but here *facinus* may be used in the archaic neutral sense of simply a "deed," "event."

novitate: abl. of cause with *memorabile*, which picks up *memoria digna* above. S. may be consciously imitating Thucydides (1.1) who began his history of the Peloponnesian War by calling attention to the uniqueness of the war as a justification for making it the subject of a detailed account.

(5) *faciam*: the subjn. indicates that this clause is not merely temporal but expresses an added notion of purpose: ". . . before I can begin my narrative."

CHAPTER 5

(1) *L. Catilina*: S. never refers to Catiline by his nomen Sergius. His cognomen may be derived from a modified spelling of the adj. *catulina* (sc. *caro*) = "puppy's flesh."

nobili genere: the participle *natus* is normally construed with an abl. of source without a preposition. The *gens Sergia* claimed descent from Sergestus, one of the Trojan companions of the hero Aeneas who traditionally settled in Latium (Verg. *Aen.* 5.121), and like the *Iulii* belonged to a select group of old patrician clans that boasted of Trojan lineage. *Nobilis* is a technical term used to describe a limited number of families, both patrician and plebeian, whose ancestors had held either the consulship, military tribunate with consular power, or the dictatorship. This hereditary nobility was almost closed to newcomers since the consulship was jealously guarded by the members of this select group—a virtual oligarchy. Catiline's family was patrician (31.7) and could point to consular forebears, but it had suffered a long period of eclipse not unlike Sulla's family (cf. 5.6, 11.4). The last Sergius known to have achieved consular rank is Cn. Sergius Fidenas Coxo (380 B.C.), and Catiline's father was apparently a man of limited means ([Q. Cic.] *Comm. Petit.* 2.9). For the probable date of Catiline's birth, vid. App. I. It is significant that not only Catiline himself but some of his supporters were also *nobiles*. The prominence of these aristocratic accomplices forms a recurring theme throughout the monograph and supports S.'s diagnosis of the decadence that gripped

Roman society (10–13). The social and political standing of those who plotted against the state made the conspiracy all the more dangerous and difficult for a "new man" like Cicero to expose and suppress.

malo pravoque: *malus* = "bad by nature"; *pravus* ("crooked," "twisted," the opposite of *rectus*) = "bent out of shape," "deformed" by habit or training.

(2)　*adulescentia*: "his youth," loosely contrasted with *iuventutem* below, a more inclusive term which denotes the period in a man's life when he is fit to bear arms. This distinction is not, however, always maintained, and the two terms overlap. S.'s description of Catiline's early devotion to wickedness and fondness for bloodshed closely resembles a comparable sketch of Catiline's youth in Cic. (*Sull.* 70).

bella intestina . . . discordia civilis: the phrase is bracketed by the arrangement of the adjs. with the first and last noun in the series.

caedes: Catiline was a partisan of Sulla and was said to have committed numerous atrocities during the proscriptions that followed Sulla's victory in the Civil War. S. does not go into detail, but Cic. gives the names of four of Catiline's victims in his *Oratio in Toga Candida* delivered in 64 B.C. (ap. Ascon. p. 84C.5–9): M. Marius Gratidianus, Q. Caecilius, M. Volumnius, and L. Tanusius. According to a late source (*Scholia Bernensia* ad Lucanum 2.173—possibly supported by S., *Hist.* 1.45M), Gratidianus was the brother of Catiline's own wife, and the claim is also made that Q. Caecilius was the husband of Catiline's sister ([Q. Cic.] *Comm. Petit.* 2.9). Plutarch (*Sull.* 32.2; *Cic.* 10.3), possibly misinterpreting one of these two accounts, alleges that Catiline murdered his own brother and subsequently persuaded Sulla to enter the name of his victim on the proscription lists.

ibique: = *in eisque* (*rebus*).

iuventutem suam: "his prime," "early manhood." This is the only instance in S. where *iuventus* has this meaning. Elsewhere it is used as a collective noun equivalent to *iuvenes*. On Catiline's early career, vid. App. I.

(3)　3–6: the traits of Catiline's personality: many of the qualities attributed to Catiline are also to be found in Livy's description of Hannibal (21.4.5–9), which appears to draw on S. Likewise Tacitus (*Ann.* 4.1.3) clearly borrowed from S. in composing his portrait of Sejanus.

inediae, algoris, vigiliae: obj. gens. in asyndeton governed by the participial adj. *patiens* used to denote a permanent quality

(= "capable of enduring"), while the acc. would indicate a particular occurrence ("experiencing"). The verb *to be* (sc. *erat* here and below with *animus*) is consistently omitted in this terse account of the conflicting ingredients in Catiline's personality. The rare and archaic *inedia* and *algor* are deliberately preferred to the synonyms *fames* and *frigus* which were used by Cic. in a comparable description of Catiline's great physical endurance (*Cat.* 1.26; cf. 3.16).

supra quam: "more than," for the more usual *ultra quam*, which is never found in S. The adv. *supra* qualifies *patiens* making it virtually comparative.

cuiquam: dat. with *credibile*. The indefinite pronoun *quisquam* is employed because of the implied negative: "no one would believe it."

(4) *audax, subdolus, varius*: *varius* ("versatile," i.e., "capable of assuming different attitudes") reinforces and explains the apparent contradiction implied by the words *audax* ("daring," suggesting open recklessness) and *subdolus* ("cunning," in a secretive sense). This versatility is further developed in the following phrase.

cuius . . . lubet: gen. of the indefinite adj. *quilubet* (-*lib*-), = *cuiuslubet rei*.

simulator ac dissimulator: these verbal substantives in -*tor*, marking a permanent quality, are used here with the value of adjs., as often in S. This usage is an extension of apposition. Due to their verbal nature, *simulator* and *dissimulator* are construed with an obj. gen. *cuius rei lubet*: "capable of pretending or concealing anything at all."

alieni adpetens, sui profusus: *alieni* and *sui* are neuter substantives. *Profusus* takes an objective gen. by analogy with the gen. which is normal with the participial adj. *adpetens*. This same influence of one adj. upon another in an antithetical pair may be observed at 7.6 where *liberalis*, meaning "generous," is made to govern a gen. to balance the regular obj. gen. with *avidus* which immediately precedes.

satis eloquentiae, sapientiae parum: sc. *ei erat*; chiasmus is used to strengthen the antithesis. S. uses *eloquentia* in the restricted sense meaning the ability to speak well or persuasively, while *sapientia* is used in the sense of prudence or wisdom that depends upon proper training in moral conduct.

(5) *Vastus*: "insatiable"; from its original meaning of "empty," "desolate," this adj. takes on the sense of "enormous," "prodigious" in size or degree. Hence it is appropriate to describe a grasping desire that is never surfeited but always has room for more.

inmoderata, incredibilia, nimis alta: the third occurrence in this chapter of a triad in asyndeton. These neut. adjs. are used substantivally in place of abstract nouns: "the extravagant, the unbelievable, the impossible (lit., too lofty)."

(6)   *post dominationem L. Sullae*: "after the despotism of Sulla"; *dominatio* is invariably used in S. to describe absolute or tyrannical power. Following his victory in the Civil War late in 82 B.C., L. Cornelius Sulla had himself appointed dictator, ostensibly for the purpose of reforming the laws of the state, and he remained master of Rome for more than two years until he voluntarily retired into private life during the course of 79. The memory of this civil strife and the policies of Sulla's regime are referred to from time to time by S. as factors that encouraged Catiline and his supporters to aim at the overthrow of the government (e.g., 16.4, 37.6, 47.2)

lubido maxuma invaserat: "a very great desire had come over him"; on *invado*, vid. 2.5n. *Lubido* conveys the notion of an unlawful desire and is a stronger word than *cupido*.

id: picks up *rei publicae capiundae* in the previous clause and supplies the direct object of *adsequeretur* within the indirect question. There is an abrupt shift of subject between these two clauses from *lubido* to *Catilina*, which was the direct object (*hunc*) of *invaserat*.

regnum: "despotism," lit., "the power of a king," the word *rex* being synonymous with tyranny after the foundation of the Republic and detested by the Romans (cf. Livy 27.19.4 *regium nomen alibi magnum, Romae intolerabile esse*).

pararet: subjn. in a clause of proviso after *dum* (= *dummodo*, which is never found in S.).

quicquam pensi: "a matter of importance," i.e., "important," predicate acc. with the verb *habebat* (= "consider," "regard") which takes a double acc. and has the indirect question as its direct object. The partitive gen. *pensi* (pf. pass. part. of *pendo*, "a thing weighed") depends on *quicquam* after the negative *neque* above and invariably occurs in a negative context in S. It is used both as a predicate (here and 23.2) meaning "to regard as of no importance" and absolutely meaning "to have no scruples" (12.2, 52.34).

(7)   *Agitabatur*: emphasized by being put first in the clause—likewise *incitabant* below. The role of Catiline's guilty conscience in driving him to extremes is also alluded to at 15.4

✗   *in dies*: "daily," always combined with a comparative or an expression denoting increase, whereas *cottidie* is used to describe the repetition of an act or event day after day.

quae utraque: standing for *quarum utramque*; for the neut. gender of the rel. pron. which has two f. sing. nouns as its antecedents, vid. 1.7n. *utrumque*. *Uterque* ("each of two") is normally pl. only when it refers to two classes or groups, but here it has been attracted into the pl. by being made to stand in apposition with the relative which has taken its place as the direct object.

(8) *Incitabant*: the direct object is not expressed but must be supplied from *animus ferox* above.

quos: the antecedent must logically be *mores* alone since the adj. *corrupti* is developed as the theme of the rel. clause.

divorsa inter se: "mutually opposed" (lit., "differing between themselves") because these two vices caused men to covet money and squander the wealth that they possessed on frivolous and wasteful pleasures. This observation concerning the contrary nature of these two vices may ultimately stem from the Elder Cato to whom Livy attributes a very similar pronouncement (vid. 52.7n.). The superlative of *divorsus*, which occurs elsewhere in S., would have been more appropriate here than the positive degree to balance *pessuma*.

(9) *Res ipsa*: "the subject itself," providing an artful pretext for the digression on the growth and subsequent corruption of the Roman state (chaps. 6–13), as if these chapters were not consciously planned in advance by the author.

de moribus: this is the only instance in S. of *de* + abl. with *admonere* (= "to remind someone about . . .")—sc. *me* as direct object. Elsewhere, S. uses either the gen. or an internal acc. to express the thing about which one is reminded.

tempus: "occasion," virtually synonymous with *res*, which S. often uses in this sense. For *res* and *tempus* together, cf. 20.15, 50.3.

supra repetere: best taken absolutely, perhaps with *memoriam* understood: "to go back in time," lit., "to call up a recollection from past times." This inf. and *disserere* below depend on *hortari* (sc. *me*) in place of the more usual subjn. *ut repetam*. Other examples of this extended use of the inf. in S. are found with the verbs *impero* (16.2), *moneo* (52.3), *coniuro* (52.24), and *dubito* (15.2) by analogy with *non dubito*.

paucis: cf. 4.3n.

instituta . . . disserere: the acc. *instituta* provides the first of three objects dependent on *disserere* (= "discuss"), the other two being the indirect questions *quo modo . . . reliquerint* and *ut* (= *quo modo*) *. . . facta sit*. This practice of combining different constructions with the same verb to produce dissymmetry may be observed elsewhere in S. (e.g., 10.4, 16.2, 17.6, 25.2, 37.10, 47.1).

habuerint: virtually equivalent to *tractare*: "administer," "treat." This meaning of *habere* is quite common in conjunction with an adv. or abl. of manner.

immutata: "altered," sc. *res publica* from above.

<atque optuma>: these words are lacking in the best MSS and restored from a citation of this passage in Augustine (*Civ. Dei* 2.18). Homoeoteleuton may account for the omission: *pulcherr <uma atque opt>uma*. In favor of adopting this supplement are S.'s fondness for arranging pairs of opposing words in chiasmus (e.g., 3.3n.) and the resemblance of this passage to the nearly identical statement made at 10.6 where the adjs. are found in symmetrical pairs.

CHAPTER 6

(1) *Urbem Romam . . . habuere*: these words provided a model for the opening of the first chapter of Tacitus' *Annales*, which is stylistically greatly indebted to S. (1.1 *Urbem Romam a principio reges habuere*). S. uses nearly the same expression in the *Jug.* (18.1) to introduce his account of the earliest inhabitants of Africa *(Africam initio habuere Gaetuli et Libyes)*, and in both passages *habere* is used in the sense of *incolere*, a meaning of this word that is also found in Cato (4.15J).

sicuti ego accepi: an indication that the author is drawing upon tradition. There were a variety of foundation legends according to which either the Trojan exile Aeneas or an eponymous native hero Romulus (the brother of Remus) founded Rome. S. does not name his source, but we are told by Servius (ad *Aen.* 1.6) that he followed Cato's account in his *Origines* of the union formed by the Trojan survivors under Aeneas and the native Aborigines. Romulus is conspicuously absent from S.'s version, yet Cato apparently attempted to reconcile the two mutually exclusive foundation legends by making Romulus a remote descendant of Aeneas through the line of kings founded by Aeneas' son Ascanius at Alba Longa (*HRR* fr. 4, frr. 8–13). This series of Alban kings was used to fill the gap of approximately 432 years between 753 B.C., when Rome was traditionally founded, and 1184 B.C., the date worked out for the sack of Troy. S. does not take this interval into account but implies that Rome was settled soon after the Trojans and Aborigines united under Aeneas.

sedibus incertis: best taken as abl. absol. standing for *cum sedes incertae essent*.

cumque his: normally the enclitic *-que* is not appended to a monosyllabic preposition but to the word following unless the preposition is repeated. Exceptions to this rule, however, do occur in Cic. and Caes. as well as S. (e.g., 48.5 *deque ea re*), and there is no need to accept the reading preserved by Servius *et cum his*, as some editors do.

Aborigines: subject nom. with *Troiani* of *condidere atque habuere*. This is the name commonly given to the indigenous population of Latium at the time of Aeneas' arrival in Italy. Cato (*HRR* fr. 6) believed that they were earlier immigrants from Greece who came to Italy some time before the Trojan War. Another tradition found in Dion. Hal. (*Ant. Rom.* 1.72) made them autochthonous.

agreste: "uncouth," "barbarous," lit., pertaining to the country as opposed to the civilization and refinement of the city.

sine legibus . . . solutum: a series of four modifiers in pairs; chiasmus is used to set off the corresponding components in the two pairs: *sine legibus* is answered by *solutum* ("unrestrained"), while *sine imperio* ("without any government") corresponds to *liberum*. As often in S., only the words in the second are joined by a conjunction. The use of a prepositional phrase as the equivalent of an attributive adj. is found elsewhere in S. (cf. 3.2n. *supra ea*) but is comparatively rare in classical prose.

(2) *Hi*: subject of both the temporal *postquam* clause and *coaluerint* below in the indirect question.

in una moenia: "into one fortified city"; *moenia* is virtually equivalent to *urbs*, but the fortifications are what distinguish a city in the early stages of its development before it is completely built up. *Unus* meaning "one" is found in the pl. only with nouns like *moenia* that are pl. in form but singular in sense.

dispari genere: abl. of quality best translated concessively: "although of different stock"—i.e., part Trojan and part native.

alius alio more viventes: the sing. *alius*, standing in partitive apposition with *viventes*, would normally describe the conduct of individuals within a single group: "each person living in a different way." Since this meaning does not suit the context, which seems to concern the dissimilar conduct of the two races that formed the new nation, it is tempting to adopt in place of *alius* the pl. *alii*, which is found in several MSS of both families. The sing., however, is supported by a fragment of a 5th cent. papyrus (*Pap. Oxyrh.* VI.884) and is retained by most modern editors on the assumption that *alius* has been attracted into the sing. by *alio*.

incredibile memoratu: *incredibile* is a predicate adj. modifying the indirect question which supplies the grammatical subject of *est*. It is best, however, to translate *est* impersonally and treat the indirect question as the object of the supine *memoratu*.

<ita . . . facta erat>: this clause is lacking in all the best MSS of both families. It is quoted by Augustine (*Epist.* 138.10) without naming his source but in a context that implies Cic. or S. Restoration of these words at this point in the text is supported by the inclusion of this clause in the 5th cent. papyrus frag. mentioned above with the slight variation *facta est* for *facta erat*.

brevi: sc. *tempore*.

diversa atque vaga: *vaga* ("unsettled," "roaming") seems to pick up *vagabantur* above (6.1) but may also be intended as a description of the uncivilized native population.

concordia: abl. of cause.

(3)   *res*: standing for *res publica* or *civitas*. *Res* is frequently used in this sense in poetry but is not common in prose until Livy and the Augustan period.

civibus, moribus, agris: a triad of abls. of respect in asyndeton with *aucta*—the three chief ingredients of national growth: population, organization (lit., "customs," "institutions") and territory. The abstract *moribus* stands out in juxtaposition with the other two nouns, which are concrete. Each of these words might be said to recall the one outstanding contribution or influence on the development of the Roman state that tradition assigned to each of the first three kings of Rome: Romulus, Numa, and Tullus Hostilius.

satis: "fairly," an adv. often used by S. to qualify adjs. for which the superlative is too strong. The symmetry of the two adjs. and advs. is emphasized by alliteration which is also produced by the collocation of *agris aucta*.

videbatur: "was beginning to appear"; the impf. indic., rather than the more usu. pf., after *postquam* is used to describe a past state of affairs that extended over a period of time as opposed to a single event in the past.

mortalium: probably part. gen of *mortalia* with *pleraque* (= "most human affairs"), rather than gen. of possession (*mortales* = *homines*, vid. 1.5n.). In either case, the meaning is virtually the same.

habentur: in place of the common idiom *se habent* (e.g., 2.3): "are constituted," or more freely "turn out."

(4)   *finitumi*: to be taken with *reges* as well as *populi*, the former referring esp. to the Etruscans north of Rome and the latter to the Latins, Volsci, and Aequi who contested Rome's increasing hegemony in central Italy.

temptare: lit., "put to the test," with the instrumental abl. *bello*, *historical inf.*

= "attacked"; the first of seven historical infs. in this and the following section which S. often employs in place of the impf. indic. for
giving a rapid account of a series of actions. *Eos* must be supplied as
the object of *temptare*, and the dat. *eis* with *auxilio esse.*

pauci: not "a few," but "only a few"; to be taken with *ex amicis*
which is the usual substitute for a partitive gen. with words expressing number.

nam: vid. 2.1n.

aberant: having an active sense indicating a conscious decision to
remain aloof: "kept themselves apart from the dangers."

(5) *intenti*: used absolutely, vid. 2.9n.

parare: "made preparations," "made (themselves) ready"; *se* is perhaps understood. This absolute sense of *paro* is very rare outside of
S. Contrast with *amicitias parabant* below where *parare* =
"acquire," "obtain."

alius alium: vid. 1.7n. *alterum.*

hostibus: dat. with the adv. *obviam* plus *ire*: "they went to meet,"
i.e., in a hostile sense.

patriam parentesque: since S. rarely uses *-que* to join the last two
components in a series of three or more words except after *ceterus*,
these two words are best taken as forming a single unit in
asyndeton with *libertatem.*

propulerant: the plupf., rather than pf. indic., is used after *ubi* to
indicate that the act was repeated on a number of occasions and
completed each time with respect to the impf. indic. in the main
clause, which describes a continuous state of affairs in past time.

portabant: a poetic equivalent for *ferebant*; *portare* is properly
applied to burdens of great weight. The choice here may be influenced by the presence of *propulerant* in the preceding clause, just
as the pl. *pericula* perhaps explains why *auxilia* is pl., rather than
sing., to increase the symmetry.

magisque dandis quam accipiundis beneficiis: abl. of means; the
notion is also found in Thucydides (2.40.4) where Pericles says of
the Athenians, "We make friends not by receiving but by conferring kindness."

(6) *legitumum*: "bound by law," modifying *imperium*, which means
"supreme power" or "government" and by itself need not imply the
existence of *leges.*

nomen imperi regium: in apposition with *imperium*: "the name of
the government (being) monarchal."

annis . . . sapientia: the two abls. are causal. Talent (*ingenium*) and *sapientia* form the two chief ingredients in S.'s definition of *virtus*. Catiline possessed the former (5.2) but lacked the latter (5.4).

consultabant: this is the only instance in S. where the frequentative stands for *consulebant* and takes the dat. (*rei publicae*) by analogy: "consulted the interest of," i.e., "looked after." Elsewhere in S., *consultare* means "to deliberate" and is found with *de* + abl. or an indirect question as its object.

patres: more likely this title is to be explained by the fact that the early senate was probably composed of the heads (*patres*) of the principal families. Since the original *gentes* (groups of families) from which the earliest senate was recruited were doubtless those that were later designated as patrician (a word derived from *pater*), the term *patres* is also sometimes used as a synonym for patrician (e.g., 33.3). S.'s explanation that they were called *patres* because of their age or the similarity of their duty is purely fanciful, but it is in substantial agreement with other attempts that were made in antiquity to rationalize this term.

(7) *conservandae . . . rei publicae*: this use of the gerundive in the gen. to express tendency or purpose is quite common in S.: "had served to preserve . . ." With verbs other than *esse*, it is easiest to understand *causa*. A few MSS unnecessarily introduce *causa* into this passage—several as an addition in another hand—in an attempt to rationalize this extended sense of the gen.

superbiam dominationemque: hendiadys for *superbam dominationem*; *dominatio* is the opposite of *imperium legitumum*, and *superbiam* provides an allusion to Rome's seventh and last king, Tarquinius Superbus, whose tyrannical behavior, according to the standard account, led to the abolition of monarchy at Rome.

imperia: pl. since the supreme authority is now vested in two magistrates.

imperatores: "chief executives" (cf. 2.3n.); these magistrates were first called *praetores* when the office was created, traditionally in 509 B.C.; later their title was changed to *consul* after the suppression of the Decemvirs in 449 B.C.   S. deliberately used this general word to avoid the anachronism committed by Livy (1.60.4), who refers to these magistrates by their later title when he describes the creation of this office.

insolescere: an extremely rare word which S. may have borrowed from Cato (Gell. 6.3.15).

CHAPTER 7

(1) *Sed*: frequently used by S. at the beginning of a sentence merely to continue the narrative, like δέ in Greek (e.g., 23.1, 43.2)—also sometimes to introduce digressions (e.g., 8.1, 18.1, 25.1, 53.2) or an afterthought (50.3).

ea tempestate: archaic and poetical for *eo tempore*, which S. uses only twice in the *Cat.* (48.7, 50.4).

quisque: nom. standing in partitive apposition with the pl. subject which is understood from *coepere*.

extollere: "to distinguish" (lit., "to raise up") with the reflexive. According to Herodotus (5.78), Athens experienced a similar burst of national confidence and energy on the part of her citizens after the tyranny of the Pisistratidae was replaced by a democracy. This celebrated event in Greek history, together with its assigned date (510 B.C.), doubtless influenced the details that became standard in the account of Rome's early history after the expulsion of the last king, Tarquinius Superbus, in 510.

in promptu: "on display," a common expression with *esse* or *habere*; *promptus*, from the original notion of exposing something to view, is used in combination with these verbs to denote that which is visible or available for use.

(2) *Nam*: frequently used by S. where the connection is not strictly logical due to the omission of a statement that can easily be understood from the context, e.g., here: "<the opposite was formerly the case> for. . . ."

regibus: dat. with the pred. adj. in the comparative *suspectiores*; likewise *eis* with *formidulosa* ("causing terror," i.e., "terrifying," the active sense, which is the only one used by S., as opposed to its other meaning "fearful," i.e., "experiencing fear").

(3) *civitas*: subject of the indirect questions introduced by *quantum* (adv.). Its position early in the sentence is meant to signal a contrast with *quisque* above. The statement is not strictly true. Historically Rome actually declined in power during the period immediately following independence from Etruscan domination and the removal of an aggressive central authority represented by the Tarquins.

adepta libertate: abl. absol.; *adepta* is treated as passive, although the verb is deponent. A few instances of *adipiscor* in a passive sense in the indicative and the infinitive may be found in early Latin, but this seems to be the first use of the participle as passive.

tanta: logically this clause should have introduced the previous statement in the form of a result clause ("such a great desire for glory had become prevalent that . . ."), but S. prefers parataxis, which gives both clauses equal weight. The second clause is almost added as an afterthought which is offered as an explanation.

incesserat: used absolutely; S. also construes *incedo* with the dat., *in* plus the acc., and once with an acc. direct obj.

(4) *iuventus*: = *iuvenes*, the usual sense in S.

simul ac: the only instance of this temporal conj. in S., who prefers *ubi primum*, which is probably avoided here due to the presence of *iam primum* just preceding.

belli: obj. gen. with *patiens*.

erat: for the impf. indic. in a temporal clause, vid. 6.3n. *videbatur*.

in castris: = *in bello*, a frequent extension of the basic meaning "camp."

usum militiae: practical experience as opposed to only theoretical knowledge. The better attested reading *usu militiam* gives an equally satisfactory sense, and it is difficult to decide in favor of one of these alternatives over the other. It might be argued, however, that *per laborem usu* is not a very pleasing combination in place of *labore et usu* and is un-Sallustian.

lubidinem: with *habebant* and *in* + abl. = "took pleasure in . . ."; something of the common pejorative connotation of *lubido* (i.e., "unlawful desire," "lust" e.g., 5.6) may be felt with the phrase *in scortis atque conviviis*, while with the first set of abls., the sense is positive (= *delectatio*).

habebant: a switch to the pl. after two verbs in the sing. (*erat, discebat*) is made possible by the collective sense of the subject *iuventus* and the distance of the verb from the noun.

(5) *viris*: dat. of reference.

non: repeated at the beginning of each of the following clauses to provide emphasis by anaphora: hence in the second clause we find *non . . . ullus* rather than the customary *nullus*.

labor: this is the unanimous reading of all the MSS, but according to Servius (ad *Aen.* 1.253) *Sallustius paene ubique "labos" posuit*. The only confirmation that S. may have adopted this archaic spelling of *labor* in the nom. sing. is provided by one MS, V, which preserves *labos* in two speeches excerpted from the *Historiae* (2.47.1M, 3.48.18M). In the other instance where *labor* occurs in a narrative passage (*Jug.* 100.4), the normal spelling is attested by the MSS. Most modern editors of S. reject Servius' broad statement but recognize the likelihood that S. may have adopted a few such archaic forms in several specific instances (vid. 15.5n. *colos*).

insolitus: pred. adj. with *erat* understood.

asper aut arduus: S. may well have borrowed this alliterative pair of adjs. from Cato (38.9J *asperrimo atque arduissimo aditu*), and the alliteration is extended further by *armatus*, while *labor* is answered by *locus* after the second *non*.

virtus . . . domuerat: another example of Sallust's fondness for parataxis.

(6) *gloriae*: objective gen. with *certamen* (a "contest for") whose verbal equivalent *certare* is construed with *de* + abl.

se: acc. subject of the following infs., while a series of simple complementary infs. would be more normal with *properare*. The reflexive is probably introduced here due to the presence of *quisque* which is often accompanied by this pronoun.

hostem ferire: an archaic expression (= *hostem occidere*) found twice elsewhere in S. (60.4; *Jug.* 85.33).

facinus faceret: alliteration is produced by the device known as *figura etymologica* (the pairing of words from the same root as in "to do a deed" in Eng.); such phrases are probably colloquial. This particular expression commonly refers to a wicked act, but in this context, *tale* must be taken in a positive sense (vid. 2.9n.). The subjn. is due to the fact that the *dum* clause expresses a thought that is in the mind of the subject of *properabat* and is therefore in virtual indirect discourse.

eas divitias: a double acc. governed by *putabant* (vid. 2.2n.). *Eas* and *eam* are both demonstrative pronouns (not adjs.) standing for *ea* (neut. acc. pl.—the things just enumerated by the infs.), which has been attracted to the gender of the predicate nouns.

pecuniae liberales: vid. 5.4n. *sui profusus*. The theme of an unselfish pursuit of glory in preference to wealth, which is freely expended when necessary, seems to be modeled on Demosthenes 22.76 (*contra Androtion*).

ingentem . . . honestas: these adjs. are to be taken predicately after the two objects of *volebant*: "on a grand scale . . . provided it was gained by honest means." This sentence virtually repeats the statement in the preceding clause and serves to conclude this topic with a reference to *gloria*, which introduced this section (7.3).

(7) *possum*: the MSS overwhelmingly favor *possem* (impf. subjn. in the apodosis of a contrary to fact condition). The indicative, however, (attested here by Servius) is normally preferred in the main clause of a contrary to fact condition when the verb is one of obligation, necessity, possibility, or ability.

parva manu fuderit: possibly a stock expression.

pugnando: "by assault," standing for *oppugnando* or *expugnando*. S. often substitutes a simple verb for the compound. *Pugnando* with *capere* is perhaps a shortened version of the phrase *vi pugnando* (with *capere* or similar verbs), which frequently occurs in military or related contexts and may be a time-honored military expression.

ni: found four times in the *Cat.* for *nisi*.

nos: pl. for the sing. after *possum* just above; one can easily interpret this shift to the pl. as a reference to S. and his readers.

CHAPTER 8

(1)   *Sed*: introducing a digression, vid. 7.1n.

ea: = *fortuna*; reference to the subject of the previous sentence by means of the demonstrative pronoun in the nom. produces parataxis and is a common feature of early Latin. S. deliberately uses this simple syntax here in preference to a relative pronoun (*quae*) or a subordinate conjunction (e.g., *quia*), which would have produced a more polished complex sentence out of the two clauses.

ex lubidine: "according to (lit., from) caprice," a common meaning of *ex* in S. Nearly the same thought is expressed at 51.25.

ex vero: *verum* = *aequum* ("fair," "reasonable"), as it often does in the expression *verum est*.

(2)   *Atheniensium*: placed first for emphasis.

aestumo: used esp. of judging the merit of a thing after estimating its weight or value; preferable to the less colorful *existimo* (simply "to judge," "hold an opinion") which is found in a few MSS.

satis: vid. 6.3n.

aliquanto: "to some extent," "somewhat"; abl. of degree of difference with *minores*, sc. *fuere*.

feruntur: the sense is virtually equivalent to *celebrare*, *extollere*, = "make known," "celebrate" (lit., "report") with *fama*, abl. of means.

(3)   *provenere*: = "came forth," "appeared"; a word used only once by S. and apparently archaic for *appareo*.

ibi: = *apud eos* (i.e., *Atheniensis*), cf. 3.3n. *ibique*.

scriptorum magna ingenia: = *scriptores magni ingeni*; by an inversion of the logical grammatical relationship, known as hypallage and commonly found in poetry, S. emphasizes the *ingenium* of these writers by making this word subject here and below.

pro maxumis: equivalent to *quasi maxuma essent*.

(4)   *qui fecere*: most MSS have *qui ea fecere* which would make the

statement refer specifically to the Athenians. S. is not adverse to the repetition of the demonstrative in such close proximity, but the sense is slightly improved if we omit *ea* following the evidence of one of our best MSS, **P**[1], and some *recentiores*, which are supported by two citations of this passage; *fecere* is then used in an absolute sense: "those who have acted," i.e., "performed deeds" (cf. 3.1).

quantum: adv. with *potuere extollere*, (lit., "however much"), correlative to *tanta*; trans. ". . . is considered as great as the illustrious intellects have been able to exalt it with their words."

(5) *ea copia*: "this advantage" (i.e., of having their deeds extolled by talented writers)—not = *copia clarorum ingeniorum*; for *copia* = "advantage," "opportunity," cf. 17.6.

quisque: with the superlative *prudentissumus* (cf. 2.6n.).

maxume negotiosus: on this form of the superlative, vid. 1.3n. S. is thinking particularly of involvement in public affairs. The early Romans looked askance at leisure (*otium*) as a betrayal of one's duty to serve the state and a sign of laziness.

ingenium . . . corpore: cf. 2.1ff. where the merits of the exclusive exercise of one or the other were considered.

optumus quisque: Cicero too laments the lack of talent among those who recorded Roman history. They were, in his words, merely *narratores rerum* and did not deserve the name historian. Cicero felt that the writing of history would never be perfected until authors applied the same techniques of composition that were the essential ingredients in shaping the style of oratory (*De Or.* 2.62–63). S. was perhaps the first Roman writer to deserve the title "historian," but he obviously earned this distinction by cultivating a style that was consciously un-Ciceronian (vid. Introd. pp. 10–14).

bene facta: "good deeds," "brave acts" (cf. 3.1 *bene facere*), sometimes written as one word; the participle, although it is being used as a substantive, is still modified by an adv. The expression seems to be archaic.

CHAPTER 9

(1) *Igitur*: signalling a return to the topic interrupted by the digression in chapt. 8 (vid. 2.1n.).

minuma: virtually equivalent to *nulla* and used here to balance *maxuma*; the antithesis is strengthened by the chiastic arrangement of the two nouns and adjs. S. delays the introduction of *avaritia* as a serious factor until 10.3ff. The insistence on *concordia* is a willful distortion because it ignores the bitter internal disputes between the plebeians and patricians that occupied so much of the first two centuries of the Republic. True concord between the two rival orders was not established until the *lex Hortensia* was passed in 287 B.C. giving the plebeian assembly the right to pass laws binding on the whole *populus*.

legibus: abl. of means; note that *ius* ("right," "justice") may be enforced by a set of laws or statutes but is never defined by these laws. It exists absolutely and provides an absolute standard according to which the laws themselves may be judged as either good or bad.

natura: "by nature," i.e., their natural disposition.

valebat: sing. because the compound subject *ius bonumque* ("right and goodness") is viewed as forming a single concept.

(2)   *suppliciis*: = *supplicationibus* ("acts of worship") here and at 52.29 (lit., "bending the knee in worshiping the gods"). This meaning of the word *supplicium* is archaic and is never found in Cic. or Caes., where it always means punishment or torture (esp. capital punishment, from the same notion of bending the knee, i.e., to receive a blow from the executioner); for this latter sense in S., vid. e.g., 49.2, 50.4.

domi: locative, contrasted with *in suppliciis*. S. deliberately varies the construction with each adj. (*in* + acc. with the third adj. *fideles*) to produce *inconcinnitas*.

(3)   *artibus*: "practices," vid. 2.4n.; abl. of means, further specified by *audacia* and *aequitate*, which are chosen for the sake of alliteration. *Audacia* is used here, and occasionally elsewhere, in a positive sense (= "daring") rather than "recklessness."

ubi . . . evenerat: deliberately substituted for *in pace* (used below 9.5) to produce *inconcinnitas* by avoiding balanced parallel phrases in chiasmus; for the plupf. indic. in a temporal *ubi* clause, vid. 6.5n. *propulerant*.

seque remque: the combination *-que . . . -que*, which S. frequently employs to join two words, is archaic and poetic. With one exception, the first member of the pair is always *me* or *se*.

(4)   *quod*: the conj. introducing the first of two substantive clauses standing in apposition with *documenta haec* ("the following proofs," "examples"): = "namely the fact that . . ."

vindicatum est: "those were punished" (lit., "punishment was exacted against those who . . ."); *in* with the acc. occurs with *vindicare* only in the passive voice, which is always impersonal.

qui . . . pugnaverant: for one well-known example, vid. 52.30n. Likewise A. Postumius Tubertus, dictator in 431 B.C., is said to have ordered his son to be executed for engaging the enemy contrary to orders (Livy 4.29.5–6; Val. Max. 2.7.6), and Q. Fabius Maximus, Master of the Horse, barely escaped the death penalty through the intervention of the senate and army after he had defied the order of his superior and fought a successful engagement against the Samnites in 325 B.C. (Livy 8.30–36; Val. Max. 2.7.8).

in hostem: the sing. is used in a collective sense in place of the more usual pl.

tardius: "too slowly," put first in the relative clause for the sake of emphasis, but to be taken with *excesserant* rather than the participle *revocati*.

quam qui: = *quam* (*in eos*) *qui*, completing the comparison introduced by *saepius*.

loco: sc. *suo*, "(their assigned) position," abl. of separation best taken with *cedere*, which corresponds to *proelio excesserant* just above, while *pulsi* ("routed") is used absolutely and balances *revocati* in the earlier clause.

(5) *agitabant*: vid. 2.1n.; sc. *Romani* as subject.

accepta iniuria: abl. absol., although logically the object of the inf. *persequi*. S. sometimes uses *ignoscere* absolutely, but with *persequi* we must understand *eam*. As usual, the verb standing first governs the choice of construction.

CHAPTER 10

(1) *reges magni*: e.g., Philip V and Perseus of Macedon, Antiochus the Great of Syria. These kings were the last representatives of the dynasties founded in the eastern Mediterranean in the 4th cent. B.C. by the successors to Alexander the Great (the so-called *diadochi*). Their kingdoms began to fall to Rome one by one in the 2nd cent. B.C.

domiti: sc. *sunt* here and with *subacti* below.

nationes . . . populi: together forming a class separate from monarchies; the first word refers to loosely organized societies such as the native tribes of Spain and North Africa. *Populus*, on the other hand, implies a higher degree of formal organization such as Carthage enjoyed and the various states in Italy and Sicily which Rome eventually incorporated into the commonwealth by grants of full or partial citizenship.

ab stirpe: "utterly" (lit., "from the root"). After the capture of Carthage in the Third Punic War (149–146 B.C.) by the Younger Scipio, the city was razed, a curse was pronounced upon the site, and the ground was symbolically ploughed up and sown with salt.

Approximately one hundred years elapsed before resettlement was successfully carried out by Julius Caesar and Augustus. The corrupting influence of peace and prosperity is a *topos* which S. may have found in Cato among others (e.g., Cato, frr. 122, 163 *ORF*[3]). Likewise, the belief that union at home is fostered by the fear of a foreign enemy is well grounded in tradition (e.g., Xen. *Cyr.* 3.1.26; Plato, *Laws* 698Bff.; Arist. *Pol.* 1334a-b; Polyb. 6.18, 6.57.5). Most historians before S., however, placed the crisis in Roman society that led to a process of accelerating moral decay well before the middle of the 2nd cent. B.C. Various dates were given for this turning point: e.g., 187 B.C. when Manlius Vulso's army returned from Asia (Livy 39.6.7 drawing on the early annalists); 168 B.C. following the collapse of the Macedonian Kingdom (Polybius 31.25.3ff.); 154 B.C. (L. Calpurnius Piso, fr. 38 *HRR*). Possibly the important role played by the Elder Cato in advocating the destruction of Carthage is what drew S.'s attention to this event and led him, in preference to the annalistic tradition, to view the removal of Carthage as the turning point in Roman history. Significantly one of the main arguments employed by Scipio Nasica, who opposed Cato and advocated the preservation of Carthage, was the danger that Rome would grow soft in the absence of a threat from abroad.

maria terraeque: here and at 53.2, S. deliberately reverses the normal order of words in this familiar combination for the sake of variety.

patebant: "lay exposed," i.e., accessible, subject to Rome's control. This is the fifth and last verb in a series dependent on the temporal conj. *ubi*; a switch in tense to the impf. is made because the statement is descriptive in contrast with the other four verbs.

fortuna: S. uses this word in two slightly different senses: (1) mere chance or fate over which man has no control whatsoever (e.g., 8.1, 34.2, 41.3, 51.25, 53.3, 58.21) and (2) good or bad fortune, as here, which is influenced by the presence or absence of *virtus* and *boni mores* (e.g., 2.5, 20.14).

(2) *Qui*: the relative clause is placed before its antecedent *eis* to stress the contrast between former times and the change that occurred after prosperity became prevalent.

otium divitiaeque: most MSS omit the *-que*; asyndeton, however, is rare with only two words except in formulas and agitated discourse; *labores, pericula* above might be cited as a parallel if we take *dubias atque asperas res* as an appositive (balancing *optanda alias*) defining the preceding pair, rather than the third member of a series.

optanda: "desirable (things)" (lit., "to be desired"). This reading is preferable to *optandae*, which is better attested in the MSS, since adjs. or participles are generally made neut. pl. when they modify two or more abstract nouns of different genders. In the same way, the demonstrative pronoun *ea* below (10.3), which stands for *pecuniae cupido et imperi cupido*, is neut. pl. rather than f.

alias: adv., "in other circumstances" in a temporal sense—the only occurrence of this word in S. An alternative reading, the dat. *aliis*, which is found in most MSS, also makes sense in this context (i.e., desirable things for others as opposed to the Romans who found them burdensome), but it is less likely to have been altered to *alias* (the *lectio difficilior*) than the other way around.

(3) *pecuniae . . . imperi*: obj. genitives depending on *cupido* and further defined in the following sections as *avaritia* (10.4) and *ambitio* (10.5). The introduction of these vices by the words *primo . . . deinde* is in apparent conflict with S.'s statement below (11.1) where he claims that at first *ambitio* rather than *avaritia* had a greater influence. This latter assertion, however, does not provide sufficient justification for emending the present passage to *primo imperi, deinde pecuniae* as Nipperdey proposed to do. Note that *avaritia* is recognized as a factor even before serious corruption was felt (9.1), and in this chapter S. takes up each vice in his analysis of its characteristics according to the order in which it is first introduced. This is the way S. ordinarily develops two separate topics that are first mentioned together and then treated individually (e.g., 9.3–5 *in bello, ubi pax*; 51.18–20 *metus aut iniuria*), although sometimes the arrangement is deliberately chiastic (e.g., 46.2 *cura atque laetitia*).

ea: cf. 10.2n. *optanda*. One might have expected that the gender would be attracted into the f. sing. by the predicate nom. *materies*, but this is not the case since *fuere* shows that the subject is pl. For the use of the demonstrative rather than the rel. pron. introducing a subordinate clause, vid. 8.1n. *ea*.

(4) *ceterasque*: vid. 6.5n. *parentesque*.

artis bonas: vid. 2.4n.

edocuit: taking four objects in pairs: 2 accs. and 2 infs. (cf. 5.9n. *disserere*); the last member of the series is the longest and provides a climax. Another acc. describing the persons taught (e.g., *homines, Romanos*) is understood with all four objects. Contrast the meaning of *habere* here (= "to treat") with its meaning below in 10.5 (= "to have"). S. often reproaches the Roman nobility for its venality.

(5) *multos mortalis*: vid. 1.5; the further alliteration of *falsos fieri* adds

weightiness to this statement.

falsos: "deceitful," amplified by the three infs. that follow *subegit*.

subegit: "impelled" (= *coegit*), a common meaning in Plautus but never used by Cic. in this sense. The inf. with *subigo* is rare outside of S. as opposed to *ut* + the subjn.

clausum . . . promptum: the antithesis is reinforced by the chiastic arrangement of the predicate adjs. and prepositional phrases. This description of the cunning man may ultimately be traced back to a well-known passage in Homer (*Il.* 9.313).

ex re: "according to its merit/true worth" as opposed to expediency; for this use of *ex*, vid. 8.1n.

aestumare: vid. 8.2n.

magisque voltum . . . habere: for the opposite characteristic, vid. the description of the Younger Cato (54.6): *esse quam videri bonus malebat*.

(6) *Haec*: i.e., *avaritia* and *ambitio*.

crescere . . . vindicari: historical infs., the latter illustrating S.'s freer use of this construction by extending it to verbs in the passive voice (cf. 27.2).

contagio: "infection," "pollution" (containing the notion of something spread by contact, cf. *contingo*); the only occurrence of this word in S. It leads naturally to the comparison with an infectious disease (*pestilentia*—the stronger and more restricted term—always physical contagion in prose). Elsewhere S. employs *tabes* in the same sense as *pestilentia* (twice with *invado*) to describe the rapid spread of some evil.

invasit: for the meaning and use of this word, vid. 2.5n.

inmutata: sc. *est* and a conjunction; also supply *est* with *factum* below. A similar statement was made at 5.9.

imperium: referring especially to the administration of Rome's overseas territories and provincial corruption in contrast with the *civitas* (affairs at home affecting Roman citizens).

CHAPTER 11

(1) *exercebat*: virtually equivalent to *vexabat*: "troubled," "disturbed" (contrast 9.2 where *exerceo* = "to practice," "carry on"). If the meaning of *exerceo* in this context is properly understood, the present statement need not be viewed as contradicting the assertion above (10.3) that first *avaritia* and then *ambitio* increased. S. wishes to point out here that *ambitio* is the more insidious of the two evils since it is more nearly related to *virtus* and hence likely

to captivate and lead astray men who might otherwise remain upright.

quod tamen vitium: the presence of *tamen* indicates that the description of *ambitio* as a *vitium* is to be taken concessively: "a failing, <to be sure>, yet one which . . ." The gender of the relative is determined by *vitium*, which is grammatically the antecedent standing in apposition with *ambitio*. It is normal for such an appositive to be incorporated into the relative clause.

propius virtutem: the comparative adj. *propius*, agreeing with *vitium*, is much like a preposition (cf. *prope*) and may be construed with the acc.: "closer (in aspect) to virtue."

(2) *ignavos*: = *ignavus*; the MSS of S. preserve traces of the archaic spelling *-os* for *-us* and *-om* for *-um* in the second declension after consonantal *u* (e.g., 23.6 *novos*; 51.18 *novom*; 61.4 *vivos*; Jug. 25.8 *pravom*) and *qu* (59.1 *aequom*).

ille: = "the former" (*bonus*) in contrast with *huic* (*ignavos*), the nearer of the two persons mentioned in the previous sentence.

vera via: i.e., *virtutis via*, expressing the "way by which" with *nititur* = "strive" (cf. 1.1).

huic: belongs to both of the following clauses; its case (dat.) is determined by the nearer verb (*desunt*), while the nom. (*hic*) must be understood as subject of *contendit*.

(3) *habet*: "involves" (lit., "has"), from the simple notion of possession.

concupivit: pf. used in a present sense: "covets" (lit., "has longed for"). The negative statement makes a generalization about the past with the implication that what has not happened does not happen and never will happen. Called the gnomic pf., it is frequently found in broad negative statements that express a general truth.

ea: i.e., *avaritia*; vid. 8.1n. *ea*.

venenis malis: lit., "harmful drugs"—*venenum* by itself originally signified a drug or medicine of any kind, not necessarily good or bad. By the time S. was writing, however, the word had generally assumed the meaning of a "poison" (synonymous with *virus*), and the addition of the epithet *malis* is therefore an archaic affectation.

virilem effeminat: the collocation of these two words is deliberate, producing an antithesis of sense as well as a play on their literal meanings; this is the only occurrence of *effeminare* (= *debilitare*) in S. S.'s reason for saying that greed weakens the body, as well as the mind, puzzled ancient critics (a lengthy discussion in Gellius 3.1). Perhaps the notion is best explained by the reference to *venenis malis*, which conjures up the effect of harmful drugs that can in fact destroy both the mind and body.

infinita, insatiabilis: the effectiveness of this alliterative pair of virtually synonymous adjs. is increased by asyndeton.

neque copia neque inopia: paronomasia adds forcefulness to this paradoxical observation which forms a *topos*; rich or poor, the greedy man is never satisfied and always wants a bit more.

(4)   *Sed, postquam*: marks the transition to the topic of *luxuria* which caused *avaritia* to surpass *ambitio* as the more prominent evil in contrast with 11.1 *sed primo*. . . .

recepta re publica: abl. absol.; *armis* abl. of means with *recepta* is made prominent by its position, a not unusual arrangement of words in an abl. absol. in S. When Sulla (cf. 5.6n.) led his army back to Italy in 83 B.C. after concluding the war with Mithridates in Asia (11.5), he put forward the claim that he was rescuing the state from his political enemies who had usurped power in his absence. After his final victory in the Civil War at the battle of the Colline Gate (1 Nov. 82 B.C.), Sulla began a ruthless purge of all those who had opposed him. A general blood bath followed, known as the Sullan proscriptions, in which many innocent victims were put to death so that their confiscated property might be used to reward Sulla's soldiers and partisans.

bonis initiis: best treated as an abl. absol. (cf. 6.1 *sedibus incertis*) rather than a dat. depending on *eventus habuit*. The sense is concessive = *cum bona initia fuissent*: "despite good beginnings, he brought about (lit., had) bad results."

omnes: nom. subj. of the historical infs. *rapere* and *trahere*, in asyndeton, which are used absolutely without reference to a specific direct object. These two verbs form a stock expression.

domum alius, alius agros: chiasmus contributes to the forcefulness of this allusion to the fact that many suffered in the proscriptions because their property excited the greed of Sulla's henchmen.

neque modum neque modestiam: these two nouns are virtually synonymous, and they are paired elsewhere by S. and in other authors for the sake of alliteration. The former refers especially to moderation in conduct, while the latter denotes moderation in character. Normally *modestia* results in *modus*.

facinora facere: vid. 7.6n.; *foeda* further adds to the alliteration.

(5)   *Huc accedebat quod*: introducing a further consideration: "to this there was added (lit., came in addition) the fact that," i.e., "moreover"; the subject of *accedebat* is provided by the substantive *quod* clause (cf. 9.4).

ductaverat: this frequentative is common in S., always to describe the leading of troops; according to Quintilian (8.3.44), it had acquired a vulgar sense (perhaps from being used in the comic poets to describe the bringing home of a prostitute).

quo: normally introduces a purpose clause that contains a comparative adj. or adv. This archaic use of *quo* (= simply *ut*) also occurs at 33.1, 38.3, 58.3. The usual construction where *quo = ut eo* with a comparative is found at 22.2, 39.2, 40.6, 48.7, 49.4, 59.1 and in a mixed construction with two verbs at 48.4.

fidum: a predicate adj. in agreement with *eum* (= *exercitum*) which is to be supplied as the object of *faceret*. Three phrases in succession produce a powerful accumulation of alliteration that gives this crucial statement a sonorous quality: *fidum faceret, morem maiorum, luxuriose . . . liberaliter.*

habuerat: vid. 5.9n. Observe that *habere* is used in this chapter in four different senses in close succession: 11.3 "involve," 11.4 with *eventus* = "bring about," with *modestiam* = "observe."

amoena, voluptaria: two adjs. in asyndeton agreeing with *loca*. The province of Asia was notorious for its corrupting influence.

(6) *Ibi*: = *in eis (locis)*, cf. 3.3n. *ibique.*

primum insuevit: vid. 10.1 note on *ab stirpe* for the corresponding annalistic tradition that traced the introduction of luxury to the return of Manlius Vulso's army from Asia at a much earlier date in 187 B.C.

potare: often used in a frequentative sense meaning "to drink habitually." The assonance of *-are* is aptly rendered by Merivale: "to indulge in wine and women."

vasa caelata: vessels decorated with raised relief work in gold or silver.

mirari: "to wonder at," in the sense of "to admire the artistic value," i.e., to appreciate in an artistic sort of way.

privatim et publice: describing the source of their plunder: from private owners and communities—esp. from temples where state treasures consisting of statues, works of art, and bullion were kept.

delubra: a frequent synonym in poetry for *templum*—usu. pl.— and also found in elevated prose.

(7) *nihil relicui . . . fecere*: "left nothing to the vanquished" (lit., "made nothing of a remainder"), more forceful than *nihil reliquere*. The gen. *relicui* may be classified as partitive, but in contrast with the more usual partitive gen. (e.g., 20.13), here and elsewhere with the verb *facio* (e.g., 28.4, 52.4), *relicui* is best regarded as adverbial since it supplies the predicate complement.

victis: dat. of reference; contrast the former treatment of the conquered described at 9.3 and 12.4 below.

(8)   *Quippe*: S. uses this word several times in the archaic sense of *nam* to offer an explanation for a previous assertion.

sapientium animos fatigant: lit., "disturb the spirit of wise men," i.e., weaken their high-minded principles; *sapientium* is put before *animos* for emphasis and is crucial to the sense since a contrast is being drawn between this class and the lawless soldiers (*illi*) in Sulla's army.

ne: standing for *nedum*, which is found in a few MSS, mostly in a correcting hand: = "still less." This use of *ne* for *nedum* with the potential subjn. is rare and usually follows a negative statement (which is implied in *fatigant*, i.e., *quippe sapientium animi secundas res ferre non possunt*).

corruptis moribus: abl. of quality or description with *illi*: "depraved," "lawless."

victoriae: dat. depending on *temperarent* meaning "set a limit to," "use moderately."

CHAPTER 12

(1)   *honori*: predicate dat. in place of a predicate nom. with *esse coepere*; likewise *probro* with *haberi* ("to be regarded as").

gloria . . . potentia: a triad in asyndeton; *potentia* is a more general word for power—often excessive or illegitimate political influence—as opposed to *imperium* or *potestas*, which is conferred by office.

sequebatur: for the impf., here in combination with the pf. in the same *postquam* clause, vid. 6.3 *videbatur*. The verb is singular probably because *gloria, imperium, potentia* are viewed as forming a single concept (cf. 9.1n.). *Sequor* is used in the sense of "follow spontaneously/of its own accord."

hebescere: "to lose its keenness"; to make sense of the metaphor, it must be extended to the subject *virtus*, = "the edge of virtue."

paupertas: "moderate means," rather than poverty (*egestas, inopia*). The Romans of S.'s day looked back with admiration to the time when their countrymen took pride in a simple existence.

innocentia: esp. as characterized by self-restraint in the acquisition of wealth.

pro malivolentia: a bad motive (viz., the desire to find fault with others) is assigned even to good conduct. The notion that the original meaning of moral terms is distorted when society undergoes a radical change is borrowed from Thucydides' description of the revolution on the Greek island of Corcyra in 427 B.C. (3.82).

coepit: normally a pass. inf. attracts *coepi* into the pass. voice, but S. seems to prefer this less common usage which is also found occasionally in Livy and the poets. The passive construction is attested only once (*Jug.* 27.1).

(2) *ex divitiis*: lit., "from," i.e., "in consequence of," "as a result of." The addition of the preposition emphasizes the source as well as the cause which is expressed by the word in the abl.

invasere: vid. 2.5n.

rapere, consumere . . . pendere . . . cupere: the statement made with the historic perfect is amplified by a series of historical infs. whose subject is to be supplied from *iuventutem* (used in a collective sense, vid. 5.2n.). The first pair of infs. is used absolutely without a direct object. The pairs are arranged to form a chiasmus: *rapere* and *cupere* refer to the property of others; *consumere* and *pendere* describe the way those young men managed their own property. The description recalls what was said earlier about Catiline (5.4): *alieni adpetens, sui profusus*.

parvi: gen. of price or value with *pendere* = "value" (lit., "weigh"). The word in the gen. is usually an adj. which is treated as a substantive. Just the opposite attitude was described at 2.1 (*sua cuique satis placebant*).

pudorem, pudicitiam: paired for the sake of alliteration and virtually synonymous (cf. 11.4 *modum . . . modestiam*). *Pudor* is the more general word for "shame" or "decency"; *pudicitia* refers especially to "chastity" or "purity" arising out of *pudor*.

divina atque humana: an expression used several times by S. to include all aspects of life: "things in heaven and on earth."

promiscua: "without distinction," a predicate adj. to be taken with *habere* (= "treat"). It seems to modify all four objects which are arranged as usual with *atque* joining the words in the second pair only (cf. 6.1n. *sine legibus*). There is an apparent zeugma, however, in construing *promiscua* with the first pair, with which an adj. such as *vilia* would be more appropriate, since *pudor* and *pudicitia* are virtually synonymous and not opposites as *divina* and *humana* are. In order to bridge this logical gap, it is perhaps best to render freely "they had no regard for."

nihil pensi neque moderati: "no scruples and no moderation" (vid. 5.6n.). This acc. is to be taken as a separate object of *habere*; it summarizes and expands the previous statement concerning their conduct with respect to themselves and towards others.

(3) *Operae pretium est*: "it is worthwhile," "worth the effort" (lit., "a

reward for the effort"—obj. gen.). The subject of *est* is provided by the inf. *visere* ("to visit," "behold").

cognoveris: best taken as pf. act. subjn. of the indefinite second person sing. (vid. 1.6n. *incipias*): "when you have become acquainted with."

(4) *Verum illi*: lit., "but those men of old"—*illi* contrasted with *hi* below, "the present-day Romans." The strong adversative (*verum*) is due to the implied statement that the temples built by the pious generation of Romans were insignificant compared with private mansions in S.'s day.

delubra: vid. 11.6n.; it contributes to the solemnity of the alliteration produced by *deorum . . . domos . . . decorabant*.

victis: dat. of separation with *quicquam . . . eripiebant*.

(5) *sociis*: technically "allies" bound to R. by treaties, but often in S. an all-inclusive word for cities or nations which were subject to Roman authority and not admitted to full Roman citizenship.

proinde quasi: "just as if," used ironically in a conditional clause of comparison. The tense of the subjn. in clauses of this type obeys the normal rule of sequence (secondary here referring to a contemporaneous act) and does not conform to the rules governing ordinary conditions.

id demum: *id* stands in apposition with *iniuriam facere*, the subject of *esset*; the predicate nom. is a second inf. phrase *imperio uti*.   S. is fond of using the demonstrative pronoun—usu. accompanied by *vero* or *demum*—to repeat a word or phrase for the sake of emphasis. This type of pleonasm is colloquial. On *demum*, vid. 2.2n.

CHAPTER 13

(1) *Nam*: vid. 7.2n.; understand: <enough has been said on this subject>.

quid . . . memorem: "why should I mention," deliberative subjn.

a privatis compluribus: private citizens as opposed to foreign monarchs like Xerxes (vid. the following note); the position of the adj. *compluribus* after the noun places more emphasis on *privatis*, which is the important word.

subvorsos montis, maria constrata esse: chiasmus is used to set off these two indirect statements in asyndeton: "mountains have been levelled and seas covered over." *Subvorsos montis* would naturally suggest the levelling of high ground for building purposes, but it is better taken as a reference to the channels that were cut through mountains to bring sea water into the artificial fish ponds (*piscinae*) that were maintained by wealthy men such as L. Lucullus and Q. Hortensius in S.'s day. Suppport for this interpretation may be found in Jerome's use of the expression *montis subvertere* to describe the canal that the Persian king Xerxes constructed to bypass Mt. Athos (*Ep.* 60.18), and in the same passage, the words *maria constravit* refer to Xerxes' bridge across the Hellespont. In S., *maria constrata* describes the practice of turning the sea into dry land and alludes to the villas that were built by wealthy Romans on foundations sunk into the sea, particularly on the Bay of Naples.

(2) *Quibus . . . ludibrio*: double dative depending on *videntur . . . fuisse*, while *mihi* goes with *videntur* only: "for whom, it seems to me, wealth served as (lit., was) a mere plaything."

quippe: vid. 11.8n.; to be taken with *properabant* rather than *quas*; *eis* (= *divitiis*), abl. with *abuti*, is to be supplied as the antecedent of *quas*.

honeste habere: vid. 5.9n.

per turpitudinem: used by S. in place of an abl. of manner or adv. corresponding to *honeste*. S. is fond of using *per* with the acc. as a substitute for an instrumental or modal abl.

(3) *ganeae*: "gluttony," a common metonymy from its lit. meaning of a "cook shop" or "eating-house," places that were notorious for riotous drinking and debauchery—esp. a haunt for prostitutes—hence *ganeo* (m.) 14.2 = a person who frequents such places, i.e., a glutton or dissipated person.

ceterique cultus: "and for other (additional) wantonness"—obj. gen. depending on *lubido*. For -*que* used to join the last two members of a series, vid. 6.5n. *parentesque*. *Cultus* rarely has this pejorative sense, = "perverted or excessive refinement." Normally the word refers to the civilizing aspects of culture. The sing. of *ceterus* here is archaic and in classical prose authors is ordinarily employed only with collective nouns. In the same way, S. employs the sing. of *plerusque* (e.g., *Jug.* 18.12).

non minor: modifying *lubido*, i.e., not less than the craze for lavish houses and fish ponds.

viri muliebria pati: a *topos* in any list of vices characterizing decadence (e.g., Xen. *Mem.* 2.1.30, which may be S.'s model for this section).

pudicitiam: vid. 12.2n.

in propatulo: with *habere*, "to offer for sale" (lit., "to hold in an open place"); S. is fond of using *habere* with prepositional phrases of this sort (cf. 7.1 *in promptu habere*).

terra marique: a common expression in the abl. without a preposition, used as a locative to indicate place where; on the word order, vid. 10.1n. Gellius (6.16.5) enumerates some of these imported delicacies of the table which he found mentioned in a satirical poem by Marcus Varro. Among the costly and exotic fare are to be found cranes from Media, tunny-fish from Chalcedon, and peacocks from Samos.

esset: subjn. rather than indicative after *priusquam* because more than simple priority of time is involved. The clause describes a state of affairs which did not in fact take place and conveys the notion of a result that is prevented by sleeping more than nature intended so that the need or desire for sleep is never experienced.

luxu antecapere: "anticipated with self-indulgent practices"; *antecapere* is a rare word outside of S. and may have two distinct senses according to the context: (1) "to obtain in advance" (e.g., 32.1); (2) "to forestall," "to act in advance of" (e.g., 55.1). Either sense is possible here, i.e., (1) they stimulated their appetites for sensual pleasures in advance by unnatural means, or (2) they did not wait for hunger, thirst, etc. If the first interpretation is what S. intended, the statement will refer to the use of emetics to induce vomiting so as to make room for larger meals and the use of hot and cold baths to stimulate thirst and fatigue.

(4) *Haec*: the various perversions just mentioned.

facinora: vid. 2.9n.

(5) *haud facile . . . carebat*: "by no means easily went without," i.e., they could not give up; *careo* + the abl. of separation (*lubidinibus*) does not mean "lack" in this context, but is equivalent to *abstineo*.

eo: causal (= *ea re*): "for this reason (i.e., because they could not curb their lusts) their spirit was more immoderately given up to. . . ."

CHAPTER 14

(1) *flagitiorum atque facinorum*: gens. depending on *catervas habebat*; by the rhetorical figure known as metonymy, the abstracts ("vices and crimes") are substituted for the corresponding concrete words denoting such persons, i.e., *flagitiosorum* and *facinorosorum* which are found in a few MSS, mostly as additions by a later hand. This explanation justifies the presence of *catervas* ("bands") in this context, a word invariably used with animate objects, esp. persons, rather than things. The alliterative pair *flagitium*, *facinus* (vid. 1.4n.) is used four times by S. in the *Cat.* (cf. 14.2, 23.1, 37.5), and here the preceding *factu facillumum* (cf. 3.2) further adds to the

alliteration.

stipatorum: "attendants," "bodyguards" (m. gen. pl.), always used of persons, hence *tamquam* is inserted to ease the transition from the abstracts to a concrete term.

(2)   *quicumque*: *ei* below (14.3) gathers up all of the different types of malefactors enumerated in this and the following clauses which provide the subject of the main verb *erant* (14.3).

inpudicus, adulter, ganeo . . .: this passage is transmitted by the MSS in a confused state. As it stands, *inpudicus* is used as a substantive (sc. *vir*) and is more inclusive than *adulter* (on *ganeo*, vid. 13.3n. *ganeae*). One attractive proposal is to treat *adulter* as a gloss on *inpudicus*, which subsequently crept into the text when it was recopied, and to expand *alea*, found in several MSS, to *aleator*: *inpudicus [adulter] ganeo alea<tor>*. The three abls. in the following series would then take up the three nominatives in reverse order, *manu* corresponding to *aleator*.

manu, ventre, pene: three abls. of means with *laceraverat*: "by gambling, carousing, and lechery" (*manus* is used in a different sense below, 14.3).

bona patria: the same as *familiares opes* above, 13.4.

alienum aes grande: S. deliberately reverses the word order in the stock expression *aes alienum*, although he writes *aes alienum grande* at 24.3. Cic. (*Off*. 2.84) states that the problem of debt reached crisis proportions in the year of his consulship. Indebtedness was a burden for both the upper and lower classes (Cic. *Cat.* 2.18–19, 21), and property values were depressed as a result of the uncertain political situation (Val. Max. 4.8.3). A contributory factor to the tight-money situation in Italy may have been the successful conclusion of the Pirate War by Pompey in 67 B.C. and the continuing repacification of Asia during 66–63 B.C., which reopened lucrative fields for investment abroad. The desire to reinvest capital abroad caused credit to become tight in Italy, and many outstanding loans were no doubt called in to generate cash for more profitable foreign investments. The flow of gold and silver out of Italy is attested by a *senatus consultum* in 63 B.C. which attempted to restrict the export of capital (Cic. *Flac.* 67; *Vat.* 12). A solution to the problem of debt was sought through legislative means in early 63 B.C. when a tribune sponsored a motion for cancelling debts (Dio 37.25.4). This measure failed to pass and added fuel to the existing discontent and desperation. In retrospect Cic. noted that the primary result of his consulship was the protection of the creditor class and public credit (*Att.* 2.1.11; *Fam.* 5.6.2; *QFr.* 1.1.6; *Off*. 2.84).

quo . . . redimeret: possibly to be taken as a relative clause of purpose rather than treating *quo* as a conjunction (cf. 11.5n.); *quo* is
then an abl. of means and refers to the antecedent *alienum aes*:
"with which to buy off . . .," i.e., by means of cash payments to the
injured party, esp. in cases of adultery, or bribes for the jury once a
case had been brought to court.

(3) *parricidae*: originally this word seems to have been applied to anyone who intentionally committed murder, although its precise ety-
mology is subject to dispute (the ancient derivation from *patri-cida*
being purely fanciful). By an extension of its basic meaning, it is
often used to describe a traitor or rebel against his country.

convicti . . . timentes: "convicted by the courts or fearing prosecution," modifying *parricidae* and *sacrilegi*.

ad hoc: lit., "(added) to this," i.e., "moreover," a very common
expression in S.

manus . . . sanguine civili: the arrangement is chiastic; bloodshed
explains how they employed their hands, while *periurio* describes
the use of their tongues.

postremo: frequently used by S. like *prorsus* (vid. 15.5n.) to sum up
a series or mark a climax.

conscius animus: "a guilty conscience"; this subjective sense of
conscius (= "conscious of wrong doing") is rare and mostly confined to poetry (L-S); for the usual sense = "sharing knowledge
with others," i.e., an accomplice or confidant, vid. 25.4, 37.1.

Catilinae: gen. of possession rather than a dat. with *proxumi*,
which is used here as a substantive rather than an adj.: "the most
intimate associates."

(4) *par similisque*: "alike in every respect," not only equal in degree
(*par*) but resembling the others as well (*similis*). The two words
refer to different aspects of the way two or more things may be
alike and are sometimes used together to qualify or limit the extent
of similarity.

(5) *adulescentium familiaritates*: the young M. Caelius Rufus is a
well-known representative of this class which is prominent among
Catiline's associates (e.g., 17.6, 43.2). Caelius supported Catiline in
his bid for the consulship in 63, and he is portrayed by Cic. as just
one of many virtuous citizens who were deceived by the semblance
of good qualities in Catiline (*Cael.* 11–12). The pl. of the abstract
familiaritas is somewhat unusual and implies that Catiline had
many such contacts.

molles etiam: "still soft," i.e., easily influenced; vid. S.'s reflection
on the susceptibility of his own tender years to corrupting

influences (3.4). The temporal sense of *etiam* predominates here
and at 14.4, 61.4, virtually = *adhuc*.

fluxi: "changeable," "fickle," i.e., "unstable" (cf. 1.4).

(6) *ex aetate*: vid. 8.1n. *ex lubidine*.

parcere: unless we adopt Madvig's emendation *molestiae* for
modestiae, *parcere* must be used in two slightly different senses
with the datives *sumptui* and *modestiae*; with *modestiae*, it will
mean to "use sparingly so as not to injure."

dum: = *dummodo*, vid. 5.6n. *pararet*.

obnoxios: probably to be taken in both the literal sense of the word
(from *ob* + *noxam*) (1) "indebted," i.e., under an obligation to, as
well as (2) "obedient" or "submissive," the meaning that is foremost
because of *fidos* which follows.

(7) *nonnullos qui*: Cic. alludes to sexual relations between Catiline and
his associates on several occasions (e.g., *Cat.* 2.8, 2.23; *Red. Sen.* 10;
Dom. 62). These charges are a standard feature of invective, and S.
quite correctly reserves judgment.

frequentabat: S. frequently employs the indicative in subordinate
clauses within indirect statements and questions instead of the more
usual subjn. The indic. may be an archaism but may also indicate
that the statements in these subordinate clauses are made from the
point of view of S. as well as the subject of the main verb.

honeste . . . habuisse: vid. 5.9n. *habuerint*.

ex aliis rebus: vid. 12.2n. *ex divitiis*.

cuiquam: dat. of agent with the passive *compertum foret*, a common construction in S. with the pf. pass. part. of verbs of perceiv-
ing or knowing. The indefinite pronoun *quisquam* is used because
the *quod* clause is felt to be negative after *magis quam*, which
makes it virtually equivalent to *non quod*.

compertum foret: plupf. subjn. because the *quod* clause states a
reason that is rejected. *Foret* for *esset* is archaic and is the form
preferred by S. in the plupf. pass. subjn. The verb *comperio* (=
"ascertain"), which occurs frequently in S., was apparently used so
often by Cic. when consul to describe his findings against the conspirators that during the next few years his enemies used this word
to taunt him (Cic. *Att.* 1.14.5; *Fam.* 5.5.2). S. may have been aware
of this fact, but there is no reason to assume that he adopted this
expression here and elsewhere out of malice towards Cic.

CHAPTER 15

(1) *Iam primum*: "now to begin with," not to be taken with *adulescens*, but introducing a new phase of the narrative after the general observations in the previous chapter (cf. 7.4).

multa nefanda stupra: normally two adjs. modifying the same substantive are joined by a conj., but occasionally the conj. is omitted when one of the adjs. is felt to belong more closely to the substantive, the whole concept being further qualified by *multus*.

cum virgine nobili: further details are lacking, unless S. perhaps refers to the scandalous affair between Catiline and a mistress who bore him a daughter (vid. 15.2n. *Aureliae Orestillae*).

cum sacerdote Vestae: ordinarily the priestesses of Vesta, the goddess of the hearth whose temple stood in the Forum, were called Vestal Virgins (*virgines Vestales*), but the title given here is also attested and obviously preferred in view of the fact that *virgo* has just been used in the preceding phrase. The six Vestals took a vow of chastity, and the penalty for breaking this vow was burial alive. The priestess referred to by S. is identified by Asconius (p. 91C. 19ff.) as Fabia, a half-sister of Cic.'s wife Terentia. She was tried and acquitted on the charge of incest with Catiline (Ascon. l.c.). The probable date of the trial (73 B.C.) is established by an allusion in Cic. (*Cat.* 3.9) to a prosecution of the Vestal Virgins ten years before his consulship. S. does not refer to the acquittal since it would undercut the claim that Catiline committed *multa nefanda stupra*. According to Orosius (6.3.1), Catiline was charged with this crime and escaped conviction through the influence of Q. Catulus. This incident will explain Catiline's reference to Catulus' *egregia fides re cognita* in the letter that he addressed to Catulus in 63 (35.1). It is doubtful, however, that Catiline's case was ever brought to trial. We hear of only two acquittals of Catiline prior to 63 (Cic. *Att.* 1.16.9; *Pis.* 95), and these obviously refer to the prosecution in 65 *de repetundis* (vid. 18.3n.) and in 64 *inter sicarios* (vid. 24.2n.).

alia: Catiline was tried for extortion in 65 B.C. after his term as governor of Africa (18.3); earlier in that same year according to S., he plotted to murder the consuls and seize power (18.5); for the various crimes committed during the Sullan reign of terror, vid. 5.2n. *caedes*.

huiuscemodi: gen. of quality; S. prefers the older and more emphatic form of *huius*, which is formed by adding the demonstrative suffix *-ce*; the simple form *huius* occurs only once in the *Cat.* (54.3).

contra ius fasque: "against human and divine law."

(2)   *Postremo*: vid. 14.3n.

Aureliae Orestillae: probably the daughter of Cn. Aufidius Orestes
(cos. 71 B.C.), an Aurelius Orestes by birth before his adoption by a
Cn. Aufidius. S. takes no notice of the charge made by Cic. and
another contemporary, L. Lucceius, that Catiline married his own
daughter by a former mistress (*Tog. Cand.* ap. Ascon. p. 91C.24–26
and p. 92C.1–3). Apparently neither author specified the name of
this woman, and it is impossible to say whether Aurelia was the
lady in question. In any case, this story, together with Cic.'s claim
(*Cat.* 1.14) that Catiline murdered his previous wife so that he
would be free to marry Aurelia, are best viewed as the products of
rhetorical invective.

cuius: best taken as a partitive gen. with *nihil* rather than a gen. of
possession with *formam*: "in (lit., of) whom . . . nothing."

nubere: lit., "to veil oneself," i.e., "to marry"; construed with the
dat. *illi*; the inf. depends upon *dubitabat* ("hesitate") which, however, normally takes this construction only when it is negative or
interrogative. For other extensions of the inf. construction in S.,
vid. 5.9n. *repetere*.

pro certo creditur: the personal construction—nom. *captus* modifying *Catilina* understood as the subject—is made slightly awkward
by the addition of *pro certo*. It would be more usual to find this
expression used impersonally followed by the acc. and inf.

necato filio: "by the murder of his son" (lit., "his son having been
killed"); the source of this charge may be the rather vague statement in Cic. (*Cat.* 1.14) that Catiline followed up the murder of
his former wife with a further act of shocking wickedness.

3)   *Quae . . . res*: this is the normal position of *res*, the antecedent,
which is attracted into the relative clause and refers to the whole
preceding statement.

facinus maturandi: only one MS, **P**, preserves the acc. governed by
the gerund rather than the easier gen. *facinoris* followed by the
gerundive (cf. 4.1n. *colundo*); *facinus*, of course, here means the
conspiracy (vid. 2.9n.).

(4)   *infestus*: "hostile," to be taken with the datives *dis hominibusque*.

quietibus: abl. of means, = "sleep," "repose." The pl. is unusual and
probably due to the antithesis with *vigiliis*, which is usually pl.
when it means "wakefulness," "going without sleep."

ita: introducing an explanation after the preceding statement, virtually = *nam*, a use that is to be found in early Latin.

conscientia: S. has already alluded to the restlessness produced in
Catiline (5.7) and his supporters (14.3) by a sense of guilt. He now

portrays Catiline as driven to the brink of madness by the murder of his own son.

vastabat: "ravaged," "troubled," a bold expression standing for the more usual *vexabat* (e.g., 3.5)—an emendation sometimes adopted by editors—or *exagitabat* (e.g., 14.3); *vastare* ordinarily refers to ruin done to physical places ("to ravage," "make desolate"); for this extended sense, cf. the expression *vastus animus* (5.5).

(5)   *colos*: sc. *erat* with the pred. adj. *exsanguis*; this is the only surviving instance of this word in the nom. sing. in S.; the archaic spelling in *-os* is not found in any of the MSS but is attested by the grammarian Probus.

ei: dat. of reference in place of the possessive *eius*, which has crept into some MSS.

foedi oculi: in place of a conjunction, S. employs chiasmus: *colos (erat) exsanguis, foedi (erant) oculi*; *foedus* (= *deformis*), lit., "foul" or "ugly," must be taken in a sense appropriate to *oculi* such as "bloodshot" or "haggard/wild."

incessus: a dignified gait, neither too fast nor excessively slow, was considered the mark of a gentleman and indicative of one's character (e.g., Cic. *Off.* 1.131); the antithesis is set off by chiasmus, *c. modo, modo t.*

prorsus: adv., "in short" (a meaning perhaps first found in S.), to be taken with *inerat* and used like *postremo* (vid. 14.3n.) to introduce a brief summary after a series of statements. This word occurs only once in S. (16.5) in the more usual sense of "thoroughly," "in every respect" (virtually = *omnino*).

in facie voltuque: virtual synonyms without, however, alliteration, which is a common ingredient in such pairs (cf. 11.4, 12.2nn.); the first word refers especially to physical features (perhaps including mannerisms and behavior in general), while the second refers to his expression or countenance. This is the only instance in S. where *inesse* is construed with *in* + the abl., rather than a dat. either expressed or understood.

CHAPTER 16

(1)   *iuventutem . . . facinora*: double acc. with *edocebat* (cf. 10.4n.); the collective sense of *iuventutem* (vid. 5.2n.) accounts for *ex illis* (i.e., *iuvenibus*), an example of synesis whereby sense, rather than grammatical form, determines gender and number.

multis modis mala: alliteration produces emphasis.

(2)   *signatores*: lit., "a sealer," i.e., one who witnesses a legal document, esp. a will, with his seal (*signum*) as on a signet ring; with *falsos*,

which also modifies *testis*, = "forgers."

commodare: historical inf., "he was accustomed to supply," i.e., to those who might require their services; ordinarily used of things rather than persons, and specifically things that are loaned with the understanding that they will be returned later. Below S. shifts from the historical inf. to the imperfect (*imperabat*)—probably because this verb takes an objective inf. (*habere*)—and then back again to the inf. (*circumvenire* and *iugulare*).

pericula: best taken in the technical sense = "prosecution on criminal charges"; the three acc. objects in asyndeton are to be construed with *habere* (= "treat") and the predicate adj. *vilia*.

habere: either an historical inf. coordinate with *commodare* (subject *Catilina*), or an objective inf. depending on *imperabat* below, which also governs a second object in the acc. (*maiora alia*—sc. *facinora*).

adtriverat: lit., "rub away," hence "weaken," "destroy"; a word that is not much used before S. and found afterwards mainly in poetry. On the tense, vid. 6.5n. *propulerant*.

(3) *in praesens*: sc. *tempus*: "for the present," equivalent to the more common expression *in praesentia*.

minus: virtually = *non*—an archaic usage—with perhaps just a slight overtone of the comparative remaining.

nihilo: vid. 3.5n.

insontis sicuti sontis: "the innocent just as though they were guilty," i.e., guilty in the sense of being offensive to Catiline, incurring his hatred; *insons* is mainly archaic and poetical, although it is also used after S. by the historians Livy and Tacitus. *Sicuti* in the sense of *quasi*, signifying a hypothetical comparison, is relatively rare outside of S. (cf. 28.1, 53.5; with the subjn. 31.5, 38.3).

gratuito: "without profit," "for nothing," i.e., without a view to gain but spontaneously and unprovoked; not to be confused with *frustra* which means "for nothing" in the sense of "without success."

potius: adv. "preferably," i.e., by choice.

(4) *amicis sociisque*: dat. with *confisus*, the usual construction with *fido* and *confido* when the object is personal. Both verbs are semi-deponent; therefore, the pf. participle is active, not passive, and it is frequently used in a present sense. The main verb is *cepit* at the very end of the sentence. The participle is best taken in a causal sense, and it is substituted for a further *quod* clause coordinate with those that follow for the sake of inconcinnity.

simul: lit., "at the same time," followed by *et* (= "both . . . and") introducing the subordinate *quod* causal clauses.

aes alienum per omnis terras: vid. 14.2n.

largius suo usi: lit., "having used their property too profusely" (*usi* + *largius* virtually = "squandered"). The soldiers in Sulla's army acquired a taste for *luxuria* while on campaign in Asia (11.5), and at the conclusion of the Civil War (vid. 11.4n. *recepta*), they were settled on land that had been confiscated from the losing side—120,000 allotments according to Appian (*BCiv.* 1.104). A large number of these allotments were made in Etruria, the region just north of Rome, which had been a stronghold of the anti-Sullan faction during the war (Plut. *Cic.* 14.1); hence the activities of Catiline in this district near Faesulae. Many of these veterans, however, were ill-suited to farming because they lacked previous experience in this line of work and had little inclination for the sound management of their new-found wealth. Soon their extravagant tastes plunged them into debt, and according to Cic. it was not even easy to raise ready cash from the sale of these plots of land because buyers were reluctant to invest in property whose title was tainted by its acquisition in Sulla's proscriptions (*Leg. Agr.* 2.68). These desperate men naturally recalled (*memores*) their former prosperity and pampering by Sulla and longed for a renewal of social upheaval to restore their sagging fortunes. According to Cic. (*Cat.* 2.20), their plight was so desperate that nothing short of a return to the days of Sulla would enable them to escape ruin.

veteris: usu. = "of long standing," but here it must be used in the sense of *antiquus* ("of bygone days").

(5) *In Italia nullus exercitus*: sc. *erat*. In this period, there was no police force in Rome or the other cities in Italy, and no standing army was stationed in Italy except in the northern province of Cisalpine Gaul. Instead, troops were levied as needed to meet sudden emergencies. A heavy drain, however, had already been imposed on the available manpower a short time before by the *lex Gabinia* of 67 B.C., which authorized Pompey to enlist a large force in the war against the pirates (vid. 39.1; 120,000 men according to Plut. *Pomp.* 26.2). By the *lex Manilia* of 66 B.C., these troops were added to those already in the East when the command in the Mithridatic War was transferred to Pompey. When the government finally mobilized its forces against Catiline in late 63, a small role was also played by the proconsuls Q. Marcius Rex and Q. Caecilius Metellus Creticus, who were still waiting just outside Rome with part of their armies in the expectation of celebrating a triumph (30.3).

in extremis terris: many of Rome's best legions were in the East at this time under the command of Pompey and were still engaged in the war against Mithridates, King of Pontus, which had been waged continuously since 74 B.C. The absence of these troops from Italy was a factor that influenced the timing of Catiline's uprising. The war against Mithridates was fast drawing to a close. News of Mithridates' death reached Pompey in 63, and final settlement of the Eastern provinces was in sight (Cic. *Prov. Cons.* 27). In 62 Pompey completed his organization of Asia Minor, and by December he had returned to Italy with his army, which he disbanded upon arrival.

petenti: dat. with *spes* (sc. *erat*). *Petere* is the *vox propria* for seeking an elective office, while the corresponding noun *petitio* means candidacy. The pres. participle is to be preferred to the gerund *petendi*, which is the reading of most MSS, since Catiline was at that time (64 B.C.—vid. 17.1) already a candidate. *Petendi spes* would look forward to a future occasion on which he expected to become a candidate.

nihil sane: to be taken with *intentus* (sc. *erat*), which is used absolutely (vid. 2.9n.); *nihil* is adverbial and emphatic for *non* (cf. 51.3). Cic. repeatedly refers to the senate's reluctance to take seriously the rumors about Catiline (e.g., *Cat.* 1.30; *Mur.* 51).

prorsus: vid. 15.5n.

CHAPTER 17

(1)   *circiter Kalendas Iunias*: "about the 1st of June." This is one of the few specific dates supplied by S. in the *Cat.* There are only five in all: three in 18; one in 30.1. S. places the meeting of the conspirators at which Catiline revealed his strategy (vid. 20.1n.) approximately one month before the consular elections which normally took place about mid-July. The year (64 B.C.) is specified in the usual fashion in the following abl. absol. by the names of the two consuls: L. Julius Caesar and C. Marcius Figulus. This Caesar was a distant relative of the future dictator. His sister, by her first husband, was the mother of the triumvir M. Antonius and was at this time married to Catiline's accomplice P. Lentulus Sura, who is mentioned below (Cic. *Cat.* 4.13; *Phil* 8.1). Despite this connection, L. Caesar recommended the death penalty for Lentulus and his fellow conspirators (Cic. *Att.* 12.21.1).

appellare: the first in a series of four historical infs.; the verb means to call upon someone in order to solicit his support. An elaborate form of double chiasmus is used to set off the first three of these four clauses in asyndeton: *singulos* (A) *appellare* (B), *hortari* (B) *alios* (A), *alios* (A) *temptare* (B).

inparatam r. p.: the leading idea is contained in the participle as it often is when a pf. pass. part. is used as an attributive adj.; translate by means of an abstract noun: "the unpreparedness (i.e., unprepared condition) of the state."

(2) *quae voluit*: sc. *explorare* ("ascertain"); *voluit* has been attracted into the historic pf. by *explorata sunt* and stands for *volebat*.

in unum: adverbial, pleonastic with *omnis convocat*; Cic. (*Leg.* 1.53) has *in locum unum convocasse*, but S. always prefers to treat *unum* as a substantive. The phrase occurs only here in the *Cat.*, but six times in the *Jug.*

quibus: dat. depending on *inerat* (vid. 15.5n.), which goes well with *plurumum audaciae*, while *erat* is best understood with *necessitudo*. As it stands, there is a slight zeugma.

necessitudo: "want" or "need" in the sense of "distress" caused by poverty. Throughout the *Cat.* and *Jug.*, S. eschews the word *necessitas*, for which he substitutes *necessitudo*, a somewhat archaic usage (Gell. 13.3.3). Rarely in S. does *necessitudo* have its more usual classical meaning of a "bond" or "tie" of friendship or obligation. [S. shows a preference for abstracts in *-tudo* rather than *-tas* (e.g., *claritudo* twice but never *claritas*) since the former were felt to be more archaic and were regarded as contributing a certain *dignitas* or solemnity because of their weightiness (Gell. 17.2.19).]

(3) *senatorii ordinis*: gen. of quality modifying the proper names that follow. The senatorial order was one of the three principal classes into which the citizen body was divided in this period according to office or wealth (vid. 17.4 on the *ordo equester* and *plebeius*). The *ordo senatorius* consisted of the 600 members of the Roman senate, who held their seats for life unless they were removed by the censors for misconduct when the roll of the senate was revised. After the reforms of Sulla in 81 B.C., admission to this body was gained by election to one of the twenty annual quaestorships, the first and lowest office in the *cursus honorum*.

P. Lentulus Sura: the most important of the conspirators after Catiline; a member of the Cornelian *gens*, grandson of a *princeps senatus* (cos. 162 B.C.), and a patrician. He was praetor in 74 B.C. and consul in 71 B.C., but in the following year the censors expelled him from the senate along with 63 others who were judged unworthy of their rank (Plut. *Cic.* 17.1). Lentulus held the praetorship for a second time in 63 B.C., which entitled him to regain his membership in the senate, but unless he had recovered his senatorial rank earlier by repeating one of the junior offices, he was technically no longer a member of the *senatorius ordo* at the date of this meeting in 64. Likewise Autronius, Curius, and probably Vargunteius had forfeited their membership in the senate prior to this date. Lentulus assumed the direction of the conspirators in Rome after Catiline left the city to join the forces that had been collected by Manlius at Faesulae, and he was one of the five who were put to death following the resolution of the senate on Dec. 5th.

P. Autronius (Paetus); a reckless, violent, and licentious man (Cic. *Sull.* 71), he was in his youth a fellow student and friend of Cic.'s and his colleague in the quaestorship in 75 B.C. (*Sull.* 18). As a result of his conviction for *ambitus* (corrupt electioneering practices) in 66, he lost his seat in the senate and was permanently disqualified from standing for office in the future. His shattered career will account for his willingness to join the conspiracy.

L. Cassius Longinus: praetor with Cic. in 66 B.C., he was a corpulent and slow-witted individual (Cic. *Cat.* 3.16). He was a member of a noble plebeian family, and since he was himself a candidate for the consulship in 64 along with Cic. and Catiline, it was probably only after his failure to attain this office that his thoughts turned to revolution. According to Cic. (*Sull.* 36–39), he played an active role in the negotiations with the Allobroges in late 63 and eagerly took charge of the arrangements for setting fire to the city (*Cat.* 3.14, 4.13; *Sull.* 53).

C. Cethegus: of the Cornelian *gens* and a patrician like Catiline and Lentulus. He was noted for his impetuous and violent nature (43.3–4; Cic. *Cat.* 3.16 *furiosa temeritas*, 4.11). At the time of the conspiracy, Cethegus was a relatively young man, and his impatience for more rapid political advancement may account for his joining the plot. After his arrest, a search of his house on 3 Dec. 63 B.C. revealed a large stockpile of armaments (Cic. *Cat.* 3.8, 3.10; Plut. *Cic.* 19.2). According to one source (Ampelius, *Lib. Mem.* 31), his own brother voted for the death penalty when the senate met on Dec. 5th to consider the punishment of the conspirators.

P. et Ser. Sullae Ser. filii: the elder Servius, their father, may have been a brother of the dictator (5.6), which would make them both patricians. Their family background and the desire for power and rapid advancement may well account for their presence among the conspirators. Both were tried and convicted early in 62 B.C. for their role in the plot (Cic. *Sull.* 2). This P. Sulla is not to be confused with the consul designate in 66 (18.2), whom Cic. successfully defended in 62.

L. Vargunteius: charged with *ambitus* probably in 66 B.C. and apparently convicted despite being defended by the distinguished orator Q. Hortensius (Cic. *Sull.* 6). This circumstance will account for the apparent allusion to Vargunteius in Nov. 63 as an *eques* rather than a senator (Cic. *Cat.* 1.9 with S. *Cat.* 28.1). In the early months of 62, he was prosecuted and presumably condemned to exile under the *lex Plautia de vi* for his part in the conspiracy (*Sull.* 6).

Q. Annius: doubtless the Q. Annius Chilo who is mentioned by Cicero as one of the prime movers in soliciting the participation of the Allobroges in the conspiracy. A warrant was issued for his arrest at the meeting of the senate on Dec. 3rd (Cic. *Cat.* 3.14), and on the 5th he was condemned to death *in absentia* by decree of the senate.

M. Porcius Laeca: the conspirators were summoned by Catiline to a meeting at his house, which was located in the street of the scythe-makers, on the night of 6 Nov. 63 B.C. (27.3–4). He was prosecuted in 62 and presumably condemned to exile (Cic. *Sull.* 6).

L. (Calpurnius) Bestia: elected tribune of the plebs in 63; after he entered office on Dec. 10th, he appears to have joined his fellow tribune Q. Metellus Nepos in criticizing Cic. for abusing the powers of his office in suppressing the conspiracy, and they prevented Cic. from addressing the people when he laid down his consulship at the end of the year on the grounds that he had put Roman citizens to death without a trial (Plut. *Cic.* 23.1; *Schol. Bob.* pp. 82, 127 St.; cf. Cic. *Sull.* 31; *Sest.* 11). Apparently a reconciliation took place some years later because in 56 Cic. defended Bestia on a charge of *ambitus* which stemmed from Bestia's candidacy for the praetorship in 57 (*QFr.* 2.3.6). He seems to have been convicted and is last heard of in Antony's camp in 43 (*Phil.* 11.11, 13.26).

Q. Curius: another senator who was deprived of his seat in the census of 70 B.C. (vid. 23.1n.). He is probably to be identified with the ex-quaestor who was a notorious dicer (Ascon. p. 93C). Through his mistress Fulvia, he was persuaded by Cic. to turn informer, and he is given credit for warning Cic. of the plot to assassinate him on Nov. 7th. Curius forfeited, however, the reward that had been voted to him by the senate when he attempted to implicate Caesar in the conspiracy (Suet. *Jul.* 17).

(4)   *equestri ordine*: as its name implies, the members of this class were originally those who served on horseback in Rome's army. In this period, the *ordo equester* appears to have included all citizens who possessed a specified property qualification (400,000 *sesterces* under the Empire when the figure is first attested) and were not members of the senate. The remainder of the citizens outside these two classes were lumped in the *ordo plebeius*. The social status of the equestrians was not too different from that of most senators.

Although they did not belong to the governing class, their influence was ever present behind the scenes. To this class belonged the *publicani*, who farmed the taxes, and the financiers who controlled the fields of banking and commerce. When the juries were reconstituted by the *lex Aurelia* of 70 B.C., senators and equites both received a share of this important function.

M. Fulvius Nobilior: mentioned only here by S. and not to be identified with the Fulvius *senatoris filius* (39.5) whom S. specifically says was among those *extra coniurationem*. His precise role in the conspiracy and fate are unknown, unless he is the M. Fulvius Nobilior who was convicted in 54 B.C. apparently on a charge of *ambitus*. He is perhaps a descendant of Q. Fulvius Nobilior, censor in 136 B.C. Since the mid 3rd century B.C., this noble plebeian family had suffered eclipse, and this may explain why Fulvius joined the conspiracy.

L. Statilius: one of the five conspirators executed on 5 Dec. 63 B.C. He and Gabinius were to direct the setting of fires in twelve designated regions of the city.

P. Gabinius Capito: Cicero (*Cat.* 3.6) singles him out as one of the most wicked ringleaders of the plot and dubs him with the nickname *Cimber*, doubtless to liken his conduct to the barbarity of the Cimbri, a Germanic tribe, who invaded Italy at the end of the 2nd century B.C. He played an active role in the negotiations with the Allobroges and was executed by order of the senate.

C. Cornelius: along with Vargunteius, he attempted to assassinate Cicero at his home on 7 Nov. 63 B.C. He was tried and apparently condemned to exile in 62 B.C. (Cic. *Sull.* 6).

ad hoc: vid. 14.3n.

coloniis et municipiis: a standard expression denoting the various towns of Italy that had their own government at the local level. After the Social War (91–87 B.C.) when Roman citizenship was granted to all Italians south of the river Po, the distinction in status between these two classes of settlements was virtually obliterated. Originally the colonies were settlements planted by the Roman government to garrison strategic regions (esp. the Italian coasts), to relieve excess population in Rome, or to settle discharged veterans. By contrast, the *municipia* were originally formerly independent Italian towns that had been incorporated into the Roman state by grants of partial citizenship (*civitas sine suffragio*, i.e., civil rights but not the right to vote or hold office) to which was added the obligation (*munus*) of serving in the Roman army.

domi nobiles: in apposition with *multi* (*eo convenere*); a stock phrase to denote men of high standing at the local level (members of the municipal aristocracy) as opposed to the more select circle of *nobiles* in Rome whose family had held high office in the Roman government (vid. 5.1n. *nobili*); *domi* is locative.

(5)   *Erant*: placed first because it is used in the substantive sense: "there were" (subject) *complures . . . nobiles*; these sympathizers were not present at the meeting, and their identity is open to speculation.

occultius: "more secretly," i.e., "less openly," comparative adv. modifying the adj. *participes*, which is construed with the gen.

huiusce: vid. 15.1n.

(6)   *Ceterum*: adv., "besides," introducing a transition to another observation.

sed maxume: the adv. *maxume* strengthens the adversative, and this combination often serves to introduce the most important member in a series (cf. 14.5).

quibus: pl. due to the collective sense of *iuventus* (cf. 16.1n.).

vivere: virtually equivalent to a complementary inf. depending on *copia erat* (cf. 8.5n.), as if S. had written *qui . . . poterant*. The gen. of the gerund *vivendi* would be more usual, and the inf. appears to be introduced by an extension of its common use as the subject of *esse* or equivalent verb that takes a predicate nominative. For other examples of S.'s freer use of the inf., vid. 5.9n. *repetere*.

pro . . . quam: S. deliberately varies the construction although both pairs stand in the same relationship to *malebant* (cf. 5.9n. *disserere*). The acc. with *malo* is rare and mainly confined to poetry; on the shift from the sing. (*favebat*) to pl. (*malebant*), which is eased by the rel. *quibus* whose unexpressed antecedent supplies the subject, vid. 7.4n. *habebant*.

(7)   *ea tempestate*: vid. 7.1n.

M. Licinium Crassum: he amassed great wealth in the Sullan proscriptions (cf. 11.4n.) and afterwards became one of the richest men in Rome. Twice consul with Pompey (70 and 55 B.C.) and censor in 65, he remained in Rome during the absence of Pompey from 67–62 and cast about for various means to strengthen his own power so that he would be in a favorable bargaining position when Pompey returned from the East with his army (vid. 16.5n.). The memory of Sulla's invasion of Italy was still fresh in the minds of most Romans, and many feared that Pompey would emulate Sulla and use his army to achieve personal domination over the government. Crassus' precise connection with Catiline at this time is difficult to determine. In his secret history, *de Consiliis Suis*, which was

not published until after his death, Cic. claimed that Crassus
engineered the alleged plot of Catiline and Piso to murder the
consuls in 65 (18.5) and that Catiline and Antonius received financial backing from Crassus in 64 in their bid for the consulship
(Ascon. p. 83C). It is not unreasonable to suppose that Crassus may
have supported the candidacy of Catiline in 64 since at that time,
contrary to S.'s account, Catiline was by no means an avowed revolutionary. The senate had arranged for the consuls elected in 64 to
govern the provinces of Cisalpine Gaul and Macedonia in 62, and
since both provinces contained armies and were strategically
located, Crassus may well have wished to secure the election of two
men friendly to his own interests as a counterweight to the vast
military resources at Pompey's disposal.

ipsi: i.e., Crassus, dat. with *invisus*, which is best translated by
means of a relative clause. In 71 B.C. Crassus brought the war
against Spartacus to a successful conclusion but was deprived of
much of the credit by Pompey, who returned with his army from
Spain in time to crush the remnants of this revolt and claim the
glory of the victory for himself (Plut. *Crass.* 11.5–7). This incident
gave rise to jealousy and hostility between Crassus and Pompey
which was only temporarily abated by a reconciliation toward the
end of their joint consulship in 70 (Plut. *Crass.* 12.2–4, *Pomp.* 23.1–
2; Suet. *Iul.* 19.2; cf. S. *Hist.* 5.51M).

ductabat: although the *quia* clause is causally related to the indirect
statement made by *voluisse* (subject *Crassum*), the indicative
rather than the subjn. indicates that this reason is added by S. as a
factual statement and is not simply attributed to the subject of the
verb (cf. 14.7n. *frequentabat*).

illius: i.e., *Pompei*.

simul: vid. 16.4n.; the participle is to be taken in a causal sense, as
at 16.4, and is deliberately substituted for a second *quia* clause to
produce dissymmetry.

valuisset: the subjn. is due to the fact that the conditional clause is
subordinate to the indirect statement (suboblique) and stands for
the fut. pf. indic. *valuerit* in *oratio recta*, while *fore* (= *futurum
esse*) stands for *ero*.

illos: sc. *coniuratos*, a sense-construction (synesis, cf. 16.1n.) from
coniuratio preceding.

CHAPTER 18

(1)   *Sed*: vid. 7.1n.; the flashback (chaps. 18–19) to the so-called first
conspiracy of Catiline in 65 B.C. (vid. App. II) appears to be
prompted by the reference to Crassus at the end of chapt. 17.
According to some accounts, Crassus and Caesar were active participants in this plot (vid. 17.7n. above on Crassus; Suet. *Iul.* 9). S.
(19.1) explicitly connects Crassus with Cn. Piso, who was commonly linked with Catiline's intrigues in 65. The technique of
interrupting the narrative to footnote an earlier related event by
means of a digression may be a device consciously borrowed from
Thucydides (e.g., 1.89–118, the "Pentakontaetia"; 6.54–59, the
Athenian tyrants).

coniuravere: the verb is made more emphatic by being placed
before the subject *pauci*.

quibus: this is the reading of all the best MSS. The archaic form
quis, which is restored by some editors here and at 31.1 on the basis
of citations of these passages, does not appear to have been used by
S. in the *Cat.*, although this alternate form of the dat. and abl. is
attested some twelve or thirteen times in the *Jug.* and also in the
Hist.

(2)   *qua*: i.e., *coniuratione* which must be supplied from *coniuravere*, as
if S. had written *coniurationem fecere*; an extreme example of a
type of synesis (cf. 16.1n.) which is found occasionally in Thucydides (e.g., 1.90.2, 1.91.1, 5.47.6), but is almost without parallel in
Latin (cf., however, Cic. *Mur.* 29 *in qua*; *De Or.* 2.5 *saepta*).

L. (Volcacio) Tullo et M.' (Aemilio) Lepido: coss. in 66 B.C.;
Volcacius conducted the consular elections in this year, and on the
advice of his *consilium* he announced that he would not accept
Catiline's candidacy since he had been accused of abusing his
power while serving as governor of Africa in 67 (Ascon. p. 89C).
Not much is known about the activities of the other consul in this
year, Manius Lepidus, a patrician, whose praenomen is invariably
corrupted to M. (= Marcus) in the MSS.

P. (Cornelius) Sulla: not to be identified with *P. Sulla, Servi filius*
(17.3); Dio (36.44.3) calls him a nephew of the dictator L. Sulla;
Cic. (*Off.* 2.29) styles him simply *propinquus*. He was married to
Pompey's sister (Cic. *QFr.* 3.3.2) and was successfully defended by
Cicero in 62 B.C. on a charge of being a member of the conspiracy. In return for this service, Cicero allegedly received a huge
loan which he used to buy a mansion on the Palatine (Gellius
12.12.2ff.; *Fam.* 5.6.2). Sulla actively supported Caesar in the Civil
War and was entrusted with the command of Caesar's right wing

at the battle of Pharsalia in 48. Cicero rejoiced at the news of his death in 46 (*Fam.* 15.17.2). On his alleged participation in the first conspiracy, vid. App. II.

designati consules: S. deliberately reverses the normal word order in this standard expression which is to be found at 50.4 and 51.18 (cf. 10.1n. *maria terraeque*). During the interval between the elections (usually held about mid-July) and Jan. 1st, when the consuls entered office, elected officials were immune from prosecution except on the charge of *ambitus*. This will explain the desire to block Catiline's intended candidacy in 66 until he could be tried for extortion.

legibus ambitus: the law in force at the time was passed by the consul C. Calpurnius Piso in 67 B.C. In addition to a stiff monetary fine, it imposed perpetual exclusion from the senate and disqualification from holding office (Dio 36.38.1; *Schol. Bob.* p. 78 St.).

(3) *Post paulo*: normally the abl. of degree of difference, *paulo*, would stand first. S. clearly implies that Catiline wished to stand at the supplementary election which was probably held in late October or November after the conviction of Autronius and Sulla. Some scholars, however, have argued that Catiline is more likely to have presented himself as a candidate at the regular election earlier in the year since his intended candidacy in 66 makes better sense if we assume that he sought the consulship at the earliest opportunity following his praetorship in 68. According to this view, carelessness has caused S. to misrepresent the correct sequence of events by mentioning Catiline's candidacy after the conviction of Sulla and Autronius, or else the text should be emended to *ante paulo*. Asconius' account of this affair (p. 89C) does not help to settle the controversy one way or the other. Two passages in Cic., however, tend to confirm S.'s chronology (*Cael.* 10; *Sull.* 68). The first implies that Catiline spent most of 66 abroad as governor of Africa, and the second reports an allegation that P. Sulla, after his conviction, recruited a band of armed men to help Catiline intimidate a rival candidate, L. Manlius Torquatus, who, we know, secured the consulship at the supplementary election.

pecuniarum repetundarum: gen. of charge with *reus*; = "extortion," a charge covering the misuse of power by a provincial governor (cf. 49.2), especially the unlawful acquisition of wealth at the expense of the provincials—hence lit., a suit for the "recovery of monies."

reus: possibly *reus* should be taken in the sense "threatened with prosecution" since Catiline was not formally charged until 65 B.C. (Ascon. p. 85C), and his trial was delayed until the summer of that year (Cic. *Att.* 1.1.1, 1.2.1).

intra legitimos dies: before an assembly of the Roman people could be convened to vote on legislation or elect magistrates, the business of the assembly had to be announced at least a *trinum nundinum* in advance (Cic. *Dom.* 41, *Phil.* 5.8; Livy 3.35.1). The period known as a *trinum nundinum* is commonly assumed to consist of three eight-day weeks, each containing a market-day (*nundinae*). Apparently a candidate's formal *professio* had to be made prior to the announcement of the assembly so that his name could be included on the list of candidates when the date for the assembly was posted at least a *trinum nundinum* in advance of the elections (Cic. *Fam.* 16.12.3). The reason given here for Catiline's disqualification fits the chronology adopted by S. if we assume that Catiline was prevented from standing at the supplementary election because he had not been a candidate at the first election and had not, therefore, met the requirement of announcing his candidacy within the appropriate interval.

profiteri: sc. *se consulatum petere* or *se candidatum consulatus*.

nequiverat: all but two MSS read the subjn. *nequiverit*, which would make the statement in the *quod* clause an alleged reason—virtual indirect discourse (cf. 7.6n.)—rather than factual, but the pf. tense will not stand in secondary sequence. The verb *nequeo* (= *non possum*), which is frequently employed by S. (seven times in the *Cat.*), is slightly poetic and archaic.

(4)   *Erat*: cf. 17.5n.

eodem tempore: S. always prefers *tempore* to *tempestate* (cf. 7.1n.) with *eodem*.

Cn. (Calpurnius) Piso: elected quaestor in 66 B.C., he took office on Dec. 5th (the Nones). In 65 he was sent out as *quaestor pro praetore* to govern Hither Spain. There was apparently a shortage of eligible governors in this year since Cicero and several of his colleagues in the praetorship in 66 declined provinces. Piso was an avowed enemy of Pompey (19.1; cf. Val. Max. 6.2.4).

summae audaciae: gen. of quality bracketed on either side by two adjectives that give first his age and social status and then his economic condition and disposition. The superlative indicates that *audacia* is pejorative here (cf. 9.3n.).

factiosus: a favorite word of S.'s (9 times); used to describe overzealous partisan activity in a *factio* ("a power clique," vid. 20.4n.); ultimately denoting a revolutionary or seditious disposition, = *seditiosus*.

mali mores stimulabant: the whole description of Piso is

reminiscent of what was said earlier about Catiline himself (e.g., 5.7–8) and his other supporters (14).

(5) *in Capitolio Kalendis Ianuariis*: since 153 B.C., the consuls entered office on January 1st and inaugurated their term with sacrifices and vows for the safety of the state during the coming year. This ceremony took place at the temple of Jupiter Optimus Maximus, which stood on the Capitoline Hill above the Forum.

ipsi: nom. agreeing with *Catilina et Autronius*, the subject of *parabant*, which also governs *mittere*. It provides the logical subject of the following abl. absol. and calls attention to the division of roles after the first phase of the plot had been carried out in concert with Piso (*cum hoc*), who now becomes the object of *mittere*. S. appears to follow Cicero (*Sull.* 67–68), who attempted to prove that his client Sulla did not participate with Autronius in this scheme to recover the consulship after their conviction and unseating for *ambitus* (vid. App. II). Livy (*Per.* 101), Suetonius (*Iul.* 9.1), and Dio (36.44.3) state that the plot was aimed at restoring the consulship to Autronius and Sulla.

fascibus correptis: the symbol (*fasces*) stands by metonymy for the office itself (the consulship). The *fasces* were bundles of wooden rods that were bound together by thongs and assigned to Roman magistrates as a symbol of their *imperium*. The number reserved for each office varied in proportion to the magnitude of *imperium* belonging to it. Each consul was accompanied by twelve lictors who bore a like number of *fasces* before the consul whose turn it was to hold the active power of command. In the regal period, the rods were bound about an axe whose blade projected, but from an early date in the Republic the axe was removed from the *fasces* when they were displayed within the boundary of the city out of regard for the Roman *populus*, which conferred the magistrate's *imperium*.

optinendas: the standard term for holding or administering a province as governor.

duas Hispanias: since 197 B.C., Spain had been divided into two provinces, Hispania Citerior and Ulterior, which were normally governed at this time by ex-praetors. Eventually Piso received only one of these provinces.

(6) *Ea re cognita*: "the plot having been discovered"; unlike the previous abl. absol., the logical subject is obviously not the subject of the main vb. (*coniurati*—understood with *transtulerant*), but rather the "government" or the "Roman people." According to Dio (36.44.4–5), the consuls were voted a bodyguard by the senate, but a tribune intervened to prevent the senate from adopting stronger

measures against the conspirators. Cicero (*Sull.* 11–12, 81) mentions a body of advisors who assisted the consul Torquatus in investigating rumors of unrest in late 66 and early 65 (vid. App. II).

rursus: "again"—not strictly appropriate with *transtulerant*. They did not repeat an earlier postponement, but they did renew their preparations.

in Nonas Februarias: S. is the only author to mention the postponement to Feb. 5th. Possibly he was led to this conclusion by the variety of dates that he found in his sources. Different rumors were in circulation, some of which put the conspiracy in late Dec. 66, others in early 65 (e.g., Cic. *Cat.* 1.15; *Sull.* 68). S. seems to have attempted to make a coherent whole out of this patchwork. His reason for selecting Feb. 5th for the second plot is unknown, unless possibly he found this date mentioned in connection with the disturbances that occurred in 65 at the trial of the ex-tribune C. Manilius (vid. App. II). The Nones were *fasti*, so court cases could be heard. There is a plethora of precise dates given in this chapter compared with the work as a whole, which may reflect Sullust's effort to relate these events *quam verissume* (18.2).

transtulerant: S. is fond of substituting the plupf. for an historic pf. in the course of a narrative passage. In this instance, he may be thinking ahead to the statement in the following sentence and assuming this as a point of reference in the past before which the action described by the plupf. occurred.

(7)   *Iam tum*: "then on that occasion," as opposed to the previous plan, or = "then already" looking ahead to the later conspiracy in 64–63 which aimed at the same goal.

plerisque senatoribus: Cic. several times alleges that Catiline envisioned the slaughter of the *optimates*, i.e., the leading conservatives (*Tog. Cand.*, ap. Ascon. p. 92C; *Mur.* 81 *consilium senatus interficiendi*). This, combined with allusions to a plot merely against the consuls (e.g., *Sull.* 68), provides the substance for this expanded view of the conspirators' aims.

(8)   *maturasset . . . dare*: virtually equivalent to *maturius dedisset*: "had given prematurely"—a rare meaning of *maturare*. Asconius (p. 92C) gives the same version as S., while Suetonius (*Iul.* 9.2) implicates Caesar and Crassus in this plot and states that the massacre was not carried out because Caesar did not give the appointed signal when Crassus failed to appear on the day set for the attack.

pro curia: the area known as the *Comitium* in front of the senate-house, the Curia Hostilia, in the northwest corner of the Forum.

post conditam urbem: vid. 17.1n. *inparatam r. p.*; the prepositional phrase limits *pessumum*.

patratum foret: on *foret = esset*, vid. 14.7n.; *patrare* (= "to accomplish," "perpetrate") had come to be used in a vulgar or equivocal sense (Quint. 8.3.44). S. was apparently attracted by its archaic quality and revived its original neutral sense which occurs three times in the *Cat.* and six times in the *Jug.*

frequentes: the adj. is to be taken predicately, "in great (i.e., sufficient) numbers."

ea res: i.e., Catiline's overeagerness to give the signal.

CHAPTER 19

(1) *quaestor pro praetore*: his title and province are confirmed by an inscription (*CIL* I² 749 = *ILS* 875 *quaestor pro pr. ex s.c. provinciam Hispaniam citeriorem obtinuit*). Possibly S. puts the adj. *citeriorem* first here to draw attention to the fact that Piso received control over only one of the Spanish provinces and not both as the conspirators had intended (18.5).

   adnitente Crasso: abl. absol.; *adnitor* is used absolutely: "exerting his influence." The decision to appoint a quaestor to a post normally occupied by an ex-praetor rested with the senate. Ordinarily when a quaestor was posted to a province, he served on the governor's staff as a financial officer.

   infestum inimicum: a pair of alliterative adjs. in asyndeton which are virtually synonymous: "hostile and unfriendly," sc. *esse* after *eum*. Cic. often pairs these words for emphasis, but they are found together only here in S. Since this is the only instance in S. where *inimicus* appears to be construed with the dat., some prefer to take this word as a substantive on analogy with *Jug.* 23.2 (*hostem infestum*).

(2) *Neque tamen*: frequently used to introduce an unexpected or surprising statement; with *invitus* here, the litotes draws attention to the fact that Crassus' influence was not the sole reason for giving this commission to Piso.

   dederat: vid. 18.6n. *transtulerant*.

   quippe: vid. 11.8n.

   foedum: = "vile," "base" when applied to character; the antithesis with *boni* below is striking.

   a re publica procul: physically removed from Rome and Italy as opposed to retirement from political life, the meaning of this expression at 4.1. Dio (36.44.5), Suetonius (*Iul.* 9.3), and Asconius

(p. 92C) all state that the appointment was merely a pretext for removing Piso from the capital. Cicero (*Tog. Cand.*, ap. Ascon. p. 93C) asserts that the same men who were supporting Catiline and Antonius for the consulship in 64 formerly planned to use Piso's appointment to undermine the authority of the government.

simul: vid. 16.4n.

boni complures: the placement of *complures* emphasizes *boni* (cf. 13.1n.). This is S.'s term for the self-styled *optimates*, a group which comprised the conservative oligarchy within the senate, many of the *nobiles* and their supporters, as well as those citizens who favored the status quo and opposed radical politicians who sought power for themselves through manipulating the popular assemblies (see Cic. *Sest.* 96–100 for a programmatic statement). S. never uses the word *optimates*, but instead he prefers to refer to this group as the *pauci potentes* or simply the *pauci*.

in eo: i.e., Piso; the prepositional phrase is to be taken as a predicate with *praesidium putabant* (vid. 2.2n.).

et: the following clause, although coordinate, in fact states the reason of the *boni* for desiring this *praesidium* or security that they hoped to find in Piso.

potentia: vid. 12.1n.; Pompey's legal position at this time gave him vast military resources which he might have been tempted to use for his own personal advantage upon his return to Italy—to say nothing of his political influence and connections within the senate.

(3) *in provincia*: quite a few of the best MSS have the acc., which would mean that Piso was murdered while going out to his province. Dio (36.44.5) and Asconius (p. 92C), however, state that he was murdered while he was serving as governor, and this is confirmed by S.'s comment (19.4) on his harsh administration. According to Asconius, Piso was killed sometime before the elections in 64, although S. makes Catiline refer to him as still alive at this time (21.3)—an apparent oversight.

(5) *alii*: sc. *dicunt*.

Gn⟨aei⟩ Pompei veteres fidosque clientis: forming a dactylic hexameter (– –/– –/–″ ◡ ◡/– –/– ◡ ◡/– –), which is probably inadvertent. These *clientes* were natives who became attached to Pompey when he was sent to Spain to help crush the rebellion of Sertorius (76–72 B.C.). It was quite common for provincials to form close ties with a particular Roman family, often the family of the first governor or of the commander who subdued the province. The provincials looked to these "patrons" as representatives of their interests in the capital (cf. Fabius Sanga, who had ties with the Allobroges, 41.4). The dependency of these foreign "clients" on a Roman "patron" is a natural extension of the client-patron relationship that formerly bound the plebeians to the patricians in early Roman society.

voluntate eius: "with his consent"; Asconius (p. 92C) also refers to this belief on the part of some. The fact that Pompey was engaged in Asia at this time in the war against Mithridates need have prevented him from exercising influence in Spain through his many personal contacts.

adgressos: sc. *esse* here and with *perpessos* below.

praeterea: adv. "besides this (one instance)"—an obvious exaggeration. We hear of at least one other Roman governor, L. Calpurnius Piso Frugi, who met his death (ca. 112 B.C.) while serving in Spain (Cic. 2 *Verr.* 4.56), and the natives were notorious for their hostility to Roman domination (*Bell. Hisp.* 42.4).

saeva multa: cf. 15.1n.

(6) *dictum*: sc. *est*; the two short clauses in asyndeton at the end of this chapter close off the digression and return the reader to the meeting called by Catiline at 17.2. S. concludes on an objective note and refuses to commit himself to either version of the motive for Piso's murder, although he records without criticism the claim made about the tolerant nature of the Spaniards, which tends to incriminate Pompey.

CHAPTER 20

(1) *Catilina*: in a prominent position as the first word in the long period to emphasize the importance of his role.

paulo ante: i.e., 17.3–4.

in rem fore: "it would be advantageous," "it would be to his purpose," an archaic expression. The subject of the indirect statement depending on *credens* is provided by the infs. *appellare et cohortari*.

secedit: a vivid historical pres., likewise *videt* in the *ubi* clause, while the final vb. *habuit*, is put in the pf.

amotis: usu. *removeo* is used to describe the removal of witnesses or eavesdroppers.

huiuscemodi: S. uses this formula to introduce his version of oral or written communications for which he makes no claim to be reproducing a verbatim copy of the original. Obviously no record was kept of the exact words spoken by Catiline when he addressed the conspirators in secret, but a general account of what transpired at these meetings was passed along to Cic. by informers, and some of this intelligence became public knowledge. Cic. (*Mur.* 50; cf. Plut. *Cic.* 14.1), in fact, gives a brief account of a speech that Catiline delivered to his supporters shortly before the elections in 63, and this *contio domestica*, as Cic. calls it, may have provided S. with a model for the meeting that he assigns to 64. In Cic.'s version, however, Catiline espouses the cause of the *miseri* ("the poor") and professes himself to be the *dux et signifer calamitosorum.* This element is absent from the speech in 64 as reported by S. since Catiline did not claim to be a champion of the poor until the following year (35.3). The rewards promised by Catiline in 64 were mainly designed to satisfy his supporters among the upper class who were eager for advancement in their careers.

(2)   *spectata . . . forent*: the sing. *foret*, which is found in a few MSS, would make *spectata* agree with the nearer subject, but the participle is best taken as neut. pl. modifying both of these f. nouns. This is the usage preferred by S. when the substantives are abstract (51.12 *pares* provides an exception).

mihi: dat. of agent.

opportuna: predicate adj. with *cecidisset* ("turned out"), which is qualified by the adv. *nequiquam.*

in manibus: qualifying *dominatio* (vid. 5.6n.) in place of an attributive adj. balancing *spes magna.*

frustra: adv., forming the predicate of *fuissent*; this alliterative combination is archaic. The use of an adv., in place of a predicate adj., after the verb *sum* appears to be characteristic of conversational Latin since it occurs most frequently in Roman comedy and Cicero's letters.

per ignaviam aut vana ingenia: standing by metonymy for *per ignavos aut vanos homines* (or *homines vani ingeni*). *Vana ingenia* refers to persons of unstable or unreliable character and corresponds to *fides* above as its opposite, just as *ignaviam* is opposed to *virtus.*

incerta pro certis: cf. 17.6.

captarem: frequentative of *capio*, found only here in S. (vid. 2.1n.).

(3)   *tempestatibus*: "critical situations"; the pl. of *tempus* is more usu. in the sense of "circumstances" or "occasions" (esp. the hazardous sort) except in metaphors of navigation where *tempestates* (lit., "storms") sometimes has this extended meaning.

fortis fidosque: a second pair of alliterative adjs. following closely upon *multis et magnis.*

eo: = *ideo*, "for that reason," i.e., the explanation contained in the preceding *quia* clause.

animus: standing for *ego* here and below 20.6.

incipere: the use of an acc. substantive with this vb. is archaic.

simul: vid. 16.4n.

(4) *ea demum*: vid. 12.5n.; the pronoun has been attracted into the f. by the predicate nom. *amicitia*. In the *Jug.* (31.14–15), S. draws a distinction between good and bad men who form an association out of common interests: among the former, such a combination may be called *amicitia*, but among the latter, the proper term is *factio* (cf. 18.4n. *factiosus*). *Factio* more appropriately describes the group fashioned by Catiline.

(5) *quae . . . agitavi*: *ea* is understood as the antecedent and direct object of *audistis* (= *audivistis*). The pf., rather than impf., more precisely defines the scheme as it was outlined to each individual on a specific occasion.

divorsi: "separately" in time, i.e., on different occasions (like *cum singulis* above 20.1; cf. 17.1), not "separately" in the sense of pursuing different courses (e.g., 2.1).

(6) *Ceterum*: vid. 17.6n.

animus accenditur: alliteration here and below (*cum considero quae condicio*) makes the statement more forceful.

nosmet: acc. pl.; the suffix -*met* intensifies the reflexive pron. Although most MSS give the acc. *ipsos*, the nom. *ipsi* is necessary to the sense which is surely: "unless we free ourselves (by means of our own efforts)" rather than, "unless we free ourselves (as opposed to others)."

vindicamus in libertatem: a standard idiom meaning "to deliver into freedom." This slogan is especially associated with the propaganda of the *populares* and provides a good example of how moral and political terms became debased in the struggle for power that was waged in the popular assemblies against the *optimates* who had the most control over the senate. The pres. indic. *vindicamus* has been substituted for the fut. pf. and conveys urgency. Since the *nisi* clause is subordinate to the indirect question depending on *considero*, the verb might well have been attracted into the pf. subjn. (cf. 17.7n. *valuisset*).

(7) *illis*: dat. of advantage with *vectigales esse* and referring to the *pauci potentes*, i.e., the conservative aristocratic faction (cf. 19.2n. *boni*).

tetrarchae: petty monarchs or rulers (*tetrarches*, a Greek term, is lit. the ruler of the quarter part of a country); this title is found in several regions of the East, notably Thessaly and Galatia, and usually is joined, as here, with *reges*. It is loosely used of any ruler who possessed supreme authority and yet was not recognized as a king (*rex*) by the Roman people.

vectigales: "tributary," a predicate adj. balanced by *stipendia pendere* ("pay taxes") in the next clause; the infs. are historical. A *vectigal* was technically revenue derived from state-owned land, mines, and quarries, and such indirect taxes as the harbor duties. The amount of these revenues varied since they were based upon a percentage of actual produce of the land or the value of the goods being traded. By contrast, a *stipendium* was a direct tax consisting of a fixed sum and was levied on the land of the provincials. The amount was calculated to equal a set quota of the average annual yield of the land. Presumably the *reges* and *tetrarchae* are said to be tributary (*vectigales*) to the *pauci* because these rulers paid cash to influential senators to secure the recognition of their status and to protect their interests at Rome.

populi, nationes: for the distinction, vid. 10.1n.

strenui, boni: best taken concessively; these two adjs. represent a time-honored description of the ideal Roman who was energetic and righteous. *Strenui* resumes the notion contained in *virtus* above (20.2), while *boni* corresponds to *fides*. The accumulation of pairs of words in asyndeton in this section is striking and serves to convey Catiline's impetuous nature and indignation.

nobiles atque ignobiles: standing in apposition with the preceding expression which defines the group as a whole: "nobles as well as those whose family lacks the distinction of a consular ancestor" (vid. 5.1n. *nobili*).

volgus: "a rabble," i.e., in the sense of the great mass of citizens who were excluded from the circles of power and influence.

sine gratia: "without regard/esteem" in a neutral sense as opposed to the next sentence (20.8) where *gratia* = "influence," i.e., the buying and selling of favors. *Gratia* lit. refers to favor gained by conferring *beneficia*, and it is what leads to *potentia* through those who are under obligation to a benefactor.

obnoxii: with the dat. *eis* (vid. 14.6n.).

formidini: predicate dat. with *essemus*.

(8)   *apud illos*: the same complaint is made by S. himself in a digression on Roman politics after the destruction of Carthage (*Jug.* 41.7).

ubi: i.e., *apud quos* (vid. 3.3n. *ibique*).

pericula: "criminal charges" (vid. 16.2n.), while *iudicia*, if it is not meant to be merely synonymous, refers more specifically to judicial judgments against some of those present—notably Autronius and Vargunteius (vid. 17.3n.). A few words in these two series of four words in asyndeton correspond (*repulsas* to *honos*, *egestatem* to *divitiae*), but there does not seem to be any conscious attempt to pair each benefit with its opposite disadvantage. The accumulation of asyndeton throughout this speech effectively conveys Catiline's indignation.

(9)   *quousque tandem*: lit., "to what length, pray," i.e., "to what extent," "how long"; a vivid reminiscence of the impatient *exordium* of Cicero's first speech against Catiline (1.1). The adv. *tandem* is frequently used by Cic. to strengthen interrogations or imperatives, but this is the only instance of this usage in S.

per virtutem: adverbially, to denote manner; likewise *per dedecus* below (vid. 13.2n.).

quam: conj. after *praestat* (= "it is preferable"), whose subj. is supplied by the inf. *emori*. The thought expressed here seems to be an adaptation of Pericles' observation in the funeral oration on the nobility of death (Thuc. 2.43.6).

inhonestam: i.e., "shameful/inglorious" because *honos* is the monopoly of the *pauci potentes*.

ubi: standing for *in qua*.

ludibrio: double dat. with *superbiae*.

(10) *Verum enim vero*: vid. 2.9n.

pro deum . . . fidem: acc. of exclamation—in origin possibly felt to depend on *imploro* or *testor* understood; *pro* is an interjection, and *deum* is an alternate form of the gen. pl. (= *deorum*), which is quite frequently found in stock expressions such as this one.

in manu nobis: the sing. in *manu* (as opposed to the pl., e.g., 20.2) normally expresses the notion of control or possession in the sense that something "depends on" the person indicated by the dat. If this is the meaning here, the reading *vobis*, which is found in several MSS, often as a correction, may be preferable to *nobis*. The context, however, favors the interpretation "victory is within our grasp" since Catiline proceeds to contrast the age and debility of their opponents (*illis*) with the youth and mental alertness of himself and his supporters. The succeeding statement is clearly meant to explain why victory is assured.

Viget . . . valet: alliteration and chiasmus draw attention to this justification of the previous remark.

illis: dat. of ref. corresponding to *nobis*.

annis atque divitiis: abls. of cause; for the debilitating effect of wealth on both the body and soul, vid. 11.3n.

consenuerunt: "have grown weak" (lit., "old," a fitting metaphor in a context where *annis* is opposed to *viget aetas*). This is one of the few instances in the *Cat.* where the pf. ends in *-erunt* (vid. 2.2n. *coepere*). Two of the other three passages in which the long form is used occur in the speech attributed to Caesar (51.9, 51.38).

incepto opus est: vid. 1.6n.; the familiar proverb states that a beginning amounts to the accomplishment of half a task (e.g., Plato, *Laws* 753E). Catiline boldly asserts that a beginning is all that is needed; events will see to the rest.

cetera: neut. acc. pl. object of *expediet* ("arrange"—lit., "disentangle"); the subj. *res* = "the way things are/existing circumstances" or possibly "action."

(11) *Etenim*: "indeed," not so much corroborating the previous statement but rather introducing a further consideration which should lead to action on the part of the conspirators. The emphasis is now on the disparity between the rich and the poor.

superare: intransitive, "exist in abundance" (= *superesse*, *abunde esse*). The inf. with subj. acc. *divitias* forms an indirect statement depending on *tolerare*, a rare usage outside of poetry and post-Augustan prose (L-S).

profundant: subjn. in a rel. clause of purpose.

in extruendo mari et montibus coaequandis: cf. 13.1n.; the arrangment is still chiastic, as in the former passage, but here the order in which these two activities are mentioned is reversed. Gronovius' emendation *extrudendo* ("pushing back") for *extruendo* is attractive. The expression appears to refer to the same practice of building houses over the water *molibus iniectis* that was described at 13.1 by the words *maria constrata*. If *extruendo* is retained, presumably an abl. of means such as *aedificiis* is to be understood but not expressed since the whole phrase is in the abl. In view of Catiline's complaint about this extravagant abuse of wealth, it is interesting to note that a member of his own *gens* was called Sergius Orata as a result of his reputation for stocking his fishponds with gilt bream (*aurata/orata*), a kind of goldfish (Varro, *Rust.* 3.3.10).

amplius: the comp. adv. is substituted for an adj. (i.e., *plures*) and may be felt to stand loosely in apposition with the statement as a whole; *continuare* refers to joining together two adjacent buildings to form an enlarged residence.

larem familiarem: standing by metonymy for *domum*; the Lar was one of the household gods who was worshiped at the family hearth and was believed to watch over the family's prosperity. The name of this household divinity serves as a symbol for hearth and home—more personal than simply *domum*, and nicely balancing *rem familiarem* above with a partial verbal echo.

(12) *toreumata*: a Greek word = *vasa caelata* (vid. 11.6n.), which is used both for the sake of variety and to convey something of the exotic nature of these imported luxury goods.

emunt: the *cum* clause is primarily temporal ("while"), hence the indic., but it is also partly concessive as can be seen from the presence of *tamen* below.

nova diruunt: "they pull down houses newly built"; cf. the story told of Julius Caesar who demolished a recently constructed country-house because it was not entirely to his satisfaction (Suet. *Iul.* 46).

postremo: vid. 14.3n.

trahunt, vexant: these vbs. denoting abuse are borrowed from the terminology of war or plunder, a metaphor which is continued by *vincere*; they treat their wealth the way an invading army lays waste enemy territory.

summa lubidine: either abl. of manner or an abl. absol. in a concessive sense: "despite the greatest wantonness."

(13) *foris aes alienum*: cf. 14.2n. Relief from debt played such an important role in Catiline's program that in 62 Cic. playfully asserted that he himself would be willing to join a fresh conspiracy, if only the revolutionaries would trust him, since he had borrowed a vast sum at 6% to pay for his new house on the Palatine (*Fam.* 5.6.2).

res, spes: this paronomastic pair of nouns in chiasmus forms a common antithesis: "actual circumstances" as opposed to "prospects for the future."

relicui: partitive gen. with *quid*.

animam: = *vitam* (vid. 2.9n.).

(14) *Quin*: from an old form of the abl. *qui* plus the interrogative particle *-ne* (lit., = "why not"); it frequently, as here, introduces a question equivalent to an exhortation.

in oculis sita sunt: the participle is to be taken as a predicate adj. (likewise below 20.17 *parati*): "are placed before (lit., in) your eyes."

posuit: the simple vb. for the compound, = *proposuit*.

(16) *Vel imperatore vel milite*: the abls. are predicative agreeing with *me*, which depends on *utimini* (imperative). In the final battle, Catiline is credited with playing the role of both an energetic soldier and a good commander (60.4).

neque . . . aberit: litotes for *aderit*. The reference to *animus* and *corpus* provides an echo of the prologue (1.2ff.). Here the two words serve to resume the contrast just above between the role of the *imperator* and *miles*.

(17) *nisi . . . me animus fallit*: "unless I am mistaken."

CHAPTER 21

(1) *abunde*: a predicative adv. (vid. 20.2n. *frustra*): lit., "to whom all evils existed in abundance," i.e., "who were overwhelmed by . . ."

neque res neque spes: cf. 20.13; the variation below (*opis aut spei*) indicates that *res* here means "resources."

quieta: n. acc. pl., object of the inf. *movere*: "stable conditions" (cf. 34.2).

movere: = *perturbare*, just as *motus* is used to describe a political disturbance or insurrection (42.1). The inf. serves as the subject of *videbatur*, while *merces* (lit., "wages," i.e., compensation for their effort) is the predicate nominative. Alliteration here (*mmm*) and in the following clauses (*pppp qu c qu pp qu*) produces weightiness and is used for emphasis.

condicio belli: "terms of the war" (cf. 20.6), i.e., the goals to be sought and the means at their disposal, as the next two indirect questions make clear. The reference to *bellum* and *arma* at this stage in Catiline's plans in 64, when his hopes of being elected consul were still high, introduces a false note and anticipates measures that were adopted out of desperation after his second defeat at the consular elections in 63 (26.5).

foret: this alternate form of *esset* may sometimes be regarded as having a future sense, here = *futura esset*, as can be seen from the corresponding expression at 20.6.

ubique: best taken in the generalizing sense, = "anywhere," although the meaning *et ubi* is also possible.

(2) *tabulas . . . omnia*: this is one of the longest series of words in asyndeton in S. (6 members) and continues the rapid-fire pace set in chapt. 20 through the frequent employment of asyndeton (e.g., 20.15 five members).

tabulas novas: lit., "new tablets," i.e., "new account books," the standard expression for the cancellation of debts. *Tabulae* were the tablets on which records of financial transactions were inscribed. Catiline held out the hope that the loans recorded in these ledgers would be abolished so that the slate would be wiped clean.

proscriptionem locupletium . . . sacerdotia: these words expand upon the incentives enumerated at 20.14 (*divitiae, decus, gloria*). The dictator Sulla was the first Roman to eliminate his political enemies systematically and confiscate their property by offering a bounty for the murder of his victims, whose names were posted on proscription lists (cf. 11.4n.). This practice was revived with even greater ruthlessness by the triumvirs in late 43 at about the time S. was writing this monograph. *Sacerdotia* refers primarily to the four major *collegia* or boards of religious officials: the 15 *Pontifices*, 15 *Augures*, 15 *Quindecimviri*, and 7 *Epulones*. The members of these boards did not form a professional priestly class, but rather they were generally the same powerful nobles who sought to monopolize high political office. Roman religion and politics were always closely connected, and religious officials exercised a considerable influence on political affairs through their supervision of the calendar and the taking of the auspices which had to accompany any important act. Vacancies on these boards were filled in this period by co-optation or by a modified form of public election under the terms of legislation passed in 63 B.C., and these appointments carried great prestige.

(3) *esse*: inf. in an indirect statement which depends upon a verb of saying that must be supplied from *polliceri* (21.2).

Pisonem: his death seems to have occurred sometime before this date (vid. 19.3n.).

P. Sittium Nucerinum: a Roman *eques* and noted financier from Nuceria in Campania. At this time, Sittius was absent from Rome and involved in financial dealings with the king of Mauretania (present-day Morocco including the NW portion of Algeria) who had apparently borrowed a large sum of money from him (Cic. *Sull.* 56). Sittius himself was heavily burdened by debts of his own and suspected of sympathizing with Catiline, but it is unlikely that he possessed an army at this date. He seems to have been able to satisfy most of his creditors by liquidating some of his assets in Italy (Cic. l.c.). Several years later, perhaps in 57, Sittius went into voluntary exile to escape prosecution arising out of a grain deal, and he spent the rest of his life in Mauretania and Northern Africa where he operated with a private army which he had recruited in Italy and Spain (Cic. *Fam.* 5.17.2; App. *BCiv.* 4.54; Dio 43.3). S. appears to antedate the existence of this mercenary army by almost a decade. It is likely that S. knew Sittius personally since they both served under Caesar in his African campaign in 46, and Sittius was rewarded by Caesar for his support with an extensive grant of land around Cirta within the new province of Africa Nova which Sallust governed (Dio 43.3–12; *Bell. Afr.* 25, 48, 93, 95; App. *BCiv.* 4.56).

Sittius administered the territory assigned to him as a virtual principality until he lost his life in a revolt soon after the assassination of Caesar (Cic. *Att.* 15.17.1).

participes: in apposition with *Pisonem* and *Sittium*.

C. Antonium (Hybridam): son of the famous orator M. Antonius (cos. 99 B.C.; censor 97) and uncle of the triumvir. He was removed from the senate along with Lentulus Sura and Curius by the censors in 70 B.C. (Ascon. p. 84C) but regained his seat by holding the praetorship with Cic. in 66. In 64, he and Catiline made a joint bid for the consulship in an effort to prevent Cic. from being elected (Ascon. p. 83C). Antonius was elected (24.1), and Cic. managed to detach him from Catiline by offering to exchange the provinces that had been allotted to them for the following year (vid. 26.4n.). Antonius took the more lucrative province of Macedonia which he governed from 62–60. When he returned to Rome, he was prosecuted (probably for *maiestas*) in 59, and despite Cic.'s defense he was convicted and forced to go into exile where he remained until he was recalled ca. 45 (Dio 43.27; App. *BCiv.* 2.107; cf. Cic. *Phil.* 2.98). Ironically he was made censor in 42, perhaps through the influence of his nephew (*ILS* 6204). Although he led the army that crushed Catiline's forces in early 62, he was understandably reluctant to oppose his former associate face to face, and on the day of the engagement he avoided assuming command by pleading illness (59.4).

necessitudinibus: vid. 17.2n.

consulem: in apposition with *se*.

(4)   *increpabat ... laudare ... admonebat*: for the historical inf. in combination with the impf., cf. 16.2–3.

bonos: vid. 19.2n.

alium egestatis: the first in a series of four objects of *admonebat*, which, as a verb of reminding, takes an acc. of the person and gen. of the thing.

suae: the reflexive is emphatic for "his own" and refers to the object, *alium*, rather than the subject of the verb.

periculi aut ignominiae: as at 20.8 where *pericula* and *iudicia* occur in the same sentence, the second word is the more definite of the two and refers to actual circumstances; *ignominia* = disgrace or dishonor of conviction, esp. the loss of one's seat in the senate and exclusion from public office. The sing. is used in a distributive sense and refers to individual cases.

ea: i.e., the *victoria Sullana*, a recurring theme, e.g., 16.4, 28.4, 37.6.

praedae: predicate dative—likewise *curae* below (21.5) with *haberent* (= "regard/consider") in place of *curae esset*.

(5) *animos alacris*: a combination perhaps suggested by Cato (20.4J).

videt: a vivid historical pres., while the main vb. is pf. (cf. 20.1). S. invariably uses the historical pres. of the vb. *video* after *postquam*.

petitionem: "candidacy" (cf. 16.5n. *petenti*). Ironically this appeal for support at the polls is addressed to a group which supposedly included one of Catiline's rival candidates, L. Cassius Longinus (vid. 17.3n.).

CHAPTER 22

(1) *Fuere . . . qui dicerent*: no allusion to this oath consecrated with blood is found in Cic. where a reference would be expected if the rumor was current at the time of the conspiracy. It was, therefore, apparently a subsequent invention as S. reports (22.3), and it is best not to take *ea tempestate* too literally as a reference to the precise time of these events. The story is found in several later sources with various embellishments (Plut. *Cic.* 10.3; Flor. 2.12.4; Dio 37.30.3). Dio, who places this event after the elections in 63, and Plutarch both mention a human sacrifice and a tasting of the flesh which S. discreetly refrains from reporting in so many words. The allegation involving human sacrifice appears to be a traditional feature in invective (cf. Cic. *Vat.* 14).

popularis: all three occurrences of this word in the *Cat.* (24.1, 52.14) are accompanied by a gen., and the meaning is always an "associate" or "accomplice." This use of *popularis* as a substantive, equivalent to *socius*, is found in comedy and appears to be colloquial. S. nowhere uses *popularis* as a political label for those who courted the common people in preference to the aristocrats, just as he never employs *optimates* to designate the conservative faction (cf. 19.2n.).

adigeret: the MSS offer *adiceret*, an obvious corruption, while the correct reading is preserved in one late citation of this passage. *Adigere* forms a stock expression with *ius iurandum* meaning to "bind with an oath," although it is more commmonly construed with a double acc. instead of the acc. and *ad*.

humani corporis: a vivid concrete expression in place of a simple adj. *humanum* modifying *sanguinem*.

(2) *inde*: = *ex eis* (i.e., *pateris*) or *ex ea potione* (vid. 3.3n. *ibique*), to be taken with *degustavissent*, which is ordinarily construed with the acc. and rarely used in classical prose with its literal meaning as here = "to take a taste (of)."

post exsecrationem: a solemn oath accompanied by a curse in case the terms of the oath are violated.

in sollemnibus sacris: the practice of ratifying an oath by tasting the blood of either a victim or the participants is attributed to various primitive peoples (e.g., the Medes and Scythians by Herodotus 1.74.6, 4.70.1). Possibly such rites were imported to Rome by various foreign religions as these words suggest, and this supplied the ingredients for the rumor about Catiline. Much misconception and exaggeration, however, surrounded these foreign cults since their rituals were shrouded in secrecy.

consuevit: "(it) is customary," the only instance of this verb used impersonally in S. in place of the more usual *solet*. With *solet* and *consuevit*, S. normally does not express the complementary inf. when it is *fieri* or *facere*.

atque eo †dictitare† fecisse: this is the reading of most MSS, and the text appears to be corrupt at this point. The simplest solution is to strike out *dictitare* as a gloss, which perhaps arose from a reader's annotation such as *dicitur*, and emend *atque* to *idque*, thus providing an object for *fecisse*: "that Catiline did this for the following reason, so that . . ." If *dictitare* is retained, it is unlikely that Catiline can be understood as the subject both because the previous infs. are perf. and because the statement of his motive would be made unnecessarily blunt. This is the only instance in S. where *eo* (= *ideo*) anticipates a purpose clause; more often this adv. is joined with a *quia* or *quod* clause.

quo: vid. 11.5n.

alius . . . conscii: standing loosely in apposition with the subject of *forent* and virtually causal here: "<since they would be> mutually aware of such a great atrocity." The reciprocal *alius alii* is used for the sake of variety after *inter se* in the *quo* clause, and the dat. *alii* depends upon *conscii*, which is construed with an objective gen. *facinoris*.

(3) *ficta*: sc. *esse*; the inf., which is part of an indirect statement depending upon *existumabant*, gains emphasis by being placed before the two subjects in the acc., *et haec et multa praeterea*.

Ciceronis: objective gen. with *invidiam* in the passive sense: "Cicero's unpopularity." S. alludes to the troubles that beset Cic. in the last days of his consulship (vid. 17.3n. *Bestia*) and his eventual banishment for more than a year, which was brought about by his political enemy P. Clodius in 58.

credebant: indic. rather than the subjn., which is more normal (vid. 14.7n. *frequentabat*).

Nobis: vid. 14.7n. *cuiquam*.

pro: "considering/in view of" (lit., "in proportion to").

CHAPTER 23

(1)   *Sed*: vid. 7.1n.

in ea coniuratione: abstract for the concrete, = *inter eos coniuratos*.

Q. Curius: vid. 17.3n.

loco: lit., "place," i.e., "rank" or "station" due to the standing of one's family. The abl. is possibly modeled on the abl. of source which often accompanies *natus* (cf. 5.1) or may be simply a locative abl. without a preposition (cf. 24.2); *haud obscuro*—an example of litotes (cf. 3.1)—stops short of asserting that Curius was *nobilis* (vid. 5.1n.) while granting the family some distinction.

flagitiis atque facinoribus: vid. 14.1n.

probri: in the lit. sense "disgraceful conduct." The use here of *gratia* with this gen. (in place of *propter* plus the acc.) to state the cause, rather than the purpose or object, is rare. Although several leading figures among Catiline's associates were removed from the senate by the censors in 70 B.C., S. reports only this one instance in the *Cat*. The precise nature of the grounds for Curius' expulsion is nowhere stated.

(2)   *Huic homini*: the second word is superfluous, but such redundancy with the relative (e.g., 4.5) or demonstrative (e.g., 25.2) is common in S.

vanitas: "folly," "want of judgment" (lit., "emptiness"), cf. 20.2n.

reticere . . . occultare . . . dicere . . . facere: the first two infs. are best taken as historical, while the second pair forms the object of *habebat*, which also takes *quicquam pensi* as a predicate acc. (cf. 5.6n.); *dicere* and *facere*, which are frequently paired (e.g., 3.1, 8.5), are both used here absolutely as at 8.5.

prorsus: vid. 15.5n.

(3)   *Fulvia*: nothing certain is known about this woman besides her role as a spy in the service of Cic. (cf. App. *BCiv.* 2.3; Diodorus 40.5). Plut. (*Cic.* 16.3) agrees with S. in describing her as a woman of high rank, while Florus (2.12.6) calls her a worthless prostitute (*vilissimum scortum*) and says nothing about her noble birth. Possibly she was related to M. Fulvius Nobilior, who is mentioned among the conspirators at 17.4, or the Fulvius who attempted to join Catiline after he had left Rome (39.5).

consuetudo: a word meaning intimacy or familiarity between two persons; with the gen. *stupri* = "an illicit union," "a love affair," in a pejorative sense.

inopia: abl. of cause.

maria montisque polliceri: possibly an expression coined by S. to produce alliteration and modeled on an older phrase that refers to promising mountains of gold (Ter. *Phorm.* 68; cf. Pers. *Sat.* 3.65).

foret: subjn. because this clause qualifies the threat made by Curius and therefore stands in virtual indirect discourse (cf. 7.6n. *faceret*); *foret* has a future sense in this context (cf. 21.1n.) since it represents *eris* of *oratio recta*.

postremo: vid. 14.3n.

agitare: vid. 2.1n.

(4)   *insolentiae*: "arrogance," but the context also suggests the meaning "unusual behavior" after *quam solitus erat*.

haud occultum: predicate acc. with *habuit*: "did not keep secret," i.e., "keep this secret to herself," as opposed to the simple expression *haud occultavit* ("conceal").

sublato auctore: "withholding the name of her source"; in S., only here and at *Jug.* 45.2 does *tollere* mean "remove" rather than "raise up," "exalt."

quoque modo: either *et quo modo*, in which case we would expect the subjn. in an indirect question; or in the distributive sense, the abl. of *quisque*: "in each way" (cf. 21.1n. *ubique*), i.e., on various occasions. The variant *quoquo modo* (= "in whatever way"), which is found in several inferior MSS, would imply that Fulvia had other sources of information about the conspiracy besides Curius.

(5)   *Ea res*: Appian (*BCiv.* 2.2) and Plutarch (*Cic.* 11.2) also attribute Cicero's election to the fear aroused by Catiline when his ulterior designs became known to the people. S., however, and the other sources give a false impression of the threat posed by Catiline, whom they portray as an avowed revolutionary in 64 (cf. 21.1n.). Although Catiline's past conduct made it possible for Cic. to portray him as a dangerous and desperate man in the speech that he delivered shortly before the elections (*Tog. Cand.*, ap. Ascon. e.g., pp. 92–3), the conservative aristocrats were probably led to support Cic. more out of the fear that the election of both Catiline and Antonius would tip the balance in favor of Crassus, who seems to have supported their candidacy (Ascon. p. 83C). Early in 63, various tribunes sponsored a number of radical legislative proposals including a land bill, a measure to cancel debts, and another to restore civil rights to the sons and grandsons of those whom Sulla had proscribed (Dio 37.25.4). If it had not been for the staunch

opposition of Cic., many of these reforms might have been carried over the protest of the conservatives. Not to be left out of account as well are the broad support that Cic. enjoyed among the *equites*, whose interests he had frequently defended in the courts, and the fact that during the past several years Cic. had actively courted the favor of Pompey, notably in his speech for the Manilian law in 66 and by accepting the cases of several clients in 65 who had ties with Pompey ([Q. Cic.] *Comm. Pet.* 51).

(6)   *invidia*: an abl. of cause; *invidia* here is being used in the active sense (= "jealousy"), cf. 22.3.

aestuabat . . . credebant: for the use of a sing. and pl. verb with a collective noun (*nobilitas*) as the subject, cf. 7.4.

homo novos: for *novos* = *novus*, vid. 11.2n.; by the late Republic *novus homo* had become a technical term for a man who was the first in his family to become a senator, and in a more restricted sense it was used to describe the first member of a given family to reach the consulate. In this period, election to the consulship was in practice vitally restricted to *nobiles* (vid. 5.1n.) or the sons of senators. Only ten consuls during the last 150 years of the Republic can be identified as *novi homines* who rose directly to this office from outside the senate, and Cic. provides the only instance of such an accomplishment for the years 93 to 48 B.C. For S.'s variation of the usual word order, vid. 10.1n.

adeptus foret: subjn. due to the fact that this clause is subordinate to the indirect statement (suboblique, cf. 17.7n.).

post: pred. adv. (vid. 20.2n. *frustra*): "were put aside."

CHAPTER 24

(1)   *comitiis habitis, consules declarantur*: the technical expression for conducting an election and declaring the victors whose names were announced by the presiding magistrate. Consuls and praetors were elected by the *comitia centuriata*, which was an assembly of the Roman people divided into census classes. Cic. was elected first, ahead of his colleague C. Antonius, and carried all of the voting units in the assembly (Cic. *Leg. Agr.* 2.4, 2.7; *Vat.* 6; *Pis.* 3).

quod factum: i.e., the victory of Cic. over Catiline.

popularis: vid. 22.1n.

concusserat: the plupf. seems to depend on the following sentence for its reference to a fixed point of time in the past (cf. 18.6n.) and is virtually concessive in relation to the sentence beginning *Neque tamen* (cf. 19.2n.).

(2)   *agitare*: vid. 2.1n.; logically Catiline is the subject of this historical

inf., but by the grammatical principle known as zeugma (cf. 12.2n.) *Catilinae furor* is made the subject of both vbs., although it is strictly appropriate with only the first. S. fails to mention that as an additional setback Catiline was indicted by L. Lucceius shortly after the elections in 64 for his part in the Sullan proscriptions (Ascon. p. 91C). He was tried before Julius Caesar and acquitted (Dio 37.10.3; cf. Cic. *Att.* 1.16.9; *Pis.* 95). The fact that many ex-consuls supported him at this trial indicates that he was still well-connected in 64 and not yet known to be openly plotting violent revolution (Cic. *Sull.* 81).

locis opportunis: abl. of place where without a preposition; this construction is often employed with *locus*, esp. when it is modified by an adj.

sumptam mutuam: with *pecuniam*, a technical expression, = lit., "taken up on loan," i.e., "borrowed." The adj. *mutuus* (= "on loan"—related to *mutare*), as opposed to *commodare* (cf. 16.2n.), seems to refer to transactions in which the thing loaned is not itself returned, but rather an equivalent amount is repaid.

Faesulas: present day Fiesole, a town situated on a hill a few miles northeast of Florence in northern Etruria. This region contained many of Sulla's veterans who had been settled on confiscated land. In 78 B.C., after the death of Sulla, it was the scene of the unsuccessful revolt led by M. Aemilius Lepidus against the government established by Sulla's reform of the constitution.

Manlium: his praenomen was Gaius (27.1); according to Dio (37.30.5; cf. Cic. *Cat.* 2.14) he was an experienced military man who had served as a centurion in Sulla's army. He profited greatly as a result of Sulla's victory in the Civil War, but like many he had squandered his new-found wealth and was ripe for revolution (cf. Cic. *Cat.* 1.7, 2.20; Plut. *Cic.* 14.2).

portare: cf. 6.5n.

princeps: first in order of time, on 27 Oct. 63 B.C., not in the sense of "leader."

(3) *quaestui . . . luxuriae*: dats. with *modum fecerat* = "had set a limit," i.e., "restricted"; *neque* stands for *et non* since the negative is to be taken closely with *luxuriae*.

(4) *servitia*: = *servos*; when referring to slaves as a class, S. prefers the abstract and reserves the concrete word for cases involving individuals. Although Lentulus urged Catiline to recruit slaves (44.5–6) and apparently went ahead on his own to sollicit their support (39.6), Catiline himself is explicitly said to have rejected the slaves who flocked to join his army (56.5, cf. 44.6). The apparent

inconsistency is most easily resolved by assuming that Catiline was not adverse to covert assistance from this class—particularly in causing intrigues and confusion in the city on the night set for the uprising—while he was unwilling to compromise his position as the avowed champion of the downtrodden Roman populace by enlisting slaves in his army.

vel interficere: the impact of these words is made more powerful by their position at the end of this series of indirect statements. According to Appian (*BCiv.* 2.2), Catiline received financial backing from many women who hoped to be able to murder their husbands as a result of the uprising. His aim, as it is stated here, resulted in the assignment of a comparable role to the youthful members of the conspiracy who were to massacre their own families on the night of the conflagration (43.2).

CHAPTER 25

(1) *Sed in eis erat*: the opening words here closely resemble the phraseology at the beginning of chapt. 23. Unlike this earlier chapter, however, the present one does not further the narrative but merely forms a digression that illustrates the type of women referred to above (24.3–4). The portrait of Sempronia corresponds in many respects to the sketch of Catiline (5.1–8; cf. 15), and she is, in a sense, his female counterpart: both were descended from noble families, talented, daring, and depraved. Sempronia herself, however, plays no part in S.'s narrative before or afterwards (apart from an allusion to the conference with the Allobroges at her house 40.5), and this causes one to wonder why S. singled her out and described her at such length. One reason for doing so at this particular point in the narrative may have been structural. This digression serves to conclude what may be viewed as the first phase of the conspiracy, which ended when the plot came out into the open towards the end of 64. The very next chapter (26) begins S.'s account of 63, which occupies most of the remaining portion of the monograph. Another reason for devoting so much attention to a comparatively minor figure may have been the need to create the impression of mounting revolutionary activity between the elections in 64 and 63, which S. is hard-pressed to document. Most of the preparations described at 24.2 are of a very general nature and seem to belong better to the following year (27.1). However, once S. committed himself to the notion that Catiline was plotting an armed revolution as early as the summer of 64, he was forced to keep his account of these events going as best he could, and the chapter on Sempronia gives the impression of adding to his

narrative of events after the elections of 64, while, in fact, it turns out to be mere padding.

Sempronia: several noble plebeian families belonged to the *gens Sempronia*, including the Sempronii Gracchi. One theory, which has not been widely accepted, would make Sempronia a daughter of C. Gracchus and, therefore, a woman in her 60's at this time. S.'s description of her, however, and his comment about the age of Catiline's female supporters in general (24.3), conjure up a woman in her late thirties to mid-forties—about the age of Catiline himself.

(2)   *viro liberis*: abls. of respect; her husband was D. Junius Brutus (cos. 77 B.C.), who was absent from Rome in Nov. 63 (40.5); among her children was D. Junius Brutus Albinus, one-time legate of Caesar in Gaul and the Civil War, and later one of his assassins.

docta: "skilled in" (lit., "taught"), used here apparently with three separate constructions: as a participial adj. with (1) an abl. of respect *litteris*; and as a participle of a verb of teaching, which may take a secondary object, with (2) the infs. *psallere, saltare* and (3) an acc. *multa alia*. Alternatively we may take the infs. separately as historical infs. and supply a verb with *multa alia* such as *ei inerant*. For S.'s use of a mixed construction with a single verb, vid. 5.9n. *disserere*, and for the acc. with the pf. pass. part., cf. 45.1, 50.4, 50.5.

psallere: a Greek word (cf. 20.12) which means both to play a stringed instrument (esp. the cithara) and to sing to this musical accompaniment, while *cantare*, which is found as a gloss in several MSS, means simply "to sing."

probae: = *pudicae*, dat. with *necesse est*, which implies that a certain degree of accomplishment in these endeavors was acceptable in this period, although the Romans generally regarded singing and dancing as unbecoming to a freeborn citizen and left these entertainments to professionals who were mostly foreigners and often of servile origin.

(3)   *fuit*: sing. agreeing with the nearer subject *decus atque pudicitia*, which forms a single concept (cf. 9.1n.), rather than pl. (i.e., *fuere* which is found in a few MSS) with *omnia*.

discerneres: a potential subjn. in the indefinite second person sing. referring to past time (cf. 61.1): "you would have decided"; the object is the alternative indirect question with *parceret*, whose subj. must be supplied from the dat. *ei* (i.e., *Semproniae*) in the previous clause. For this abrupt shift of subj. from one clause to the next, cf. 5.6n. *id*.

accensa: sc. *est*; a number of MSS offer *lubidine*, which was introduced, no doubt, as an emendation to avoid the sudden and jarring change of subject in the *ut* clause from *lubido* to Sempronia.

(4)   *Sed ea*: Sempronia is once more the subject of the main clause after the variation beginning in 25.3 with *sed ei*.

antehac: "previously"; normally this adv. relates a past event to the present, but here the reference point in time is already in the past (25.1 *in eis erat*); hence the following vbs. are in the pluperfect.

creditum: neut. subst. from *credo*, either "that which has been entrusted for safe keeping," or more especially in the sphere of business a "loan."

abiuraverat: a legal word, "had denied under oath," i.e., claimed that she had never received it.

praeceps abierat: "had rushed headlong to ruin" (*abire* = "to go astray"—a unique sense of this word in S., which occurs twelve times in the *Jug.* with its literal meaning "to go away")—with the abls. of cause *luxuria atque inopia*.

(5)   *posse*: historical inf. governing three complementary infs. Normally the historical inf. is restricted to verbs of action, but S. extends this construction to copulative verbs (e.g., 20.7 *esse*, 38.1 *fieri*) as well as *posse*.

prorsus: vid. 15.5n.

inerat: sing. agreeing with the nearer subj.; sc. the dat. *ei*.

CHAPTER 26

(1)   *nihilo minus*: i.e., in spite of his preparations for revolution. The abl. absol. *his rebus conparatis*, which refers to the arrangements described in chapt. 24, is virtually concessive and resumes the narrative after the digression on Sempronia.

in proxumum annum: "for the next year," i.e., 62 at the elections conducted by Cic. in 63. In that year, Catiline's competitors were D. Junius Silanus, L. Licinius Murena, and Ser. Sulpicius Rufus, a fellow patrician and learned jurist. Since by law at least one of the consuls elected each year had to be a plebeian, Cic. supported the candidacy of Sulpicius (*Mur.* 7) in the hope that he would receive more votes than Catiline and thus block Catiline's election. Sulpicius and Catiline, however, were both defeated by Murena and Silanus. When Sulpicius prosecuted Murena in Nov. for *ambitus* (vid. 18.2n.)—perhaps not without just cause—Cicero vigorously defended the consul-elect and won an acquittal rather than risk the necessity of repeating the elections or allowing the new year to begin without two consuls in office while Catiline was still at the head of his rebel army.

designatus foret: standing for a fut. pf. indicative (*designatus ero*) in *oratio recta*.

ex voluntate: vid. 8.1n.

insidias: Cic. claims that Catiline made numerous attempts on his life both before he assumed office and while he was consul (*Cat.* 1.15).

(2) *dolus aut astutiae*: both words normally have a negative connotation which tends to undercut the apparent compliment to Cic. (*illi*). S., however, perhaps intended to revive an earlier positive sense of *dolus* (= *sollertia*), which it once possessed in archaic Latin. Likewise *astutia* (sing. & pl.) assumed a pejorative sense very early—a craftiness in one's own self-interest—and a more favorable judgment would have been conveyed if S. had written either *providentia* or *diligentia*.

(3) *proderet*: subjn. in a substantive *ut* clause of result which forms the object of *effecerat*; the reflexive pronoun *sibi* refers to the subject of the main verb.

(4) *Ad hoc*: vid. 14.3n.

pactione provinciae perpulerat: alliteration draws attention to this important act on Cic.'s part and the effort that it involved. As early as 1 Jan. 63 Cic. let it be known that he might decline a province for the following year (*Leg. Agr.* 1.26). He purchased his colleague's cooperation, or at least his neutrality, in the struggle against Catiline by offering to exchange the provinces that had been allotted to them. According to this arrangement, Antonius received the more lucrative province of Macedonia in place of Gallia Cisalpina. Since Cic. later publicly relinquished the province of Gaul in a speech that was delivered at a *contio*, probably shortly before the elections (Cic. *Att.* 2.1.3; *Pis.* 5), the deal with Antonius can be dated to the first half of 63.

praesidia amicorum: Cic. several times refers to his bodyguard of personal friends who stood between him and Catiline's assassins (*Cat.* 1.11; cf. 3.5).

clientium: besides his personal friends, Cic. relied upon a bodyguard of young men whom he summoned from Reate, a town in the Sabine territory, which was loyal to Cic. because he had acted as their *patronus* in Rome (*Cat.* 3.5; cf. *Scaur.* 27).

(5) *dies comitiorum*: on the day before the elections were to be held in 63, the senate voted a postponement on the motion of Cic. in order to investigate a rumor concerning certain inflammatory remarks that Catiline had addressed to a meeting of his supporters (Cic.

Mur. 51; cf. Plut. *Cic.* 14.3–4). This famous *contio domestica*, as Cic. calls it, appears to lie behind S.'s report of the meeting in 64 (vid. 20.1n.). When the senate met on the date originally set for the elections, Catiline refused to clear himself of suspicion and uttered veiled threats against the safety of the state. The senate, however, took no firm action, and the elections were held probably a day or two later.

consulibus: the pl. rather than the sing. both here and below (27.2) is difficult to explain since S. says that Catiline was counting on the support of Antonius if elected (26.1) and regarded Cic. as the main obstacle to the success of his plans (27.4; cf. 26.1). The sing. at 29.3 makes it unlikely that S. intended *consulibus* to stand for the office of consul in general and therefore refer to Cic. in particular since he was chiefly responsible for directing the affairs of this office (cf. 32.1). Unless we assume that S. used the pl. inadvertently, the statement must mean that Catiline attempted to murder both Cic. and Antonius. This strategy may have been dictated by the occasion and site chosen for the attack (*in Campo*, vid. n. below), and the obscurity may arise from the compressed nature of S.'s account. Doubtless Catiline's specific objectives varied from day to day. Also, by this time Catiline may have become aware of the fact that Cic. had purchased the cooperation of Antonius by exchanging provinces with him shortly before the elections were to be held.

in Campo: sc. *Martio*, the meeting place of the *comitia centuriata* (vid. 24.1n.). Cic. several times refers to Catiline's plot to assassinate him on the Campus Martius when he was conducting the elections (*Cat.* 1.11; *Mur.* 52; *Sull.* 51). Since the senate refused to take firm precautions to insure the consul's safety, Cic. had to rely upon the means at his disposal. He surrounded himself with a firm bodyguard of personal friends and wore a breastplate under his toga, partly to protect himself and partly to make the people aware of the danger to his life and arouse them against Catiline (*Mur.* l.c.; Plut. *Cic.* 14.5; Dio 37.29.4). These measures are said to have frightened Catiline's henchmen from carrying out their assignment.

aspera foedaque: pred. adjs. in place of advs. probably due to the desire to produce variety after *prospere cessere* just above.

CHAPTER 27

(1) *C. Manlium*: vid. 24.2n. Apparently Manlius had returned to Rome to support Catiline at the elections (Plut. *Cic.* 14.2), and he brought with him a large number of colonists from Faesulae and Arretium (vid. 36.1) who were eager to see Catiline elected (Cic. *Mur.* 49).

in eam partem Etruriae: i.e., the northern district in the vicinity of Faesulae and Arretium.

Camertem: adj. "of Camerinum," a city in eastern Umbria on the border with Picenum where unrest broke out during the Catilinarian disturbances (Cic. *Sull.* 53). Nothing further is known about Septimius, whom S. dismisses with the indefinite *quendam*, or about C. Julius, who is not to be confused with C. Julius Caesar the future dictator. For uprisings in Picenum and Apulia later in the year, vid. 30.2, 42.1. Both districts are situated on the Adriatic coast: Picenum to the east of Etruria, and Apulia in the extreme southeast of the peninsula.

alio: an adverb going closely with *alium*: "others to various places."

ubique: lit., "anywhere" (vid. 21.1n.); with *quem*, translate: "wherever he thought that anyone would be serviceable to him."

(2)   *Interea Romae*: S. breaks off his description of preparations outside Rome to narrate the events that led up to Catiline's departure from the city in Nov. He then resumes his narrative of the simultaneous developments in Etruria (28.4) and the countermeasures adopted by the senate in Oct. (29ff.). This arrangement causes an apparent disruption of the chronology and at first glance gives the impression that the meeting of the senate called by Cic. at 29.1 immediately followed the attack on the consul's life (28.1–3).

consulibus: vid. 26.5n.; this word upsets the balance with the following inf. and its object, which are arranged so as to produce a chiasmus.

hominibus: an abl. of means.

cum telo esse: a stock expression meaning "to carry a weapon." The *lex Cornelia de sicariis* passed by the dictator Sulla made it unlawful to carry a weapon for the purpose of committing a murder, but it apparently did not prevent a person from arming himself in self-defense (*Digest* 48.8.1; Cic. *Mil.* 11).

item: sc. *cum telis esse*.

alios: standing loosely for *ceteros* as often in S.

uti: for the conj. *ut*, an older spelling employed for archaic effect some 26 times in the *Catiline* and more frequently still in the *Jug.* and *Hist.*

(3)   *agitanti*: dat. with *procedit* (historical pres., cf. 28.2 below) meaning "to prosper," "succeed"; the participle is concessive. As examples of plans that miscarried, Cic. claims that Catiline's plot to murder the *optimates* on Oct. 28th failed because the targets of this massacre had been warned in advance. Some fled the city; those who remained were protected by Cic.'s armed guards (*Cat.*

1.7). Similarly Catiline was prevented from seizing the town of Praeneste (23 miles SE of R.) as he had planned on the night of Nov. 1st because the town had been provided with a garrison (*Cat.* 1.8).

intempesta nocte: "late at night," a common expression; the dead of night was so described either because it is an inactive period and hence "timeless" in the sense of having no clear division of time, or because these hours were regarded as "untimely" (*intempestivus*) for conducting affairs. Cic. (*Sull.* 52) reports that this meeting of the conspirators was held on the night of Nov. 6–7th.

per M. Porcium Laecam: vid. 17.3n. Since the meeting took place at his house in the street of the scythe-makers (*inter falcarios*, Cic. *Cat.* 1.8; *Sull.* 52), it is difficult to explain why S. did not write *ad* rather than *per* which implies that Laeca merely called the conspirators together in compliance with Catiline's instructions. The expression as it stands surely obscures Laeca's role, although the statement need not be taken as contradicting our other sources or mean that S. was necessarily unaware of where the meeting took place. Various emendations have been proposed (e.g., *penes*; *propere ad*, cf. 28.2) without, however, any MS authority. In addition to the attempt on Cic.'s life which was planned at the meeting, Catiline set the date for his own departure from the city and assigned specific tasks to his various supporters (Cic. *Cat.* 1.9; *Sull.* l.c.).

(4) *ibique*: = *in eoque conventu*, "at that meeting."

paraverat: the indic., rather than the subjn., which is more usual in subordinate clauses within an indirect statement, stresses the factual nature of this assertion (cf. 14.7n.).

facerent: subjn. in a rel. clause of purpose.

oppressisset: subjn. within the indirect statement standing for a fut. pf. (*oppressero*) in *oratio recta* (vid. 17.7n. *valuisset*).

suis consiliis: dat. with *officere*.

CHAPTER 28

(1) *C. Cornelius*: vid. 17.4n. Cic. specifically names him as one of the assassins who undertook this assignment although he states that Autronius was chiefly responsible for inciting this attack (*Sull.* 18, 52). Plut. (*Cic.* 16.2) and Appian (*BCiv.* 2.3) confuse this C. Cornelius, an *eques*, with the senator C. Cornelius Cethegus.

L. Vargunteius: vid. 17.3n. S. is the only authority for his role on this occasion. Cic. mentions his connection with Catiline's plot several times (*Sull.* 6, 67) but fails to implicate him in the attempt on his life. Plut. (l.c.) and Appian (l.c.) give the name of the second assassin as Marcius or Lentulus respectively. Dio (37.32.4) simply refers to the plot without naming the two conspirators.

paulo post: i.e., on the morning of Nov. 7th; confirmed by Cic. (*Cat.* 1.9 *illa ipsa nocte paulo ante lucem*, and *Sull.* 52 *prima luce*).

cum armatis hominibus: the specific role of these additional men is obscure because of the compressed nature of S.'s account. Perhaps they were to help Cornelius and Vargunteius force their way into the house if they were not readily admitted on the pretext of calling on Cic., or they may have been required to overcome Cic.'s bodyguards who might hinder the escape of the assassins after the deed had been accomplished. Apparently Cic. anticipated a strong show of force because he states that he fortified his house with additional guards when he learned of this plot (*Cat.* 1.10).

salutatum: a supine (from the vb. *salutare*) expressing their purpose, or rather the pretext for their early morning call since it is qualified by *sicuti* (= *quasi*, vid. 16.3n.). It was customary for the clients and retainers of rich and powerful Romans to call upon them at their homes in the early morning hours and to accompany them, as a mark of respect, when they set out for the Forum. This everyday occurrence, which was known as the *salutatio*, provided an opportunity for visitors to seek advice on legal or business matters and for politicians to consult with their supporters and advisers. More and more, however, the custom turned into a social obligation that could be burdensome for both the callers and for the person honored by the visit.

suae: i.e., *Ciceronis* (cf. 21.4n.).

confodere: S. appears to be the first author to use this verb in the sense of "strike down," "stab." It occurs only once elsewhere in S. (60.7) in the context of a battle and is common later in military historians.

(2)   *intellegit*: historical pres. for the sake of vividness (cf. 20.1).

(3)   *ianua*: abl. of separation with *prohibiti*: "kept away from the entrance," "denied admission."

(4)   *Interea*: the scene now shifts back in time and place to where S. left off at 27.1, several months prior to the meeting on Nov. 6–7th.

egestate simul ac dolore iniuriae: the abls. are causal and to be taken with *cupidam*; *dolore iniuriae* is explained by the following *quod* clause.

novarum rerum: "revolution" (lit., "new things") obj. gen. depending on *cupidam*. The very expression for "revolution" in Latin reveals the fundamentally conservative outlook of Roman society.

latrones: the second object of the historical inf. *sollicitare*. These brigands were mainly runaway slaves who had been employed as agricultural labor on the vast estates in this region.

nihil relicui: vid. 11.7n.

fecerat: sing. because the compound subject is treated as a single concept (cf. 9.1n.).

CHAPTER 29

(1) *ancipiti malo*: the evil or danger is said to be twofold (lit., "double headed") because the state was threatened both from within the city and without, as explained in the *quod* clause.

privato consilio: Cic. states that he protected the state from Catiline as long as he could by using private means rather than arousing alarm (*Cat.* 1.11–12). In fact, Cic. was forced to proceed with caution because the senate refused to believe the rumors about Catiline (*Cat.* 1.30; *Mur.* 51).

longius: this is the only instance in S. where this adv. denotes time rather than distance (cf. 7.7). Elsewhere he prefers *diutius* (e.g., 39.4, 58.6).

quo consilio: abl. of quality or description supplying, with *quantus*, the predicate of *foret*: "of what intention," i.e., "what was its aim."

satis compertum: vid. 14.7n., a predicate acc. in the neut. agreeing with the indirect question *exercitus . . . foret*, which forms the direct object of *habebat*. Actually Cic. claimed to be better informed than S. implies. In the published version of his *First Catilinarian*, which Cic. prepared nearly three years later in 60 B.C. (*Att.* 2.1.3), he states that at the meeting of the senate on Oct. 21st, he accurately predicted that Manlius would commence an armed uprising on Oct. 27th (*Cat.* 1.7). This statement, however, may well be a boastful exaggeration after the fact.

ad senatum refert: a technical expression for laying a matter before the senate. According to Plutarch (*Cic.* 15; cf. *Crass.* 13.3) and Dio (37.31.1–2), Cic.'s decision to consult the senate on this occasion was precipitated by some anonymous letters that had been delivered to Crassus and warned of an impending massacre in the city— probably the *caedes optimatium* set for Oct. 28th (Cic. *Cat.* 1.7). When Crassus showed these incriminating documents to Cic., the consul seized upon this concrete evidence of a conspiracy to rouse the senate from its lethargy. Furthermore, the senate must have been reassured by Crassus' behavior on this occasion that he was not willing to back Catiline's scheme, and this may account for the strong measures taken by the senate at this time.

exagitatam: *exagitare* usu. means "to arouse" or "excite" in S., but in this context the participle must bear the extremely rare sense of "discussed" or "bandied about." Therefore, the emendation *exagitatum*, which makes this word modify *senatum*, rather than *rem*, is attractive. Previously the senate was described as not sufficiently energetic (16.5).

(2)   *solet*: sc. *fieri* (vid. 22.2n. *consuevit*); the subject *quod* is neut. because its antecedent is the whole statement that follows.

decrevit darent: *ut* is rarely omitted after *decernere* but often after verbs of similar type (e.g., *mandare* 32.2; *obtestari* 33.5; *permittere* 45.1; *censere* 52.26), thus preserving the original hortatory nature of these subordinate commands. The wording of this decree, which is commonly known as the *senatus consultum ultimum* (first so-called by Caes. *BCiv.* 1.3), is variously given. The language here is very similar to that in Cic. (*Cat.* 1.4). This decree served as a substitute for the dictatorship, which had formerly been employed to meet grave emergencies down to the end of the 3rd cent. B.C., and it was first passed in 121 B.C. to crush the ex-tribune C. Gracchus and his supporters. It invested the consuls with exceptional powers (29.3) and effectively suspended a citizen's right of *provocatio*, which ordinarily protected him from coercion by a magistrate (vid. 51.22n.), if the consul judged the state to be threatened. According to Asconius (p. 6C.3–8), Cic. delivered his first speech against Catiline on the 18th day after the senate passed the *s.c.u.* If we take Nov. 8th as the date of the *First Catilinarian* (vid. 31.6n.), then the *s.c.u.* was passed on Oct. 21st (or 22nd if we count the days inclusively). Cic. (*Cat.* 1.7) confirms that the senate met on this date to receive a report on the state of affairs in Etruria, and Dio (37.31.1–2) and Plutarch (*Cic.* 15.3–4) both declare that the senate placed affairs in the hands of the consuls when it learned of the unrest in Etruria.

(3)   *maxuma*: modifying *ea potestas*, but the adj. is separated from its substantive for the sake of emphasis: "this power is the greatest entrusted. . . ."

parare: this and the following infs. are in apposition with *potestas*.

domi militiaeque: i.e., within the city as well as in the field.

aliter: = *alioquin*, introducing a consequence that will result if the conditions in a previous statement are not fulfilled (cf. 44.1); i.e., without the *s.c.u.*

nullius earum rerum: the gen. *nullius* depends upon *ius* (= "power," "authority over"), while *earum rerum* is partitive. The

statement is not strictly accurate since the people (*populus*) normally left the levying of troops (e.g., 30.5, 36.3) and the regulation
of allies (*socii*) to the senate's discretion. In other matters involving
jurisdiction over citizens, however, the people claimed the right to
hear cases on appeal from a magistrate's verdict.

consuli: dat. of possession; the sing. designates the office of the
consulship rather than the two individuals occupying this office (cf.
26.5n.).

CHAPTER 30

(1)   *L. Saenius*: S. is the only source to mention this senator by name in
connection with the confirmation of events in Etruria (cf. Dio
37.31.3). Nothing further is known about him.

adlatas: sc. *esse*, pf. pass. inf. in the indirect statement depending
on *dicebat*. The date is probably the 1st or 2nd of Nov. since we
must allow time for the letter to travel from Etruria (*Faesulis*) to
Rome after the uprising on Oct. 27th.

scriptum erat: impersonal passive whose subj. is supplied by the
indirect statement *C. Manlium . . . cepisse. . . .*

ante diem VI Kalendas Novembris: Oct. 27th; this is the only precise date given by S. in the year 63 (cf. 17.1n.) and agrees with the
testimony of Cic. (*Cat.* 1.7).

(2)   *id quod . . . solet*: cf. above, 29.2.

portenta . . . prodigia: paired for the sake of alliteration (cf. 1.4n.).
Cic. mentions among other heavenly signs of the impending crisis a
glow seen in the western sky at night, lightning bolts, and earth-
quakes (*Cat.* 3.18; cf. Plut. *Cic.* 14.3).

portari: vid. 6.5n., and cf. 42.2 *portationibus*; the three indirect
statements depend upon *nuntiabant* which is to be supplied with
the second *alii* from above.

Capuae: locative, a town in Campania south of Rome noted for its
schools (*ludi*) of gladiators (vid. 30.7 below). It was from this place
that Spartacus escaped in 73 B.C. and raised the well-known servile
war. Cic. sent the quaestor P. Sestius with some troops to secure
Capua against the conspirators (Cic. *Sest.* 9).

in Apulia: cf. 27.1.

(3)   *senati*: this alternate 2nd decl. form of the gen. sing. is preserved in
a few MSS of S. and is confirmed by the grammarians who attest it
in S. It occurs altogether six times in S., all but once in the set
phrase *senati decretum*. With words other than *decretum*, S.
prefers the usual form of the gen. in *-us* (e.g., 53.1), and also with

decretum if it depends on a preposition (e.g., 51.36). The form in -*i* appears to be archaic.

Q. Marcius Rex: cos. in 68 B.C. and procos. in Cilicia the following year. He was replaced by Pompey in 66 under the provisions of the *lex Manilia* and waited in vain outside Rome for permission to celebrate a triumph. The family traced its ancestry back to Ancus Marcius, Rome's fourth king (Suet. *Iul.* 6.1), although this branch of the family was plebeian and did not bear the cognomen Rex until the late 3rd cent.

Q. (Caecilius) Metellus Creticus: cos. in 69 B.C. and assigned as procos. to Crete and Greece (68–65 B.C.) where he waged war against the pirates. He eventually pacified the island of Crete— whence his surname—and organized it as a Roman province. He was forced, however, to wait until 62 before being allowed to cele- brate a triumph.

(4)   *hi utrique*: = *horum uterque* (cf. 5.7n.).

ad urbem: a set phrase meaning "near the city" just outside the *pomerium* where a promagistrate was required to wait if he wished to celebrate a triumph since he was not allowed to retain his mili- tary *imperium* once he crossed this sacred boundary. In order to enter the city at the head of his conquering army, it was necessary for a promagistrate to be exempted from the restriction barring his *imperium* within the city. Originally the people had the sole right to grant such a dispensation, but later the prerogative was assumed by the senate.

imperatores: pred. nominative to be taken closely with *ad urbem*. Theoretically every official holding *imperium* was an *imperator*, but in practice the title was reserved for the commander of an army in the field since *imperium* within the city of Rome was more limited in scope. Furthermore, it was customary for this title to be conferred officially only upon commanders who had won a significant victory over Rome's enemies. Until a commander won such a battle and was saluted *imperator* by his victorious troops, he was not permitted to add this title formally to his list of honors.

calumnia paucorum: abl. of cause, "due to the quibbling obstruc- tion of a few men." Pompey and his supporters blocked Marcius and Metellus from triumphing on the grounds that they had won their victories while acting as Pompey's subordinates (*alieno auspicio*) under the provisions of the *lex Gabinia* and the *lex Manilia*. One of the requirements for being allowed to celebrate a triumph was that the general who claimed this honor had to be the supreme commander when he won his victory.

vendere: the inf. supplies the subject of *mos erat* (cf. 17.6n. *vivere*)
rather than *ut* plus the subjn., which is the more usual construction.

(5)   *praetores*: *missi sunt* is understood from above.

Q. Pompeius Rufus: praetor 63 B.C., procos. in Africa 62–59 B.C.
Possibly he was sent to relieve Sestius, who is credited by Cic. with
securing Capua against the conspirators (vid. 30.2n.).

Q. (Caecilius) Metellus Celer: praetor 63 B.C., procos. in Cisalpine
Gaul in 62 B.C. after Cic. gave up his option on this province,
which he had received from Antonius in exchange for Macedonia
(vid. 26.4n.); cos. 60 B.C. His father, Q. Metellus Nepos (cos. 98
B.C.), was a cousin of Metellus Creticus (30.3), and his half-sister
Mucia was Pompey's wife at this time. His brother Metellus Nepos
was elected tribune for 62 and blocked Cicero from addressing the
people when he laid down the consulship (vid. 17.3n. *Bestia*). Both
brothers had served as legates on Pompey's staff in the East, and
Nepos was sent to Rome by Pompey to represent his interests as
tribune in 62. Metellus Celer played a significant role in suppressing Catiline's men in the field, while Cic. looked after the safety of
the city (Cic. *Cat.* 2.5, 2.26; *Fam.* 5.2.1; Plut. *Cic.* 16.1). His army
in Picenum and the *ager Gallicus* prevented Catiline from
escaping from Italy by crossing the Alps and forced him to face
Antonius at Pistoria (57.2–3). When he died suddenly in 59, his
wife, the notorious Clodia, was suspected of having poisoned him
(Cic. *Cael.* 59–60).

permissum: sc. *est*: the subject is supplied by the *uti* clause.

pro: "according to," "in keeping with," i.e., as these circumstances
necessitated and permitted the preparations to be made.

exercitum: we learn of a levy conducted by Metellus *in agro
Piceno et Gallico*, a region in which Pompey had great personal
influence (Cic. *Cat.* 2.5).

(6)   *indicavisset*: subjn. because this clause formed part of the senate's
decree (cf. 36.2) and therefore stands in virtual indirect discourse
replacing a fut. pf. indicative (cf. 23.3n.).

praemium: *decrevere* is to be supplied from the clause below.

sestertia centum: "100,000 sesterces." The *sestertius* (= 4 *asses* or
1/4 of a *denarius*) was a small silver coin—about half the diameter
of a U.S. dime—which was rarely minted but served as the standard unit of reckoning. The word *sestertia* (neut.) is used as an
adj., with *milia* understood, and denotes the sum of 1000 sesterces.
The reward offered by the senate was rather considerable when
compared with what is known about the purchasing power of the
sestertius at this time. We learn, for instance, that Julius Caesar

granted relief in 46 B.C. to poor tenants who were paying as little as 2000 sesterces annual rent in Rome, or 500 sesterces outside the city. At the same time, he paid out as bounties 24,000 sesterces to each of his soldiers, twice this amount to centurions, and about 96,000 sesterces to the military tribunes and cavalry officers (Suet. *Iul.* 38; App. *BCiv.* 2.102). It is worth recalling that in the late Republic 100,000 sesterces (= 400,000 *asses*) was the minimum requirement for membership in the first census-class, and under the empire, 400,000 sesterces represented the minimum census qualification for the equestrian order (vid. 17.4n.). The fact that the senate's very generous terms led to no betrayal of the conspiracy (36.5) may demonstrate how deeply rooted the social problems were that fostered Catiline's attempted revolution. Alternatively, the failure to break silence may also be interpreted as a sign that very few people were involved in the conspiracy and had anything to report.

(7)   *familiae*: this is the usual term for a gang of slaves or a troop of gladiators who were trained by a *lanista* and offered for hire at public spectacles (*munera*). The removal of these professional fighters from the city was especially desirable in view of their potential recruitment by the conspirators.

Capuam: apparently treated as though *distribuerentur* were a verb of motion followed by the acc. of place to which. It is difficult to explain why Capua was selected for this purpose since this town was noted for the number of gladiatorial schools located there on a permanent basis, and there were rumors of unrest in this region (vid. 30.2n.).

vigiliae: "watches"; in all probability, arrangements were made for posting these guards earlier, at the time of the *s.c.u.* in Oct. when the senate was alarmed by the threat of bloodshed in Rome (so Dio 37.31.3; cf. 29.1–2nn.). Rome had no regular police force or fire brigade until Augustus instituted the *cohortes vigilum*, numbering about 7000 men, in A.D. 6 and the three urban cohorts of 1000 men each.

minores magistratus: officials below the rank of praetor, esp. the *tresviri capitales*, who were charged with maintaining public order (Ascon. p. 37C) and oversaw the prison and punishment of offenders (55.1); also possibly the aediles and the quaestors.

CHAPTER 31

(1) *rebus*: the preparations signifying danger, as well as the reports that were coming in from Etruria.

laetitia atque lascivia: paired for the sake of alliteration (cf. 1.4n.); *lascivia* adds a pejorative coloring to the pair as a whole which *laetitia* would not ordinarily convey by itself.

quae: neut. acc. pl., although both antecedents are f. (cf. 3.4n.).

diuturna: the city had been at peace since the bloody civil war with Sulla (83–82 B.C.), although the revolt led by Lepidus in 77 B.C. and the war with Spartacus (73–71 B.C.) temporarily threatened the safety of the city.

invasit: used transitively with *omnis* as the direct object (vid. 2.5n.).

(2) *festinare*: the first in a series of six historical infs. used to evoke the feeling of panic and disarray.

cuiquam: to be taken with *loco* and *homini*, both dats. depending on *credere*. *Quisquam* is the usual indefinite pronoun after a universal negative, but it is rarely used as an adj. in place of *ullus* except with personal substantives (e.g., 61.5 *quisquam civis*). Here *homini* permits the extension to *loco*.

suo . . . metu: abl. of the standard of measurement with *metiri*.

(3) *quibus*: dat. with *incesserat* (vid. 7.3n.).

magnitudine: abl. of cause explaining *insolitus*. Their fear was "unaccustomed" because the extent of Rome's power normally shielded the city from the fear of attack.

adflictare: the first of seven historical infs. in asyndeton, and the only instance of this vb. in S., which is replaced by *adfligere* in the *Jug.* and *Hist*. Although *se adflictare* can be used figuratively to describe merely a state of distress or anxiety, in this context it appears to approach the meaning of *adflictatio*, which Cic. (*Tusc.* 4.8) defines as *aegritudo cum vexatione corporis*, and refers to the physical blows that women commonly inflicted on themselves as a sign of mourning: "they beat their breast and tore their cheeks."

miserari: "they expressed their pity for" (cf. 51.9), as opposed to *misereri* which simply refers to the feeling of pity or compassion.

rogitare omnia: frequentative (cf. 2.1n.), "kept asking about everything"; a rare word outside of Plautus and Terence and found only here in S.

<*omni rumore*>: not found in the MSS of S. but supplied by a citation of this passage in Fronto (p. 168 H.II), which also has *adripere omnia* ("eagerly grasped at every scrap of information").

If the MS reading is retained, *omnia* must be construed with either *pavere* ("were terrified at") or *rogitare*, and the remaining verb will then be left to stand on its own in an absolute sense. Either interpretation yields a tolerable sense but results in a rather weak statement when compared with the fuller version found in Fronto. In favor of adopting the supplement is the striking resemblance to a similar expression in the *Jug.* (72.2) where *pavescere* is construed with an abl.: *circumspectare omnia et omni strepitu pavescere.*

(4) *At Catilinae*: S. here resumes his account of Catiline's maneuvers which was broken off at 28.3 after the failure to assassinate Cic. The description of the senate's countermeasures in the month leading up to the meeting at Laeca's house and the reaction to these preparations of the senate in the city (31.1–3) provides a smooth transition back to the former scene of action and the month of Nov. With *postremo* (31.5) the narrative is brought back to the day following the early morning visit of the assassins (vid. 31.6n.).

lege Plautia: this is the earliest prosecution on record under this law which covered acts of violence (*vis*) against the state as well as against private individuals. Among the offenses covered by this law were the unlawful use of a weapon and the occupation of public places with armed men (Ascon. p. 55C.12). It was perhaps passed in 70 B.C. by the tribune who sponsored the bill to recall the followers of Lepidus and the agrarian law for the Spanish veterans of Pompey and Metellus. It apparently supplemented an earlier *lex Lutatia de vi*, which seems to have been limited in scope to acts of violence against the state and was passed by the consul Catulus in 78 B.C. to suppress the insurrection of his colleague M. Lepidus (Cic. *Cael.* 70; cf. 1). Catiline's supporters were tried under the *lex Plautia* in 62 B.C. (Ps. Sall. *in Cic.* 2.3; *Schol. Bob.* p. 84St; cf. Cic. *Cael.* 70).

interrogatus erat: the time element is left rather indefinite. Dio (37.31.3) implies that Catiline was charged soon after news of the insurrection in Etruria reached Rome, ca. Nov. 1st or 2nd (vid. 30.1n.). This would certainly provide an adequate justification for the indictment, and Cic. confirms that a hearing on this charge was pending at the time the *First Catilinarian* was delivered on Nov. 8th (vid. 31.6). According to Cic. (*Cat.* 1.19), Catiline attempted to avoid suspicion by offering to surrender himself voluntarily into the custody of various leading citizens, including Cic. himself, until the case was decided, but no one would receive him into his house except his accomplice M. Metellus.

L. Paulo: L. Aemilius Lepidus Paulus, son of the cos. in 78 B.C., who led the revolt that was crushed by Catulus, and brother of the triumvir. He was consul in 50 B.C. and supported Caesar in the Civil War. The only other source to allude to Lepidus' role in this prosecution is Cic. (*Vat.* 25; cf. *Schol. Bob.* p. 149St. 3–6).

(5)   *sicut*: = *quasi* (vid. 16.3n.), with the subjn. *lacessitus foret*, plupf. subjn. in secondary sequence with reference to a prior act (cf. 12.5n. *quasi*). Catiline tried to give the impression that there were ✕ no grounds for the attack against him other than personal animosity.

iurgio: "abuse," i.e., a groundless charge arising from spite or malice rather than a genuine belief in his guilt.

in senatum: according to Cic. (*Cat.* 2.12, cf. 1.33; Plut. *Cic.* 16.3), the senate met on this occasion in the Temple of Jupiter Stator, which was located near the Via Sacra at the foot of the Palatine Hill. The Palatine had been earlier provided with a garrison in response to the threat posed by the conspiracy (Cic. *Cat.* 1.1), and a large body of Roman Knights surrounded the temple on the day of this meeting as an additional precaution against an outbreak of violence (Cic. *Cat.* 1.21).

(6)   *praesentiam*: Cic. explicitly refers to his apprehension so long as Catiline remained within the city (*Cat.* 1.10).

orationem: the *First Catilinarian*; within this speech Cic. alludes to the meeting of the conspirators at Laeca's house which was held on the night of Nov. 6–7th (vid. 27.3n.), and states that this gathering took place on the "night before last" (*priore nocte*) relative to the time at which he was speaking (*Cat.* 1.8; cf. 1.1). Apparently Cic. allowed one more night to elapse after the unsuccessful attempt had been made against his life on Nov. 7th to see if Catiline would take this opportunity to leave the city voluntarily. It seems that Catiline had announced this intention and even perhaps set the date of his departure at the meeting on Nov. 6th (*Cat.* 1.9; *Sull.* 52). When Catiline showed no signs of departing since the consul was still alive, Cic. brought the matter before the senate on Nov. 8th.

luculentam: Cic. uses this same word to describe the effective speech that Cato delivered on Dec. 5th when the punishment of the conspirators was debated (*Att.* 12.21.1).

scriptam: published in 60 B.C. (Cic. *Att.* 2.1.3). Not surprisingly S. refrains from including his own version or paraphrase of this famous oration. To do so would have spoiled the proportions of his monograph and served no useful purpose. Livy (45.25.3) and Tacitus (*Ann.* 15.63.3; cf. 15.67.3) both follow the same practice of omitting from their histories well-known published documents, which their readers could consult, if they wished, in their original form.

(7)   *adsedit*: the technical term for resuming one's seat in a gathering after concluding a speech which one delivered while standing.

ut erat paratus: in a causal sense. This is the only instance in S. of *ad* plus the acc. with *paratus*, which normally is construed with the inf. and once with *ut*. For Catiline's adeptness at dissembling, cf. 5.4. According to Cic. (*Orat.* 129; cf. *Cat.* 2.13), Catiline made no reply to the charges that were levelled against him in the *First Catilinarian*, but this need not, of course, preclude the possibility that Catiline offered an extemporaneous disclaimer of guilt such as the one S. invents to suit this occasion.

demisso voltu, voce supplici: chiasmus intensifies the alliteration.

a patribus: on this title for Roman senators, vid. 6.6n. S. neglects to mention the silence and suspicion with which the other senators greeted Catiline when he attended this meeting and the fact that all the consulars vacated the seats near him (Cic. *Cat.* 1.16, 2.12).

ea familia ortum: to be taken with *se*, subject acc. of the indirect statement depending on a verb of saying that is to be supplied from the preceding *postulare*, which governs the two indirect commands introduced by *ne*. On his family, vid. 5.1n. and below. This is one of the few instances in S. where *ortum* is construed with an abl. of source without a preposition, a common construction with participles indicating birth or origin, e.g., *natus* (5.1, 23.1).

in spe haberet: an idiom meaning "to expect" or "count upon." *Omnia bona* are to be taken together as the object of *haberet*: "nothing but good things" (lit., "all good things").

sibi: dat. with *opus esse*.

maiorum pluruma beneficia: the only surviving evidence for Catiline's immediate family concerns his great-grandfather, M. Sergius Silus, who distinguished himself on the battlefield during the 2nd Punic War (Pliny, *HN* 7.104–106, derived from Varro). He was wounded 23 times during his military service (cf. Amm. Marc. 25.3.13), suffered the loss of his right hand, and twice escaped from imprisonment by Hannibal. A catalogue of his military exploits was preserved in a speech that he delivered in 197 B.C. when he was praetor urbanus (Pliny, l.c.; Livy 32.27.7, 32.28.2).

in plebem Romanam: the emendation *populum Romanum* (Dietsch and Schmalz) is attractive and can be supported by the assumption that the MS reading is derived ultimately from the abbreviation *p.R.* If *plebem R.* is retained, it provides a striking antithesis to *patricio* just above and may be intended to stress

Catiline's avowed sympathy with the anti-aristocratic faction.

essent: subjn. because the relative clause is part of the indirect statement depending upon *existumarent*.

perdita re publica: abl. with *opus*, "need for" (cf. 1.6n.).

cum: "while," circumstantial, and at the same time the use of the subjn. here is closely related to that in relative clauses of characteristic.

inquilinus: normally this word is a noun, not an adj., and may be taken here as standing in apposition with *civis*. This term (from *in + colo*), which properly refers to a lodger in a house that he does not own, is intended as a slur on the municipal origin of Cicero, who was a native of Arpinum, a town approximately 60 miles SE of Rome in the Volscian highlands. This town, however, had possessed the private rights of R. citizenship since 303 B.C. and full rights since 188 B.C. Therefore the remark merely reflects the haughty bias of a patrician like Catiline towards a man of municipal origin whose ancestors had not been ennobled by holding office in Rome (cf. 23.6n. *homo novos*). Cic. met with similar abuse in the following year from the young Torquatus, also a patrician, who styled the ex-consul a *peregrinus rex* (*Sull.* 22–23). S. may well have misplaced the contemptuous reference to Cic. as a "foreign resident" since Appian (*BCiv.* 2.2) connects the remark with the campaign for the consulship in 64, and this agrees with Asconius' comment that Cicero's chief rivals heaped abuse upon his humble origins (*novitas* pp. 93C.25–94C.1). S. makes a similar error below (vid. 31.9n. *ruina*).

(8) *hostem*: later Catiline and Manlius were formally declared *hostes* (i.e., enemies of the state who had forfeited their claim to the rights of a citizen) when news of Catiline's arrival in Manlius' camp reached Rome (36.2).

parricidam: vid. 14.3n.

(9) *ruina*: "general destruction"; this is an allusion to the practice of pulling down buildings in order to block the path of a fire that is burning out of control. S. misplaces this remark since we know from Cic. that it was addressed to Cato sometime before the elections in 63 when he threatened to prosecute Catiline for corrupt campaign practices (*Mur.* 51 *Catoni . . . respondisset si quod esset in suas fortunas incendium excitatum, id se non aqua sed ruina restincturum*). Florus (2.12.7) and Valerius Maximus (9.11.3) both follow S. in assigning these words to Catiline's response to the charges made by Cic.

CHAPTER 32

(1) *ex curia*: by failing to mention that the senate met on Nov. 8th in the Temple of Jupiter Stator (vid. 31.5n.), S. causes his account to be potentially misleading when he substitutes *curia*, by a common metonymy, for *senatus* (cf. Cic. *De Or.* 3.167) since this word can also designate the regular meeting-house of the senate in the Forum (e.g., 18.8, apparently).

consuli: a dat. of reference (disadvantage), which must be taken with *insidiae*, rather than the verb as it is at 27.3 where the word in the dative refers to the person who experienced failure (cf. 32.2, 40.2, 40.3): "his plots against the consul were not succeeding."

optumum: predicate adj. agreeing with the infs. *augere* and *antecapere*, which form the object of *credens* and are to be taken as verbal sustantives.

scriberentur: subjn. because of the prospective nature of the *prius quam* clause. The levy is that provided for at 30.5.

antecapere: vid. 13.3n.

forent: the subjn. is probably due to the generic nature of the rel. clause.

nocte intempesta: vid. 27.3n.; this refers to the night of Nov. 8–9th.

cum paucis: Cic. laments that more of Catiline's supporters did not leave with him (*Cat.* 2.4), while Plutarch (*Cic.* 16.4) states that as many as 300 armed men accompanied him.

(2) *possent*: subjn. because the relative clause occurs within the indirect command that depends upon *mandat*; the omission of *ut* (cf. 29.2n.) emphasizes the jussive nature of *confirment*, *maturent*, and *parent*. For the combination of secondary and primary sequence following a verb in the historic present, cf. 34.2. For the sake of vividness, the imperatives of *oratio recta* are put in the pres. subjn., while the imperf. subjn. stands in the subordinate clause, which was originally cast in the indicative.

factionis: normally a pejorative term designating any narrow association of political partisans whose interests are selfish (cf. 18.4, 20.4nn.).

accessurum: sc. *esse*; the indirect statement depends upon a verb of saying, e.g., *pollicetur*, which is understood from *mandat* above.

(3) *ex suo numero*: = *ex numero suorum* (cf. 42.3).

Marcium Regem: vid. 30.3n.

huiscemodi: vid. 20.1n.

CHAPTER 33

(1) *imperator*: vid. 30.4n.

cepisse: the indirect statement depends upon *testamur*, which takes an acc. of the w̄itness invoked (*deos hominesque*) and an object clause of fact.

quo: a purpose clause without, however, a comparative (vid. 11.5n.). S. deliberately pairs this purpose clause with the prepositional phrase *contra patriam* to produce *inconcinnitas*. For the combination of *quo . . . uti*, cf. 58.3.

qui: the antecedent must be supplied from *nostra*.

violentia . . . crudelitate: abls. of cause.

patriae . . . fama . . . fortunis: both the gen. and abls. depend on *expertes* and are combined to produce dissymmetry (cf. *Jug.* 74.3 *potior* with the gen. and abl.); of the two cases, the abl. is archaic and poetic. Some editors choose to adopt the reading *patria*, which is also amply attested in the MSS, and emend *sed* to *sed<e>* on the grounds that the adversative conj. is awkward in pointing up a contrast without a concessive word such as *tamen* (cf. 61.3). The alteration to *patria sede* ("ancestral abode") yields an expression that is attested elsewhere in S. (*Hist.* 1.55.12M) and makes the complaint refer to the loss of property rather than exile or flight from Rome to avoid the consequences of insolvency.

lege uti: the following reference to *liberum corpus* implies that this is an allusion to the *lex Poetelia et Papiria* of 326 B.C., which forbade imprisonment for debt. Apparently under the earlier regulation of the XII Tables (451–450 B.C.), while interest was set at the ceiling of 1/12 the principal per annum (= 8 1/3%, Tac. *Ann.* 6.16.2), a debtor could be imprisoned and sold into slavery for defaulting (Gellius 20.1.45–47). Aulus Gellius (20.1.18–19) asserts that under the earlier law, creditors were allowed to cut up a debtor's body in proportion to the money owed to them. [In the Ciceronian period, interest rates might legally range as high as 12% (Cic. *Att.* 1.12.1), but the law was commonly circumvented. For instance, a sydicate of businessmen, to which M. Brutus belonged, loaned money to provincials on one occasion at 48% (Cic. *Att.* 5.21.11), and Horace (*Sat.* 1.2.14) alludes to businessmen who charged five times the going rate of interest as a matter of course.]

amisso patrimonio: according to Cic., however, a number of Catiline's supporters joined the conspiracy in an attempt to avoid the necessity of liquidating their assets to settle with their creditors (*Cat.* 2.18).

praetoris: the urban praetor had jurisdiction over civil suits involving debts, and by his edict, which he issued at the beginning of his term, he indicated the guidelines according to which he would enforce the laws and judge cases. In 89 B.C. the urban praetor A. Sempronius Asellio was murdered by an angry mob of creditors when he attempted to alleviate a financial crisis arising out of the Social War by ruling in favor of debtors (Livy, *Per.* 74; Val. Max. 9.7.4; App. *BCiv.* 1.54). In 63 B.C., the urban praetor apparently aggravated the financial crisis (vid. 14.2n.) by favoring the claims of creditors—hence the allusion to *iniquitas praetoris* below 33.5.

(2) *vostrum*: this reading is preserved only in Gellius (20.6.14), who states that texts of S. were already being altered in his day to *vestri*. This use of the gen. (usually partitive, e.g., 33.1 *cuiquam nostrum*), in place of the adjectival possessive pronoun (e.g., 51.37 *maiores nostri*), is rare in this period but more common later. Here the gen. may be used to convey a tone of familiarity between Manlius and Marcius.

decretis: by legislation as well as by subsidizing the cost of grain or distributing it free. Among other laws, the *lex Licinia-Sextia* of 367 B.C. permitted the interest already paid to be deducted from the outstanding principal, and the *lex Genucia* of 342 B.C. temporarily outlawed the charging of interest on loans, while the *lex Flaminia* of 217 B.C. attempted to relieve debtors by assigning a higher value to the *denarius*.

inopiae . . . opitulati sunt: this *figura etymologica* (vid. 7.6n.) adds emphasis to the statement; *opitulor*, which is construed with the dat. like its synonym *succurro*, is colloquial.

novissume: Cic. used this word sparingly, apparently because it seemed to be a *novum et improbum verbum* (Gell. 10.21), although it is attested in the Elder Cato (89.24J). S. employs it only once in the *Cat.* and twice in the *Jug.*

memoria nostra: abl. of time within which.

bonis: vid. 19.2n.; in this context, however, it refers especially to men of substance (cf. 37.3).

argentum aere: doubtless a reference to the consular *lex Valeria* of 86 B.C., which permitted debts to be settled by payment of one quarter of the remaining principal. Since in this period each silver sesterce was worth four bronze *asses*, the provisions of this law entailed the payment of one *as* for each sesterce owed.

(3) *a patribus secessit*: according to one tradition, which S. followed (*Jug.* 31.17), the plebeians twice withdrew to the Aventine Hill: once in 494 B.C. to protest the harsh laws relating to debt and to secure the recognition of the tribunate (vid. 38.1n.); and once in

449 B.C. in reaction to the tyrannical power of the Decemvirs. The last of these formal withdrawals, by which the plebeians attempted to enforce their demands, occurred in 287 B.C. when the *plebs* occupied the Janiculum Hill, again to protest the heavy burden of debt. The resolution of the protest on this occasion resulted in the *lex Hortensia*, which empowered the plebeian assembly to pass legislation (plebiscites) binding on the whole population, and this victory effectively ended the struggle between the plebeians and patricians. For *patribus* in the sense of patricians, vid. 6.6n.

(4)   *bonus*: the sense here is moral rather than political (cf. 3.2). Both the thought and diction in this section are Sallustian (e.g., 2.2, 6.3) and confirm the judgment that this document does not purport to be a faithful copy of an original (vid. 32.3 *huiuscemodi* and 20.1n.). Note that unlike Catiline and his aristocratic supporters, Manlius disavows the claim that *imperium* and *divitiae* are the objects of the uprising (cf. 20.14, 21.2).

(5)   *consulatis*: as in 32.2, the *ut* has been omitted to emphasize the jussive nature of the subjn. after *obtestamur*, which is a verb of petition (cf. 33.1 *testamur* followed by an ind. statement of fact).

quaeramus: subjn. following the analogy of *ut* clauses with verbs of necessity or obligation such as *oportet* or *necesse est*.

ulti: the leading idea is contained in the participle rather than *pereamus*: "how in laying down our lives we may most avenge our bloodshed." This is put in the form of an indirect deliberative question depending on *quaeramus*.

CHAPTER 34

(1)   *discedant . . . proficiscantur*: the pres. rather than the impf. subjn. is employed to emphasize the imperative nature of these verbs in *oratio recta* despite the fact that they depend upon *respondit*, which is in the historic perfect. The impf. *vellent* stands for a pres. indic. of direct address. For a similar combination of primary and secondary sequence, cf. 32.2n. where, however, the historic present makes the mixing of tenses less striking. Perhaps S. wished here to avoid the possibility of the impf. subjn. being misinterpreted in a hypothetical sense. Following the jussive subjns., the construction after *respondit* shifts to an indirect statement of fact (*senatum . . . fuisse*) in the next clause. *Ab armis discedere* is a technical expression for laying down arms.

ea mansuetudine . . . misericordia: abls. of quality; this alliterative pair of words (vid. 1.4n.) is employed four times in all by S. (52.11, 52.27, 54.2), and these concepts figure prominently in Cato's analysis of the position adopted by Caesar in the debate concerning the punishment of the conspirators. Cic. (*Cat.* 4.2) echoes Marcius' judgment on the protection afforded by ·the senate to oppressed people, but elsewhere (e.g., *Cat.* 2.8) he observes that many followers of Catiline joined the conspiracy because they despaired of finding relief in other quarters—presumably the senate. This view is reflected in the complaint made by the Allobroges (40.3).

petiverit: this use of the pf. subjn. in a result clause to represent a pf. indic. (i.e., actual as opposed to a potential consequence) is quite normal even after a main verb in a secondary tense (here *fuisse*).

(2)   *optumo*: in the political sense, alluding to the aristocratic faction, the self-styled *optimates* (vid. 19.2n.). For the superlative with *quisque*, vid. 2.6n.

criminibus: these false charges refer to the accusations made by Cic. in his *First Catilinarian*, and more especially to the pending prosecution under the *lex Plautia* (31.4).

circumventum: sc. *esse*, a pf. pass. inf. forming with its subject *se* an indirect statement depending upon a verb of reporting implied in the expression *litteras mittit*.

nequiverit: subjn. because the *quoniam* clause occurs within an indirect statement. Primary sequence is employed here after the main vb. (*mittit*) in the historic pres. (cf. 32.2n.), while immediately below a shift is made to secondary sequence (*esset, foret, oreretur*). On S.'s fondness for *nequeo*, vid. 18.3n.

fortunae: vid. 10.1n.

Massiliam: Marseilles was in origin a Greek colony founded by Phocaeans ca. 600 B.C. and in this period enjoyed the status of an allied state with respect to Rome. Therefore, although it was located in the Roman province of *Gallia Narbonensis*, it was technically a sovereign state and could serve as a haven for Roman exiles. Cicero's client Milo retired to Massilia in 52 B.C. after he was convicted of the murder of P. Clodius, as did Verres in 70 B.C. when he was prosecuted by Cic. for extortion. In the *Second Catilinarian*, delivered on the day after Catiline's departure, Cic. alludes to the false report that Catiline intended to go into voluntary exile at Massilia (2.14, 2.16).

non quo . . . sed uti: contrast with 33.1; here *non quo* is causal, and the subjn. is normal because the reason given is expressly denied and therefore hypothetical (cf. 14.7).

conscius: vid. 14.3n. for the subjective sense of *conscius*; for the dat. and obj. gen., vid. 22.2n.

foret: the future sense of this form of the impf. subjn. (cf. 21.1n.) may explain the shift from *esse* in the previous clause, which refers to a contemporaneous circumstance.

oreretur: the spelling of this word in the MSS of S. fluctuates between *oriretur* and *oreretur*. Both forms are apparently correct, although the forms borrowed from the 3rd conj. are generally preferred for the pres. indic. and impf. subjn.

(3) *Q. (Lutatius) Catulus*: cos. in 78 B.C., he was instrumental in suppressing the rebellion raised by his colleague M. Lepidus in 77, and was censor with M. Crassus in 65. He was a leading spokesman of the conservative faction (*optimates*) and vigorously opposed the extraordinary commands entrusted to Pompey by the *lex Gabinia* in 67 and the *lex Manilia* in 66. Earlier in 63, he was defeated by Julius Caesar when he stood for the office of *pontifex maximus* recently left vacant by the death of Metellus Pius (49.2). [His father, Q. Lutatius Catulus (cos. 102 B.C.), who shared a triumph with C. Marius over the Cimbri at Vercellae in 101 B.C., perished in the Marian massacres of 87 B.C. Revenge was perhaps the motive when Catiline executed Marius Gratidianus (vid. 5.2n.) at the graveside of the elder Catulus during the Sullan reign of terror ([Q. Cic.] *Comm. Pet.* 10; Val. Max. 9.2.1; Florus 2.9.26; Lucan 2.173ff), and this incident may provide an early indication of the bond of friendship that seems to have existed between Catulus and Catiline for some time (vid. 35.1n.).]

exemplum: the same formula is used only once elsewhere in S. (44.4) to introduce the letter that Lentulus sent to Catiline. The latter document can be compared with the version of it given by Cic., and S. is found to be in substantial agreement. This fact tends to establish the authenticity of the letter attributed to Catiline, and its genuineness is further supported by a number of un-Sallustian words and expressions (e.g., *commendatio, satisfactio, conscientia de culpa, me dius fidius, statum dignitatis non obtinebam, aes alienum meis nominibus, honore honestatos, commendo*). Where S. does not claim to reproduce a faithful copy of an original document, he prefers the expression noted at 20.1n.

CHAPTER 35

(1) *L. Catilina Q. Catulo*: sc. *salutem dicit*, the standard salutation in letters, commonly abbreviated *S.D.*

re cognita: a cryptic allusion to Catulus' support when Catiline was accused of incest with the Vestal Fabia (vid. 15.1n.); *cognita* is nom. in agreement with *fides*.

fiduciam: "confidence," a word that S. uses elsewhere only in the *Hist.*; substituted here for the more usual *fidem*, which the author has already used just above in a slightly different sense ("loyalty") and wishes to avoid repeating.

commendationi: this looks ahead to the request at the end of this letter that Catulus look after the interests of Catiline's wife (35.6).

(2)   *defensionem*: a formal defense in response to one's critics as opposed to *satisfactionem*, which is a personal apology or explanation offered to a friend.

in novo consilio: "in <adopting> this new course of action" (cf. 51.8); these words appear to be deliberately ambiguous. Possibly they are intended as a subtle allusion to his decision to adopt the course of revolution (*res novae*) and join Manlius at Faesulae; alternatively, they could be designed to keep up the pretense that he was going into self-imposed exile.

de culpa: a colloquial expression in place of the more usual obj. gen. It is all the more awkward from being made to depend on *conscientia*, which is itself the obj. of a prep. The same assertion was attributed to Catiline in his explanation of his decision to go into voluntary exile (34.2).

quam: acc. object of *cognoscas*, which is the only instance in S. of the subjn. depending on *licet*; elsewhere S. prefers the inf. (e.g., 3.1, 13.2, 33.1). The antecedent of the relative pronoun is *satisfactionem*.

me dius fidius: sc. *iuvet*, an expression meaning "believe me" (lit., "so help me the god of truthfulness"). The expression is especially common in comedy and the colloquial prose of letters, but it is also used sparingly by Cic. in his orations.

(3)   *fructu*: abl. of separation with *privatus*, which, despite its literal meaning here, provides an awkward verbal contrast with *publicam* in the next clause.

statum dignitatis: "the position of my prestige"; *status* refers to the political or social standing that one possesses, not that to which one aspires. Therefore, *obtinere* is used in the usual sense of "maintain," "preserve," rather than "obtain." By these words Catiline does not refer to his recent failure to obtain the consulship, which he has already mentioned (*fructu . . . privatus*), but he describes the effect of his defeat in the past two elections on his social and political prestige which is now impaired (35.4 *relicuae dignitatis*). *Dignitas* describes both the respect and worthiness that were felt to belong to an individual and ultimately rested upon the tenure of high political office. It could be acquired by holding office, but it could also, like *nobilitas* (vid. 5.1n.), be inherited from one's ancestors. Catiline's complaint is reminiscent of Caesar's appeal to his slighted *dignitas* as one of the justifications for beginning the Civil War in 49 B.C. (e.g., Caes. *BCiv.* 1.7.7, 1.9.2).

miserorum: vid. 20.1n.; Catiline claims to look after the interests of the *miseri* according to his custom, just as S. later remarks that it was the custom of Crassus to favor the *mali* (48.8).

meis nominibus: a technical expression (abl. of description) with *aes alienum*, which is to be supplied with *alienis nominibus* below. The former debts were loans that Catiline raised on his own account, and therefore his name appeared in the ledgers (*tabulae*, vid. 21.2n.) next to these sums. The pl. suggests that a number of these personal debts were outstanding with various creditors. The latter debts (*alienis nominibus*) were either loans to Catiline's friends, for which he agreed to stand surety, or more likely the loans referred to at 24.2, which were contracted by the friends of Catiline for his use in financing the conspiracy, especially the activities of Manlius at Faesulae.

possem: although quite a few of the best MSS offer the reading *non possem*, several (**A**, **D**, **F**) show signs that *non* was inserted by a corrector who perhaps misunderstood the force of *quin*. Since *non quin* is equivalent to *non quod . . . non* and is intended to put forward a rejected reason that is stated in the form of a negative proposition, the addition of *non* before *possem* is not desired, and it should not be retained unless it can possibly be justified as a colloquialism. Instances of a further *non* after *quin* may be found in Cic. (e.g., *Pis.* 3), but the additional negative always cancels, rather than reinforces, the original negative sense of *quin*, which is just the opposite of the desired sense in this passage: "not because I was not able." Another solution, if *non* is retained, is to emend *quin* to *quia*, an easy change to justify paleographically and one that has already been made in some MSS, usually by a second hand. Catiline's claim that he is financially solvent is contradicted by 5.7. There were, however, according to Cic., a number of conspirators who could have liquidated their assets and settled with their creditors if they had been willing to make the sacrifice (vid. 33.1n.).

persolveret: the loose connection of this clause with the one preceding has given rise to great confusion in the MSS. If *et*, which is adopted by most modern editors, is the correct reading, the statement is best viewed as a parenthetical aside. The subjn. is then most easily interpreted as potential referring to past time ("would have satisfied"), rather than depending on *non quin*.

non dignos homines: clearly a reference to Cic., who was a *novus homo*, and possibly meant to include L. Murena as well, who was one of the successful candidates for the consulship in 63 and was the first member of his family to hold this office.

honore honestatos: the alliteration with *homines* is heightened by this *figura etymologica*, which is a feature of archaic Latin and is perhaps designed to emphasize Catiline's indignation. This is the only instance of the verb *honestare* in S., but it is used often by Cic. in the sense of "to dignify" or "embellish."

alienatum: "discarded," "abandoned" by those who ought to have supported him. This word provides another example of inelegance after the repetition of the word *alienus* just above.

(4) *Hoc nomine*: "on this account," an expression borrowed from the sphere of business and frequently used, especially in letters, as a synonym for *causa*.

pro: vid. 22.3n.; the prepositional phrase is to be taken with *satis honestas*, which echoes *honore honestatos* above.

relicuae dignitatis: cf. 35.3n. *statum dignitatis*. This is no idle boast since S. asserts that Catiline died mindful of his *dignitas* on the day his rebel forces were crushed by the consular army (60.7).

(5) *vellem*: an epistolary impf. standing for the present at the time of writing, but the act is described as past relative to the time when the recipient of the letter will read about it (cf. 53.6n.). Apparently Catiline wrote this letter on the night of his departure from Rome.

(6) *fidei*: this picks up the opening words of the letter; dat. to be taken with both *commendo* and *trado*. Its postponement after the first verb is perhaps another indication of hasty composition.

defendas: a colloquial use of the jussive subjn. in place of the more usual imperative. It is loosely connected with a verb of petition that is to be supplied from the expression *per liberos tuos rogatus* (= *rogo*).

Haveto: an archaic fut. imperative (= *ave*) in place of the more formal *vale*, which is the word preferred by Cic.

CHAPTER 36

(1) *C. Flaminium*: nothing further is known about this figure. Possibly he was, like Manlius, one of Sulla's veterans who had been settled in the region (vid. 16.4n.).

Arretino: a district taking its name from the town Arretium in northern Etruria (cf. 27.1n.) through which Catiline had to pass on his journey to Faesulae. According to Cic. (*Cat.* 2.6), Catiline left

Rome by the *via Aurelia*, apparently in order to effect a rendez-vous with some of his supporters who were waiting for him at Forum Aurelium (*Cat.* 1.24).

exornat: "equipped," pres. indic. as usual in a *dum* clause.

fascibus: vid. 18.5n. Cic. several times refers to these insignia of *imperium*, which Catiline illegally assumed (*Cat.* 2.13; *Sull.* 17). By this act, Catiline behaved as though he had been invested with the promagisterial *imperium* which was commonly granted to field commanders (Plut. *Cic.* 16.4; App. *BCiv.* 2.3).

(2) *hostis*: "public enemies" (cf. 31.8n.) predicate acc. with *iudicat*. By this act, the senate outlawed Manlius and Catiline and declared a state of war to exist against them.

quam: its antecedent is *diem*, although elsewhere S. usually treats this word as m. even when it refers to a fixed day. The only other example of the f. occurs at *Jug.* 68.2.

liceret: on this use of the subjn., vid. 30.6n. Secondary sequence is employed in this subordinate clause after *statuit*, which is probably historical present, while below after *decernit*, primary sequence is used for the sake of vividness.

sine fraude: "without penalty" (= *damno*), an old legal sense of the word (lit., "dishonesty," "deception").

ab armis discedere: vid. 34.1n.

praeter: conj. = *praeterquam*, *nisi*, to be taken with *condemnatis*. This is a comparatively rare usage of this word outside poetry and later prose authors.

condemnatis: dat. to be taken either with *liceret*, or more likely as balancing *multitudini*, which goes with *diem statuit* as a dat. of ref. It takes a gen. of the crime (*rerum capitalium*).

(3) *dilectum habeant*: this supplements the *s.c.u.* of 29.2 and the preparations to be carried out by the proconsuls (30.3) and praetors (30.5).

(4) *Ea tempestate*: vid. 7.1n. The digression on Roman political affairs that is introduced at this point (down to 39.5) serves to divide the monograph roughly in half and provides a pause before S. describes the suppression of the dangers that he has recounted in the first part of his narrative. By stressing the wide support enjoyed by Catiline among the urban masses, S. draws attention to the danger from within the city that seriously threatened Cicero's attempts to suppress the conspiracy.

multo: this use of *multo* to intensify the superlative is archaic. It is used sparingly by Cic. and in his later works seems to be confined mainly to the adj. *maximus*. *Longe* is preferred by Cic. and Caes.

with the superlative, but this usage is found only once in S. (*Jug.* 9.2).

maxume miserabile: for this means of forming the superlative, vid. 1.3n. The statement is intensified by the alliteration of *m*.

ad occasum ab ortu: the usual order of these words is reversed for the sake of variety (vid. 10.1n.).

otium atque divitiae: cf. 10.2; this whole digression resumes the general analysis (chapts. 6–13) of the growth of corruption in Roman society that S. offered as a preface to the conspiracy proper. He now focuses on the conditions in the post-Sullan era and brings his account down to the year 63.

affluerent: by zeugma (cf. 12.2n.) this verb is made to describe the abundance of *otium* as well as *divitiae*, although it is strictly appropriate only with the latter.

seque remque: vid. 9.3n.

perditum irent: an archaic expression consisting of a supine of purpose with a verb of motion: "they were proceeding/undertaking to destroy." The subjn. is due to the generic nature of the relative clause.

(5) *Namque*: this introduces a reason corroborating *obstinatis animis* above.

duobus senati decretis: abl. absol. to be taken concessively (cf. 11.4): "despite the existence of . . ." The two decrees are the one referred to above (36.2) and the one passed earlier that offered a reward for information about the conspiracy (30.6). On the form *senati*, vid. 30.3n.

inductus: *quisquam* must be supplied from the following clause.

patefecerat . . . discesserat: the plupf. (cf. 18.6n.) implies that these acts are being described relative to a later point in the past, e.g., the day fixed by the senate's decree (36.2).

tanta vis morbi: the logical subject is supplied by the word in the gen.: "a disease of such great intensity" (vid. 8.3n.). Hypallage is introduced because there is no gen. sing. of *vis*.

atque uti: this is the reading of all the principal MSS (*uti* confimed by Festus 490.33L). The presence of *atque* makes it necessary to take *uti* in the sense of *quasi* qualifying this bold expression. Since this is an extremely rare meaning of *uti* (but, cf. *Hist.* 4.46M *qui quidem mos ut tabes*), several modern editors adopt the emendation *ac veluti*, which brings this passage in line with a strikingly similar expression in the *Jug.* (32.4) which contains many verbal echoes: *tanta vis avaritiae* [*in*] *animos eorum veluti tabes invaserat*.

plerosque: an example of a transferred epithet which logically should modify *civium*.

CHAPTER 37

(1) *aliena*: the metaphor of disease introduced above by *morbi* and *tabes* suggests that *aliena* in this context means "disturbed," "frenzied" (a sense which may be illustrated by the expression *alienata mens* = "insanity").

cuncta plebes: the proletariat in general; it is not meant to be taken in this instance as merely the plebeians proper as opposed to the patricians. The older spelling *plebes* (as opposed to *plebs*) is used only twice in the *Cat.* (cf. 37.4) but is the preferred form in the *Jug.* and *Hist.* (11:2).

studio: abl. of cause (cf. *odio* 37.3) with the obj. gen. *novarum rerum* (cf. 28.4n. and *nova* below, 37.3).

(2) *adeo*: "indeed," strengthening the demonstrative pronoun as at 37.11, where emendation is accepted by most editors for *ideo* of the MSS.

(3) *bonis*: cf. 33.2n.

invident: the unexpressed subject (*ei*) of this vb. supplies the antecedent of *quibus*. The rapid succession of six clauses in asyndeton provides a striking example of S.'s fondness for this device, which is a characteristic feature of his plain and simple style.

turba: "turmoil," in the abstract rather than the concrete sense ("crowd"); abl. of means with *aluntur*.

sine cura: explained by the *quoniam* clause; poverty places one in the position of having nothing to lose.

(4) *ea vero*: the demonstrative refers to and emphasizes *urbana plebes* (cf. 12.5n.).

praeceps: "reckless," i.e., headlong in their eagerness to join the conspiracy (cf. 25.4).

(5) *Primum omnium*: answered by *deinde* below; *omnium* is neut. and a partitive gen. Five classes in all are distinguished by S.—the third through fifth being introduced by *praeterea*, *praeterea*, and *ad hoc*—while the first group is subdivided into three categories by *qui ubique*, *alii*, and *postremo omnes*.

ubique: "anywhere," cf. 21.1n.

probro . . . petulantia: abls. of respect with *praestabant* ("excel"), a verb which normally is used in connection with virtues rather than vices. Here it contributes to the alliteration of *p*.

per dedecora: adverbial, cf. 13.2n.

patrimoniis amissis: the abl. absol. is employed for the sake of variety in place of a relative clause parallel to the one above and serves almost as an abl. of description.

sicut in sentinam: "as if into the bilge of a ship"; Cic. often uses this metaphor likening the urban rabble to the dregs of a ship's hold.

(6)   *multi*: this may be a reference to Sulla's veterans themselves (cf. 16.4), but since S. is enumerating classes of the *urbana plebes* who favored Catiline's schemes, he is probably still referring to those in the city populace who witnessed the rise of Sulla's followers.

ex gregariis militibus: it is true that in 81 B.C. Sulla replenished the senatorial order, which had been seriously depleted by the civil wars of the 80's, and permanently increased the total membership of the senate by doubling its previous size from 300 to 600. However, despite S.'s sweeping assertion that common soldiers were elevated to the rank of senator, only one such soldier is known by name, the centurion L. (?) Fufidius (S. *Hist.* 1.55.22M; Oros. 5.21.3), and it is more likely that most of the Sullan additions were drawn from the equestrian order (vid. Livy, *Per.* 89).

ita divites: enrichment of Sulla's partisans came from the proscriptions (cf. 51.33–34). One centurion alone, L. Luscius, is reported to have amassed a fortune amounting to 10 million sesterces (Ascon. p. 90C.25–26)—vid. 30.6n. for comparative figures.

regio victu atque cultu: abls. of manner; the two nouns are virtually synonymous, but when distinguished, *victus* refers especially to food and drink, while *cultus* refers to other refinements of civilization (vid. 13.3n.). *Regio* in the sense of "lavish," "befitting a king" is mainly poetic and chosen deliberately to emphasize the excessive nature of this wealth (cf. 5.6n.).

χ *foret*: subjn. standing for a future indicative in *oratio recta*. The conditional clause is in virtual indirect discourse since it expresses a thought within the mind of the subject of *sperabat*.

sperabat: attracted into the singular by *quisque*, which stands in apposition with the grammatical subject *multi*. Ordinarily the verb would be in the pl. (cf. 38.3), but here the distance between the subject and verb has brought about the change to the singular.

(7)   *iuventus*: the collective sense of this noun (vid. 5.2n.) accounts for the pl. demonstrative below, *eos = iuvenes* (cf. 16.1n.).

manuum mercede: "by manual labor" (lit., "the wages of their hands").

privatis atque publicis largitionibus: the former refers especially to the banquets and gifts furnished by patrons to their clients and by candidates for office to the general populace. The latter would include the public festivals and monthly grain dole which was further subsidized by the state in 62 B.C. through legislation passed by Cato (Plut. *Caes.* 8.4; *Cat. Min.* 26.1) and extended to an estimated 200,000 recipients.

malum publicum: "the general state of corruption," "public ills," a term coined by analogy with the more common expression *bonum publicum*, "the common good" (e.g., 38.3). S. perhaps adopted it from Cato (37.17J).

(8) *Quo*: "wherefore" (vid. 1.3n.).

mirandum est: the subject is supplied by the acc. and inf. *homines . . . consuluisse*.

malis moribus, maxuma spe: abls. of description qualifying *homines* and introduced for variety after the adj. *egentis*. The alliteration of *m* serves to emphasize the enormity of this depravity.

iuxta ac: "just as," used to relate the two dats. dependent on *consuluisse*, and in this context, the meaning is: "they had as little regard for the commonwealth as they had for themselves" (cf. 2.8n.).

(9) *quorum*: to be taken as a possessive gen. with *parentes, bona*, and *ius*. The unexpressed antecedent *ei* is supplied by the subject of *exspectabant*.

ius . . . inminutum erat: in addition to suffering the personal loss of family members and family property, the children of the proscribed were prohibited by the *lex Cornelia* (82 B.C.) from holding public office for two generations (Vell. 2.28.3–4; Plut. *Sull.* 31). An attempt was made to rescind this disqualification in 63, but the proposal was successfully opposed by Cic. and others on the grounds that the repeal of this admittedly unpopular law would cause turmoil in the state (Cic. *Pis.* 4; Quint. 11.1.85). Eventually the restrictions on the descendants of proscribed persons were lifted in 49 when Caesar became dictator (Plut. *Caes.* 37.1; Suet. *Iul.* 41.2).

haud sane alio animo: i.e., with the same attitude as those described above.

(10) *atque*: to be taken with *aliarum*: "other than." *Partes senatus* is a periphrasis for the *optimates* (vid. 19.2n.), just as in the *Jug.* (43.1) S. uses *partes populi* for the corresponding faction that is commonly styled the *populares* in other authors.

ipsi: for the sake of variety *malebant* is construed with both an acc.

and inf. (*conturbari rem publicam*) and a complementary inf. (*valere*), whose subject *ipsi* is put in the nom. since it is identical with the subject of the main verb.

(11) *Id <ad>eo malum*: vid. 37.2n.; the "evil" referred to is the divisive opposition to the senate's leadership that led some politicians to prefer a state of turmoil if they could not prevail by constitutional means. The source of this opposition lay chiefly in the tribunate, which was curtailed by Sulla in 81 but restored to its former potency in 70, an interval of time which S. loosely describes as *multos post annos*.

CHAPTER 38

(1) | *tribunicia potestas restituta est*: ten tribunes were elected annually in this period by the plebeian assembly (*concilium plebis*). They were not technically magistrates of the Roman people since they were not elected by the whole populace, but originally they were chosen to protect the interests of the humbler plebeians. In 81, the dictator Sulla restricted the tribunes' right to veto and pass new legislation and also disqualified tribunes from holding any subsequent office. The bar placed on a tribune's career was lifted in 75, and the unrestrained right of *intercessio* and legislative prerogatives were restored through legislation supported by the consuls Pompey and Crassus in 70.

adulescentes: vid. 3.3n.; apparently there was no minimum age requirement for this office since it was not part of the official *cursus honorum*. It was customary, however, in this period to hold the tribunate after the quaestorship and before the praetorship, for which the minimum age requirements were 30 and 39 respectively. S. himself was probably 34 years old when he was tribune in 52.

summam potestatem: since the tribunes were not elected by the whole *populus Romanus*, they did not possess *imperium*, and their power is always designated *tribunicia potestas*. This power, however, was considerable (hence *summam*) since they possessed the right to propose new legislation and could obstruct the action of other magistrates and the senate by means of their veto.

ferox: elsewhere in the *Cat.*, this adj. is mainly used to describe the boldest members of the conspiracy (e.g., 5.7 Catiline; 43.4 Cethegus; cf. 52.18). Only once is it used in a positive sense to describe warlike courage befitting a soldier (11.5). S.'s criticism of the excesses perpetrated by those who opposed the conservative faction in the senate tends to balance his account which is mainly critical of the *optimates*. It also reminds one of the turmoil caused by S. himself in his tribunate of 52 (vid. Introd. pp. 2–4).

senatum criminando: cf. 4.1n. *agrum colundo*.

fieri: historical inf., not dependent on *coepere* as *exagitare* and *incendere* are.

(2) *summa ope*: cf. 1.1n.

senatus specie: the gen. with *specie*, the abl. used adverbially and meaning "under the pretence," stands for *specie pro senatu*, in contrast with <*re vera*> *pro sua magnitudine*.

(3) *paucis . . . absolvam*: vid. 4.3n.

post illa tempora: i.e., since the consulship of Pompey and Crassus when the tribunate was revitalized.

agitavere: "disturbed," "troubled," as a result of striving for their own ascendancy (cf. 2.1n.).

honestis nominibus: *nomen* is used here in the sense of a name given to one's motives that disguises their true nature, i.e., a "professed reason." The description of this factional rivalry in which political slogans were used as a fair-sounding excuse for the pursuit of selfish domination appears to be inspired by Thucydides (3.82.8). On the perversion of moral terms and political slogans as reported elsewhere by S., cf. 12.1, 52.11.

alii . . . pars: cf. 2.1n.; in partitive apposition with the group denoted by the *quicumque* clause.

sicuti: = *quasi*, vid. 16.3n.

quo: = *ut*, vid. 11.5n. This purpose clause corresponds to the *sicuti* clause after *alii* and produces further dissymmetry.

bonum publicum: vid. 37.7n. *malum publicum*.

simulantes: *se defendere*, which may be understood from the context, is omitted to make this expression more terse.

quisque: standing in partitive apposition with the subject of *certabant* (cf. 37.6n. *sperabat*).

potentia: vid. 12.1n., and cf. below, 39.1.

(4) *modestia neque modus*: vid. 11.4n.; *illis* (dat.) refers to both factions mentioned above.

CHAPTER 39

(1) *ad bellum . . . Mithridaticum*: vid. 16.5n.

imminutae: sc. *sunt*. The long absence of Pompey from Rome (67–62 B.C.) left the forces opposed to the conservative faction of senators without their strongest military leader. Crassus, however, remained in the capital and was actively engaged in maintaining his own *potentia* by supporting popular causes (vid. 17.7n.).

paucorum potentia: vid. 19.2n. *boni*.

(2) *Ei*: i.e., the *pauci*, while *ceteros* below refers to their opponents, especially the tribunes, who sought power by championing the rights of the common people (38.1); cf. Catiline's complaint about this same state of affairs (20.7).

innoxii: "secure," "unmolested"; this meaning is rare and mainly confined to poetry and post-Augustan prose. More often this adj. is used in the active sense of "harmless" or "innocent" (e.g., 40.6).

quo . . . placidius tractarent: vid. 11.5n.; the oligarchs used the threat of prosecution (*iudiciis*, cf. 14.3) to restrain potential demagogues. *In magistratu* must refer especially to the tribunes, although the office was not technically a magistracy (vid. 38.1n.). S., however, uses the word *magistratus* elsewhere to describe the tribunate (e.g., *Jug*. 37.1). *Placidius* is apparently to be taken in the sense of "more moderately"; with *tractarent* ("manage," "govern," cf. 51.28), it denotes the opposite of *plebem exagitare . . . incendere* (38.1). Those (*ceteros*) who were not in sympathy with the aims of the conservative faction were forced by the threat of prosecution to keep the commons in line with the policy of the senate.

(3) *dubiis rebus*: abl. absol., "in a perilous state of affairs" (cf. *secundis rebus* = a condition of prosperity or success).

novandi spes: "hope of bringing about a revolution." S. seems to be the first author to use *novandi* absolutely in the sense of *res novandi* (cf. 55.1); doubtless the expression is influenced by the desire to avoid the repetition of the word *res* immediately following *rebus*.

eorum: referring especially to *ceteros* above.

(4) *aut aequa manu*: the addition of the abl. of manner introduced by *aut* (= "or at least") serves to correct or modify *superior* and states the minimum degree of success necessary for the hypothesis to remain valid. *Aequa manu* is a military expression meaning "with equal advantage," i.e., "a draw."

clades atque calamitas: virtual synonyms paired for the sake of alliteration; the two words are treated as forming a single entity, hence the number of *oppressisset*.

illis: dat. depending upon *licuisset* and defined by the relative clause. S. refers either to Catiline and those who favored revolution or, more probably, to the factions on either side. Everyone stood to lose if Catiline was even partially successful in the first encounter. Chaos was bound to follow, and the situation would pass beyond

the control of the existing government as well as the revolutionaries.

adepti forent: the subjn. is probably due to the fact that the antecedent *illis* is indefinite. Therefore, the relative clause is one of
characteristic and may be translated concessively: "although victorious." If, however, *illis* is intended as a reference to the Catilinarians, then the subjn. is best interpreted conditionally in an
essentially contrary to fact supposition in past time as if S. had
written *si* in place of *qui*.

quin: = *ut non* (cf. 53.6), introducing a negative result clause
employed in a limiting sense after the negative *neque . . . licuisset*:
"they would not have been permitted to enjoy it for long without
someone snatching. . . ."

defessis et exsanguibus: dat. of separation with *extorqueret* and
referring to the group denoted by *illis* above; *exsanguis* (lit.,
"bloodless," "pale," cf. 15.5) is used here as a virtual synonym for
defessus. The struggle would exhaust them and drain them of
energy and resources.

qui plus posset: *plus* is an internal acc. with *posset*, the combination being equivalent to *potentior esset*. This clause defines the
subject of *extorqueret*, and the subjn. is employed because of the
indefinite nature of the antecedent. Possibly this is an allusion to
Crassus, who was suspected of being active behind the scenes (vid.
17.7n.). More likely, however, S. is thinking of Pompey, who had
vast military resources at his disposal and might welcome a pretext
for not disbanding his army upon returning to Italy (cf. 19.2n.).
Pompey had adopted similar tactics in 71 when he returned with
his army from Spain and blunted Crassus' victory in the war with
Spartacus (vid. 17.7n.). Pompey's former lieutenant Metellus
Nepos, who was tribune in 62 (vid. 30.5n.), unsuccessfully attempted to pass a bill early in the year that would have empowered
Pompey to restore order in Italy. This maneuver apparently took
place before Catiline's army was decisively defeated early in
January—perhaps Jan. 3rd (Plut. *Cic.* 23.2, *Cato Min.* 26; Dio
37.43.1–3; cf. Cic. *Fam.* 5.2.8). Many suspected that the general
was displeased that Cic. had handled the crisis so successfully. Cic.,
in fact, complains of the cool reception with which Pompey
greeted the news that the commonwealth had been preserved from
danger (*Fam.* 5.7.3). According to Plutarch (*Cic.* 18.1), the conspirators planned to kidnap Pompey's children on the night when the
massacre was to be carried out in Rome so that they could bargain
with the general and neutralize the danger to the success of their
new regime from that quarter.

(5) *Fuere tamen*: S. has just described the likelihood that many would
     have joined the fighting if Catiline had held his own in the first
     battle. To prove this contention, he refers to another sizeable group
     that actually set out to join the insurgents even before the outcome
     of the first engagement had been decided.

     Fulvius, senatoris filius: the father and son are not otherwise
     known, but Val. Max. (5.8.5) and Dio (37.36.4) both report this
     incident (cf. 17.4n.). It was rare in this period for a father to exer-
     cise his *patria potestas* against the life of his children. Although a
     pater familias technically had the power of life and death over his
     children, the relatively few recorded instances of the application of
     this power are mainly confined to the early Republic.

(6) *Isdem temporibus*: with these words S. resumes his narration of the
     conspiracy which was interrupted by the digression at 36.4. On the
     orthography of *isdem* for *eisdem*, vid. Cic. *Orat*. 157.

     quoscumque: the unexpressed antecedent supplies the direct object
     of *sollicitabat*.

     moribus . . . fortuna: abls. of respect with *idoneos*, which is to be
     construed with the dat. *novis rebus*.

     cuiusque modi: gen. of description virtually equal to *quodlibet* and
     modifying *genus*: "men of every sort" (lit., "a class of every sort of
     men"). The expression is pleonastic and substituted for the simpler
     cuiusque generis homines, which S. uses elsewhere (e.g., 24.3). In
     addition to Roman citizens, Lentulus not only attempted to recruit
     the support of the Allobroges, who were foreigners and thus likely
     to compromise the claim of the conspirators to represent the down-
     trodden *plebs*, but he also advocated the enlistment of slaves (vid.
     24.4n.).

     quod modo: a relative clause of characteristic qualifying *genus* and
     stating a proviso or restriction (= *dummodo*): "which at least would
     be of use in war," i.e., provided that they were useful in war.

     foret: = *futurum esse* (vid. 21.1n.).

CHAPTER 40

(1) *P. Umbreno*: Cic. calls him a freedman (*libertinus*) and confirms
     that he was responsible for introducing the ambassadors of the
     Allobroges to Gabinius (*Cat*. 3.14). Along with Cassius, Annius (vid.
     17.3n.), and Furius, he escaped immediate arrest when the conspir-
     acy was detected but was sentenced to death together with the
     other five conspirators who were in custody (50.4).

     legatos Allobrogum: the Allobroges were a Celtic tribe whose terri-
     tory was situated in the foothills of the Alps within the province of

Gallia Transalpina. They inhabited the region between the Isère and Rhône rivers and were brought under Roman control in 121 B.C. by Q. Fabius Maximus, who took the agnomen *Allobrogicus* in honor of his conquest (Caes. *BGall.* 1.45; Livy, *Per.* 61). Financial conditions in Transalpine Gaul were apparently worsened when L. Murena (cos. 62 B.C.) assisted Roman creditors in collecting the debts that were owed to them by the provincials when he was governor of this province in 64 (Cic. *Mur.* 42). This will account for the presence of the ambassadors in Rome whom the Allobroges sent to request relief from the senate (cf. 40.3).

requirat: the *ut* clause expresses an indirect command depending upon the expression *negotium dat* which contains the notion of a verb of requesting. Primary sequence is employed for the sake of vividness after the main verb in the historical pres.

possit: subjn. because the *si* clause is part of the indirect command.

existumans: this governs the indirect statement *facile eos . . . posse*.

publice privatimque: "both as a nation and individually."

oppressos: the participle is to be taken in a causal sense and is used in place of a *quod* clause, which would balance the following *praeterea quod*.

natura: abl. of respect with *bellicosa*; on their warlike disposition, vid. 41.2.

esset: subjn. (suboblique) because the *quod* clause is subordinate to the indirect statement. The sequence, however, after the main verb in the historical pres. has shifted to secondary.

(2) *negotiatus erat*: "had engaged in business"; Cic. reports that the province of Gaul contained a large number of Roman *negotiatores* (traders and bankers), who were involved in every aspect of the provincial economy (*Font.* 11).

civitatium: this is one of the commonest 3rd decl. f. nouns in -*tas* to preserve the i-stem form in the gen. pl. This spelling of the gen. pl. is attested 66 times in Livy, for instance, as opposed to *civitatum* only three times.

notus . . . noverat: "was known to and knew"; the perf. of *nosco* ("learn") is used in a present sense meaning "to know," while the plupf. serves as the simple past.

eius: i.e., *civitatis*; *casum* refers to the difficult circumstances in which the Allobroges found themselves.

tantis malis: best taken as a dative depending upon *exitum* (sc. *fore*), an indirect statement governed by *sperarent*.

(3)   *Postquam . . . videt*: vid. 21.5n.

   auxili: partitive gen. with *nihil* (cf. *consili* 41.1): "no aid."

   esset: subjn. because this clause states a reason that is attributed to the Allobroges and not given as S.'s own opinion. The main verb *videt* in the historical pres., which governs the indirect statements, accounts for the secondary sequence (cf. 40.1n. *esset*).

   miseriis suis: dat., cf. 40.2n. *tantis malis*.

   si modo: the indic. is normal after *si modo*, which adds a proviso that limits the statement contained in the main clause (cf. 51.37).

   effugiatis: a rel. clause of characteristic defining *rationem*.

(4)   *sui misereretur*: an indirect petition depending on the historical inf. *orare*. The reflexive pronoun refers to the subject of the main verb.

   nihil . . . esse: the indirect statement depends upon a verb of saying which is implied by *orare*.

   facturi essent: a relative clause of result anticipated by *tam asperam* and *tam difficile*.

(5)   *D. Bruti*: vid. 25.1–2n.

   aliena consili: this is the only instance in S. of the gen. with *alienus* (= "unfavorable"). Elsewhere it is used absolutely, apart from being construed once with *a* and the abl. (51.17) and once with the simple abl. or dat. (56.5) in the sense "inconsistent with." There seems to be a deliberate play on the words *alienus* and *propinquus*.

   nam: understood is the thought: "there was no danger of their conversation being overheard" (cf. 7.2n.).

   ab Roma: normally a preposition is not used with the names of cities and towns to indicate separation unless the word is meant to denote the district surrounding the place named. This will account for the absence of *ab* in most of our MSS, which must be corrected from the citation of this passage in the grammarians. S. always employs a preposition, rather than the simple ablative, with *absum*, and this usage with place names seems to be archaic.

(6)   *Gabinium*: vid. 17.4n. Gabinius was an *eques* and would inspire more confidence in the foreign ambassadors than Umbrenus, a mere freedman.

   inesset: normally in the *Cat.*, S. prefers primary sequence in a clause that depends directly on a verb in the historical pres., while secondary sequence is freely used in subordinate clauses.

   cuiusque generis: cf. 39.6n.

   innoxios: vid. 39.2n. Cic. (*Sull.* 36–39) describes a similar conference that the Allobroges had with the conspirator L. Cassius (vid. 17.3n.). According to Cic., Cassius implicated Autronius and many others to inspire confidence in the ambassadors, but he refused to commit himself when he was asked if Cic.'s client P. Sulla was a member of the plot.

operam suam: according to Cic. (*Cat.* 3.4, 3.9), the ambassadors were asked to raise a revolt in Gaul and furnish Catiline with horsemen for his cavalry.

CHAPTER 41

(1)   *caperent*: the subjn. in the indirect question stands for a deliberative subjn. *capiamus* in *oratio recta*.

(2)   *in spe victoriae*: by qualifying the prospects of their success in this way rather than writing *in victoria*, S. emphasizes the uncertainty of success which is picked up below by *incerta spe*. The Allobroges ran less risk by supporting the government, whose resources were greater than those of the conspirators.

maiores opes: in antithesis with *aes alienum*, while *tuta consilia* and *certa praemia* correspond to *studium belli* and *magna merces*.

certa praemia: the ambassadors were in fact rewarded by a vote of the senate on Dec. 4th (vid. 50.1n.).

(3)   *fortuna*: vid. 10.1n.

(4)   *Q. Fabio Sangae*: it was customary for the conqueror of a new territory and his family to become the unofficial representative (*patronus*) of the inhabitants of the region after it had been organized as a province and to look out for their interests in Rome (vid. 19.5n.). This man's name suggests that he was a descendant of Q. Fabius Maximus Allobrogicus (vid. 40.1n.).

(5)   *per Sangam*: to be taken with the following abl. absol.

praecipit: all the MSS read *praecepit*, which is generally emended to the present tense in virtue of the primary sequence in the jussive clauses. In the other two instances in S. where *praecipio* is construed with the pres. subjn., the MSS fluctuate between *praecepit* and *praecipit*. In this instance, if *praecepit* is retained, the pres. subjn. may possibly be explained as an example of the graphic construction, more vividly representing the imperatives of *oratio recta* (cf. 34.1n.).

ceteros: they were to extend their contacts beyond Umbrenus and Gabinius. This will account for the conference with Cassius mentioned above, 40.6n.

bene polliceantur: the adv. is used predicatively: "make grand promises."

quam maxume manufestos habeant: "bring out into the open to
the greatest possible extent," "get the most positive proof of their
guilt," as opposed to circumstantial or hearsay evidence—a technical term belonging to the legal sphere. *Manufestus* (lit., "caught in
the act") is commonly applied to criminal acts, but rarely to
persons outside of poetry and post-Augustan prose. For this form of
the superlative, vid. 1.3n.

CHAPTER 42

(1) *in Gallia citeriore atque ulteriore*: *Gallia citerior* comprised the
northern part of Italy south of the Alps and north of the Rubicon
River, while the further province of Gaul (*ulterior*) occupied the
southeast corner of modern-day France and was bounded by the
Rhône River on the north and the Cévennes Mts. on the west.

in agro Piceno, Bruttio, Apulia: a further instance of dissymmetry
which is produced by the triad in asyndeton consisting of the two
adjs. *Piceno* and *Bruttio* modifying *agro*, and the noun *Apulia*. For
the *ager Picenus* and Apulia, vid. 27.1n.; the *ager Bruttius* is the
district in the extreme southwestern part of the peninsula (the toe),
south of Lucania and across the Gulf of Tarentum from Apulia.
Cicero's brother Quintus is credited with putting down disturbances among the *Bruttii* during his praetorship in 62, while his
colleague M. Calpurnius Bibulus checked similar uprisings among
the *Paeligni* in central Italy (Oros. 6.6.7; cf. Dio 37.41.1). Apparently, however, not all of the Catilinarian sympathizers were
repressed since the senate in 61 commissioned C. Octavius, the
father of the future Emperor Augustus, to crush some refugees
from the army of Catiline and Spartacus who were still at large in
the countryside about Thurii (Suet. *Aug.* 31.1, 7.1).

motus: vid. 21.1n. *movere*.

(2) *quos ante . . . dimiserat*: vid. 27.1, 27.4.

inconsulte ac veluti per dementiam: for the dissymmetry, cf.
13.2n.

cuncta simul: "all things at once" (cf. 27.2 *multa simul*); below S.
uses the word *festinando* to describe this rash haste which recalls
the Elder Cato's definition of the verb *festinare*: *qui multa simul
incipit neque perficit, is festinat* (44.5–6J).

consiliis: "meetings."

armorum atque telorum: virtual synonyms, but where the two
words are used together, the former refers especially to defensive
equipment and weapons for close combat, while the latter denotes
offensive weapons, such as spears and javelins, that are thrown

from a distance.

portationibus: an extremely rare word, first attested in S.

(3)   *Ex eo numero*: i.e., *ex eorum numero*.

ex senatus consulto: possibly the *s.c.* that Cic. secured for Metellus soon after the sortition of the praetorian provinces (*Fam.* 5.2.3–4). In addition to the judicial authority mentioned here, the *s.c.* may have conferred consular *imperium* on Metellus and allowed him to enter his province while he was still praetor in 63.

causa cognita: a technical expression belonging to the legal sphere meaning "after a formal hearing" or "judicial investigation."

in citeriore Gallia: S. is in error, unless the fault lies with the trans-mission of the text, which should read *ulteriore*. L. Licinius Murena left his brother Gaius in charge of Gallia Transalpina when he returned to Rome to stand for the consulship in 63 (Cic. *Mur.* 89). The praetor Metellus Celer was sent to Picenum and charged with securing that region and the *ager Gallicus* (vid. 30.5n.). Pre-sumably his sphere of control was extended to include Cisalpine Gaul by the *s.c.* mentioned above.

C. Murena: sc. *in vincula coniecerat*.

CHAPTER 43

(1)   *ut videbatur*: the position of this clause within the abl. absol. favors the view that it is meant to qualify *paratis* rather than *magnis*.

constituerant: plupf. rather than pf. doubtless because this act is described relative to the events mentioned above, which occurred at a later date. The verb is made pl. by synesis as if S. had written *Lentulus ceterique*.

in agrum †Faesulanum†: either S. has committed a serious blunder, or the text is corrupt, since Catiline's plans called for the uprising in the city to break out when he had brought his army from Faesulae (*ex agro Faesulano*) to the vicinity of Rome (32.2, 43.2, 44.6). Clearly he had reached Faesulae long before Bestia entered office as tribune on Dec. 10th (36.1–2), and there is only a slight hint elsewhere that Catiline expected his supporters to raise a disturbance in Rome before he moved his army (56.4, 58.4). The fact that Appian (*BCiv.* 2.3) follows the version given here by our text implies that the error may have been due to S.'s carelessness rather than the poor transmission of the text. Various emendations have been proposed to make the passage designate a region in the vicinity of Rome (*Aefulanum, Falerianum*), but the matter must remain in doubt.

venisset: since the *cum* clause is strictly temporal, the subjn. is due to its subordinate nature within the *uti* clause depending upon *constituerant* and stands for a fut. pf. indic. of *oratio recta*.

L. Bestia: vid. 17.3n.

contione: S. does not date this public meeting, but Cic. (*Cat.* 3.10, cf. 3.17) and Plut. (*Cic.* 18.2) report that according to the testimony of the Allobroges on Dec. 3rd Lentulus and the other conspirators wanted the massacre and burning of Rome to take place on the *Saturnalia*, a festival on Dec. 17th when everyone would be in a relaxed and careless mood, while Cethegus was impatient and favored an earlier date. S., however, need not refer to the *Saturnalia* by the words *proxuma nocte* since the speech may well have been planned for Dec. 10th, when Bestia entered office as tribune, only to be postponed because of the uncertainty that Catiline and his army would arrive on time (cf. 43.3). Since the Saturnalia was a public festival, on which it would not be legal to hold an assembly of the people, if Bestia's speech is to be connected with the account given by Cic., perhaps it was postponed until Dec. 16th, which we know from surviving pre-Julian calendars was a *dies comitialis*, on which it was lawful to address the people.

actionibus: "acts," "measures," a rare meaning of this word in the pl., which normally refers to lawsuits.

optumo consuli: Cic. (*Att.* 12.21.1) complains that he received faint praise from Brutus, who described him with these very words in his pamphlet on Cato. Apparently Cic. took offense because Brutus magnified the role played by Cato's speech (vid. 52) in deciding the fate of the conspirators, and it may also have been the tone of his account and the context of the words *optumus consul* that injured Cic.'s pride. S. uses the superlative *optumus* sparingly in the *Cat*. In fact, this is the only instance of this word in the *Cat*. where it is applied directly to an individual rather than used in a distributive sense with *quisque* (e.g., 2.6, 8.5, 34.2). Finally, since the only surviving reference to Cic.'s displeasure is contained in a private document, which was not published until after the death of S., there is no reason for assuming that S. selected this description out of malice. If he had an ulterior motive for using the word *optumus*, it is more likely intended as an allusion to Bestia's criticism that Cic. was acting as a champion of the self-styled *optimates* (vid. 19.2n.).

coniurationis: by metonymy (vid. 14.1n.), an abstract is substituted for the concrete *coniuratorum*.

suum quodque: standing for *suum quisque*, which is the reading of several late MSS; *quodque* is a conjecture for the obviously corrupt *suum quaeque*, which is found in the bulk of the better MSS.

Quisque is quite often attracted into the case and gender of an accompanying *suus* (K-S i.645), and the two words may be taken together as virtually equivalent to a compound adj. = "their several."

(2) *ea*: "these," probably referring to the *negotia* rather than *multitudo* from the previous sentence since S. invariably treats the collective noun *multitudo* as sing. when it is the subject of a verb; with *divisa* sc. *esse*. According to Cic. (*Sull.* 52), the various tasks were assigned to the conspirators at the meeting on the night of Nov. 6–7th at Laeca's house (27.4).

Statilius et Gabinius: (vid. 17.4n.) subjs. of the first *uti* clause, which is governed by a verb of commanding implied by *divisa*; *uti* is also understood with the verbs *obsideret, aggrederetur, interficerent*, and *erumperent* below. Contrary to S., Cic. states on several occasions that Cassius Longinus was to oversee the firing of the city, a task that he had eagerly requested (*Cat.* 3.14, 4.13; *Sull.* 53). Possibly S.'s account reflects a change of plans since Cassius set out for Gaul in advance of the Allobroges, who left on Dec. 2nd (44.2).

duodecim: Plutarch (*Cic.* 18.2) inflates the number to 100.

quo tumultu: cf. 14.2n.; the confusion (*tumultus*) caused by the fires and efforts to contain them would cover the assaults against the house of Cic. and other senators. Plut. (l.c. above) reports that some of the conspirators were to block up the aqueducts and attack those who might try to extinguish the fires.

alius . . . alium: sc. *aggrederetur.*

filii familiarum: the singular *familias* (gen.) is the preferred form in set phrases such as *pater familias, mater familias*, etc., even when pl. S. seems to have adopted the less conventional *familiarum* (cf. 51.9) from the historian Sisenna, whom Varro cites as authority for this usage of the gen. pl. (*Ling.* 8.73). A *pater familias* exercised great control over the person and property of his children throughout his lifetime (vid. 39.5n.), and this will account for the desire on the part of some of these young men to gain their independence by means of parricide. Cic. probably alludes to this group when he refers to Catiline's effeminate and luxurious supporters who were to be seen lounging about the Forum and senate-house (*Cat.* 2.5; cf. *Att.* 1.14.5 *barbatuli iuvenes, totus ille grex Catilinae*).

(3) *parata atque decreta*: the former refers especially to their material resources (*copiis* above), the latter to their plans: "all the time those preparations and plans were being made."

illos . . . corrumpere: this indirect statement depends upon a verb of saying which is implied by *querebatur*.

dies prolatando: elsewhere S. uses *prolatare* to describe the postponement of events, but never with words denoting time; *dies*, therefore, probably means "the arrangements made for a certain day" which kept being moved up from one day to the next.

facto . . . consulto: abls. with *opus esse*.

adiuvarent: subjn. within an indirect statement (suboblique) standing for a fut. indic. of *oratio recta*.

languentibus aliis: abl. absol. best taken concessively; *aliis* probably stands loosely for *ceteris* (cf. 27.2n.), unless Cethegus deliberately uses *alii* rather than *ceteri* to show his contempt.

curiam: vid. 32.1n.

(4) *Natura*: abl. of respect with *ferox* and *vehemens*.

in celeritate putabat: vid. 2.2n.

CHAPTER 44

(1) *ex praecepto Ciceronis*: cf. 41.5.

item: elsewhere this word is sometimes used to add a final member to a series almost as an afterthought (e.g., 54.1), but here and at 46.3 it sets apart the person mentioned last as somehow exceptional. In both passages, the first group is summed up by *ceteri*, while the last member is dealt with separately.

signatum: the oath was to be in the form of a written document to which the conspirators would affix wax seals (*signa*) with their signet rings (cf. 47.3).

perferant: subjn. in a relative clause of purpose.

aliter: vid. 29.3n.

posse: the indirect statement depends upon a verb of saying which must be supplied from *postulant*.

(2) *dant*: the direct object *ius iurandum* must be supplied from the previous sentence.

eo: adv. = *in Galliam*, which is to be understood from the context, esp. *ad civis* above.

(3) *T. Volturcium . . . Crotoniensem*: apart from his role in giving evidence against the conspirators and the fact that he was a native of Croton in Bruttium and acquainted with the praetor Pomptinus (45.4), nothing further is known about this figure. He is doubtless a member of the class whom S. refers to at 17.4 as *domi nobiles*. S. implies that he was unaware of the plans that Cic. had made with the Allobroges since he resisted arrest on the night of the ambush (45.4).

pergerent: subjn. because the *prius quam* clause is part of the *ut* clause of purpose; secondary sequence after *mittit*, which is in the historical pres.

fide: = "guarantee," "confirmation," a common meaning with the verb *dare*; cf. 47.1 where *fide publica* means an assurance of protection on the part of the state, i.e., immunity from prosecution.

(4) *exemplum*: vid. 34.3n. S. gives a slightly more polished version of this letter than Cic., who appears to copy the original verbatim (*Cat.* 3.12): *Quis sim scies ex eo quem ad te misi. Cura ut vir sis et cogita quem in locum sis progressus. Vide ecquid tibi iam sit necesse et cura ut omnium tibi auxilia adiungas, etiam infimorum.* S. eliminates the colloquial expressions *scies ex eo* and *cura ut*, the latter of which occurs twice in the original, doubtless as a result of its hasty composition. The first sentence is made more periodic by shifting the verb *cognosces* to the final position, while the expressions *in quanta calamitate* and *quid tuae rationes postulent* are substituted for the vague abstractions in the original.

(5) *Qui sim*: as a precaution, Lentulus did not refer to himself or Catiline by name (confirmed by Cic. *Cat.* 3.12 *sine nomine*). The letter, however, bore his seal, which guaranteed its authenticity, and was in Lentulus' own handwriting. For the standard salutation, vid. 35.1n.

Fac: the subjns. *cogites, memineris, consideres,* and *petas*, with *ut* omitted as usual, all depend upon this word, which provides a polite periphrasis for the imperative when one person is addressing another who is his equal.

infimis: a veiled allusion to the slaves whom Lentulus urged Catiline to recruit more openly in the oral part of his message (44.6; cf. 24.4n.).

(6) *mandata*: an oral (*verbis*) message (cf. 32.3). Cic. (*Cat.* 3.8), upon whom S. may have relied here as his source, gives a similar account of this message which urged Catiline to avail himself of the support offered by slaves and to lead his army to Rome as quickly as possible.

quo consilio: this indirect question depends upon a verb of inquiry which is to be supplied from *mandata*, while the next two clauses presume a verb of saying and a verb of urging respectively.

iusserit: standing for *iussisti* in *oratio recta*, i.e., at 32.2.

CHAPTER 45

(1) *constituta nocte*: chiasmus is employed in lieu of a conjunction to set this abl. absol. apart from the one that precedes. As at 18.6 (vid. n.), and contrary to the usual practice, the logical subject of the verbs in the abl. absols. is not the subject of the main verb (*Cicero*), but rather we are to understand from the context a phrase such as "by the conspirators." *Cuncta* serves to establish the proper relationship between the subject of the main clause and the statements put in the abl. absols. The date is the night of Dec. 2nd–3rd; on the following day, Dec. 3rd, Cic. delivered his *Third Catilinarian* (3.5).

proficiscerentur: subjn. in a relative clause of purpose.

cuncta: one of the two accs. governed by *edocere* in the active voice is retained in the passive (cf. 25.2n. *docta*).

L. Valerio Flacco: son of the *consul suffectus* in 86 B.C., who was the author of the *lex Valeria* referred to at 33.2n. He had a wide range of military experience, first as a military tribune in Transalpine Gaul (ca. 82 B.C.) and Cilicia (78–76 B.C.), and later as a legate of Metellus Creticus (vid. 30.3n.) in Crete (68–66 B.C.) and of Pompey in Asia (66–65 B.C.). For his role on this occasion, vid. Cic. *Flacc.* 102. Following his praetorship, he governed the province of Asia in 62 and was successfully defended by Cic. in 59 on a charge of extortion arising out of his propraetorship. He is last heard of in 54.

C. Pomptino: possibly to be identified with the legate who served under Crassus in the war against Spartacus in 71 B.C. (Frontin. *Str.* 2.4.7). He relieved C. Murena of his command over Transalpine Gaul (vid. 42.3n.) in 62 and governed this province during the next two years in which he repressed a rebellion of the Allobroges (vid. 50.1n.). He was not allowed to celebrate a triumph, however, until 54, due to the opposition of Caesar's supporters. Later he served as a legate under Cic. in Cilicia (51–50 B.C.).

ponte Mulvio: this bridge (the modern Ponte Milvio), which lies about three miles north of the Forum, carries the *via Flaminia* across the Tiber River. Once they had passed over the bridge, the conspirators would have proceeded to Arretium and Faesulae along the *via Cassia*, which branches off the *via Flaminia* just after it crosses the Tiber and leads into northeastern Etruria.

Allobrogum comitatus: both the Gauls and their escort were to be taken into custody, but the main object of the seizure is emphasized by being made the direct object, while *Allobroges* stands in the gen. The pl. *comitatus* is unusual and perhaps intended to stress the size of this escort.

opus sit: "as the situation might require" (lit., "as there might be need for action"). The subjn. is employed owing to the subordinate nature of the *uti* clause within the indirect command (suboblique). Normally in S., secondary sequence is preferred in a clause that depends on a verb in the historical present if the subordinate clause stands first, but here the previous historical presents prepare the way for the pres. subjn.

permittit: sc. *ut* with *cetera . . . ita agant* (cf. 29.2n.); *eis* (dat.) is understood from *Flacco* and *Pomptino* above.

(2) *militares*: both were experienced military men (vid. 45.1nn.). The appositive may be taken almost in a causal sense explaining the smoothness of the operation.

sine tumultu: Cic. says that the preparations for the ambush were made *sine cuiusquam suspicione* (*Cat.* 3.5).

praesidiis conlocatis: Cic.'s personal bodyguard from Reate was among the forces under the praetors' command on this occasion (*Cat.* 3.5).

(3) *utrimque*: Cic. reports that the praetors concealed their troops in houses near either side of the bridge and closed in as soon as the Allobroges and conspirators began to cross (*Cat.* 3.5).

cito cognito consilio: the adv. *cito* is essential to the meaning of this abl. absol. since the Allobroges were apparently not advised of Cic.'s plans in advance (Cic. *Cat.* 3.6) but quickly sized up the situation and realized that this trap had been set by the consul to capture the documents that they had been urged to request (44.1).

(4) *multa*: an inner acc. object of the depon. participle *obtestatus*, which takes an acc. of the person to whom the appeal is made (cf. 33.5) and is here construed with *de* plus the abl.: "having made many appeals to Pomptinus for his own safety."

vitae: dat. with *diffidens* = "giving up hope in" (cf. 31.3); *vitae* is used for the sake of variety after *salute* just above.

dedit: historical pres. of *dedo*.

CHAPTER 46

(1) *propere*: according to Cic. (*Cat.* 3.6), the conspirators were captured *tertia fere vigilia exacta* (i.e., between three and four A.M.) and were brought to him *cum iam dilucesceret*.

(2) *cura atque laetitia*: taken up in the reverse order below by *laetabatur* and *anxius erat*, thus producing chiasmus; *gaudium* would have been a more flattering description of Cic.'s pleasure

since it describes the inner feeling of satisfaction, while *laetitia* commonly denotes the outward manifestation of joy, esp. unrestrained gladness (Cic. *Tusc.* 4.13). The words *cura . . . occupavere* are strikingly reminiscent of an expression in Homer (*Od.* 19.471) describing someone's reaction to a dramatic revelation.

porro: lit., "next," here equivalent to an adversative: "but," "on the other hand."

tantis civibus deprehensis: best taken as an abl. absol. rather than dat. or abl. depending upon *facto* within the indirect question. *Tantis* (= "such important") refers especially to the praetor Lentulus and the senator Cethegus, both of whom were patricians.

quid facto opus esset: "what ought to be done" (lit., "what should be necessary to be done"); when the logical object of the participle is expressed by an indefinite or interrogative pronoun (in this instance *quid*), it is often made the subject of the verb *esse*, and *opus* becomes a predicate nominative. According to Cic. (*Cat.* 3.7), many leaders of the state called upon him at his home after they had learned of the arrest on the Mulvian Bridge. Although they urged him to break the seals and examine the contents of the letters before he summoned the senate in case these documents should fail to justify bringing the matter before the senate, Cic. insists that he never wavered in his resolution to consult the senate in this crisis. Plut. (*Cic.* 19.4–20.2) assigns the doubts that assailed Cic. to a conference on the night preceding the debate on the punishment of the conspirators which took place on Dec. 5th. This conference was attended by Cic.'s brother Quintus (praetor 62 B.C.) and P. Nigidius Figulus (praetor 58 B.C.), who was one of the four senators chosen by Cic. to keep a written record of the interrogation of the witnesses on Dec. 3rd.

oneri: although Cic. was armed with the *s.c.u.*, his authority to punish Roman citizens without due process hinged upon the appropriateness of the circumstances in which he exercised this exceptional authority, and he could be called to account later after he had laid aside his office.

perdundae reipublicae: predicate gen. expressing tendency, vid. 6.7n.

(3)   *itemque*: vid. 44.1n.

Caeparium Terracinensem: another minor figure (cf. 44.3n.) identified here as a native of Tarracina, a town in Latium about sixty-five miles south of Rome on the *via Appia*. The description of his role in the conspiracy is confirmed by Cic. (*Cat.* 3.14), but beyond this nothing further is known about him.

(4)   *sine mora*: actually Cic. (*Cat.* 3.6) says that Lentulus came *tardissime*—probably because he had been up late the night before arranging the departure of the ambassadors.

cognito indicio: "having learned of the disclosure of the plot." At this point Caeparius could only know of the arrest of Volturcius and the ambassadors at the bridge and the summons of Cic. The sequel would not have been hard to imagine. The plupf. indicates that he fled before the others were brought before the senate.

(5)   *in aedem Concordiae*: the temple of Concord stood at the foot of the Capitoline Hill to the right of the *clivus Capitolinus* and overlooked the Forum. It was built in 367 B.C. by the dictator M. Furius Camillus to celebrate the reconciliation of the plebeians and patricians marked by the senate's acceptance of the Licinio-Sextian laws. It was rebuilt by the cos. L. Opimius in 121 B.C. to commemorate the restoration of order after the suppression of C. Gracchus and his supporters.

(6)   *Eo*: adv. referring to the Temple of Concord; likewise *eodem* below.

magnaque frequentia: best taken as an abl. absol. loosely used to describe the accompanying circumstances of the verb; with *eius ordinis*, understand *senatorii* (vid. 17.3n.). Cic. (*Cat.* 3.7) confirms that the meeting was well-attended, and S. says the same about the meeting on the 4th (48.6; cf. 50.3). Frequently meetings of the senate were sparsely attended in the late Republic except in times of crisis such as this one. Ordinarily many of the 600 members would be absent from the capital or unable to be present owing to official or private business. The *lex Cornelia* of 67 B.C. set a quorum of 200 members for certain types of important business, and apparently a meeting that drew up to 400 members qualified for the description *frequens* in the late Republic (e.g., Cic. *Att.* 1.14.5).

Volturcium cum legatis: Cic., however, (*Cat.* 3.8) states that Volturcius was brought before the senate first *sine Gallis*.

introducit: *introducere aliquem in senatum* is the standard expression for bringing a speaker or witness before the senate.

CHAPTER 47

1–4. Introductory Note: Cic. on his own authority appointed four senators to keep a written record of the interrogation of the witnesses on this occasion (*Sull.* 42), and similar arrangements seem to have been made for the meetings on Dec. 4th and 5th (Plut. *Cato Min.* 23). The men selected were C. Cosconius (praetor 63 B.C.), M. Valerius Messalla (cos. 53 B.C.), P. Nigidius Figulus (praetor 58 B.C.), and App. Claudius

Pulcher (cos. 54 B.C.). Not until 59 were the minutes of the senate published on a regular basis (Suet. *Iul.* 20.1), and even on the rare occasions before this when a record was made of a debate, it was customary for the magistrate to keep this documentary evidence in his private possession. There was, therefore, no official account of the senate's proceedings, and even in the case of *senatus consulta*, which were committed to writing and deposited in the *aerarium*, the Roman record office, it was not unheard of for forgeries to occur. Accordingly, Cic. took the additional precaution of having the minutes of this important meeting transcribed and published throughout Italy and the provinces without delay so that the testimony of the witnesses would be known to all and not subject to misrepresentation later when the immediate danger of the conspiracy had passed.

(1)   *consili*: partitive gen. with *quid*, the object of *habuisset*; *qua de causa* asks for his motive in adopting a certain course of action. The change of construction with *interrogatus* from *de* + abls. *itinere* and *litteris* to an indirect question provides another example of S.'s fondness for variation.

      alia: i.e., different from the truth, object of the historical inf. *fingere*.

      dissimulare: this is the only place in S. where *dissimulare* is construed with *de* + the abl. In classical Latin it normally takes an acc. or an acc. + inf.

      fide publica: vid. 44.3n.; best taken as an abl. absol. with *data* understood (cf. 48.4). This immunity was granted by the senate (Cic. *Cat.* 3.8 *iussu senatus*).

      omnia uti gesta erant: the main points of his testimony are summarized at 48.4.

      legatos: sc. *scire*: "he knew nothing more than the Allobroges knew <about the matter>."

      solitum: sc. *esse*; this inf. governs the complementary inf. *audire* and continues the indirect statement introduced by *docet*, while *audire* governs the further acc. and inf. *P. Autronium . . . esse.*

(2)   *sermonibus*: oral conversations in addition to the captured documents that bore Lentulus' seal (47.3). The following indirect statements stand in apposition with this word and depend upon a verb of saying which is easily supplied from the context (cf. 52.13).

      ex libris Sibyllinis: the official collection of Sibylline oracles was contained in three books which, according to legend, had been sold to Tarquinius Superbus, the last king of Rome, by the Cumaean Sibyl. These books were stored in the temple of Jupiter Capitolinus under the care of the *Quindecimviri Sacris Faciundis* (vid. 21.2n.)

and were consulted only in times of emergency by order of the senate. They were apparently written in Greek hexameters, and rather than being prophetic they generally prescribed the means for appeasing the gods in times of crisis, frequently by recommending the introduction of a new god or new rites for an existing god. When the original collection perished in the fire that destroyed the Capitoline temple of Jupiter in 83 B.C., the senate commissioned a fresh collection to be made from various sources in Italy and Asia. In addition, many forgeries, masquerading as genuine Sibylline oracles, continued to remain in private hands, and it is probably these unofficial oracles that inspired Lentulus' expectation that he would be the third Cornelius to become master of Rome (cf. Cic. *Cat.* 3.9; Plut. *Cic.* 17.4; App. *BCiv.* 2.4).

regnum: vid. 5.6n.

antea: sc. *fuisse* from *esse* which follows. The first of the Cornelii, L. Cornelius Cinna, dominated the Roman government during Sulla's absence in Asia (vid. 11.5) and held the consulship for four years in a row (87–84 B.C.). He was killed in 84 in a mutiny by his own army which he was preparing to lead across the Adriatic to Epirus, possibly to train these raw recruits in anticipation of an armed conflict with Sulla, who was about to return to Italy with his seasoned veterans. On L. Cornelius Sulla, the second Cornelius within recent memory who held absolute power at Rome, vid. 5.6, 11.4nn.

cui fatum foret: "to whom it was fated" (lit., "for whom it was fate"). The subject is supplied by the inf. *potiri*, which is construed with the gen. (*urbis*), as often in S., rather than the more usual abl. S. uses the abl. and gen. interchangeably with *potior*.

ab incenso Capitolio: the participial construction (vid. 17.1n.) is preferred to the abstract *incensio*, which is not attested in S. but is found in the corresponding description of this event by Cic. (*Cat.* 3.9). The word *incendium*, which S. might also have used, is perhaps rejected because it is commonly employed by S. to refer to a fire that is deliberately set, and the participle better describes the destruction caused by the fire on the Capitoline which was apparently accidental. The Temple of Jupiter Optimus Maximus on the south summit of the Capitoline was burnt on 6 July 83 B.C., during the disturbances that broke out when Sulla invaded Italy, and the cause of the fire was never determined. According to tradition, the foundations of this temple were laid by Tarquinius Priscus, the 5th king of Rome, and it was dedicated in the first year of the Republic, 509 B.C. It became at an early date a symbol of Rome's divine favor and stability and was the site at which the new consuls took their vows each year (cf. 18.5n.) and triumphing generals offered prayers of thanksgiving for their victories. After the fire, Sulla began the project of rebuilding the temple on a grander scale. This new temple was completed after the dictator's death and dedicated by Q. Lutatius Catulus (cos. 78 B.C.) in 69 B.C.

illum: standing for *hic est vicesimus annus* in *oratio recta*.

haruspices: these were not official priests of the state but practitioners of the Etruscan art of foretelling the future by inspecting the entrails of sacrificial animals and observing lightning. They could be consulted by private citizens as well as magistrates, and they are to be distinguished from the augurs (vid. 21.2n.), who interpreted the will of the gods by observing the flight of birds. The verb *respondissent* is appropriate to the pronouncement of a seer or *jurisconsultus*.

bello civili: abl. of cause with *cruentum fore*, whose subject is *quem* (*annum*). Possibly Lentulus alluded to the dire predictions of the *haruspices* who were consulted in 65 after various shrines and statues on the Capitoline had been struck by lightning. They foretold the coming of a bloody civil war unless the gods could somehow be appeased. Special games were celebrated to solicit the gods' favor, and a new statue of Jupiter, the protector of the city, was commissioned. As a symbolic gesture, it was proposed that the statue should be made to face east so that the god could overlook the Forum and senate-house. Two years elapsed, however, before this project was carried out, and doubtless due to skillful stage-managing on the part of Cic., the new statue was set in place on the very day that the conspirators were brought before the senate (Cic. *Cat.* 3.19–21; *Div.* 2.46).

(3)   *prius*: each of the letters was bound with a thread (*linum*) which was tied in a knot and sealed with a wax impression (cf. 44.1n.). All of the conspirators were asked whether they recognized (*cognovissent*) their own seals before the seals were broken and the letters read out loud to the senate.

decernit: S. neglects to mention that in addition to the provisions for the custody of the prisoners, the senate voted Cic. a *supplicatio* on the motion of L. Cotta (cos. 65 B.C.), commended the two praetors for their role in making the arrest, and expressed gratitude to Cic.'s colleague Antonius for his loyalty to the state (Cic. *Cat.* 3.14–15; *Phil.* 2.13). A *supplicatio* was a period of days set aside for the public adoration of the gods and was commonly decreed following a national calamity or to mark a significant victory by one of Rome's generals. Cic. took great pride in the fact that he was the first magistrate to be so honored for his acts in a civilian capacity.

abdicato magistratu: the usual expression is *abdicare se magistratu*, but *abdicare* is occasionally construed with an acc. of the office, and this usage makes possible the abl. absol. here. The senate decreed that Lentulus should resign from his praetorship since a Roman magistrate was immune from prosecution until he became a private citizen. Technically there was no constitutional means of removing a magistrate from office short of bringing pressure on him to abdicate of his own accord.

in liberis custodiis: Romans who were awaiting trial or sentencing were rarely confined to prison, especially if they were persons of prominence. They were, however, occasionally placed in the custody of distinguished citizens who would guarantee their appearance in court (cf. Catiline's offer to surrender himself voluntarily into custody, 31.4n.).

(4) *P. (Cornelio) Lentulo Spintheri*: as cos. in 57 B.C., he was one of the chief supporters of Cicero's recall from exile.

aedilis: two curule and two plebeian aediles were elected each year. These junior magistrates were responsible for supervising the markets and public buildings of Rome, for maintaining public order in the city, and for celebrating many of the annual games (*ludi*), which they sponsored largely at their own expense. Since Lentulus Spinther was a patrician, he was eligible only for the curule aedileship.

Q. Cornificio: he was one of Cic.'s six competitors for the consulship in 64, and although he was not the first member of his family to become a senator, as Cic. himself was, he had no consular ancestors (Ascon. p. 82C.4–9).

C. (Julio) Caesari: the future dictator. There were rumors that Caesar (49.2–4) and Crassus (48. 4–9) were both in sympathy with the conspirators. We must assume, therefore, that these suspicions were not taken seriously by the majority of the senate, or else these men were deliberately chosen to watch over two of the conspirators so that they would be compelled to make their true intentions clear one way or the other. Statilius and Gabinius, it should be noted, were both equestrians (17.4n.) and of comparatively lesser importance than the two senators and ringleaders Lentulus and Cethegus.

ante: contrary to the impression given by S., Caeparius was apparently not recaptured until after the senate had adjourned (Cic. *Cat.* 3.14).

Cn. Terentio: otherwise unknown.

CHAPTER 48

(1)   *quae*: the antecedent is *plebs*, while the abl. absol. *coniuratione patefacta* is doubtless an allusion to Cic.'s *Third Catilinarian*, which was delivered to the people on Dec. 3rd after the senate adjourned.

bello favebat: Cic. in his *Fourth Catilinarian* (16ff.) alludes to the support that the government enjoyed in this crisis from even the lower classes and slaves in comparison with the conspirators, many of whom were members of very distinguished families.

exsecrari: historical inf. in asyndeton with the second historical inf. *tollere*.

gaudium atque laetitiam: vid. 46.2n.

(2)   *alia belli facinora*: i.e., as opposed to *incendium*, with which *fore* is also understood and forms a second indirect statement depending on *putabat*.

maxume calamitosum: standing for *calamitosissimum*, vid. 1.3n.

quippe cui: this is the only instance in the *Cat.* of *quippe* with the relative in a causal sense. S., contrary to the standard usage, perfers the indicative, rather than the subjn., in this type of clause.

in usu cotidiano et cultu: abstracts for the concrete: "since all their possessions consisted of articles for everyday use and clothing"; on *cultus*, vid. 37.6n. The poor might expect to derive some profit from the looting (*praedae*) that would be possible if the conspiracy succeeded. They had no valuable property to protect, and hence they would not be targets themselves of assassins. The fires, however, that the conspirators planned to set would affect rich and poor alike and would be especially disastrous for the lower classes who would be left homeless and without resources, since they owned no property outside of the city to which they could retire in the event of an urban conflagration.

(3)   *Post eum diem*: "on the following day," i.e., Dec. 4th; a periphrasis for the adv. *postridie*, which S. eschews.

quidam L. Tarquinius: the indefinite *quidam* normally follows the name of a person. Nothing further is known about this Tarquinius.

(4)   *data esset*: subjn. (suboblique) within the indirect statement introduced by *diceret*; it stands for a fut. pf. indic. in *oratio recta*.

eadem fere quae Volturcius: "the same things for the most part as Volturcius <had stated>," one of two accusatives (the other *senatum*) depending on *docet*, a verb of instructing in the historical pres. After *praeterea* the construction changes to acc. and inf. depending on *docet*, as a verb of saying. Dio (37.35.1–2) follows S.

closely in his account of this attempt to implicate Crassus and the reaction of the senate.

bonorum: in the political sense (vid. 19.2n.).

nuntiaret: subjn. in a rel. clause of purpose.

deprehensi: the leading idea is contained in the participle which should be translated as an abstract noun: "the arrest of."

eoque magis properaret: in this second clause depending upon *nuntiaret* in the sense of urging or advising (*ut* is understood after *ne* above), the subject abruptly shifts to *Catilina* (understood), the object (*eum*) of the preceding clause (cf. 5.6n. *id*); *-que* is to be taken in an adversative sense, and *eo* qualifies *magis*.

quo: vid. 11.5n.; *illi* refers to those conspirators under house arrest.

(5) *summa potentia*: the second of two abls. of description modifying *hominem* in apposition with *Crassum*; *potentia* (cf. 12.1n.) refers especially to Crassus' considerable influence behind the scenes.

alii . . . pars . . . plerique: the subject of *conclamant* is divided into three groups, and after his usual fashion S. deliberately varies the construction in giving the reason for each group's protest (a participle *rati*, a *quia* clause, and adj. *obnoxii*).

in tali tempore: with the preposition and the adj. *talis*, the word *tempus* commonly means "crisis," "critical situation."

tanta vis hominis: vid. 36.5n.; *tanta* contributes to the alliteration produced by *t*.

ex negotiis: causal (vid. 12.2n.), "as a result of business transactions" (esp. loans).

obnoxii: with the dat. *Crasso*: "bound," "indebted" (cf. 14.6n.).

deque: vid. 6.1n. *cumque*.

referatur: sc. *a consule ad senatum* in the technical sense of this word (vid. 29.1n.); *consulente* in the following abl. absol. refers to the role of the presiding magistrate who seeks the advice of the senate on a particular question or issue.

(6) *frequens*: vid. 46.6n.

decernit: this vb. takes the acc. and inf. rather than *ut* + the subjn. (e.g., 29.2) when it refers to deciding certain matters of fact as opposed to issuing instructions. The steps taken to insure that Tarquinius would not be able to persist in his accusation of Crassus are also framed as an indirect statement with the passive periphrastic.

videri: no uncertainty is implied, but *videor* is used here in the technical sense connected with reaching a judicial verdict (Cic.

Acad. 2.146 *maiores voluerunt quae iurati iudices cognovissent, ea non ut esse facta, sed ut videri pronuntiarent*).

potestatem: sc. *indicandi.*

indicaret: suboblique subjn., standing for a fut. indic. in *oratio recta.*

tantam rem: the acc. with *mentior*, meaning "to assert falsely," is mainly poetical and generally confined to post-Augustan prose.

(7)   *machinatum*: sc. *esse*; although deponent, *machinor* is here used in a passive sense, perhaps for the first time in Latin literature (cf. 7.3n. *adepta*).

appellato Crasso: abl. absol. with the force of a conditional clause ("if he should . . ."). Although the participle might equally well have been made to agree with *illius*, which refers to Crassus, it is given more prominence by being turned into an abl. absol. *Appellare* is meant to be taken in the technical sense of "accuse" rather than "name,". and *periculi* may also be connected with the vocabulary of the criminal courts (cf. 16.2n.).

(8)   *inmissum*: sc. *esse*, "instigated" (lit., "sent against in a hostile manner").

more suo: qualifying the participle *suscepto*: "by undertaking after his usual fashion. . . ." Crassus had a reputation for defending clients whose cases had been turned down for one reason or another by Cic., Caesar, and Pompey. Cic. (*Off.* 1.109) criticizes Crassus for his willingness to use any means to further his own power and influence.

(9)   *ego postea*: this is one of the rare instances where S. names his source; the participle *praedicantem*, rather than an inf., after *audivi* indicates that this is first-hand knowledge. Plut. (*Crass.* 13.2–4) confirms that Crassus resented Cic. for casting suspicion upon him in connection with the anonymous letters that were delivered to Crassus in Oct. to warn him of an impending massacre in Rome (vid. 29.1n.). Unfortunately, S. does not indicate the specific occasion on which he heard Crassus make this charge, but a *terminus post quem non* is provided by Crassus' final departure from Rome near the end of 55. Since 55 is also the first year in which S. is likely to have gained admission to the senate (vid. Introd. p. 2), and our sources report that the enmity between Cic. and Crassus broke out into the open during this year (Dio 39.60.1; Cic. *Fam.* 1.9.20), it is possible that S. may allude to a meeting of the senate at which he witnessed an altercation between Cic. and Crassus.

CHAPTER 49

(1)   *Q. Catulus*: vid. 34.3n.

C. (*Calpurnius*) *Piso*: cos. 67 B.C. and governor of Cisalpine and
Transalpine Gaul as proconsul 66–65 B.C., during which time he
laid himself open to prosecution for extortion by Caesar in 63. He
was a staunch opponent of the *populares* and opposed Gabinius'
bill in 67, which conferred extraordinary powers on Pompey to
clear the Mediterranean of pirates.

precibus . . . gratia . . . pretio: although the arrangement of these
words varies considerably in the MSS, this word order, which rests
upon the best authorities, provides an effective crescendo beginning
with entreaties and ending with an outright attempt at bribery.

falso: this clearly represents S.'s view of Caesar's complicity in the
plot. Not only did Cic. refrain from attempting to implicate Caesar
publicly, but in the following year Caesar was apparently able to
quash the accusations of Curius and Vettius by citing Cic.'s testimony in his favor (Suet. *Iul.* 17).

(2)   *oppugnatus*: this is the only source that connects Caesar with this
prosecution; on the charge of *res repetundae*, vid. 18.3n. The
Transpadani were those inhabitants of Cisalpine Gaul (cf. 42.1n.)
who lived north of the Po River. Although most of the inhabitants
of this province to the south of the Po (*Cispadani*) had enjoyed full
Roman citizenship since 89, the *Transpadani* generally possessed
only the more limited rights conferred by the *ius Latii*. Their aspirations to become full Roman citizens had been supported by both
Crassus (Dio 37.9.3–4) and Caesar (Suet. *Iul.* 8) in the 60's, and this
prosecution will have provided Caesar with a further opportunity
to demonstrate his sympathy with their cause. Piso was successfully
defended by Cic. (*Flacc.* 98), but his trial served as a warning to
future governors and gained further support for Caesar in this
important region of northern Italy.

ex petitione pontificatus: "in consequence of the canvass for the
<chief> priesthood"; on the use of *ex* + abl. for stating a cause, cf.
12.2n. The office of chief priest (*pontifex maximus*) fell vacant at
the death of Metellus Pius in late 64 or early 63 B.C. Caesar
defeated his two chief rivals for this life-time appointment, Q.
Catulus and P. Servilius Isauricus (cos. 79), by means of lavish
bribery which plunged him still deeper into debt (Plut. *Caes.* 7.1–
3; Suet. *Iul.* 13; Vell. 2.43.3; Dio 37.37.2).

maxumis honoribus: Catulus, who had served as consul and censor

(65 B.C.), was near the end of his career, while Caesar had not yet been praetor.

adulescentulo: on the flexible meaning of this word, vid. 3.3n. Caesar was 37 years old at the time of his election, while Catulus was his senior by about 20 years. Since the appointment was for life, *adulescentulus* may well have been a word used by Catulus to express his disappointment at being defeated by such a junior rival who would, in all probability, long outlive him.

(3)   *Res*: either (1) Caesar's present condition of being heavily in debt and hence likely to be suspected of favoring Catiline's scheme for the cancellation of debts (vid. 21.2n.), or (2) the plan of his enemies to trump up charges against him.

privatim . . . publice: these advs. are to be loosely construed with the following ablatives of cause and not with the verb *debebat*. The verbal notion contained in *liberalitate* makes this extended use of the adv. possible.

liberalitate: cf. 54.2–3.

muneribus: this refers esp. to the lavish shows that Caesar sponsored as curule aedile in 65. Caesar's personal debts, which were allegedly in excess of 30 million sesterces even before he began his political career (Plut. *Caes.* 5.4), had more than tripled by late 62 (App. *BCiv.* 2.8). His creditors held up his departure from Rome to govern Farther Spain in 61 until Crassus provided sufficient funds to satisfy the most pressing demands for payment (Plut. *Crass.* 7.6).

(4)   *dicerent*: the vb. of saying has been attracted into the subjn. under the influence of the subjn. notion (virtual indirect discourse) contained in the inf. *audisse* (contrast 30.1). S. might well have written instead: *quae, ut dicebant, audissent*, in which case the mood of *audissent* would have indicated that this was merely the claim made by Piso and Catulus, but not a true statement of fact.

illi: i.e., Caesar, dat. of ref. (disadvantage).

praesidi causa: Cic. posted this security force on the ascent to the Capitol (*clivus Capitolinus*) on Dec. 5th (cf. 50.3), and Cic.'s close friend T. Pomponius Atticus, who was a member of the equestrian order, apparently played a leading role on this occasion (Cic. *Att.* 2.1.7). According to Dio (37.35.3–4), Cic. took steps to garrison the Forum and Capitoline Hill when he learned of the plans to rescue the conspirators who had been placed under arrest.

aedem Concordiae: vid. 46.5n.

quo: this purpose clause is to be taken closely with *minitarentur*.

egredienti ex senatu: this is the only instance in S. where *egredior* is construed with *ex* + abl. rather than the abl. alone. The event referred to took place on Dec. 5th after Caesar had delivered his speech contained in chapt. 51 (Suet. *Iul.* 14.2; Plut. *Caes.* 8.2).

Caesari: dat. of the person threatened with the intransitive verb *minitarentur*, which is construed with an instrumental abl. *gladio.*

CHAPTER 50

(1) *Dum haec . . . aguntur*: with these words S. resumes the narrative broken off at 48.7ff. The transition is somewhat awkward since just above (49.4) S. has reported out of order an event that took place on the following day.

praemia: the rewards were voted on Dec. 4th, and Cic. (*Cat.* 4.5; cf. 4.10) refers to them as *amplissima*. Presumably Volturcius benefited under the terms of the decree mentioned at 30.6. Despite the cooperation of the ambassadors in obtaining evidence against the conspirators and the rewards granted to them, their mission on behalf of their countrymen was apparently unsuccessful. In 62 the Allobroges raised a rebellion, which was ultimately suppressed by C. Pomptinus (pr. 63 B.C., 45.1), who served as governor of Transalpine Gaul during 62 and 61.

liberti: this word is used to describe a freedman with respect to his former owner (*dominus*), here *Lentuli*, while *libertinus* denotes a freedman in contrast to a freeborn citizen (*ingenuus*, e.g., 61.5).

clientibus: these were freeborn citizens who looked to Lentulus as their *patronus.*

opifices atque servitia: manual laborers and craftsmen were often of servile origin and generally shared the same low social status; on *servitia*, vid. 24.4n.

eripiundum: sc. *ex custodia* (cf. 48.4); Cic. in his speech to the senate on Dec. 5th (*Cat.* 4.17) contemptuously referred to the attempts that had been made by an agent of Lentulus to rescue him from custody by stirring up the rabble. He deliberately minimized the danger of such a rescue attempt to reassure the senate that the popular will was on their side.

partim: the adv. introduces a second group seeking to achieve the same objective along other lines.

duces multitudinum: the pl. of *multitudo* (= "mobs," "gangs") is unusual. S. refers to the leaders of armed street gangs who played an increasing role in Roman politics during the next decade. The senate attempted to arrest this trend by outlawing most private societies (*collegia*) in 64 since these associations frequently served as a cover for professional street fighters. This evil reached a climax when the tribune P. Clodius lifted the senate's ban on *collegia* in 58 and formed a powerful gang of cutthroats to intimidate his rivals and ultimately even Pompey.

(2)   *familiam*: "the slaves belonging to his household," as opposed to the servile population (*servitia*) in general.

in audaciam: some editors bracket this as a gloss. Since, however, S. once uses *ad* + acc. with *orare* (*Hist.* 4.69.1M), possibly this example of *in* + acc. should be regarded as an extension of this usage, = *ut audaces esset*. In the same way, *vocare*, when it means "urge" or "exhort," which seems to be the sense of *orabat* here, may be construed with either *ad* or *in* + acc.

(3)   *dispositis praesidiis*: vid. 49.4n. *praesidi*. Appian (*BCiv.* 2.5) credits these guards with putting down the disturbances caused by the agents of Lentulus and Cethegus.

convocato senatu: Dec. 5th (Cic. *Att.* 2.1.3).

refert: vid. 29.1n. Although the *s.c.u.* (vid. 29.2n.) armed Cic. with broad powers for dealing with the crisis—including, as he claimed (*Cat.* 1.2, 2.3), the right to inflict capital punishment—he apparently hoped to shield himself from prosecution in the future on the charge that he had executed Roman citizens without due process by obtaining authority for this act from the senate (vid. *Phil.* 2.18 *comprehensio sontium mea, animadversio senatus fuit*).

Sed: this statement is added almost as an afterthought (vid. 7.1n.). *Tum* below resumes the narrative proper.

paulo ante: either Dec. 3rd, or more likely the 4th since further testimony was heard on that day (48.3–6), at the conclusion of which rewards were voted for the informers (50.1).

contra rem publicam fecisse: an expression denoting acts of treason. The documentary evidence and oral testimony linking these individuals with Catiline, who had been declared a public enemy (36.2 *hostis*), would be sufficient grounds for this resolution.

(4)   *D. Iunius Silanus*: consul with Murena in 62 and married to Cato's half-sister Servilia, who was the mother of M. Brutus, the tyrannicide, by a previous husband.

primus: it was customary in the latter part of the year, after the elections had been held, for the magistrate presiding over a meeting of the senate to call upon the consuls-elect first in the order of debate. The normal rotation would then pass to the ex-consuls, praetors-elect, ex-praetors, etc., until it was felt that the issue had been adequately debated. Those junior senators who had held only the quaestorship were probably seldom called upon to express their views, and these "back-benchers" were known as *pedarii*. Within the consulars, the first speaker to be called upon was determined early in the year by the presiding consul, and the order, once established, seems to have been maintained for the remainder of the year. Precedence was no doubt given to the coss.-elect because the responsibility for executing the senate's decree would fall to these magistrates in the following year, and therefore it was desirable to ascertain their probable suppport for any given course of action.

sententiam: one of the two accs. governed by *rogare* in the active voice is retained in the passive (cf. 25.2n. *docta*).

P. Furio: mentioned here by S. for the first time. Cic. (*Cat.* 3.14) identifies him as one of the settlers in the colony planted by Sulla at Faesulae and connects him with Annius in the negotiations carried on by the conspirators with the Allobroges. Since he escaped arrest, possibly he is to be identified with the *Faesulanus quidam* who commanded the left wing of Catiline's army at the battle of Pistoria (59.3). On Cassius and Annius, vid. 17.3n.; on Umbrenus, vid. 40.1n.

deprehensi forent: subjn. (suboblique) standing for a fut. pf. indic. in *oratio recta*, while *tenebantur* above is put in the indic.

supplicium: "capital punishment," *summum* (cf. 51.39) must be understood. The expression, however, is potentially ambiguous as it stands, and apparently Silanus himself, when he wavered in his opinion under the influence of Caesar's speech, attempted to justify his reversal by arguing that he had not intended to indicate the death penalty but imprisonment by his words "extreme penalty" (Plut. *Cic.* 21.3, *Cato Min.* 22.3; Suet. *Iul.* 14.1). The consulars who spoke immediately after Silanus and Murena all advocated capital punishment (list of 14, probably in the order in which they spoke, Cic. *Att.* 12.21.1). Crassus was conspicuously absent on this occasion (Cic. *Cat.* 4.10 with *Att.* l.c.).

sumundum: sc. *esse*; the passive periphrastic appears to have been the standard form in which a senator cast his recommendation (cf. *referundum* below, and 51.43, 52.14, 52.36).

decreverat: in reference to individuals, as opposed to legislative bodies, this verb means "to announce one's judgment," "to declare." The plupf. here and in the following clause (*dixerat*), rather than the pf., describes these acts as completed relative to a later point in past time (cf. 18.6n.). The participial phrase *permotus oratione C. Caesaris* in conjunction with *dixerat* makes it clear that the point of reference is not Caesar's speech, as we might have expected from the order in which these events are reported, but rather the final vote (*discessio*), since Silanus altered his opinion after Caesar's speech, and Nero (vid. n. below) apparently spoke after Caesar.

pedibus . . . iturum: a technical expression meaning "to support" or "vote for." During the course of a debate, senators sometimes showed their support for a given proposal by changing their seat to sit near the member with whose views they agreed. Later, when the question was put to a formal vote, the presiding magistrate instructed the house to divide into groups according to their support or opposition to the proposal being considered. Silanus indicated by these words that he would support Nero's recommendation if it was put to a vote, but as it turned out Cic. asked for a division on Cato's motion. When this motion passed (53.1), all other proposals were nullified.

sententiam: Nero's proposal apparently was simply a motion to table the issue until a later date. According to Appian (*BCiv.* 2.5), the only other source to record this detail, the conspirators were to be kept in custody until Catiline's forces had been defeated and a more thorough investigation could be made. Virtually the same account is given in some sources (vid. 51.43n.) concerning Caesar's recommendation, while others, including S., make Caesar propose life imprisonment and confiscation of their property.

Ti. (Claudi) Neronis: grandfather of the future emperor Tiberius. He served as a *legatus* on Pompey's staff in 67 and had apparently held the praetorship sometime prior to 63. He will, therefore, have spoken after Caesar, who took precedence as praetor-elect, and before Cato, who was tribune-elect. Some slight confirmation of this fact may be derived from Cic.'s claim that all senators advocated the death penalty until the debate reached Caesar (*Att.* 12.21.1). Appian (*BCiv.* 2.5), probably misled by the order of events in S.'s narrative, places Nero's proposal before Caesar's.

qui: the conj. *quod*, which is found in most MSS, gives a less satisfactory sense and is probably to be explained as an attempt to resolve the corruption *quid de* which arose from dittography and is attested by one MS.

additis: apparently there was a feeling on the part of some senators that the guards already posted by Cic. needed reinforcement, a view that Cic. (*Cat.* 4.14) attempted to refute.

(5)   *huiuscemodi*: vid. 20.1n. Although the following does not purport to be a verbatim report of Caesar's actual speech, a number of the sentiments and views expressed are confirmed by allusions in Cic.'s *Fourth Catilinarian* to the arguments used by Caesar. As for the general tone, S. in composing this speech appears to have been influenced by the debate reported by Thucydides on the

punishment of the Mytileneans, who had unsuccessfully revolted from Athens during the Peloponnesian War. In two points at least, Caesar is made to adopt the position of Diodotus (Thuc. 3.42ff.), who opposed the death penalty and argued that haste and anger were detrimental to reaching a rational decision, and that capital punishment, while justified by the enormity of the offense, was not expedient under the circumstances.

verba locutus est: the expression *verba loqui* appears to be borrowed from Cato (73.15J).

CHAPTER 51

(1) *Omnis homines . . . qui*: the opening words of this speech bear a striking resemblance to the first words of S.'s preface (1.1). The thought expressed here seems to be modeled on the *exordium* to Demosthenes' oration *On the Affairs in the Chersonese*.

patres conscripti: cf. 6.6n. The epithet *conscripti*, as explained by Livy (2.1.11), was originally applied to only part of the senate and designated those senators who were "enrolled" (*conscribere*) from among the plebeians to fill vacancies after the expulsion of the last king, Tarquinius Superbus. According to this view, the expression arose as a result of the conflation of *patres et conscripti*. More likely, however, the title reflects the change from automatic membership, based upon one's status as the head of a patrician *gens*, to membership based upon considerations other than kinship, which had formerly been the sole criterion for enrollment.

(2) *illa*: those considerations mentioned just above.

usui: in contrast with *lubidini* ("impulses"), *usus* = "one's true interest or advantage."

paruit: gnomic pf. (vid. 11.3n.).

(3) *intenderis*: subjn. of the indef. 2nd person sing.

valet: *animus* is to be supplied as subject forming an antithesis to *animus nihil valet* below; for the adverbial acc. *nihil* = *non*, cf. 16.5n. For the sake of dissymmetry, the *ubi* clause is answered by the conditional *si* clause in the contrasting proposition.

possidet: used absolutely without an expressed object: "takes control."

(4) *copia*: vid. 17.6n. *vivere*.

quae: an internal acc. governed by *consuluerint*, which by an extension of this use of the acc. is also capable of being cast into the passive voice (e.g., 52.35); *qui*, which is also amply attested in the MSS, would shift the emphasis from illustrations drawn from certain types of decisions to instances of nations and monarchs who had been misled by their emotions. The difference is slight, but the former reading provides a better parallel to *quae . . . fecere* below.

recte atque ordine: the coupling of this adv. and abl., which seems to be a set phrase, is to be taken as hendiadys for "in due order" in contrast with *male* above.

(5) *Bello Macedonico*: the Third Macedonian War, which was waged against Perses, the last king of Macedonia, and brought to a successful conclusion by L. Aemilius Paullus at the battle of Pydna in 168 B.C. The island of Rhodes, which was allied to Rome and had rendered valuable naval service to the Romans in their war against Antiochus of Syria (192–189 B.C.), made the mistake of offering to mediate the conflict between the Romans and Perses. Their motive was doubtless a desire for settled conditions in the Aegean so that they could carry on commerce, which was the mainstay of their economy. As it turned out, the battle of Pydna took place before the Rhodian ambassadors reached Rome, and the Rhodian policy was interpreted by the Romans as a hostile act. Although the mood to declare war on Rhodes was successfully combated by the Elder Cato, the Romans stripped Rhodes of the territory in southwest Asia Minor that had been awarded to their ally after the war against Antiochus and elevated the island of Delos to a duty-free port, thereby utterly crippling the mercantile economy of Rhodes. It is ironic that Caesar is made to cite this incident, in which Cato played such a major role as an advocate of clemency (his speech *pro Rhodiensibus* was well-known, Livy 45.25.1–3), while in this debate Cato's descendant was the chief spokesman for the opposite policy.

magna atque magnifica: paired for the sake of alliteration.

opibus: abl. of cause; this refers to the alliance with Rome, and especially the territorial gains made in 188 B.C. after the war with Antiochus.

atque advorsa: *atque*, not *et*, which is found in the majority of the MSS, should be preferred as providing a better contrast with *magna atque magnifica* just above.

inpunitos: a gross exaggeration in view of the punitive measures actually adopted.

(6) *bellis Punicis*: three wars were fought against Carthage for supremacy over the western Mediterranean (264–241 B.C.; 218–201 B.C.; 149–146 B.C.). The last of these wars resulted in the annihilation of Carthage.

cum: concessive.

in pace et per indutias: the preposition is doubtless varied to avoid the collocation of *in* + *indutiis*; the same consideration, however, does not apply at 52.15 where the sense probably accounts for the change. Both may be taken as examples of S.'s fondness for avoiding balanced phrases (cf. 9.3n.).

facinora fecissent: cf. 7.6n.; the assonance produced by *nefaria* with *facinora* lends further weightiness to this archaic construction, and the combination is perhaps inspired by Cato (39.12J). The treachery of the Carthaginians (*Punica fides*) was proverbial in Roman propaganda, but it is far easier to document cases of bad faith on the part of the Romans (vid. n. following).

per occasionem: i.e., although there was no lack of opportunity. In fact, the Romans frequently exploited favorable circumstances to extort further concessions from Carthage; e.g., the seizure of Sardinia and Corsica after the peace treaty ending the First Punic War had been ratified; and the negotiations leading up to the third war, in which Rome continued to hold out the prospect of a peaceful settlement of the dispute until the Carthaginians had been tricked into making major concessions.

se: "themselves," i.e., the Romans; abl. with *dignum*, the normal construction, while below (51.8) *digna* seems to be construed with *pro* + abl., a usage mainly confined to poetry.

foret: = *futurum esset* (cf. 21.1n.).

(7)   *scelus*: the "villainy" of the conspirators is so great that it may exercise more influence (*plus . . . valeat*) over the decision to adopt punitive measures than considerations of the senate's *dignitas*.

dignitas: both here and above (*se dignum*), the stress that Caesar is made to place upon considerations of *dignitas* is reminiscent of his slogan at the commencement of the Civil War more than a decade later (vid. 35.3n. *statum dignitatis*).

consulatis: used by zeugma with *irae* as well as *famae*, with which it is strictly appropriate. With *irae* a verb such as *obsequamini* would be more natural.

(8)   *pro factis*: vid. 51.6n. *se*; possibly, however, *digna* should be taken absolutely, and *pro* understood to mean "in return for" (cf. 14.3). In that case, *digna* will refer to the worthiness of the punishment both with respect to the culprits and with respect to the *dignitas* and judgment of the senate.

novom consilium: "new proposal"; legally the senate had no right to sentence Roman citizens to death. This power belonged to the people, and the tribune C. Gracchus had passed a law in 123 B.C. (the *lex Sempronia* alluded to at 51.22, vid. n.) which even restricted the senate's right to establish special tribunals for the express purpose of trying capital cases unless the senate first received approval from the popular assembly. It rested with the magistrate who had been granted broad powers by the *s.c.u.* (vid. 29.2n.) to decide whether the crisis justified disregarding the existing laws, and he alone could later be held responsible for abusing his power. Despite Cicero's attempts to portray the senate as being responsible for imposing the death penalty on the conspirators (e.g., *Pis.* 14; *Phil.* 2.18; cf. *Dom.* 33), ultimately the senate only had the power to recommend a certain course of action to the magistrate who consulted it. The circumstances were somewhat unusual in 63 since previously the *s.c.u.* had always been used to crush enemies of the state who were under arms and in open rebellion, while in the present instance, it could be argued that these accomplices of Catiline were safely in custody and could be given an opportunity to have their case tried in one of the established courts.

ingenia: by metonymy, the means used to devise a suitable punishment ("ingenuity") is substituted for a word denoting punishment itself.

his: abl. with *utendum* (sc. *esse*), i.e., "the penalties," "punishment."

(9)   *composite*: "elaborately," referring esp. to the careful arrangement of words, while *magnifice* describes the choice of words as striking or elevated. Cato (52.13) passes a similar judgment on Caesar's speech.

enumeravere: by zeugma, this verb governs both of the preceding indirect questions, while it is strictly appropriate only to the second.

rapi virgines, pueros: these words introduce a series of six indirect statements, all in asyndeton, which stand in apposition with *quae victis acciderent*. The horrors that Caesar mentions here do in fact provide one theme in Cic.'s *Fourth Catilinarian* (11–12), which was delivered at a slightly later point in the debate.

familiarum: vid. 43.2n.; Cic. by contrast writes *lamentationem matrum familias* (*Cat.* 4.12).

conlibuissent: impersonal verbs are rarely found in the pl. except where their subject is a neut. pl. pronoun, as here, or an adj. of quantity. This is the only instance in S. of this compound verb, which is an archaism for *libet*. The subjn. is employed because this clause is subordinate within the indirect statement (suboblique).

luctu: it is not common for an abstract to be included in a series of concrete nouns, but this is not the only instance in S. (cf. 6.3n.

moribus).

(10)   *illa oratio*: standing for *oratio illorum qui ante me sententias dixerunt*.

An *uti*: a hypothetical question in reply to *quo . . . pertinuit* above: "is it to make? . . ."

Scilicet: an indication that the following statement is to be taken as a sarcastic comment. It is immediately denied by *Non ita est*.

(11)   *iniuriae suae*: the reflexive *suae* refers to the person denoted by *cuiquam* (cf. 2.1n.), and it is to be taken objectively: "one's own injuries," in the sense of the injuries that one suffers.

gravius . . . habuere: cf. 5.9n.; the pf. is gnomic and is to be understood as standing for *habere solent*. S. often shows a preference for the verb *habere* in contexts where another verb would be considered more usual; here *habuere* is substituted for *tulere*, while below (51.12) *habent* takes the place of *agunt* in the phrase *vitam habent*. The more common expression meaning to tolerate or bear with difficulty is *aegre ferre*.

(12)   *licentia*: freedom to act as one pleases and follow one's inclinations to anger, etc.

demissi: best taken with the unexpressed antecedent of the rel. pron., while *in obscuro* goes with *habent*: "if persons in humble circumstances who . . ."

quid: an internal acc. object of *deliquere*: "if they have committed any fault"; *iracundia* is an abl. of cause.

pares: cf. 20.2n. *spectata*.

in excelso aetatem agunt: the observation that the most illustrious men are necessarily exposed to public scrutiny is a *topos* (e.g., Xen. *Ages*. 5.6).

(13)   *fortuna*: cf. 2.5n.

studere: "to show favoritism," very rare in this absolute sense, a usage which appears to be archaic.

(14)   *Quae . . . ea*: gender and number have been determined by the predicate nominatives; *ea*, the postponed antecedent of *quae*, refers to the acts just enumerated by the infs. *studere*, etc.

in imperio: by metonymy, an abstract is substituted for a concrete expression such as *in eis qui imperio praediti sunt*. It stands in antithesis to *apud alios*.

(15)   *Equidem*: in S. this word is confined to speeches and letters. It is normally used with the 1st person sing. to emphasize that the speaker is speaking for himself, but it is not limited to the first sing. in S., who employs *equidem* on several occasions as merely an

emphatic particle.

severior: since Caesar below (51.17) characterizes Silanus' proposal as *non crudelis*, the alternative reading *s<a>evior*, which is found in the bulk of the MSS, is less likely to be correct.

(16) *eos . . . eamque*: predicate accusatives, sc. *esse*, with *cognovi*: "such I know is his character and such the restraint of that man." On *modestiam*, which produces alliteration with *mores*, vid. 11.4n.

(17) *sed*: answers *non crudelis* just above.

aliena a re publica: vid. 40.5n.

(18) *metus . . . iniuria*: taken up below in this order by *de timore* (51.19) and indirectly by *de poena* (51.20). Both prepositional phrases receive emphasis by being placed first in each sentence.

subegit: vid. 10.5n.

genus poenae novom: cf. 51.8n.; Cic. attempted to answer this objection, which Caesar may well have raised, by observing: *hoc genus poenae saepe in improbos cives in hac re publica esse usurpatum recordatur* (*Cat.* 4.7).

decernere: vid. 50.4n.

(20) *equidem*: here S. follows the usage preferred by Cic. and leaves *ego* unexpressed.

id quod res habet: "that which is relevant to the issue"; here *habere* seems to be used in the sense of "involve" (cf. 11.3n.).

aerumnarum: obj. gen. with *requiem*: "rest from troubles"; for this slightly archaic word, Cic. substitutes *laborum ac miseriarum quietem* in a corresponding reference to Caesar's description of death (*Cat.* 4.7).

ultra: adv., here the meaning is *post mortem*. Cic. (l.c.) confirms that Caesar used such an argument to refute the appropriateness of the death penalty, and Cic. himself was willing on occasion to adopt this same position when it suited his purposes to do so (e.g., *Clu.* 171; for just the opposite view, cf. *Phil.* 14.32). Cato (52.13) is made to counter this essentially Epicurean doctrine, which denies the immortality of the soul, by alluding to the traditional belief that the virtuous and wicked receive their just deserts in an after-life. It is ironic that Cato, who was well-known for his devotion to philosophy, found it necessary in this debate to answer his opponent by appealing to a belief that Cic. (*Clu.*, l.c.) characterizes as the product of fables and nonsense, while Caesar, the *pontifex maximus*, exploited a philosophical argument which could be interpreted as calling into question the very existence of the gods. It should be noted, however, that Roman religion generally left questions concerning morality and life after death to the philosophers.

Therefore Caesar's position as chief priest was no hindrance to such philosophical speculation. Furthermore, if Cic.'s allusion to Caesar's position on this issue is accurate, he credited the gods with establishing death as a release from cares, while S. is the one responsible for presenting the argument on a purely philosophical level without reference to the gods.

(21) *in eos animadvorteretur*: impersonal construction in the pass. voice: "that they be punished."

(22) *lex Porcia*: three *leges Porciae* were enacted at the beginning of the 2nd century B.C. Their precise nature remains subject to dispute. According to Cic. (*Rep.* 2.54), all three imposed further sanctions to strengthen the right of *provocatio*, which limited a magistrate's authority to inflict corporal punishment or execute a Roman citizen without allowing an appeal to the assembly. Several references to one of these laws in other sources confirms the impression given by S. that it somehow abolished or restricted a magistrate's right to scourge a Roman citizen (Cic. *Rab. Perd.* 12 *Porcia lex virgas ab omnium civium Romanorum corpore amovit*; Livy 10.9.4 *pro tergo civium lata videtur*). It is a further bit of irony that in this debate with Cato, Caesar cites the provisions of a law that may have been passed by his opponent's great-grandfather.

aliae leges: probably the *lex Sempronia* in particular (vid. 51.8n.). Cic. (*Cat.* 4.10), who implies that Caesar may have cited this law as part of his argument, attempts to demonstrate that it does not apply in the present case because Lentulus and the others had forfeited their status as Roman citizens by taking up arms against their country.

civibus: dat. of separation with *eripi*, while it supplies the indirect object of *permitti*.

exilium: custom at any rate, if not an actual law, generally recognized the practice of granting to a condemned man an interval of time before the execution of a capital sentence during which he could go into self-imposed exile outside Roman territory (Cic. *Caecin.* 100). After his departure, the magistrate or *comitia* would impose a formal sanction in the form of an interdiction from fire and water (*aquae et ignis interdictio*) to prevent his return.

(23) *facinoris*: gen. governed by *convictos*, the pf. pass. part. of a verb of condemning.

(24) *Sin*: understand *in sententiam non addidisti uti* . . . from above.

levius: sc. *verberari quam necari*.

qui: interrog. adv., "how."

negotio: a word that S. likes to substitute for the less colorful noun *res.*

neglegeris: an archaic spelling for the more usual *neglexeris*.

(25) *At enim*: used to introduce a hypothetical objection which the speaker will presently refute.

parricidas: vid. 14.3n.

Tempus: esp. with respect to changing circumstances, while *dies* denotes the mere passage of time; the verb *reprehendent* must be supplied.

cuius lubido: cf. 8.1.

(26) *ceterum*: adversative, = "but," a meaning not found in Cic. or Caes., but frequently so used by S. in the *Jug.*

(27) *ex rebus bonis*: *bonae res* would ordinarily mean "prosperity," but here the context suggests that it stands for "good measures." A dangerous precedent is instituted under a given set of circumstances that justify harsh measures, but later this precedent is used as an excuse for tyrannical behavior against innocent persons.

Sed: S. apparently wished to set this statement apart from the one that precedes while the reader might have expected him to continue with *et*. In fact, the two observations are related but concern two separate aspects of the threat posed by setting a dangerous precedent. Either those same men who adopt a new course of action may carry it to extremes in the future (illustrated by the first set of examples, 29–34); or a precedent set by one government may provide a weapon in the hands of a future government that is less scrupulous (illustrated by 35–36).

eius: i.e., *imperi*; persons not acquainted with power and therefore likely to misuse it.

idoneis: pejorative here, = "fit (for such harsh treatment)," a rare sense of this word (cf. Cic. *Clu.* 130).

(28) *devictis Atheniensibus*: probably abl. absol. rather than dat. with *imposuere*, which is used absolutely elsewhere by S. The Spartans, who were victorious in the Peloponnesian War (431–404 B.C.), suspended Athens' democratic constitution and appointed a board of thirty to administer the affairs of the city (Xen. *Hell.* 2.3.2). This oligarchic regime came to be known as the "Thirty Tyrants" and was eventually overthrown by the Athenians. The democracy was restored after the lapse of approximately one year (June 404–summer 403 B.C.).

tractarent: vid. 39.2n.

(29) *omnibus invisum*: the addition of *omnibus* makes the adj. virtually equivalent to a superlative so that it balances *pessumum*. These

words refer especially to the sycophants, a class of informers at Athens, who were feared and hated for their activity in the courts, especially during the Peloponnesian War.

laetari . . . dicere: historical infs.; *ea* (sc. *facta*) is an internal acc. governed by *laetari*, which is normally construed with the abl., and also supplies the acc. subj. of *fieri* in the indirect statement dependent on the historical inf. *dicere*.

(30) *iuxta*: vid. 2.8n.

metu: those whom they did not kill lived in constant dread. The Spartans furnished a garrison to enforce the rule of the Thirty.

(32) *Nostra memoria*: vid. 33.2n.

cum: strictly temporal and therefore construed with the indic.

Damasippum: L. Junius Brutus Damasippus, praetor urbanus in 82 B.C., executed a number of leading senators and suspected supporters of Sulla when he was instructed to do so by the consul, C. Marius, the son of the elder Marius. He was captured and put to death by Sulla after the battle of the Colline Gate in Nov. of 82.

malo: "due to the corruption of the state," with *creverant* (cf. 51.5, 37.7n. *malum publicum*).

(33) *magnae initium cladis*: Caesar's analysis is in harmony with the views expressed by S. in his own person (cf. 11.4).

vas aut vestimentum: paired for the sake of alliteration to heighten the rhetorical effect and possibly borrowed by S. from Cato (72.22J *neque vasum neque vestimentum*).

is: referring to *alicuius* above.

proscriptorum: vid. 21.2n.

(34) *laetitiae*: predicate dat.; on the meaning of this word, vid. 46.2n.

trahebantur: *ad necem* is understood.

(36) *Potest*: placed first for emphasis: "it is possible." The grammatical subject *aliquid* is postponed until near the end of the sentence.

alio consule: abl. absol.

cui . . . sit: the subjn. is due to the hypothetical nature of this clause and is virtually equivalent to the protasis of a future less vivid condition. It was unusual in this period for a consul to have an army at his disposal. Possibly S. is alluding to the events that he himself witnessed after the assassination of Julius Caesar in 44 and not long before he began writing this monograph. One is reminded of the fact that in August of 43 Caesar's heir, C. Octavius, assumed command of an army after the death of the two consuls and marched on Rome to demand that he be made consul although he was only 19 years old at the time.

in manu: vid. 20.10n.

hoc exemplo: abl. of cause: "as a result of this precedent."

illi: dat. of reference, referring to *consul* above.

(37) *consili . . . audaciae*: gen. with *eguere* (cf. 1.7n.). *Audacia* is used here in a positive sense (cf. 9.3n.).

quo minus: used to introduce the object of a verb of hindering and found only three times in S.

si modo: vid. 40.3n.

(38) *Arma atque tela*: vid. 42.2n.; the adj. *militaria* is pleonastic and seems to be designed to balance *magistratuum*.

ab Samnitibus: a warlike people who lived in the mountainous districts of south-central Italy. Apparently the Romans adopted from this nation the *veru*, which was a type of javelin (Verg. *Aen.* 7.665 *veruque Sabello*).

ab Tuscis: the Etruscans introduced to Rome a number of external symbols of office: the twelve lictors and the *fasces*, which they carried as a symbol of *imperium*; the purple-bordered *toga prae-texta*, which was worn by curule magistrates, some priests, and boys until they reached manhood; and the *sella curulis*, which was assigned to the consuls, praetors, and curule aediles.

pleraque: to be taken with both *arma atque tela* and *insignia*. Here it is best understood in the restricted sense of "very many," which is common in S., rather than its ordinary meaning of "most."

ubique: vid. 21.1n.

bonis: although this word supplies the object of both infs., its case (dat.) is determined by *invidere*, the nearer of the two (cf. 11.2n. *huic*). Probably *institutis* is to be supplied, since the character of the nations from whom the Romans borrowed is not the point at issue; *invidere*, however, is more often used with a personal object. The Greek historian Polybius, writing near the middle of the 2nd century B.C., notes the willingness of the Romans to assimilate the best institutions that they encountered in foreign cultures (6.25.11).

(39) *Graeciae morem imitati*: both scourging and capital punishment are attested as recognized penalties under Roman law as early as 451 B.C. by the provisions of the XII Tables. Since it was com-monly believed by the Romans that this first written code was based upon Greek models, this may account for Caesar's assertion, although there is no basis for assuming that either practice was borrowed by the Romans from the Greeks.

summum supplicium sumebant: cf. 50.4n. *supplicium*; alliteration emphasizes the gravity of this ultimate punishment.

(40) *factiones valuere*: cf. 32.2n.; an allusion to the shattering of the *concordia* that, according to S.'s view, existed between the senate and people until after the destruction of Carthage and removal of this restraining *metus hostilis*.

coepere: despite the omission of a conj. after *valuere*, *coepere* appears to be the third in a series of verbs governed by *postquam*, as can be seen from *tum*. Although both infs. are passive, S. prefers the active to *coepta sunt*, which would be more usual (cf. 12.1n.).

legibus: the repetition of the antecedent within the relative clause is a common feature of Caesar's own prose and is perhaps deliberately used by S. for this reason. It does, however, serve to show that this clause modifies only *aliae leges*, and this is confirmed by the statement at 51.22.

(41) *Hanc*: i.e., the precedent set by their ancestors; for the attraction of the demonstrative pronoun into the gender of the predicate noun, cf. 7.6n.

causam: in the sense of a "reason for not doing," it is construed with *quo minus*: "I consider this the chief reason why we should not . . ." (cf. 51.37n.).

in primis magnam: virtually equivalent to a superlative (cf. 51.29n.).

(42) *illis*: i.e., *maioribus nostris*, dat. of possession in contrast with *in nobis* below. As usual, S. deliberately varies the construction for the sake of dissymmetry.

fuit: sing. because the compound subject is viewed as a single concept.

ea: this refers to *imperium*. The pronoun is neut. pl., rather than sing., because it is being used to denote the many components of *imperium Romanum*: the city itself, foreign territories, revenues, human and natural resources, etc. Often *haec* is used in this sense when the speaker regards himself and his audience as participating in this concept (e.g., 52.10), but here *imperium* is not being described from the viewpoint of Caesar's immediate audience but with respect to those who made it great—hence *ea*.

(43) *Placet*: sc. *mihi*, an expression virtually equivalent to *censeo* below or *decerno* (cf. 50.4n.), respecting a recommendation made by the speaker.

pecunias: this is apparently intended to include all their property (cf. Cic. *Cat.* 4.10 *publicationem bonorum*).

per municipia: vid. 17.4n.; according to Cic. (*Cat.* 4.8), Caesar included in his proposal penalties for any community that allowed the conspirators to escape. Cic. remarks that it will be difficult to find towns willing to assume this burden.

neu quis: at this point, the construction after *censeo* shifts to two jussive noun clauses and concludes with an indirect statement (*senatum existumare*). The first part of this proposal is expressed in the standard form consisting of the two passive periphrastics (cf. 50.4n. *sumundum*) which stand in indirect discourse (sc. *esse*).

cum populo agat: this is the technical expression for submitting a proposal to a vote in a Roman assembly, just as *ad senatum referat* describes consultation of the senate (vid. 29.1n.). By the way these provisions are worded, S. implies that Caesar recommended imprisonment for life, and this agrees with the version given by Cic. (*Cat.* 4.7 *vincula sempiterna*, cf. 4.10; Suet. *Iul.* 14.1; Dio 37.36.1-2). Since, however, confinement was seldom used by the Romans as a punishment but served more often as a precaution against the flight of the accused, possibly Caesar envisioned that the detention of the conspirators would last only until Catiline's army had been defeated and his accomplices could be brought to trial. Plutarch (*Cic.* 21.1) and Appian (*BCiv.* 2.6), in fact, support this interpretation. Perhaps Cic. deliberately exaggerated the anticipated length of confinement to stress the severity of Caesar's recommendation and thereby bring it more in line with Silanus' proposal.

CHAPTER 52

(1)   *verbo*: to be taken with *adsentiebantur*. Rather than stating his views in a formal speech (*sententiam dicere*), a senator could merely signify his support for a proposal that had already been made by stating his agreement with the author of the proposal (*adsentiri alicui*).

alius alii: *alius* stands in partitive apposition with the subject *ceteri*; *alii* (dat.), rather than *alteri*, would normally imply that more than the two proposals of Silanus and Caesar had been made, but here *alius* doubtless influences the choice of *alii*.

varie: the adv. emphasizes the lack of a clear consensus for the one proposal or the other. Dio (37.36.2) no doubt exaggerates the effect of Caesar's speech when he reports that all the senators who spoke after Caesar endorsed his recommendation until the debate reached Cato (cf. Plut. *Caes.* 8.1; Suet. *Iul.* 14.2). It was at this point, prior to Cato's speech, that Cic., as the presiding magistrate, intervened to deliver his *Fourth Catilinarian* in an attempt to rally the senate's support for a common policy against the conspirators. Since Cic. does not refer to the motion of Nero or the vacillation of Silanus (vid. 50.4n.), possibly they both followed Cic.'s speech, unless he deliberately ignored Nero's proposal since it was so similar to Caesar's.

M. Porcius Cato: great-grandson of the Elder Cato (cos. 195 B.C.; censor 184 B.C.) and quaestor in 65 or 64. At this time he was only thirty-two years old and an extremely junior member of the senate since he had not yet held any curule magistracy. Therefore, his turn to address this issue came late in the debate (vid. 50.4n.), and he spoke as one of the tribunes-elect for 62. According to our sources, Cato criticized Silanus for altering his position, praised the measures that had been taken by Cic., and insinuated that Caesar had a personal interest in advocating clemency in view of the suspicion that he was himself implicated in the plot (Plut. *Cato Min.* 23, *Caes.* 8.1, *Cic.* 21.2; Vell. 2.35.3–4; cf. Cic. *Sest.* 61, *Att.* 12.21.1). There is general agreement that Cato's strong stand arrested the wavering of the senate, and although he never reached the consulship, Cato went on to become a leading spokesman for the conservative Optimate faction until his career was ended by suicide at Utica in the civil war against Caesar—hence his later surname *Uticensis*.

huiuscemodi: vid. 20.1n.

(2)   *Longe mihi alia*: just as the opening words of Caesar's speech appear to be modeled on Demosthenes (vid. 51.1n.), S. appears to have borrowed this *exordium* from Demosthenes' *Third Olynthiac*.

res atque pericula: hendiadys for "perilous affairs."

(3)   *disseruisse*: this word implies a detached discussion, after the fashion of a philosophical debate, as opposed to a realistic consideration of the actual circumstances. One is reminded especially of Caesar's appeal to the Epicurean doctrine concerning the nature of death (51.20); and lest the connection be missed, it is emphasized by the repetition of this verb at 52.13 to describe Caesar's treatment of this theme. The speech that S. attributes to Cato is singularly devoid of such philosophical theorizing although Cic. (*Paradox.* 1. praef. 1) states that Cato frequently employed philosophical theories to support his argument when he addressed the senate.

aris atque focis: these two nouns are so frequently joined, esp. in the pl., that they form a *topos*.

cavere . . . consultare: infs. rather than the more usual *ut* + the subjn. after *monet* (vid. 5.9n. *repetere*).

statuamus: the subjn. within the indirect question stands for a deliberative subjn. in *oratio recta*.

(4)   *cetera maleficia . . .*: a *topos* concerning treason. Vegetius attributes to the Elder Cato (81.1–3J) a similar observation respecting

cowardice or lack of discipline on the battlefield. By their very nature, these faults must be corrected before they occur, or else it will be too late. *Cetera* is put first in anticipation of *hoc*, with which it is contrasted.

persequare: potential subjn. of the indefinite second person sing.; likewise *provideris* and *implores*.

hoc: subject of both *accidat* and *evenit*.

relicui: vid. 11.7n. Significantly this expression was used on two previous occasions (11.7, 28.4) to describe the behavior of Sulla's soldiers during and after the proscriptions. It will be remembered that Caesar (51.32–34) cited the Sullan proscriptions as a warning example against imposing the death penalty on the conspirators.

(5)   *pluris*: gen. with *fecistis*, a verb of valuing.

cuiuscumque modi sunt: a remark loaded with contempt as can be seen from *ista* and the choice of *amplexamini*, a word denoting excessive devotion. The same theme is treated by S. himself (13.1–2) and plays a role in Catiline's criticism of the nobility (vid. 20.11).

(6)   *de vectigalibus*: vid. 20.7n.; to be taken with *agitur* (impersonal): "it is not a matter concerning . . ."

(7)   *Saepe numero*: a rhetorical exaggeration in view of Cato's junior status as a mere *quaestorius*. It is doubtful that he had played a significant role in senatorial debates up until this time, although he had apparently been active in attacking Catiline in the senate during the election campaign in this year (vid. 31.9n.).

in hoc ordine: i.e., the senate (vid. 17.3n.).

de luxuria atque avaritia . . . questus sum: these words closely resemble those attributed to the Elder Cato by Livy (34.4.1) in a speech that he delivered against the repeal of a sumptuary law, the *lex Oppia*, in 195 B.C. (*saepe me querentem de . . . sumptibus audistis; diversisque duobus vitiis, avaritia et luxuria, civitatem laborare*).

multosque mortalis: vid. 1.5n.

ea causa: a somewhat archaic expression (cf. Cato, 27.5J) for the more usual *propter eam causam*.

(8)   *Qui . . . fecissem*: subjn. because the relative clause is causal. This seems to be the only instance of this construction in S., who prefers the indicative even after *quippe qui* (vid. 48.2n.).

animo: contrasted with *lubidini* in the main clause. Cato was a staunch adherent of the Stoic school of philosophy, which regarded the intention to commit a fault no less blameworthy than the actual commission of a misdeed. For this sense of *animus* (= "intention"), cf. 58.6.

gratiam fecissem: a relatively rare idiom meaning "to grant indulgence" or "pardon."

condonabam: normally the word in the dat. expresses the person for whose sake pardon is bestowed on an offense. Accordingly, *alterius lubidini* is virtually equivalent to *alteri lubidinoso*, an adj. not found in S. Cic. in the *pro Murena* (61) chides Cato, who was one of the prosecutors, with adhering too rigidly to the Stoic creed, and he criticizes the Stoic attitude towards granting pardon as one of the less humane and less practical aspects of this school of philosophy: *sapientem gratia numquam moveri, numquam cuiusquam delicto ignoscere*. By contrast, Cato's great-grandfather is credited with saying that he was accustomed to pardon all except himself (Plut. *Cato Mai.* 8.9).

(9) *ea*: i.e., *ea verba*.

parvi: cf. *pluris* 52.5.

opulentia: either nom. or abl. of means if *res publica* is taken as the subject of both *erat* and *tolerabat* (cf. 53.5 for a possible parallel).

(10) *haec*: standing for *imperium populi Romani* (cf. 51.42n. *ea*). The interrogative particle *-ne* is understood and answered by *an* below in the second half of this alternative indirect question.

hostium: predicate gen. of possession corresponding to the possessive adj. *nostra*, which forms the predicate in the first part of this alternative indirect question: "whether it is going to be ours or belong to the enemy."

(11) *Hic*: adv., meaning "in such circumstances as these."

mihi: an ethical dative expressing surprise or indignation, equivalent to a parenthetical "don't tell me" (lit., "for me," "in my presence"). It is mainly a colloquial usage.

quisquam: the indefinite pronoun *quisquam* is employed because of the implied negative contained in this sentence ("surely no one") whether it is to be punctuated as a statement or rhetorical question.

mansuetudinem et misericordiam: paired for the sake of alliteration. According to S. (54.2), Caesar was noted for displaying these two qualities, while the Stoic creed, to which Cato subscribed, regarded *misericordia* as a weakness to be avoided (e.g., Cic. *Mur.* 62). In the speech that S. attributes to him, however, Caesar is made to disclaim an appeal to *misericordia* (51.1).

equidem: vid. 51.15n.

vera vocabula: the following observation is borrowed from the same passage in Thucydides (3.82.4) which provided a model at 38.3.

largiri: the inf. and *audacia* in the following clause are to be construed as subjects with *vocatur*; *liberalitas* and *fortitudo* are predicate nominatives.

eo: best taken as causal ("for this reason") answering *quia* above (cf. 20.3), rather than construing it as a demonstrative adj. with *in extremo*.

(12) *Sint sane*: a jussive subjn. used in a concessive sense.

se . . . habent: vid. 2.3n.

ne: adding a proviso to the above concessions, = *dummodo ne*: "only let those men not." *Illi* picks up the indefinite subject of *sint* above.

perditum eant: for the supine, vid. 36.4n.

(13) *Bene et composite*: similar to the observation made by Caesar, cf. 51.9.

disseruit: vid. 52.3n.

credo: parenthetical, to be taken after *falsa existumans ea*.

a bonis: to be construed with *divorso*; *boni* is used in the moral (cf.3.2) rather than the political sense (19.2). The indirect statement stands in apposition with *ea*, the antecedent of the relative clause.

foeda atque formidulosa: the alliteration serves to intensify the grim nature of this statement; *habere* is equivalent here to *tenere*.

(14) *videlicet*: qualifies the participle as an ironical statement. Primary sequence is employed in the clauses governed by *timens*, rather than secondary after *censuit*, to suggest that the fear is still felt at the present moment and not simply limited to the time of the proposal.

popularibus: vid. 22.1n.

a multitudine conducta: "by a hired mob," vid. 50.1n.

(15) *in urbe . . . per totam Italiam*: cf. 51.6n.

sint: subjn. with *quasi*, vid. 12.5n.

plus: vid. 39.4n.

(16) *solus non timet*: an insinuation that Caesar was in sympathy with the conspirators and perhaps a member of the plot (vid. 52.1n.).

mihi atque vobis: to be construed with *timere*, = "to fear for."

(17) *habetote*: in exhortations, the fut. imperative is the regular form of the verbs *scio* and *habeo* when they mean "consider."

(18) *illis*: dat. of reference; it denotes those members of the conspiracy who were still at large, especially the *exercitus Catilinae*.

aderunt: be at hand in a hostile sense, = "attack." *Feroces* is a predicate adj. and is best translated adverbially.

(19) *maiores nostros*: in the following sections (19–23), Cato takes up the observation made by Caesar at 51.42 when he asserted that the present generation of Romans was surpassed by their ancestors in wisdom and courage.

(20) *multo*: vid. 36.4n.

quippe: vid. 11.8n.

illis: i.e., *maioribus nostris*. The contrast that is drawn here between material resources and other qualities that made the nation great in former times seems to be borrowed from Demosthenes (*Phil.* 3.40).

(21) *nulla*: more emphatic and colloquial than *non*, = "not at all."

delicto . . . lubidini: dats. with *obnoxius* (= "addicted to"), which further clarifies the meaning of *liber*.

(22) *publice egestatem, privatim opulentiam*: cf. S.'s description of the conditions that prevailed before the onset of *avaritia* (9.2). *Egestatem* no doubt refers to the mismanagement of public resources and the drain that was placed upon the treasury by corruption and the grain dole among other popular acts of largess.

omnia virtutis praemia: as can be seen from the presence of the word *ambitio* (vid. 3.4n.), *virtutis praemia* refers especially to public office (cf. 12.1).

(23) *separatim sibi quisque*: a similar observation is attributed by Thucydides (1.141.6–7) to Pericles who notes as a weakness of the Spartans and their allies their tendency to consult their own selfish interests to the detriment of their united goal.

hic: i.e., "in the senate," as opposed to *domi*.

eo: cf. 52.11; here *ubi* seems to be used as if it had a causal sense.

vacuam: "unattended"; on one level, this word can mean "exposed," "vulnerable" (sc. *ab defensoribus*, "devoid of defenders"), but it may also be used, as it frequently is in legal terminology, to mean "unoccupied," "without an owner or master." Under Roman law, control over such property could be gained by occupation (*Auct. ad Her.* 4.29.40).

(24) *haec*: referring to the previous theme concerning *maiores nostri* (cf. 51.35).

incendere: S. appears to be the first author to use an inf. with *coniurare* rather than *ut* + subjn. or *ad* with a gerundive to express the goal aimed at.

infestissumam: ever since the sack of Rome by the Senones, a Gallic nation, traditionally in 390 B.C., the Romans looked upon the Gauls as a deadly enemy.

supra caput: a vivid metaphor expressing imminent danger. Cic. (*Mur.* 79) uses the expression *in capite* to describe the threat posed by Catiline's supporters who remained behind when Catiline set out to join his army in Nov.

(25) *vos cunctamini*: an abrupt rhetorical question in asyndeton. Possibly this is intended as an allusion to Nero's motion for tabling the matter (50.4).

hostibus: best taken as abl., *aliquo facere* forming a common idiom meaning "to do with," although the dat. is equally possible in the sense "to do to" (cf. 55.2).

(26) *Misereamini*: an ironic jussive subjn., as can be seen from the postponement of *censeo*, which may be taken parenthetically, and the omission of *ut*. The second half of this proposal is similar to the proposition dismissed by Caesar at 51.43.

(27) *ne*: to be taken either as standing for *dummodo ne* (cf. 52.12), adding a proviso which would remove some of the irony from *misereamini*, or better as the affirmative particle, sometimes written *nae*, which is invariably followed by a pronoun or demonstrative adj., as here, often with a potential subjn.: "truly that clemency and pity of yours may develop into misery for yourselves if . . ."

convortat: intransitive here in a reflexive sense meaning "to develop into." Only once in S. (6.7) is *convortere* used in this sense with the reflexive pronoun expressed.

(28) *Scilicet*: used to introduce an ironic objection.

maxume: sc. *eam timetis.*

dis . . . confisi: vid. 16.4n.

(29) *suppliciis*: vid. 9.2n.

prospere: the adv. rather than the predicate adj. *prospera*, which is better attested in the MSS, is the normal complement of *cedo* meaning "to turn out" (cf. 26.5; *Jug.* 20.5), while *evenio* is at times construed with a predicate adj. (e.g., 26.5) as well as an adv. (*Jug.* 63.1).

implores: either a potential subjn. as at 52.4 or possibly to be taken in a conditional sense (fut. less vivid) with *ubi* + the pf. subjn. standing for a *si* clause supplying the protasis.

irati . . . sunt: an explanatory clause in asyndeton; *nam* (cf. 2.1n.) is to be supplied.

(30) *A. Manlius Torquatus*: all other authorities give Titus as his praenomen (Livy 8.7.1; Cic. *Off.* 3.112; Gellius 9.13.1).

bello Gallico: 361 B.C. Apparently S. confuses the date of this incident, which according to most accounts took place in the Latin War (340 B.C.), with the earlier occasion when the elder Manlius won the surname Torquatus in the war against the Gauls.

(31) *parricidis*: vid. 14.3n.; the prepositional phrase is to be taken with *statuatis*.

quid statuatis: one of the rare instances of an indirect question governed by *cunctor*, which is more often construed with an inf. (e.g., 44.6).

cetera vita: on the sing. *cetera*, vid. 13.3n.

obstat: "offsets," "stands in contrast to," a rare meaning of this word (cf. Livy 1.26.5).

(32) *dignitati*: vid. 35.3n.; in this instance, a reference to Lentulus' position as praetor in this year.

(33) *iterum*: this seems to imply that Cethegus had been involved in an earlier plot. Possibly this is an allusion to the conspiracy in 65 B.C. (chapt. 18) or to the charge made by Cic. (*Sull.* 70) that Cethegus attempted to assassinate Metellus Pius (cos. 80 B.C.) when the latter was serving in Spain as commander in the war against Sertorius.

(34) *quibus*: case (dat.) is determined by the nearer verb (cf. 11.2n.). It stands for *qui si eis quicquam . . . fuisset . . . habuissent*.

quicquam . . . pensi: "any scruples" (vid. 5.6n.). The indefinite *quicquam* is employed owing to the implied negative (cf. 52.11).

(35) *mehercule*: "by Hercules," a common interjection in oaths. In S., it is confined to speeches.

locus: "scope" or "room," with the dat.; i.e., if no harm would result from the mistake of showing clemency.

ipsa re . . . verba: the familiar contrast of deeds (actual events) with words.

faucibus: probably an abl. of the part affected: "by the throat," a common metaphor with the verbs *teneri* and *premi*. With *urget* (= "press upon," "squeeze") *nos* must be supplied. Possibly, however, *faucibus* should be viewed as an instrumental abl., "with his jaws," likening Catiline to a wild beast. Cic., in fact, (*Cat.* 2.2) uses this very imagery to describe the city as snatched from the peril of Catiline's many plots (*urbem quam e suis faucibus ereptam esse luget*).

in sinu urbis: a reference to the Forum as the bosom of the city, and more particularly the senate. The presence of these fifth columnists within the senate itself explains Cato's assertion that no countermeasures can be adopted *occulte*. Possibly this should be interpreted as another veiled accusation of Caesar himself (cf.

52.16n.).

consuli: vid. 51.4n.

(36) *consilio*: abl. of cause; the *cum* clause forms the preamble to Cato's *sententia*, which is cast in the usual form (cf. 50.4n. *sumundum*). The double alliteration produced by *more maiorum supplicium sumundum* adds gravity (cf. 51.39) and allows Cato to conclude his argument with an appeal to *mos maiorum* in answer to his opponent Caesar, who rested so much of his case on this principle.

de confessis: to be taken with *supplicium sumundum* (cf. 50.4, 55.6).

manufestis: vid. 41.5n.; here this word is used in the technical legal sense of "caught in the act." Culprits who were caught red-handed did not enjoy the right of *provocatio* and were subject to summary justice. Therefore, the laws cited by Caesar (51.22) which safeguarded the rights of a defendant would not apply.

CHAPTER 53

(1) *adsedit*: vid. 31.7n.

consulares omnes: the consulars are singled out for separate mention because their status added weight to their opinions (cf. 50.4n. *primus*).

ad caelum ferunt: cf. 48.1.

alii alios: these words should probably be taken with *increpantes*, which may be transitive, as well as supplying one of the two objects of *vocant*, which takes a double accusative: "they rebuked each other and called each other cowardly."

clarus atque magnus: although these two adjs. are frequently paired, possibly they are intended in this context to recall the opening words of the history written by Cato's great-grandfather (*Orig.* 4.2–3] *clarorum virorum atque magnorum non minus otii quam negotii rationem extare oportere*).

senati: vid. 30.3n.; just above we find the usual gen. *senatus*.

sicuti ille censuerat: according to Cic. (*Att.* 12.21.1), he put Cato's motion to a vote because it was the most satisfactory statement of the position that had been adopted by the other speakers who had also advocated capital punishment. S. neglects to mention the unsuccessful attempt that was apparently made to adopt a motion modeled on Caesar's proposal calling for the confiscation of the conspirators' property (Plut. *Cic.* 21.4).

(2) *Sed*: vid. 7.1n. The following sections (2–5) pick up the theme in Cato's speech found at 52.19–23.

mihi: dat. with *forte lubuit*: "it by chance was agreeable to me," "a desire stirred in me to."

multa: agreeing with *facinora*, the antecedent of *quae*, which has been attracted into the relative clause. Anaphora of *multa* with the two participles is used in lieu of a conj.

mari atque terra: cf. 10.1n.; the standard expression *terra marique* is no doubt varied to avoid the repetition of *-que*.

facinora fecit: vid. 7.6n.; further alliteration is produced by *forte*.

sustinuisset: in the sense "made possible," "supported," a word denoting by implication exertion or strenuous activity. The indirect question supplies the object of *adtendere*.

(3) *legionibus*: normally this word refers to a unit of a Roman army which contained from 4200 to 6000 men depending on the period, but here, since it is applied to foreign armies, it is equivalent to *exercitibus*, a sense that is mainly archaic and poetical.

contendisse: *populum Romanum* must be supplied from above as the subject of the inf. and below with *toleravisse*.

parvis copiis: not "troops" since this has already been treated above (*parva manu*) but "resources" (= *opibus*), as can be seen from the contrast with *opulentis regibus*.

facundia: S. came to prefer this comparatively rare and archaic word to *eloquentia*, which he uses only twice (5.4, 54.1).

ante Romanos fuisse: "before them in rank," "above" (= *praestitisse*), a meaning of *ante* not found in Cic. or Caes.

(4) *multa agitanti*: "turning over in my mind many factors" (cf. 2.1n.)

constabat: the impf. is used to describe the dawning of this realization: "it became evident."

paucorum: to be taken in the literal, as opposed to the political sense (e.g., 39.1). This view at first glance seems to be just the opposite of the one attributed by Cic. (*Rep.* 2.2) to the Elder Cato who maintained that Rome surpassed other nations because her laws and institutions had been designed by many men over the generations rather than a single lawgiver. S., however, wishes to highlight the scarcity of such talented men in any given generation.

divitias paupertas: by metonymy, the abstracts stand for nations of this sort. This and the following pair of words pick up the observations made at 53.3 in the reverse order.

(5) *rursus*: elsewhere in the *Cat.* (18.6, 27.3) this adv. means "once more," but here it = *contra*: "on the contrary," "by contrast," indicating that the roles were reversed.

sicuti effeta parentum <*vi*>: "as if the vigor of their ancestors were worn out with childbearing." All of the major MSS give simply *effeta parentum*, which is obviously corrupt; *vi* is the supplement adopted by Ahlberg based upon a conjecture by Ritschl. We must either assume that some such word has dropped out of the text— other proposals include *virtute* (Allen) or *aetate* (Dietsch)—or emend *parentum* to *parente*, which is indeed found in several late MSS, no doubt in an attempt to make sense out of the corruption: "as when the parent stock is past childbearing." Some editors, how- ever, prefer to take *effeta* as nom. modifying *res publica* since S. does not use *sicuti* elsewhere with an abl. absol. In this case, *esset* must be supplied, and one of the various emendations which have been proposed for *parentum* will have to be adopted: *partu* (Kurfess) or *pariendo* (Kunze).

multis tempestatibus: "in many periods," "on many occasions" (cf. 20.3n.).

virtute: abl. of respect with *magnus*, which may be intended as a cryptic reproach aimed at Pompey, who adopted the surname *Magnus* and deliberately set out to liken himself, according to S. (*Hist*. 3.88M), to Alexander the Great.

(6)   *obtulerat . . . fuit*: past with respect to the viewpoint of the reader. This use of the past tense (epistolary) is especially common in let- ters (e.g., 35.5n.), where the writer puts himself, as it were, in the position of the reader.

quin: "without" (vid. 39.4n.).

possum: the subjn. *possem*, which is found in the bulk of the MSS, would accord better with the normal rule for attraction of mood within subjn. clauses, but S. often shows a tendency to use the indicative for the sake of vividness.

CHAPTER 54

(1)   *genus*: both were *nobiles* (vid. 5.1n.), but while Caesar belonged to an ancient patrician *gens* which claimed to be able to trace its descent from a Trojan ancestor in the person of Aeneas' son Iulus, Cato was of plebeian stock, and his great-grandfather was the first in his family to hold the consulship (195 B.C.).

aetas: Caesar, born in 100 B.C., was only 5 years older than Cato.

eloquentia: although neither man is best remembered for his achievements in the field of oratory, both are praised by Cic. for their eloquence (*Brut.* 118 on Cato; *Brut.* 251ff. on Caesar, cf. Quint. 10.1.114).

gloria: sc. *par*.

alia alii: *alia* is to be taken with *gloria*. Although only two persons are being compared, the appropriate word for "different" is *alius*, and this influences the choice of the dat. *alii* in place of *alteri*.

(2) *mansuetudine et misericordia*: cf. 52.11n. S. deliberately avoids the word *clementia*, for which Caesar became famous in the Civil War, because this word has the connotation of mercy shown by one of superior rank or power to an inferior.

severitas: Cato's rigid and inflexible rectitude is criticized on several occasions by Cic. as being unsuited to the reality of Roman politics (*Att.* 1.18.7, 2.1.8).

dignitatem: ironically S. attributes *dignitas* to Cato and not to Caesar, although this concept played a major role as one of Caesar's slogans in the Civil War.

(3) *dando*: vid. 49.3 on Caesar's *liberalitas*, and cf. Cato's criticism of this practice in general (52.11).

ignoscendo: another allusion to Caesar's well-known *clementia* ✳ which he showed towards his defeated enemies.

miseris perfugium: Catiline attempted to portray his conduct in this light (35.3), and S. himself apparently sought refuge in Caesar's camp when he was expelled from the senate by the censors in 50 (vid. Introd. p. 4). When the proceeds from the Gallic campaigns enabled Caesar to satisfy his own debts (vid. 49.3), he employed his vast financial resources to place many in his debt (Suet. *Iul.* 27.2).

malis pernicies: just the opposite method of treating the *mali* is attributed to Crassus (48.8).

(4) *in animum induxerat*: apparently an archaic expression meaning "to form an intention."

intentus: with *negotiis*, vid. 2.9n.

neglegere . . . denegare: best taken as historical infs. rather than complementary infs. governed by *in animum induxerat* since these acts of self-denial and generosity are doubtless offered by S. as typical features of Caesar's character and not as further goals that Caesar had adopted.

dono: the concrete noun has the meaning of a verbal substantive here: "giving."

bellum novom: in contrast with Pompey, who was sent to support Metellus Pius in the war against Sertorius and replaced Lucullus as commander in the war against Mithridates, Caesar broke new ground in his wars against the Gauls, Britons, and Germans; *novom* here is virtually equivalent to *integrum*.

enitescere: the inchoative for *enitere* seems to be poetical and found mainly in post-Augustan prose.

posset: subjn. of purpose.

(6)   *Non divitiis . . . abstinentia*: this description of Cato seems to be inspired by a maxim attributed to his great-grandfather, who claimed to adhere to such a standard of conduct (Plut. *Cat. Mai.* 10.5). The field of rivalry is expressed by the abls. of respect, and chiasmus is used to set off the antithesis between the two areas scorned by Cato and the other three in which he strove to be pre-eminent.

innocente: vid. 12.1n., *innocentia*.

Esse quam videri bonus malebat: this ideal description of the truly virtuous man recalls Aeschylus' eulogy of the Greek hero Amphiaraos (*Sept.* 592), who, like Cato, perished fighting for a losing cause.

assequebatur: the subject *gloria* is to be supplied from the previous clause where it is the object of *petebat*; the resulting reversal of subject and direct object from one clause to the next is typical of S.'s style. The observation that *gloria* attends *virtus* of its own accord forms a *topos*.

CHAPTER 55

(1)   *discessit*: a technical term describing the division *(discessio)* on a motion that is submitted to a vote in the senate (cf. 50.4n. *pedibus . . . iturum*).

ratus: in a present sense as can be seen from the parallel expression at 32.1.

antecapere: vid. 13.3n.; *noctem* here means "nightfall."

novaretur: in the absolute sense, cf. 39.3: "lest any new attempt <at a rescue> be made."

tresviros: cf. 30.7n.; the *III viri capitales* were junior magistrates elected annually who assisted the *aediles* in maintaining public order and were in charge of administering the prison and carrying out sentences of execution.

[ad] supplicium: if *ad*, which is amply supported by the MSS, is retained, *consul* must be understood as the subject of *postulabat*.

(2)   *in carcerem*: this building stood next to the *comitium* and to the east of the Temple of Concord at the foot of the Capitoline Hill. It may still be viewed today beneath a Christian church built in the 16th century. The structure, which legend assigned to Rome's fourth king, Ancus Marcius (Livy 1.33.8), consisted in this period of two chambers, of which the lower one was the first to be constructed, probably ca. 250 B.C. This is the room known as the

Tullianum, and although it was not originally subterranean, by Cic.'s day the level of the *comitium* had been raised so that the Tullianum could be described as *humi depressus* (55.3). The upper chamber seems to have been added towards the end of the second century B.C. and served as a place of detention for arrested persons awaiting sentencing.

ceteris: dat. (cf. 52.25n.).

(3)   *quod*: the gender of the relative pronoun is determined by the predicate nominative *Tullianum* rather than by the antecedent *locus*.

ubi . . . ad laevam: subjn. of the indefinite 2nd person sing. Logically this clause should give the location of the Tullianum rather than the prison as a whole, and therefore the reading *descenderis*, which is found in one MS, is attractive. Since the Tullianum was located below the ground level, if *ascenderis* is retained, it would seem to refer to the building as a whole viewed as one mounts the slope of the Capitoline Hill from the Forum or possibly to some internal feature of the structure above the Tullianum.

(4)   *camera lapideis fornicibus iuncta*: "a vault formed by stone arches." The older subterranean chamber was originally circular, and it was probably at first covered with a cone-shaped dome resembling the *tholos* or beehive tombs at Mycenae. This dome seems to have been cut off and replaced by a flat stone vault at the time the second chamber was added so as to provide a floor for the room above. Access to the Tullianum was gained through an opening in this floor (hence 55.5 *demissus est*).

incultu: the three abls. in asyndeton are abls. of cause. The resemblance of this description to the passage where Tartarus is described (52.13) no doubt accounts for the variant *inculta* which is found in the bulk of the MSS.

(5)   *vindices rerum capitalium*: probably the public executioners, who were known as *carnifices*, rather than the *III viri* themselves, who merely supervised the execution of capital sentences.

praeceptum erat: impersonal since *praecipio* is used here in the absolute sense with the dat.: "to give orders (or instructions) to."

(6)   *consulare imperium*: vid. 17.3n.

exitium vitae: this is the reading of all the best MSS, and there is no need to emend to *exitum* [*vitae*] if we assume that S. is using *exitium* in the archaic sense of *exitus* ("end"), which it once had according to the grammarian Festus (71L.7–8). Elsewhere in S., *exitium* appears to be employed in the usual sense of "death" or "destruction."

CHAPTER 56

(1) *Dum ea Romae geruntur*: this stock formula (cf. 32.3) breaks off
the narrative of events that took place in Rome and resumes S.'s
account of Catiline's preparations, which was suspended at 36.1. S.
neglects to mention Cic.'s brief address to the crowd that had gathered in the Forum on the night of the execution when he made the
famous pronouncement *vixerunt*, and the triumphal escort given to
Cic. by torch light to his home (Plut. *Cic.* 22.2–4; App. *BCiv.* 2.6;
Vell. 2.35.4).

duas legiones: vid. 53.3n.; this was the usual number of legions in a
consular army, and Catiline had already illegally assumed the symbols of this office (36.1).

pro numero: "according to the number at his disposal" (cf. 30.5n.);
each legion was normally divided into ten cohorts, a unit which
contained approximately 600 men when it was up to full strength.
Since Catiline apparently had only 2000 men to start with (56.2),
each of his cohorts would consist of only 100 men.

(2) *voluntarius*: those referred to at 39.5 as *extra coniurationem*, while
sociis (sc. *coniurationis*) describes those who were members of the
plot, his confederates (cf. 16.4, 40.6, 56.4).

distribuerat . . . expleverat: the plupf. is used to indicate that these
events took place prior to the arrest and execution of the conspirators in Rome, which S. has already described. *Venerat*, by contrast,
is the normal tense in an *ut* clause used to describe action that kept
occuring on a number of occasions.

numero: abl. of respect, while in other respects (56.3) these two
legions were still not up to full fighting strength. According to
Appian (*BCiv.* 2.7) and Plutarch (*Cic.* 16.4), Catiline's forces
totaled 20,000 men, which would equal more than the complement
of two legions.

cum: concessive.

(3) *pars quarta*: the same proportion is given by Appian (*BCiv.* 2.7),
who in other respects follows S. closely in his account of these
events.

militaribus armis: the adj. is more functional here than at 51.38
since a contrast is being drawn between regulation army equipment and weapons such as a private citizen might have at his disposal.

sparos: a short hunting spear.

alii: a corresponding *alii*, both in partitive apposition with *ceteri*, is
to be understood with *sparos aut lanceas*: "some . . . others."

(4) *adventabat*: for the impf. indic. after *postquam*, vid. 6.3n.; the progressive nature of this act is further brought out by the frequentative form of the verb. Catiline probably moved his camp from Faesulae towards the end of Nov. Antonius was commissioned to lead an army against Catiline about the middle of Nov. (36.2–3), and at this time Catiline had not yet received news of the arrest and execution of his accomplices (57.1).

per montis: the context makes it clear that these words refer to the hills north of Faesulae, which provided a place of safety to await the outcome of events in Rome.

Galliam vorsus: *vorsus* ("towards"), in classical prose construed with the acc. of the names of cities, towns, and small islands as a post-positive preposition, is extended by S. to govern the names of geographical regions, as here with *Galliam* (cf. *Jug.* 19.3).

patravissent: cf. 18.8n.; on the mood, vid. 17.7n. *valuisset*. This statement appears to contradict the arrangements described elsewhere (32.2, 43.1, 44.6) where it seems that Lentulus and the others were to await Catiline's arrival in the vicinity of Rome before giving the signal for arson and murder, but possibly the forces under Antonius led Catiline to alter his original plans (cf. 58.4).

(5) *servitia repudiabat*: vid. 24.4n.

cuius: an extreme example of synesis (vid. 16.1n.); while it is not unusual for a pl. pronoun to refer to the individuals denoted by a sing. collective noun, here just the opposite relationship exists between the antecedent (*servitia*) and the relative pronoun. Apparently the pl. *servitia* is viewed as forming a class, and with *cuius*, *generis* is to be understood.

suis rationibus: most likely abl. with *alienum* meaning "inconsistent," "not in keeping with" (vid. 40.5n.), but the dat. is also possible if *alienum* is employed in the sense of "unfavorable"; for *rationes* = "interests," cf. 44.5.

CHAPTER 57

(1) *nuntius*: a verb of reporting is to be supplied from this word governing the following indirect statements. The disheartening effect that this news had on Catiline's forces tends to vindicate Cic.'s strategy not to delay the punishment of the conspirators who had been apprehended but to press for a speedy execution.

pervenit: probably perfect since *video* is the only verb that S. uses in the historical pres. after *postquam* in the *Cat.*

relicuos: it is difficult to say how many of the approximately 12,000 men who had joined Catiline's army according to S. (56.2) remained after the desertions. Dio (37.40.1) reports that 3000 died in the final battle, in which Catiline's whole army perished to the last man. Of the forces opposed to Catiline, Metellus had three legions (15,000–18,000 men), and the army of Antonius was larger still (Dio 37.39.2).

in agrum Pistoriensem: "the region about Pistoria," modern Pistoia, a town in Etruria which is situated about 20 miles northwest of Faesulae on the southern slopes of the Apennine Mts. Catiline was apparently prevented from taking the direct route across the plains from Faesulae to Pistoria by the presence of Antonius' army near Faesulae (56.4 *hostibus occasionem pugnandi non dare*). Hence he marched over the rugged terrain to the north (*per montis asperos*).

in Galliam Transalpinam: no doubt his ultimate goal was to reach the Allobroges in Transalpine Gaul, whose smoldering discontent with the Roman government (40.3) broke out into an open revolt in the following year (50.1n.). It was necesssary, however, for Catiline first to break out of Etruria and cross the Apennine Mts. into Cisalpine Gaul where he could hope to replenish his dwindling provisions (58.6) before attempting to cross the Alps into Transalpine Gaul. The lack of provisions and the difficulty of the terrain make it unlikely that Catiline planned to reach Transalpine Gaul by way of Liguria to the northwest. The quickest route across the Apennines lay between Pistoria and Bononia along the course of the Rhenus River. It was probably Catiline's intention to proceed northeast along this route to Bononia or Mutina where he could turn into the *via Aemilia* and press on to Transalpine Gaul. The praetor Metellus Celer, however, who was stationed on the northeast coast of Italy (57.2), learned of Catiline's plans from deserters (57.3) and blocked the northern end of the pass across the Apennines, probably just south of Bononia at a strategic point in the valley (*sub ipsis radicibus montium*).

(2)   *in agro Piceno*: vid. 30.5n., more correctly *in agro Gallico Picenoque* (Cic. *Cat.* 2.26). His headquarters were doubtless at Ariminum in the *ager Gallicus* to the north of Picenum, and he probably moved north to Bononia along the *via Aemilia* when he surmised Catiline's probable course of action.

praesidebat: a rare use in the absolute sense of "hold command," "be in charge."

ex difficultate rerum: "as a result of Catiline's difficult position" (cf. 12.2n.), to be taken with *existumans*.

agitare: "to set in motion" in the sense of "to meditate" a certain course of action.

(3)   *sub ipsis radicibus montium*: at the northern end of the pass (vid. 57.1n. above).

   consedit: a common military expression equivalent to *castra posuit*.

   illi descensus erat: an archaic turn of phrase for *illi descendendum erat*, where the verbal substantive is used in place of the gerundive.

(4)   *expeditos*: this is the reading of the principal MSS, confirmed by a citation in the grammarian Priscian (*pace* Kurfess who falsely attributes the reading *expeditus* to Priscian). Most modern editors emend to *expeditus* on the assumption that *utpote qui* is causal (equivalent to *quippe qui*) introducing an explanation for the statement that Antonius was not far off. *Utpote qui*, however, is to be taken here in a limiting sense (= "considering the fact that"), and the acc. *expeditos*, going closely with *in fuga*, is needed to provide the direct object of *sequeretur* (for this meaning of *utpote qui*, cf. Plaut. *Mil.* 530; Cic. *Att.* 2.24.4). Catiline's men were *expediti* in comparison with Antonius' army because they were less fully equipped and not loaded down with baggage. Antonius was forced by the size of his army to take a less direct route over more level terrain (*locis aequioribus*).

(5)   *praesidi*: a reference to the *praesidia* that Catiline hoped to receive from his confederates in the city (58.4).

   in tali re: cf. 48.5 *in tali tempore*.

   cum Antonio: according to Dio (37.39.3), Catiline chose to face Antonius, although his forces were larger than those of Metellus, because he hoped that Antonius would allow himself to be defeated in view of his former participation in the conspiracy.

CHAPTER 58

(1)   *Conpertum ego habeo*: vid. 14.7n.; the predicate acc. *conpertum* agrees with the following indirect statements (cf. 29.1n.).

   neque . . . neque: the first *neque* does not stand for *et non* but answers the one following; this clause is not strictly coordinate with the preceding statement but is causal in nature explaining why the opening observation is true.

   ex ignavo . . . ex timido: chiasmus and alliteration (*verba virtutem*) embellish the exordium of this final speech attributed to Catiline.

(2)   *animo*: for the dat. with *inesse*, cf. 15.5n.

   natura aut moribus: abls. of cause, i.e., "inborn or acquired by training."

   patere: below (58.9) this word is used in its literal sense; here it means "to be visible."

(3)   *quo . . . uti*: cf. 33.1n.; *advocavi* is historical pf. as can be seen from the sequence of tenses in the two purpose clauses.

  mei consili: i.e., his decision to give battle.

(4)   *socordia atque ignavia*: subject nom. of the indirect question *quantam . . . attulerit*; the verb is sing. because these nouns are viewed as forming a single concept.

  quoque modo: = *et quo modo*.

(5)   *quo loco*: in the figurative ("in what a difficult position") as opposed to the literal sense of locality.

  iuxta mecum: vid. 2.8n.; apparently a colloquial expression, used just this one time by S., = *aeque atque ego*.

(6)   *ab urbe*: "in the direction of the city," Antonius' army to the south near Faesulae.

  si: virtually concessive, = *etiam si*: "even if our intention (*animus*) should very greatly incline in that direction." The indicative is used in the main clause to convey the certainty of the prohibition.

(8)   *forti . . . animo*: abl. of description forming the predicate of *sitis*.

  divitias . . . patriam: apart from the addition of *patriam*, this list of considerations is the same as the one found in the speech that S. attributes to Catiline before the elections in 64 B.C. (20.14).

(9)   *vincimus*: the pres., rather than fut. pf., which is used below to describe the alternative (*si metu cesserimus*), emphasizes the likelihood of victory (cf. 20.6n. *vindicamus*). The contrast of conditions that attend victory as opposed to defeat is a *topos* in pre-battle orations.

  abunde: a predicate adv. (vid. 20.2n.); sc. *erit* with *commeatus*, which is probably nom. sing. rather than pl.

(10)   *metu*: abl. of cause.

  quisquam: vid. 31.2n.

(11)   *supervacuaneum*: "needless" (cf. 51.19); although both armies were compelled to fight by *necessitudo* (= *necessitas*, vid. 17.2n.), Catiline argues that the forces opposed to them have nothing to gain because they are merely carrying out the orders of the government and not fighting for their own interests but *pro potentia paucorum*. For just the opposite assessment of their relative positions by the commander of the government's legions, vid. 59.5.

(13)   *Licuit vobis*: "you might have," the protasis "if you had wished" is suppressed.

  alienas opes: relief from others as their dependents (*clientes*, e.g., 50.1) or as legacy hunters.

(14)   *illa*: the options just mentioned, while *haec* refers to the present

course of action, their decision to throw in their lot with Catiline. An adversative conj. must be supplied before *quia*.

(15) *mutavit*: a gnomic pf. (vid. 11.3n.); the acc. denotes the thing given up or exchanged for the condition denoted by the abl. (of price).

(16) *avorteris*: subjn. of the indefinite 2nd person sing.; the sentiment forms another *topos* in such addresses before battle.

ea: the demonstrative pronoun, which refers to *in fuga salutem sperare*, has been attracted into the gender (f.) of the predicate nominative.

(17) *pro muro*: "the equivalent of a rampart," a common meaning of *pro*, especially when it stands in the predicate (e.g., 12.1).

habetur: cf. 1.4n.

(18) *Cum vos considero*: cf. 20.6 for a similar turn of phrase in Catiline's first speech.

(19) *Animus, aetas*: these words pick up another theme in Catiline's first speech (20.10).

(20) *Nam*: introducing a reason given to dispel a fear (the superior number of the enemy) that is left unexpressed (cf. 7.2).

queat: this is the only instance of this verb in the *Cat.*

(21) *fortuna*: vid. 10.1n.; Catiline deliberately avoids the expression *si victi eritis* by using this euphemism.

inulti: sc. *ne* coordinate with *neu* after *cavete*. Nearly the same thought is expressed by the ambassadors whom Manlius sent to Marcius Rex (vid. 33.5).

CHAPTER 59

(1) *signa canere*: a common military idiom; *signa* is best taken as the acc. subject of the inf. *canere*, which is used intransitively: "the trumpet-calls to sound."

instructos ordines: i.e., in battle array into which the soldiers were arranged following the dismissal of the *contio* (cf. 57.6).

exaequato: the compound in place of *aequato*, which appears to form a standard expression with *periculo*, may be slightly colloquial and conforms with S.'s preference for compound verbs elsewhere.

pro loco atque copiis: vid. 30.5n.; *loco* here refers to the physical features of the battle field which are treated in the following section.

(2) *uti*: in a causal sense (= *quod*), an archaic usage.

et ab dextra rupe<m> aspera<m>: "and the rugged rock on the right"; *rupem asperam* is an emendation for *rupe aspera*, which is found in the principal MSS. The reference to conditions on the left and right make it logical to expect a second acc. governed by *inter* after the conj. Those who defend the reading of the MSS take *aspera* as a neut. subst. in the acc. pl. (sc. *loca*) qualified by the causal abl. *rupe*, but in the *Cat.*, only adjs. of quantity or size are commonly employed in this fashion.

signa: "standards"; by metonymy this word stands for the divisions themselves (*reliquas cohortes*). A cohort was subdivided into three maniples, each consisting of two centuries, and each cohort, or possibly each maniple, had its own regimental emblem (*signum*) affixed to a staff. Of his twenty cohorts, Catiline, therefore, placed twelve in reserve (*in subsidio*), but since his army was no longer up to full strength (57.1), he reinforced his front line by calling up the best of his reserves.

artius: referring to military formations, the adv. means "in close order." Here the comparative degree indicates that these twelve cohorts were more tighly packed than the eight in the front line.

(3)   *centuriones*: there were two of these commanders per maniple. They were seasoned non-commissioned officers.

omnis lectos et evocatos: best taken as standing in apposition with *centuriones*: "all picked men and veterans" (whom Catiline had made officers) rather than describing a separate group in contrast with the centurions and those selected from the *gregarii milites*. The *evocati* were veteran soldiers who re-enlisted after they had served their required term, and this whole class is sometimes spoken of as if it enjoyed a status nearly equal to that of a centurion (e.g., Caes. *BCiv.* 1.17.4). No doubt this group included many of the *Sullani milites* (16.4) who rallied to Catiline's cause.

armatum: unless this is a gloss, it must denote those soldiers who were fully armed (56.3 *pars quarta*) as opposed to the majority who carried makeshift weapons.

Faesulanum quendam: possibly P. Furius, vid. 50.4n.

curare: "to be in command"; this absolute sense is found on a number of occasions in S., and it is always accompanied by an expression referring to the location of the person in charge.

libertis: his own freedmen (vid. 50.1n.). It is tempting to identify the L. Sergius, whom Cic. (*Dom.* 13) calls Catiline's armor-bearer, as one of these freedmen.

colonis: apparently Sulla's verterans (28.4), unless we accept the emendation *calonibus* ("soldiers' servants"), which rests upon the corruption *colonibus* found in several MSS. Ordinarily picked soldiers would form the commander's personal bodyguard, but possibly Catiline had already committed his best troops to the battle line and was forced to rely upon freedmen and ordinary soldiers' attendants to make up the number of his praetorian cohort (cf. 60.5n.).

propter aquilam: *propter* denoting nearness to is found only here in S. Marius introduced the silver eagle as a standard for the legion when he reorganized the army in the last decade of the 2nd century B.C. (Pliny, *HN* 10.16). Cic. (*Cat.* 1.24, 2.13) several times refers to this Marian trophy, which was cherished by Catiline and seems to have been used to lend an aura of legitimacy and good luck to his cause.

bello Cimbrico: the war waged against the Cimbri and Teutones who menaced Italy with the threat of an invasion for over a decade at the end of the 2nd century B.C. The Teutones were defeated by Marius at Aquae Sextiae in 102, and the Cimbri were overwhelmed in 101 near Vercellae by Marius and the procos. Catulus.

(4)   *pedibus aeger*: apparently a case of gout (*podagra*), which is characterized by lameness (*pedibus*, abl. of resp.). These words, standing in apposition with Antonius, account for the statement in the following *quod* clause. According to Dio (37.39.4), Antonius only pretended to be incapacitated so that he would not have to come face to face with Catiline, his former associate, on the field of battle.

M. Petreio: his role on this occasion is highly praised by Cic. (*Sest.* 12). As a *legatus*, he afterwards governed one of the two Spanish provinces for Pompey from late 55 until the outbreak of the Civil War when he was outmaneuvered and forced to surrender by Caesar. He fought with the Pompeians at Pharsalus, and after the final defeat of the Republican forces at Thapsus in 46, he died in a suicide pact that he made with Juba, the King of Numidia.

(5)   *tumulti*: in the technical sense, this word was used especially to describe wars that posed an immediate threat to the state such as uprisings in Italy or invasions by the Gauls on the northern frontier. The declaration of such a state of emergency suspended the normal rules governing exemptions from military service (Cic. *Phil.* 8.2–3). The adoption of this archaic form of the gen. sing. in -*i* (cf. 30.3n.) rests upon a citation of this passage by the grammarian Nonius (489.34), while the usual 4th declension form, *tumultus*, is attested in all the MSS. Since the version given by Nonius is faulty in other respects (*frontem* for *fronte* and *subsidio* for *subsidiis*), perhaps this testimony should be treated with caution.

unum quemque nominans: apparently it was not unusual for a commander to know the names of his centurions at least (e.g., Caes. *BGall.* 2.25.2) and perhaps some of the common soldiers as well.

latrones: a derogatory word, "bandits" (cf. 28.4) rather than true soldiers.

pro patria . . . pro aris atque focis suis: cf. 52.3 where, apart from the substitution of *parentes* for *liberi*, the same words are used to enumerate those things that are held dear by a Roman. The anaphora of *pro* adds weight to this appeal.

(6)   *Homo militaris*: "a man of military experience" (cf. 45.2), which is explained by the following *quod* clause.

amplius annos triginta: the words used to make a comparison after *plus, amplius*, or *minus* may retain the case that expresses their grammatical relationship to the rest of the sentence (here acc. of duration of time) as if *quam* had been expressed, or they may be put in the abl. (e.g., 56.2).

tribunus: sc. *militum*; there were six of these officers per legion, and each held command in turn.

praefectus: an officer appointed to command the auxiliary forces that were attached to a legion and generally supplied by the allies.

legatus: an officer second in command who could act as deputy for the commander in chief as Petreius did for Antonius on this occasion.

praetor: since the eight praetors who were elected annually in this period rarely served as military commanders, either this word is used archaically in its literal sense of "commander," or more likely it stands loosely for propraetor and refers to the period when Petreius governed a province after holding the praetorship sometime prior to 63.

plerosque ipsos: *ipsos* seems to imply that he knew them on a personal basis (cf. *nominans* above, 59.5).

CHAPTER 60

(1)   *paulatim*: "a little at a time," i.e., "slowly."

(2)   *ventum est*: impersonal passive of the intransitive verb *venio*.

ferentariis: these were the skirmishers, who hurled missiles from a distance. The word is extremely rare and probably archaic.

cum infestis signis: a common military expression—usually without *cum*—which signifies the joining of battle: lit., "with hostile standards," i.e., "with opposing ranks." The preposition was probably introduced here to set off this phrase from the preceding abl. of manner.

pila omittunt: following the skirmishing by the light-armed troops (*ferentarii*), normally the *pilum*, a heavy throwing spear, was used to fire a volley from a distance (*eminus*) as a prelude to fighting at close quarters (*comminus*) with the *gladius*, a short thrusting sword. Occasionally, however, as here, the opposing forces proceeded directly to hand to hand combat without pausing to discharge their javelins.

gladiis res geritur: a stock military expression.

(3)　*Veterani*: i.e., the *cohortes veteranae* (59.5), while *illi* refers to Catiline's forces. The change from the historical inf. (*instare*) in the first clause to historical pres. (*resistunt*) in the second is abrupt and adds animation to the narrative.

(4)　*militis . . . imperatoris*: of the six historical infs. in asyndeton (cf. 31.3 for a similar series) that precede this clause, the first four refer primarily to Catiline's role as a commander, while the last two concern his conduct as a soldier. Therefore, *militis* and *imperatoris* gather up these activities in the reverse order producing chiasmus. Catiline is made to fulfill the offer that he made in his first speech (20.16 *vel imperatore vel milite me utimini*).

(5)　*tendere*: this use of the simple verb instead of the more usual compound *contendere*, which is found in several MSS, seems to be mainly poetical, but it is common after S. in the historical writers.

　　cohortem praetoriam: this elite corps was assigned to the commander (cf. 59.6n. *praetor*) as a bodyguard. It comprised seasoned veterans in addition to the close friends of the commander and young aristocrats who were serving their apprenticeship on their way to becoming magistrates and military commanders themselves.

　　alios alibi: this further explains *perturbatos*. The enemy no longer made a unified resistance but put up a fight as best they could here and there.

　　utrimque ex lateribus: "on both sides," i.e., from his position within the shattered center (*in medios hostis*; cf. 61.3) of Catiline's forces which left the inner flanks exposed.

(6)　*in primis*: to be taken with the participle rather than *cadunt*.

(7)　*dignitatis*: this word recalls an important theme in Catiline's letter to Catulus (vid. 35.4n.).

　　confoditur: vid. 28.1n.

CHAPTER 61

(1)   *tum vero*: an emphatic restatement of the time reference, which is defined by the preceding abl. absol.

      cerneres: a potential subjn. of past time.

(2)   *vivos*: = *vivus* (vid. 11.2n.) in contrast with *amissa anima*. The considerable variation in the word order that is found in the MSS has caused this word to be suspected as an interpolation from 61.4.

      pugnando: a modal abl. which is used colloquially as a substitute for the present participle (cf. *Jug.* 103.2 *Bocchus seu reputando* [= *reputans*] . . . *seu admonitus*). This use of the gerund is quite common in the Roman historians after S.

      locum: this word, which is the logical antecedent of *quem*, has been attracted into the relative clause, which is put first for for emphasis.

(3)   *divorsius*: understand *ab eo loco quem pugnando ceperant.*

      advorsis volneribus: a common expression describing honorable wounds that are received in the front while fighting, rather than in the back while fleeing.

(4)   *etiam*: = *adhuc*. According to Dio (37.40.2) Catiline's head was cut off and sent to the city to establish his death beyond any doubt.

(5)   *civis ingenuus*: cf. 50.1n. *liberti.*

(6)   *iuxta*: vid. 2.8n.

(7)   *incruentam*: S. appears to be the first writer to use this adj. The outcome of this battle accords with the wish attributed to Catiline (58.21).

      strenuissumus: the superlative is first attested in Cato (*Agr.* praef. 4; 19.1J), from whom S. probably borrowed it.

(8)   *amicum alii, pars hospitem aut cognatum*: chiasmus reinforces the contrast. The ties are presented in ascending order: friendship, hospitality, and finally kinship.

(9)   *laetitia, maeror, luctus atque gaudia*: as usual in S., *atque* is used to join only the words in the second pair (cf. 6.1). The arrangement is chiastic; *laetitia* corresponds to *gaudia* = "manifestations of joy," which is made pl. to reinforce the correspondence by means of homoeoteleuton. The first two words concern especially the outward expression of these emotions (cf. 46.2n; Cic. *Tusc.* 4.18 *maeror* = *aegritudo flebilis*), while the second pair describes the inner feeling (Cic. *Tusc.* l.c. *luctus* = *aegritudo ex eius qui carus fuerit interitu acerbo*): "exultation and tears, mourning and rejoicing."

APPENDIX I

CATILINE'S BIRTH DATE AND EARLY CAREER

The date of Catiline's birth must be no later than 108 B.C. since he was an ex-praetor and a potential candidate for the consulship in 66 (18.3). The minimum age requirement for the praetorship in this period seems to have been 39 (42 for the consulship), and although the precise date of Catiline's praetorship is not attested he probably held this office in 68. This assumption allows for the statutory two year interval between offices and agrees with the evidence that Catiline was governor of Africa in 66 (Cic. *Cael.* 10 *praetor me . . . Africam tum praetor ille* [i.e., *Catilina*] *obtinebat*). His term as governor, with the official title *pro consule* (Cic. *Cael.* 73), presumably extended from about the spring of 67 up to just before the consular elections in 66.

The details of Catiline's early career, before and after the Sullan proscriptions, can be partially reconstructed from other sources. According to Cicero, Catiline took an active interest in military affairs (*Cael.* 12). His early training was apparently acquired in the camp of Cn. Pompeius Strabo, the father of Pompey the Great. The name *L. Sergi(us) L. f. Tro(mentina)* appears on an inscription of 89 B.C. listing the officers on the staff of Strabo at Asculum (*ILS* 8888). This list also contains the name of the commander's son and hence indicates early contact between Catiline and Pompey. Furthermore, Catiline may well have become acquainted with Cicero on this same campaign since Cicero too served for a time under the consul Pompeius Strabo in 89 (Cic. *Phil.* 12.27). Later, possibly in the 70s, Catiline acted in the capacity of a *legatus* during a siege operation (S. *Hist.* 1.46M). Conceivably this post was held in 78 under P. Servilius Vatia (cos. 79) in Cilicia where Caesar also served for a short time on Servilius' staff during the same year (Suet. *Iul.* 3).

The pattern that emerges is typical of the training received by the sons of senators preparatory to seeking public office. S. refrains from including these details in his account of Catiline's past life (5.1–8, 15) because the monograph is not meant to be a biography, and the author deliberately passes over facts that would not contribute to his characterization of Catiline as a wicked man and monster from his earliest youth. This record of military service, however, tends to balance the one-sided picture given by S. and Cicero and reveals the probable early acquaintance of Catiline with three of the leading figures in Roman politics at the time of the conspiracy.

APPENDIX II

EVIDENCE FOR THE "FIRST CATILINARIAN CONSPIRACY"

Evidence for this so-called first conspiracy is extremely flimsy. The earliest extant reference is a charge made by Cicero during the election campaign in 64. He claimed that Catiline plotted with Cn. Calpurnius Piso (vid. 18.4n.) to massacre a number of leading senators (*Tog. Cand.* ap. Ascon. p. 92C). The departure of Piso for Spain in 65 (19.1) and his subsequent death before the summer of 64 (vid. 19.3n.) provide a *terminus ante quem* for this intrigue. The allusion itself is extremely vague and occurs in a speech that Cicero delivered in the senate shortly before the elections to blacken the character of his two chief opponents, C. Antonius (vid. 21.3n.) and Catiline.

The next reference chronologically is found in Cicero's *First Catilinarian*, which was delivered on 8 Nov. 63 (vid. 31.6n.). It is a bit more specific: Catiline was observed in the *comitium*—the area in the Forum in front of the senate-house—on 29 Dec. 66 with a weapon; it was common knowledge, according to Cicero, that Catiline had recruited a gang to murder the consuls and leading members of the state (*Cat.* 1.15). Later in the same month, Cicero asserted in his defense of Murena (*Mur.* 81), and also in a letter written to Pompey at the end of 63 or early 62 (*Sull.* 67), that the origins of the conspiracy that broke out in his consulship could be traced back two years to an earlier plot formed by Catiline and Piso.

T. Manlius Torquatus, the son of the consul of 65 who was allegedly one of the targets of assassination, prosecuted P. Sulla in 62 on the grounds that he had been Catiline's associate, and he attempted to use Cicero's own statements concerning the activities of Catiline in 66–65 as evidence against Sulla, whom Cicero defended. Unfortunately, Cicero's *pro Sulla* deals primarily with the conspiracy in 63, since Hortensius, who shared the brief for the defense, responded to the charges connected with the earlier plot (*Sull.* 12). There are, however, several tantalizing references in Cicero's speech to the events of 65. According to the version put forward on this occasion, Catiline and presumably Autronius (vid. 17.3n.) planned to murder Aurelius Cotta and Manlius Torquatus, the consuls designate, on 1 Jan. 65 and seize office themselves. Cn. Piso and Vargunteius (vid. 17.3n.) were privy to this plot, but not Sulla, who, like Autronius, had been convicted of bribery in 66 and deprived of his victory in the consular elections (*Sull.* 67–68).

The absence of Sulla's name in S.'s account of this first plot is significant (18.5) and doubtless attributable to the influence of Cicero's pleading in the *pro Sulla*. Furthermore, Cicero makes the point that Catiline's guilt was far from established at the time of this earlier plot: many consulars supported Catiline at his trial for extortion in the summer of 65. Among them was the elder Torquatus, supposedly one of Catiline's intended victims. At the time, Torquatus refused to believe the rumors that implicated Catiline in a plot against his life, although he had apparently changed his mind a year later since he did not support Catiline when he was prosecuted soon after the elections in 64 for his role in the Sullan proscriptions (*Sull.* 81; cf. 24.2n.).

Several facts are certain: the conviction of Sulla and Autronius for bribery in the autumn of 66 had an unsettling effect. Perhaps Vargunteius can be added to the list of candidates who succumbed to the charge of corrupt electioneering in this year (vid. 17.3n.). Autronius attempted to stir up violence to disrupt the court proceedings (*Sull.* 15). At the same time, Catiline was threatened with prosecution for extortion and prevented from standing at the consular elections (vid. 18.3n.)— further fuel for the discontent that was brewing in Rome. Then late in the year, the enemies of Pompey instituted a prosecution for extortion against C. Manilius soon after he ceased to be tribune on Dec. 10th. The case came before Cicero, who as praetor presided over the extortion court in 66, and the motive of the prosecution was doubtless revenge for Manilius' bill that transferred the command in the war against Mithridates to Pompey in the face of bitter opposition from the *optimates*. Cicero set the hearing for the last day of his term as praetor, Dec. 29th, but a mob demonstration caused a postponement (Dio 36.44.1–2; Plut. *Cic.* 4–6). Early in the following year, Manilius employed gangs to disrupt his trial (vid. 18.6n.), and when this tactic was foiled by armed reinforcements under the command of the consuls Cotta and Torquatus, Manilius let the verdict go against him by default (Ascon. p. 60C).

Catiline and Piso were perhaps implicated in the demonstrations that attended Manilius' trial (Ascon. p. 66C). This assumption will neatly account for the presence of Catiline in the Forum on 29 Dec. 66, the date set for the first hearing. Likewise, the subsequent mob violence in 65 will explain the bodyguard that was voted by the senate for the consuls (Dio 36.44.4). This measure need not have been aimed specifically at Catiline and his co-conspirators as Dio believed, but the intent was doubtless to restore order so that Manilius would be forced to answer the charge against him. Whatever role Catiline played in this affair, whether it was in support of Manilius and the Pompeian faction or of their opponents, there is no reason to suspect that he was involved in a sinister plot to murder the consuls and seize the consulship by force since at the time he had every reason to hope that he could gain this office at a later date by means of election.

SELECTED BIBLIOGRAPHY

A comprehensive bibliography for the years 1879–1964 is provided by A.D. Leeman, *A Systematical Bibliography of Sallust*, 2nd edn., Leiden, 1965. More recent scholarship pertinent to the *Catiline* is registered by N. Criniti, *Bibliografia Catilinaria*, Milan, 1971. Below is a short list of titles, mostly in English, that were found useful in preparing this edition of the *Catiline*.

I. TEXTS AND COMMENTARIES

Cook, A.M. *C. Sallusti Crispi Bellum Catilinae.* London, 1884.

Ernout, A. *Salluste.* 3rd ed. Paris, 1958.

Hellegouarc'h, J. *C. Sallustius Crispus, De Catilinae Coniuratione.* Paris, 1972.

Kurfess, A. *C. Sallusti Crispi Catilina, Iugurtha, Fragmenta Ampliora.* 3rd ed. Leipzig, 1957.

McGushin, P. *C. Sallustius Crispus, Bellum Catilinae.* Leiden, 1977.

Maurenbrecher, B. *C. Sallusti Crispi Historiarum Reliquiae.* Leipzig, 1891–93.

Merivale, C. *Gaii Sallusti Crispi Catilina.* rev. ed. London, 1882.

Nall, G.H. *The Catiline of Sallust.* London, 1900.

Summers, W.C. *C. Sallusti Crispi Catilina.* Cambridge, 1900.

Vretska, K. *C. Sallustius Crispus, De Catilinae Coniuratione.* 2 vols. Heidelberg, 1976.

II. BOOKS AND ARTICLES

Ahlberg, A. *Prolegomena ad Sallustium.* Göteborg, 1911.

Allen, W. "Catullus XLIX and Sallust's *Bellum Catilinae.*" *CJ* 32 (1936–37), 298.

_____ . "In Defense of Catiline." *CJ* 34 (1938), 70–85.

_____ . "The Acting Governor of Cisalpine Gaul in 63." *CP* 48 (1953), 176–77.

_____ . "Sallust's Political Career." *Studies in Philology* 51 (1954), 1–14.

Austin, R.G. *M. Tulli Ciceronis Pro M. Caelio Oratio.* 3rd ed. Oxford, 1960.

Badian, E. "The Early Career of A. Gabinius (cos. 58 B.C.)."

Philologus 103 (1959), 87–99.

————— . "Waiting for Sulla." *JRS* 52 (1962), 47–61.

————— . "Notes on *Provincia Gallia* in the Late Republic." *Mélanges Piganiol* (Paris 1966) II. 901–18 (913–16 the governor of Cisalpine Gaul in 63 and the appointment of Q. Metellus Celer).

————— . "Lucius Sulla, the Deadly Reformer." *Seventh Todd Memorial Lecture.* Sydney, 1970.

————— . *Publicans and Sinners: Private Enterprise in the Service of the Roman Republic.* Oxford: Blackwell, 1972.

Bennett, A.W.   *Index Verborum Sallustianus.* Hildesheim, 1970.

Boissier, G.   "Les Prologues de Salluste." *Journal des Savants* n.s. 1 (1903), 59–66.

————— . *La conjuration de Catilina.* 5th ed. Paris, 1905.

Bolaffi, E.   "I proemi delle monografie di Sallustio." *Athenaeum* 16 (1938), 128–57.

Broughton, T.R.S.   "Was Sallust Fair to Cicero?" *TAPA* 67 (1936), 34–46.

————— . "More Notes on Roman Magistrates." *TAPA* 79 (1948), 63–78 (pp. 76–78 S.'s praetorship).

————— . *The Magistrates of the Roman Republic.* 2 vols. New York, 1951–1952. Suppl. vol. 1960.

Brunt, P.A.   "Three Passages from Asconius." *CR* n.s. 7 (1957), 193–95 (the first conspiracy of Catiline).

————— . "The Army and the Land in the Roman Revolution." *JRS* 52 (1962), 69–86.

————— . "The Conspiracy of Catilina." *History Today* 13 (1963), 14–21.

————— . "The *Equites* in the Late Republic." *Second International Conference of Economic History,* 1962 (Paris, 1965), I.117–37.

————— . "*Amicitia* in the Late Roman Republic." *Proc. Cambr. Philolog. Soc.* 11 (1965), 1–20.

————— . "The Roman Mob." *Past and Present* 35 (1966), 3–27.

————— . *Italian Man Power.* Oxford, 1971.

Büchner, K.   *Sallust.* Heidelberg, 1960.

Douglas, A.E.   *M. Tulli Ciceronis Brutus.* Oxford, 1966.

Eagle, E.D.   "Catiline and the *Concordia Ordinum.*" *Phoenix* 3 (1949), 15–30.

Earl, D.C.   *The Political Thought of Sallust.* Cambridge, 1961.

————— . "The Early Career of Sallust." *Historia* 15 (1966), 302–11.

Ernout, A.   "Salluste et Caton." *Information Litteraire* 1 (1949), 61–65.

Fighiera, S.L.   *La lingua e la grammatica di C. Crispo Sallustio.* Savona, 1896.

Frank, Tenney. "The Tullianum and Sallust's *Catiline*." CJ 19 (1923–24), 496–98.

Frederiksen, M.W. "Caesar, Cicero, and the Problem of Debt." *JRS* 56 (1966), 128–41.

Frisch, H. "The First Catilinarian Conspiracy. A Study in Historical Conjecture." *ClMed* 9 (1948), 10–36.

Gelzer, M. *Caesar: Politician and Statesman*. Cambridge, Mass., 1968.

—————. *The Roman Nobility*. Oxford: Blackwell, 1969.

Gruen, E.S. "Notes on the 'First Catilinarian Conspiracy'." *CP* 64 (1969), 20–24.

—————. "Some Criminal Trials of the Late Republic: Political and Prosopographical Problems." *Athenaeum* 49 (1971), 54–69. (p. 59f. trial of Catiline in 65 B.C.).

—————. *The Last Generation of the Roman Republic*. Berkeley, 1974.

Hardy, E.G. "The Catilinarian Conspiracy in Its Context." *JRS* 7 (1917), 153–228.

Holmes, T. Rice. "Three Catilinarian Dates." *JRS* 8 (1918), 15–25.

—————. *The Roman Republic*, Vols. I-II. Oxford, 1923.

Innes, D.C. "Quo usque tandem patiemini?" *CQ* 27 (1977), 468.

John, C. "Sallust über Catilinas Candidatur in Jahre 688." *RhM* 31 (1876), 401–31.

—————. "Die Entstehungsgeschichte der catilinarischen Verschwörung." *Jahrbücher für cl. Phil.* Supp. 8 (1876), 703–819.

Kroll, W. "Die Sprache des Sallust." *Glotta* 15 (1927), 280–305.

Laistner, M.L.W. "Sallust." *The Greater Roman Historians*. Berkeley, 1947.

Last, H.M. "Sallust and Caesar in the *Bellum Catilinae*." *Mélanges offerts à J. Marouzeau* (Paris, 1948), 355–69.

Linderski, J. "Cicero and Sallust on Vargunteius." *Historia* 12 (1963), 511–512.

Lintott, A.W. *Violence in Republican Rome*. Oxford, 1968.

Lowrance, W.D. "The Use of *forem* and *essem*." TAPA 62 (1931), 169–91.

McDermott, W.C. "Cato the Younger: *loquax* or *eloquens*." *Cl. Bull.* 46 (1970), 65–75.

McDonald, A.H. "Theme and Style in Roman Historiography." *JRS* 65 (1975), 1–10.

MacKay, L.A. "Sallust's *Catiline*, Date and Purpose." *Phoenix* 16 (1962), 181–94.

Marshall, B.A. "Cicero and Sallust on Crassus and Catiline." *Latomus* 33 (1974), 804–813.

—————— . *Crassus: a Political Biography*. Amsterdam. 1976.

—————— . "Catiline: Court Cases and Consular Candidature." *Scripta Classica Israelica* 3 (1976–1977), 127–37.

—————— . "The Date of Catilina's Marriage to Aurelia Orestilla." *RivFC* 105 (1977), 151–54.

Mitchell, T.N.   "Cicero and the *senatus consultum ultimum*." *Historia* 20 (1971), 47–61.

—————— . *Cicero, the Ascending Years*. New Haven, 1979.

Mohler, S.L.   "*Sentina Rei Publicae*: Campaign Issues, 63 B.C." *Class. Wk.* 29 (1936), 81–84.

Nash, E.   *A Pictorial Dictionary of Ancient Rome*. London, 1961.

Nicolet, C.   "Arpinum, Aemilius Scaurus et les Tulli Cicerones." *REL* 45 (1967), 276–304.

—————— . "*Amicissimi Catilinae*: à propos du *Commentariolum Petitionis*." *REL* 50 (1972), 163–87.

—————— . "Les noms des chevaliers victimes de Catilina dans le *Commentariolum Petitionis*." *Mélanges offerts à Seston* (Paris, 1974), 381–95.

Nisbet, R.G.M.   "The *Invectiva in Ciceronem* and *Epistula Secunda* of Pseudo-Sallust." *JRS* 48 (1958), 30–32.

Ogilvie, R.M.   *A Commentary on Livy, Books 1–5*. Oxford, 1965.

Paul, G.M.   "Sallust." in *Latin Historians*, ed. T.A. Dorey. London, 1966.

Perl, G.   "Sallusts Todesjahr." *Klio* 48 (1967), 97–105.

Perrochat, P.   *Les modèles grecs de Salluste*. Paris, 1949.

Phillips. E.J.   "Cicero, *ad Atticum* I.2." *Philologus* 114 (1970), 291–94 (concerning Catiline's trial for extortion in 65 B.C.).

—————— . "Asconius' *Magni Homines*." *RhM* 116 (1973), 353–57 (concerning the activities of Catiline and Cn. Piso in 65 B.C.).

—————— . "Catiline's Conspiracy." *Historia* 25 (1976) 441–48.

Platner, S., and T. Ashby.   *A Topographical Dictionary of Ancient Rome*. London, 1929.

Rambaud, M.   "Les prologues de Salluste et la démonstration morale dans son oeuvre." *REL* 24 (1946), 115–30.

Renehan, R.   "A Traditional Pattern of Imitation in Sallust and His Sources." *CP* 71 (1976), 97–105.

Salmon, E.T.   "Catilina, Crassus and Caesar." *AJP* 56 (1935), 302–16.

Seager, R.   "The First Catilinarian Conspiracy." *Historia* 13 (1964), 338–47.

—————— . "Cicero and the Word *Popularis*." *CQ* 22 (1972), 328–38.

—————— . "*Factio*: Some Observations." *JRS* 62 (1972), 53–58.

—————— . "*Iusta Catilinae*." *Historia* 22 (1973), 240–48.

Shackleton Bailey, D.R. "The Prosecution of Roman Magistrates-elect." *Phoenix* 24 (1970), 162–65.

Shaw, B.D. "Debt in Sallust." *Latomus* 34 (1975), 187–96.

Sherwin-White, A.N. "Violence in Roman Politics." *JRS* 46 (1956), 1–9.

Stevens, C.E. "The 'Plotting' of B.C. 66/65." *Latomus* 22 (1963), 397–435.

Sumner, G.V. "The Last Journey of L. Sergius Catilina." *CP* 58 (1963), 215–19.

————. "The Consular Elections of 66 B.C." *Phoenix* 19 (1965), 226–31.

————. "Cicero, Pompeius, and Rullus." *TAPA* 97 (1966), 569–82 (concerning the role of Caesar and Crassus in the politics of 64–63 B.C.).

————. *The Orators in Cicero's BRUTUS: Prosopography and Chronology.* Toronto, 1973.

Syme, R. *The Roman Revolution.* Oxford, 1939.

————. *Sallust.* Berkeley, 1964.

Taylor, L.R. *Party Politics in the Age of Caesar.* Berkeley, 1949.

Todd, O.J. "Dates in the Autumn of 63 B.C." *Studies in Honour of Gilbert Norwood* (Phoenix Suppl. 1952), 156–62.

Ward, A.M. "Cicero's Fight against Crassus and Caesar in 65 and 63 B.C." *Historia* 21 (1972), 244–58.

————. *Marcus Crassus and the Late Roman Republic.* Columbia, Mo., 1977.

Waters, K.H. "Cicero, Sallust, and Caesar." *Historia* 19 (1970), 195–215.

Weinrib, E. "The Prosecution of Magistrates-Designate." *Phoenix* 25 (1971), 145–50.

Wiseman, T.P. "The Census in the First Century B.C." *JRS* 59 (1969), 59–75.

————. "The Definition of 'Eques Romanus' in the Late Republic and Early Empire." *Historia* 19 (1970), 67–83.

————. *New Men in the Roman Senate.* Oxford, 1971.

Yavetz, Z. "The Failure of Catiline's Conspiracy." *Historia* 12 (1963), 485–99.

Zimmermann, R. *Der Sallusttext im Altertum.* Munich, 1929.

INDEX NOMINUM

(References to the notes are by chapter and section of the text; references to the Introduction are by page number.)

Aborigines, 6.1
Aemilia (*via*), 57.1
M.' Aemilius Lepidus (cos. 66), 18.2
L. Aemilius Lepidus Paullus (cos. 50), 31.4
Aeneas (Trojan hero), 5.1, 6.1
Africa Nova, 21.3
Alba Longa, 6.1
Allobroges, 40.1
Amiternum, p. 2
Q. Annius (Chilo) (conspirator, sen. 63), 17.3
C. Antonius Hybrida (cos. 63), 21.3, 26.4, 26.5
Apulia, 27.1
Arpinum, 31.7
Arretium, 36.1
Ascanius (son of Aeneas), 6.1
Athenienses, 2.2, 7.1, 51.28
Aurelia (*via*), 36.1
Aurelia Orestilla (wife of Catiline), 15.2
P. Autronius Paetus (conspirator, cos. desig. 65), 17.3, 18.3, 18.5, 28.1, App. II

Bestia v. Calpurnius
Bruttius (*ager*), 42.1
Brutus v. Junius

M. <Caecilius?> Metellus (conspirator), 31.4
Q. Caecilius Metellus Celer (pr. 63, cos. 60), 30.5
Q. Caecilius Metellus Creticus (cos. 69), 30.3
Q. Caecilius Metellus Nepos (tr. pl. 62, cos. 57), 30.5, 39.4
M. Caelius Rufus (friend of Catiline, pr. 48), 14.5
M. Caeparius (conspirator), 46.3, 47.4
Caesar v. Iulius
L. Calpurnius Bestia (conspirator, tr. pl. 62), 17.3
C. Calpurnius Piso (cos. 67), 49.1
Cn. Calpurnius Piso (qu. 65), 18.4, 19.2, 19.3, App. II

Camerinum, 27.1
Capua, 30.2
Carthago, 10.1
Cassia (*via*), 45.1
L. Cassius Longinus (conspirator, pr. 66), 17.3, 43.2
Catilina (cognomen) 5.1, v. Sergius
Cato v. Porcius
Catulus v. Lutatius
Cethegus v. Cornelius
Cicero v. Tullius
Cimbricum (*bellum*), 59.3
Cinna v. Cornelius
Ti. Claudius Nero (pr. before 63), 50.4
L. Coelius Antipater (Roman historian), Introd. n.10
Concordiae (*aedes*), 46.5
C. Cornelius (conspirator, *eques*), 17.4, 28.1
C. Cornelius Cethegus (conspirator, sen. 63), 17.3, 52.33
L. Cornelius Cinna (cos. 87, 86, 85, 84), 47.2
P. Cornelius Lentulus Spinther (cos. 57), 47.4
P. Cornelius Lentulus Sura (conspirator, cos. 71, pr. 63), 17.1, 17.3
P. Cornelius Scipio Nasica Corculum (cos. 162, 155), 10.1
L. Cornelius Sulla (cos. 88, 80, dict. 82-79), 5.2, 5.6, 11.4, 16.4, 18.2
P. Cornelius Sulla (cos. desig. 65), 18.2, 18.3, 18.5, App. II
P. Cornelius Ser. f. Sulla (conspirator, sen. 63), 17.3
Ser. Cornelius Ser. f. Sulla (conspirator, sen. 63), 17.3
Q. Cornificius (pr. ca. 66), 47.4
Crassus v. Licinius
Q. Curius (informer, qu.? by 71), 17.3, 23.1
Cyrus (king of Persia), 2.2

Fabia (Vestal Virgin, half-sister of Terentia), 15.1
Q. Fabius Sanga (*patronus* of Allobroges), 41.4
Faesulae, 16.4, 24.2
Flaccus v. Valerius
Flaminia (*via*), 45.1
C. Flaminius (conspirator), 36.1
Fulvia (mistress of Curius), 23.3
Fulvius (*senatoris filius*), 39.5
M. Fulvius Nobilior (conspirator, *eques*), 17.4
P. Furius (conspirator), 50.4

P. Gabinius Capito (Cimber) (conspirator, *eques*), 17.4
Gallia Cisalpina (*citerior*), p. 16, 16.5, 17.7, 26.4, 42.1, 42.3
Gallia Transalpina (*ulterior*), 40.1, 42.1, 42.3

Hispania *citerior* and *ulterior*, 18.5
Q. Hortensius Hortalus (cos. 69), 13.1, 17.3

C. Iulius (conspirator), 27.1
C. Iulius Caesar (cos. 59, 48, 46, 45, 44), pp. 3–5, 17.3, 18.1-2, 18.8, 20.12, 21.3, 24.2, 34.3, 47.4, 49.2, 49.4, 52.1, 54.1-4, App. I
L. Iulius Caesar (cos. 64), 17.1
D. Iunius Brutus (cos. 77), 25.2
L. Iunius Brutus Damasippus (pr. 82), 51.32
D. Iunius Silanus (cos. 62), 50.4
Iupiter Optimus Maximus (temple of), 18.5, 47.2
Iupiter Stator (temple of), 31.5

Lacedaemonii, 2.2, 51.28
Laeca v. Porcius
Lentulus v. Cornelius
Lepidus v. Aemilius
M. Licinius Crassus (cos. 70, 55), 17.7, 18.1, 18.8, 19.1-2, 23.5, 29.1, 34.3, 39.4, 47.4, 48.8-9
L. Licinius Lucullus (cos. 74), 13.1
C. Licinius Murena (leg. 63), 42.3
L. Licinius Murena (cos. 62), 26.1, 35.3, 40.1, 42.3
Longinus v. Cassius
L. Lucceius (Roman historian, pr. 67), pp. 7–9, 15.2, 24.2
Q. Lutatius Catulus (cos. 78), 15.1, 34.3, 49.2

C. Manilius (tr. pl. 66), 18.6, App. II
C. Manlius (conspirator), 24.2, 27.1
A. (T.?) Manlius Imperiosus Torquatus (cos. 347, 344, 340), 52.30
L. Manlius Torquatus (cos. 65), 18.3, 18.6, App. II
L. Manlius Torquatus (pr. 49), 31.7
Cn. Manlius Vulso (cos. 189), 10.1, 11.6
C. Marcius Figulus (cos. 64), 17.1
Q. Marcius Rex (cos. 68), 30.3
Martius (*campus*), 26.5
Massilia, 34.2
Metellus v. Caecilius
Mithridates (king of Pontus), 11.4
Mithridaticum (*bellum*), 16.5
Mulvius (*pons*), 45.1
Murena v. Licinius

Numa (second king of Rome), 6.3

Orestilla v. Aurelia

M. Petreius (pr. ca. 64), 59.4

Picenum, 27.1

Pisistratidae, 7.1

Piso v. Calpurnius

Pistoria, 57.1

Cn. Pompeius Magnus (cos. 70, 55, 52), p. 3, 16.5, 17.7, 18.4, 19.2, 19.5, 23.5, 30.4-5, 31.4, 39.4, App. I

Q. Pompeius Rufus (pr. 63), 30.5

Cn. Pompeius Strabo (cos. 89), App. I

T. Pomponius Atticus (friend of Cicero), 49.4

C. Pomptinus (pr. 63), 45.1

M. Porcius Cato (Roman historian and one of S.'s models, cos. 195), pp. 11–12, 2.2, 2.4, 3.5, 5.8, 6.1, 6.7, 7.5, 10.1, 51.5, 51.6, 51.33, 52.7, 53.1, 54.6

M. Porcius Cato Uticensis (tr. pl. 62, pr. 54), 31.9, 37.7, 52.1, 52.3, 54.1-2, 54.6

M. Porcius Laeca (conspirator, sen. 63), 17.3, 27.3

Praeneste, 27.3

Reate, 26.4

Remus (brother of Romulus), 6.1

Rhodii, 51.5

Romulus (founder and first king of Rome), 6.1, 6.3

L. Saenius (sen. 63), 30.1

Sallustiani (*horti*), p. 5, 4.1

Samnites, 51.38

Sempronia (wife of D. Brutus), 25.1

A. Sempronius Asellio (pr. 89), 33.1

Septimius (conspirator), 27.1

Sergestus (Trojan companion of Aeneas), 5.1

Sergia (*gens*), 5.1

L. Sergius (*armiger Catilinae*), 59.3

L. Sergius Catilina (pr. 68), pp. 15–22, 5.1-2, 15.2, 18.2-3, 19.2, App. I and II, *passim*

Sergius Orata, 20.11

M. Sergius Silus (pr. 197), 31.7

P. Sestius (qu. 63, tr. pl. 57), 30.2

Silanus v. Iunius

P. Sittius (Campanian financier), 21.3

Spartacus (leader of slave revolt), 17.7, 30.2

L. Statilius (conspirator, *eques*), 17.4

Sulla v. Cornelius

Ser. Sulpicius Rufus (cos. cand. 63, cos. 51), 26.1

L. Tarquinius (informer), 48.3

Tarquinius Superbus (seventh king of Rome), 6.7, 7.1
Cn. Terentius (sen. 63), 47.4
Thucydides (Greek historian and one of S.'s models), pp. 10–11, 3.2, 4.4,
        6.5, 12.1, 18.1, 18.2, 20.9, 38.3, 50.5
Torquatus v. Manlius
Transpadini, 49.2
Tullianum, 55.2-4
M. Tullius Cicero (cos. 63), p. 3, pp. 7–10, 22.3, 23.5, 24.1, 26.1, 26.4,
        30.5, 46.2, *passim*
Q. Tullius Cicero (pr. 62), 42.1, 46.2
Tullus Hostilius (third king of Rome), 6.3
Tusci, 51.38

P. Umbrenus (conspirator, freedman), 40.1

L. Valerius Flaccus (pr. 63), 45.1
L. Vargunteius (conspirator, sen. 63?), 17.3, 28.1
L. Vettius (informer), 49.1
L. Volcacius Tullus (cos. 66), p. 16, 18.2
T. Volturcius (informer), 44.3

Xerxes (king of Persia), 13.1

INDEX RERUM

adverbs
- in place of predicate adj., 20.2, 21.1, 23.6, 58.9
- standing for attributive adj., 20.11
- substituted for pronoun & prep., 3.3, 5.2, 8.3, 11.6, 20.8, 20.9, 22.2, 27.4
- in *-tim*, 4.2

aes alienum, problem of debt in 64-63, 14.2

alliteration, 3.2, 6.3, 7.6, 11.5, *passim*
- pairs of adjs., 1.4, 2.8, 7.5, 11.3, 19.1, 20.3
- pairs of nouns, 11.4, 12.2, 14.1, 30.2, 31.1, 34.1, 39.4, 51.33

ambitus, 18.2

anaphora, 3.3, 7.5, 53.2, 59.5

archaic words, pp. 12–13

artes (bonae/malae), 2.4

assonance, 11.6

asyndeton, 2.3, 3.2, 5.3, 6.5, *passim*
- triad, 3.3, 4.2, 5.5, 6.3, 12.1
- six members, 21.2, 37.3
- seven members, 31.3

battle of the Colline Gate, 11.4

boni (= *optimates*), 19.2

carcer, 55.2

chiasmus, 2.2, 3.1, 3.3, 5.4, 5.9, 6.1, 9.1, *passim*
- double, 17.1
- chiastic elaboration of two statements, 46.2

clientes, 19.5

colonia, 17.4

comitia centuriata, 24.1

compound for simple verb, 59.1

cum populo agere, 51.43

curia, 32.1

dactylic hexameter, 19.5

dates given by S., 17.1

dative
- of agent, 14.7, 20.2

ethical, 52.11
debt, 14.2, 16.4
deponents as passives, 7.3, 48.7
dignitas, 35.3
domi nobiles, 17.4

epistolary past tense, 35.5, 53.6
equester ordo, 17.4
-ere = -erunt (3rd pl., pf. act. indic.), 2.2
-erunt (3rd pl., pf. act. indic.), 20.10

factio, 32.2
fasces, 18.5
figura etymologica, 7.6 (defined), 33.2, 35.3
fortuna, 10.1
frequens senatus, 46.6
frequentative verbs, 2.1

gerund
　　+ acc. direct object, 4.1, 15.3, 38.1
　　modal abl. = pres. partic., 61.2
gerundive, in gen. expressing tendency, 6.7, 46.2
gnomic perfect, 11.3, 51.2, 51.11, 58.15
gratia, 20.7

haruspices, 47.2
hendiadys, 2.2, 6.7, 51.4, 52.2
homoeoteleuton, 5.9, 61.9
hypallage, 8.3, 36.5

imperator, 30.4
inauguration of new consuls, 18.5
inconcinnitas, resulting from dissymmetry and deliberate variation, 1.4,
　　2.6, 9.2, 9.3, 16.4, 17.6, 17.7, 33.1, 38.3, 40.1, 42.1, 42.2, 47.1,
　　51.3, 51.42
indicative
　　in place of subjn. in suboblique clauses, 14.7, 17.7, 20.6, 22.3, 27.4
　　with *quippe qui*, 48.2
infinitive
　　expanded use of, 5.9, 15.2, 16.2, 17.6, 30.4, 52.3, 52.24
　　historical, p. 13, 6.4, 12.2, 16.2, 17.1, 20.7
　　historical in passive voice, 10.6
　　historical in combination with finite verb, 24.2

integri MSS, p. 14
interest rates on loans, 33.1
invective *in Sallustium*, p. 2, p. 4

Jupiter, new statue on the Capitoline, 47.2

Lar, 20.11
lex
    Aurelia iudiciaria, 17.4
    Cornelia de privilegiis, 46.6
    Cornelia de proscriptione, 37.9
    Cornelia de sicariis, 27.2
    Flaminia, 33.1
    Gabinia, 16.5
    Genucia, 33.2
    Hortensia, 9.1, 33.3
    Licinia-Sextia, 33.2
    Lutatia de vi, 31.4
    Manilia, 16.5
    Oppia, 52.7
    Plautia de vi, 17.3, 31.4
    Poetelia et Papiria, 33.1
    Porcia, 51.22
    Sempronia de capite civis, 51.8
    Valeria, 33.2
litotes, 3.1 (defined), 3.2, 19.2, 20.16, 23.1

metonymy, 13.3, 14.1, 18.5, 20.2, 20.11, 32.1, 43.1, 51.8, 51.14, 53.4, 59.2
moral terms and slogans perverted, 38.3
municipium, 17.4
mutili MSS, p. 14

nobilis, 5.1
novus homo, 23.6
number
    sing. verb with compound subj. treated as a single entity, 9.1, 12.1,
        25.3, 39.4, 51.42
    verbs in sing. and pl. with collective noun as subj., 7.4, 23.6

orationes in Catilinam
    I, 31.6
    II, 34.2
    III, 48.1
    IV, 52.1
ordo v. *equester, plebeius, senatorius*
orthography, Introd. n. 12
-os = -us (nom. sing., 2nd decl.), 11.2

pactio provinciae, 26.4
papyrus fragments of text, p. 15

parataxis, 2.1, 3.3, 7.3, 7.5, 8.1
paronomasia, 11.3, 20.13
pater familias, 43.2
patres = senatores, 6.6
patres conscripti, 51.1
pedibus ire, 50.4
piscinae, 13.1
plebeius ordo, 17.4
pleonasm, 17.2, 39.6, 51.38
pluperfect for historic perfect, 18.6, 24.1, 36.5, 43.1, 46.4, 50.4, 56.2
populares (political term), 20.6
praetorian cohort, 60.5
prepositional phrases
    employed as substantive, 3.2
    substituted for attributive adj., 6.1, 20.2
pronouns
    demonstrative, subj. nom., 8.1, 10.3, 11.3
    demonstrative, resumptive for emphasis, 12.5, 20.4, 37.4, 58.16
    gender, neut. following series of nouns in f. (m.), 1.7, 3.4, 5.7
    reflexive, redundant with prolative inf., 1.1, 7.6
    relative, antecedent attracted into rel. clause, 4.2, 11.1, 53.2
        antecedent repeated in rel. clause, 51.40
proscriptions, 5.2, 11.4, 16.4, 17.7, 21.2
    children of proscribed, 37.9

res repetundae, 18.3

salutatio, 28.1
Saturnalia, 43.1
senatorius ordo, 17.3
senatus consultum ultimum, 29.2
sestertium, 30.6
Sibylline Books, 47.2
simple verb for compound, 7.7, 20.14, 60.5
slaves in the conspiracy, 24.4
socii, 12.5
stipendium, 20.7
stock expressions altered, 10.1, 14.2, 18.2, 23.6, 36.4
subject, abrupt shift between clauses, 5.6, 25.3
subjunctive
    primary sequence preceding main vb. in historical pres., 45.1
    primary and secondary sequence after historical pres., 32.2
    primary and secondary sequence after historical pf., 34.1
    virtual indirect discourse, 7.6, 23.3, 30.6, 36.2, 37.6, 49.4
Sullan veterans, 16.4

supplicatio, 47.3

synesis (*constructio ad sensum*), p. 13, 16.1 (defined), 17.7, 18.2, 43.1, 56.5

syntax

    case of common predicate determined by nearer of two verbs, 11.2, 51.38

    influenced by analogy within pairs, 5.4

    influenced by first of two verbs, 9.5

tabulae novae, 21.2

tetrarches, 20.7

Thirty Tyrants, 51.28

title, *Bellum Catilinae*, Introd. n. 9

topos, 1.1, 1.3, 1.6, 3.2, 10.1, 11.3, 13.3, 51.12, 52.3, 52.4, 54.6, 58.9, 58.16

tribunate of the *plebs*, 38.1

trinum nundinum, 18.3

triumph, 30.4

-tudo, abstracts in, 17.2

Twelve Tables, 33.1, 51.39

variation of construction with single verb, 5.9, 10.4, 16.2, 17.6, 25.2, 37.10, 47.1

vectigal, 20.7

Vestal Virgins, 15.1

vindices rerum capitalium, 55.5

virtus, 1.4

zeugma, 12.2, 17.2, 24.2, 36.4, 51.7, 51.9

INDEX VERBORUM

adeptus (= pass.), 7.3
admonere de, 5.9
adulescentulus, 3.3
agitare, 2.1
alienus (+ gen.), 40.5
alii (= *ceteri*), 43.3
alius (attracted into sing.), 6.2
      (for *alter*), 52.1
alter (redundant), 1.7
anima, 2.8
animus (= *ego*), 20.3
antecapere, 13.3
audacia (positive sense), 9.3
avaritia, 9.1

carere (= *abstinere*), 13.5
ceterus (sing.), 13.3
coepi (act.) with pass. inf., 12.1, 51.40
colos, 15.5
commodare, 16.2
comperiri, 14.7
confodere, 28.1
conscius (subjective), 14.3
consuevit (impers.), 22.2
consultare (= *consulere*) + dat., 6.6
copia est + inf., 17.6
cultus (pejorative), 13.3
cupido, 3.5
curare, 59.3

demum, 2.2
dies (f.), 36.2
dolus, 26.2
ductare, 11.5
dubitare + inf., 15.2
dum (= *dummodo*), 5.6

egeo (+ abl./gen.), 1.7

eo (= *ideo*), anticipating purpose clause, 22.2
equidem, 51.15, 51.20
etiam (= *adhuc*), 14.5
ex ("according to"), 8.1
   (= cause/source), 12.2
exemplum, 34.3
exercere (= *vexare*), 11.1
exitium, 55.6
expers (+ gen. & abl.), 33.1

facinus, 2.9, 4.4
factiosus, 18.4
facundia, 53.3
fama (= "ill repute"), 3.5
ferox, 38.1
filii familiarum, 43.2
foret (= *futurus esset*), 21.1, 23.3, 34.2, 39.6, 51.6
    (= *esset*), 14.7
formidulosus, 7.2

gratia (+ gen.) = *propter* + acc., 23.1

habere (+ prep. phrase), 13.3
    (= *incolere*), 6.1
    (= *tractare*), 5.9
hortor (+ inf.), 5.9
huiusce, 15.1

id (pleonastic), 12.5
igitur (1st word in sentence), 2.1
imperare (+ inf.?), 16.2
in rem esse, 20.1
incedere (various constructions), 7.3
incruentus, 61.7
inesse (*in* + abl.), 15.5
innoxius, 39.2
inquilinus, 31.7
insons, 16.3
intempesta nox, 27.3
intentus (+ abl./dat.), 2.9
ita (virtually = *nam*), 15.4
item, 44.1
iuventus, 5.2
iuxta, 2.8
iuxta cum, 58.5

labos, 7.5
legio, 53.3
licet (+ subjn.), 35.2
longius (= *diutius*), 29.1

machinor (pass.), 48.7
malle (+ acc.), 17.6
    (with acc. & inf. and complementary inf.), 37.10
malum publicum, 37.7
manufestus, 41.5, 52.36
maturare, 18.8
maxume (+ positive degree for superlative), 1.3, 8.5
mentior (+ acc.), 48.6
mortales (= *homines*), 1.5
multo (+ supl.), 36.4
multus (+ 2nd adj. without conj.), 15.1

nam (parenthetical/explanatory), 2.1
    (with ellipsis), 7.2
ne (= *nae*), 52.27
    (= *nedum*), 11.8
necessitudo (= *necessitas*), 17.2
neglegeris (= *neglexeris*), 51.24
neque tamen, 19.2
nequeo (= *non possum*), 18.3
nihil (= *non*), 16.5
novare (absol.), 39.3
novissume, 33.2

opus est (+ pf. pass. part. in abl. = subst.), 1.6
oreretur, 34.2

parare (absol.), 6.5
paratus (with *ad* + acc.), 31.7
parricida, 14.3
pars . . . alii, 2.1
patrare, 18.8
pensi, 5.6
per + acc. (= adv.), 20.9
        (= instrumental, modal abl.), 13.2
plebes, 37.1
popularis (= *socius*), 22.1
portare (= *ferre*), 6.5
postquam (+ impf. indic.), 6.3
potior (+ gen.), 47.2
praeter (= *praeterquam*), 36.2

prolatare, 43.3
propius (+ acc.), 11.1
prorsus (= *postremo*), 15.5
provenire (= *apparere*), 8.3
putare (+ double acc.), 2.2

quae utraque (= *quarum utramque*), 5.7
-que, 6.5
-que (+ prep.), 6.1
-que . . . -que, 9.3
quippe (= *nam*), 11.8
quippe qui (+ indic.), 48.2
quis (= *quibus*), 18.1
quisquam (adj.), 31.2
quo (= *ut*), 11.5

relicui (with *nihil facere*), 11.7
rursus (= *contra*), 53.5

sed, 7.1
sed maxume, 17.6
senati (gen. sing.), 30.3
servitia (= *servos*), 24.4
sicuti (= *quasi*), 16.3
simul ac, 7.4
subigere (= *cogere*), 10.5
superare (= *superesse*), 20.11
supplicium (= *supplicatio*), 9.2
supra quam (for *ultra quam*), 5.3

tempestas (for *tempus*), 7.1, 20.3
tendere (= *contendere*), 60.5
tolerare (+ acc. & inf.), 20.11
tollere (= "remove"), 23.4
toreuma, 20.12
tumultus, 59.5

ubi (+ plupf. indic.), 6.5
uterque (attracted into pl.), 5.7
utpote qui, 57.4

venenum (= "drug"), 11.3
vorsus (prep.), 56.4
vostrum (= *vestri*, possessive adj.), 33.2